CULTIVATING PEACE

CULTIVATING PEACE

Conflict and Collaboration in Natural Resource Management

Edited by Daniel Buckles

INTERNATIONAL DEVELOPMENT RESEARCH CENTRE
Ottawa • Cairo • Dakar • Johannesburg • Montevideo • Nairobi • New Delhi • Singapore

WORLD BANK INSTITUTE
Washington, DC, USA

Published by the International Development Research Centre
PO Box 8500, Ottawa, ON, Canada K1G 3H9

In collaboration with the World Bank Institute of the International Bank for Reconstruction and Development/The World Bank.

The World Bank
1818 H Street, N.W.
Washington, D.C. 20433, USA

© International Development Research Centre 1999

Canadian Cataloguing in Publication Data

Canadian Cataloging in Publication Data

Main entry under title :
Cultivating peace : conflict and collaboration in natural resource management

Co-published by the World Bank.
Includes bibliographical references.
ISBN 0-88936-899-6

1. Natural resources — Management — Developing countries — Congresses.
2. Conservation of natural resources — Developing countries — Congresses.
3. Conflict management — Developing countries — Congresses.
4. Sustainable development — Developing countries — Congresses.
I. Buckles, Daniel.
II. World Bank.
III. International Development Research Centre (Canada)

HC59.7C84 1999   333.7'09'12'4   C99-980392-1

IDRC Books endeavours to produce environmentally friendly publications. All paper used is recycled as well as recyclable. All inks and coatings are vegetable-based products.

CONTENTS

CONCEPT: SOCIETY

Part 2. Coastal Areas

CONCEPT: PEACE

Part 3. Land Use

CONCEPT: POLICY

FOREWORD

In May 1998, an international workshop on community-based natural resource management (CBNRM) was jointly organized by the Economic Development Institute of the World Bank (now the World Bank Institute), Canada's International Development Research Centre (IDRC), the Ford Foundation, and other agencies. Held in Washington, DC, the workshop was attended by 200 policymakers, practitioners, and researchers from about 60 countries who were involved in some aspect of CBNRM in developing and transition economies.

Twenty years ago, such a workshop would have been unthinkable, since the conventional wisdom viewed "community-based natural resource management" as an oxymoron. Communities who derived their livelihood from common-pool resources (such as pastures, water, forests, or fisheries) could not be expected to manage these resources in a sustainable manner since they were trapped in a "tragedy of the commons" in which they were helpless to prevent individual users from overexploiting the resource. Rather, it was necessary for some external authority (the government) to impose an outside solution, either to manage the resource directly — the "command and control" solution — or to facilitate private-sector management of the resource by establishing individual, exchangeable property rights in the resource — the "market-based" solution.

Twenty years of detailed research on common-pool resources has now brought greater realism to this issue. It is now widely accepted that local communities are more likely than central governments or the commercial private sector to pay attention to the long-term consequences of resource use, precisely because they depend upon the sustainable harvesting of the resource for their livelihoods. As the case studies in this book illustrate, local communities are able to organize themselves to allocate property rights and to regulate individual resource use, but they often run up against constraints imposed from the outside that limit their effectiveness. In today's interconnected world, actions by one group of people or institutions may also generate environmental problems and social conflict far off-site. Neither governments nor local communities can solve these clashes alone.

Central governments who are genuinely concerned about the sustainable use of their country's natural resources must, at a minimum, involve local communities in their management. This means taking local communities into confidence and having confidence in them. It means engaging with their ideas, experiences, values, and capabilities and working with them, not on their behalf, to achieve resource-conservation objectives and community benefits. It means being prepared to adjust national policies so that they can accommodate local interests, needs, and norms that are compatible with the long-term preservation of national ecosystems and their biological diversity. Outsiders, including governments, have a burden of proof when proceeding contrary to local interests in the use of natural resources.

The international workshop explored various dimensions of this community-based approach to natural resource use in plenary sessions, case study sessions, and working groups. It focused on four aspects of institutionalizing CBNRM:

- Organizing effective community-based groups, at both the local level and scaling up to the regional level;

- Working out effective operational linkages between the public sector, the private sector, and community-based groups to manage resources in a mutually beneficial and sustainable way;

- Examining alternative approaches to managing conflict in the use of natural resources at all levels — local, national, and regional; and

- Codifying the above three aspects in a legal and institutional framework that fosters the emergence of community-based institutions to manage natural resources locally.

IDRC organized plenary and case study sessions in relation to the third theme: alternative approaches to managing conflict. This book brings together seven of the case studies presented at the workshop, plus three others, around this theme. It also includes four concept essays on broader themes — culture, society, peace, and policy — that situate the lessons from the case studies in on-going debates on the causes of conflict and their resolution. Most of the studies were originally supported by IDRC as part of its ongoing programs on sustainable development and peacebuilding. IDRC seeks to contribute to the generation of new thinking and more effective solutions to persistent development problems through research that is locally grounded but globally relevant. Several of IDRC's current programs deal specifically with the local, national, and regional dynamics of natural resource management. Its peacebuilding program addresses the complex interlinkages between peace, socioeconomic development, and environmental security. The contributions to this volume by six IDRC program staff reflect the range and multidisciplinarity of the Centre's programs.

The World Bank Institute jointly organized the 1998 international workshop with IDRC, the Ford Foundation, and other agencies as part of its ongoing program on policy and institutional reform for sustainable rural development. A worldwide program with a special emphasis on Africa, its overall objective is to help countries formulate and implement policy initiatives and institutional reforms for sustainable rural development and natural resource use, so that the rural sector can play a vital role in economic development, poverty alleviation, and food security. The program seeks to advance and contribute to the policy dialogue on these issues primarily by strengthening management, analytical, and training capacity not only in participating governments and universities but also in the private sector and in civil society. The World Bank Institute provides training and other learning activities that support the World Bank's mission to reduce poverty and improve living standards in the developing world. The Institute's programs help build the capacity of World Bank borrowers, staff, and other partners in the skills and knowledge that are critical to economic and social development.

Both IDRC and the World Bank Institute are delighted to collaborate in the publication of this book. It is our hope that the ideas presented herein are used by policymakers, practitioners, and researchers to develop strategies to transform conflict over natural resources into opportunities for social change and collaboration.

Maureen O'Neil
President
International Development Research Centre
Ottawa, Canada

Vinod Thomas
Director
The World Bank Institute
Washington, DC, USA

ACKNOWLEDGMENTS

This book developed over a year, and I am grateful to those who helped in its preparation. The chapters were reviewed by various readers, whose comments and suggestions greatly improved the logic of the arguments and the style of presentation. Thanks are extended to Jessica Blitt, Lisa Burley, Ken Bush, Galil Elmekki, Karen McAllister, Erik Nielsen, Robert Opp, Gerett Rusnak, and Stephen Tyler. Chris Gerrard of the World Bank Institute was very supportive during the months leading up to the International Workshop on Community-based Natural Resource Management held in Washington, 10–14 May 1998 and made it possible to bring together an exceptional group of presenters. Simon Carter, Necla Tschirgi, and Stephen Tyler, team leaders for three International Development Research Centre (IDRC) program initiatives in natural resource management and peace-building, were unwavering in their support and encouragement in the preparation of papers for the workshop and development of a manuscript for publication. Participation in a half-day workshop organized by IDRC immediately following the main event also helped consolidate thinking on lessons learned and key research gaps, information that was incorporated into a number of the chapters. This event included John Ambler, Jacqueline Ashby, Daniel Buckles, Simon Carter, Jacqueline Chenier, Jacques Chevalier, Larry Fisher, Pascal Girot, Phil Hirsch, Shashi Kant, Doug McGuire, Ilya Moeliono, Robert Opp, Paola Oviedo, Carlos Pérez Arrarte, Khamla Phanvilay, Tahnee Robertson, Gerett Rusnak, Terry Smutylo, Mohamed Suliman, Liana Talaue-McManus, Kaneungnit Tubtim, Stephen Tyler, and Kadi Warner. Sandy Garland provided exceptional editorial support during the preparation of the manuscript, as did Bill Carman. Gerett Rusnak, Helen Raij, and Kevin Conway helped develop the website for discussion of earlier drafts of the manuscript. I owe a special debt to the book's coauthors for the patience and diligence with which they made revisions to their draft chapters. I would also like especially to acknowledge the contribution of the late Madelaine Audet, long-time reference specialist at IDRC in Ottawa. Madelaine's assistance in identifying relevant resource material for various authors and supporting web-based communication of research results was greatly appreciated. I dedicate this book to her memory.

Daniel Buckles

Introduction

CONFLICT AND COLLABORATION IN
NATURAL RESOURCE MANAGEMENT

Daniel Buckles and Gerett Rusnak

Why does conflict occur over the use of natural resources? How are external factors built into local conflicts? What governing mechanisms are conducive to equitable and sustainable natural resource management by communities? When do local strategies for conflict management need to be complemented or replaced by external or new mechanisms? How can research help identify opportunities for turning conflict into collaboration? Why is collaboration in natural resource management so difficult?

This book grapples with those questions. Case studies analyze specific natural resource conflicts in 10 countries and the interventions of people close to the conflicts (in some cases, the authors themselves). Four concept papers draw the case stories together around particular themes: culture, society, peace, and policy. The concept papers illustrate their main points with examples from the case studies, grounding concepts in concrete experience and raising broader questions for further study. Chevalier and Buckles (this volume) present differences in cultural perspectives on community-based natural resource management (CBNRM). Through the use of a conversational style, the authors attempt to bring the reader closer to oral forms of community-based politics, learning, and teaching. Ramírez (this volume) examines the theory and practice of stakeholder analysis and develops a series of propositions that shed light on how it can be used to identify opportunities for turning conflict into collaboration. Bush and Opp (this volume) challenge development practitioners, including the case-study authors, to answer fundamental questions regarding the causes of conflict before launching an intervention. They argue that answers to these questions would not only inform the intervention, but also allow parties to assess the "peace and conflict impacts" of attempts to introduce more collaborative modes of natural resource management. Tyler (this volume) examines policy disincentives for CBNRM and outlines the policy changes needed to support local forms of governance over natural resources.

The cross-fertilization of case experience with conceptual insight creates a unique dialogue on lessons learned and strategic gaps in our understanding of the conditions that need to be met to move from conflict to collaboration. It shows that conflict management is a critical but constructive way of looking at natural resource problems, involving two basic steps: conflict analysis and planned multiparty intervention. Conflict analysis involves the study, conducted by those directly involved and those seeking to assist in this endeavour, of the various dimensions, levels, and consequences of conflict, with a view to understanding the causes. Multiparty interventions, when based on study of the conflict, involve the use of a variety of techniques, such as mediation and negotiation, leading to changes in the management of natural resources. Our hope is that the critical assessment of conflict management experience presented in this volume will inform the practice of all of us concerned with communities' equitable and sustainable natural resource management.

Conflict and natural resource management

Conflict over natural resources such as land, water, and forests is ubiquitous (Anderson et al. 1996; Ayling and Kelly 1997; Ortiz 1999). People everywhere have competed for the natural resources they need or want to ensure or enhance their livelihoods. However, the dimensions, level, and intensity of conflict vary greatly. Conflicts over natural resources may have class dimensions, pitting those who own the resource against those who own nothing but whose work makes the resource productive (Chenier et al., this volume). Political dimensions may dominate where the state has a keen interest in a public good such as conservation (Fisher et al., this volume) or in maintaining the political alliances it needs to remain in power (Suliman, this volume). Differences in gender, age, and ethnicity may inform the use of natural resources, bringing to the fore cultural and social dimensions of conflict (Hirsch et al., this volume). Even the identification of natural resource problems may be contested in light of different information sources, world views, and values (Pérez Arrarte and Scarlato, this volume). Although each case study presented in this book does not explore all of these dimensions equally, the dialogue between them is multifaceted.

Conflicts over natural resources can take place at a variety of levels, from within the household to local, regional, societal, and global scales. Furthermore, conflict may cut across these levels through multiple points of contact. Conflicts occurring mainly in local contexts may extend to national and global levels because of their special legal relevance (Talaue-McManus et al., this volume; Weitzner and Fonseca Borrás, this volume) or as a result of efforts by local actors to influence broader decision-making processes (Chenier et al., this volume; Oveido, this volume). All the cases presented in this volume pertain to conflicts that involve fairly localized, site-specific interactions among stakeholders. Most, however, stretch beyond local interactions to engage actors and processes at other levels as well.

The intensity of conflict may also vary enormously — from confusion and frustration among members of a community over poorly communicated development policies (Kant and Cooke, this volume) to violent clashes between groups over resource ownership rights and responsibilities (Chenier et al., this volume; Suliman, this volume). With reduced government power in many regions, natural resource management decisions are increasingly influenced by the resource users, who include small-scale farmers and indigenous peoples as well as ranchers, large scale landowners, and private corporations in industries such as forestry, mining, hydropower, and agribusiness. Resources may be used by some in ways that undermine the livelihoods of others. Power differences between groups can be enormous and the stakes a matter of survival. The resulting conflicts often lead to chaotic and wasteful deployment of human capacities and the depletion of the very natural resources on which livelihoods, economies, and societies are based. They may also lead to bloodshed. Several of the cases presented here address the extremely difficult question of the limits of collaborative approaches to natural resource management and the role of violence in redressing entrenched economic and political interests.

Why does conflict occur?

The use of natural resources is susceptible to conflict for a number of reasons. First, natural resources are embedded in an environment or interconnected space where actions by one individual or group may generate effects far off-site. For example, the use of water for irrigation in the upper reaches of the Calico River, Nicaragua, pitted upstream landowners and communities against downstream communities in need of water for domestic use and consumption (Vernooy and Ashby, this volume). Linked biophysical or ecological processes in a specific environment disperse cumulative, long-range impacts such as erosion, pollution, or loss of plant and animal habitats. The nature of the problem may not be apparent because ecological relationships are often poorly understood.

> Implicit conflicts are those in which communities are affected by a process of environmental degradation they do not recognize [or] although they might be aware of the degradation, they are unable to associate it with the activity of specific social agents. The environmental conflict is thus made explicit when communities establish an immediate logical connection between environmental degradation and the activities of certain social agents.
>
> (Ascerlad 1992, p. 35)

Research and communication can help establish this connection and may, consequently, become proximate causes of conflict, as well as catalysts for social learning about how to manage the resources and conflicts. Scientists showed that the proliferation of fish pens and fish cages for aquaculture in the Caquiputan Channel of Bolinao, Philippines, reduced water flow and the amount of dissolved oxygen in the water to levels that were lethal to fish (Talaue-McManus et al., this volume). Navigation was also impaired. This information helped to diffuse the growing conflict among resource users and provided guidance for the development of a plan for optimal resource use.

Second, natural resources are also embedded in a shared social space where complex and unequal relations are established among a wide range of social actors — agro-export producers, small-scale farmers, ethnic minorities, government agencies, etc. As in other fields with political dimensions, those actors with the greatest access to power are also best able to control and influence natural resource decisions in their favour (Peet and Watts 1996). For example, absentee Jellaba landlords (merchants, government officials, and retired generals) in northern Sudan made use of their direct connections to the State Agricultural Bank to channel international credit for mechanized farming into their operations in the Nuba Mountains in southern Kordofan (Suliman, this volume). The ruling government also helped divert attention and consolidate the Jellaba hold on the best lands in the area by inflaming historical tensions between Arab Baggara and the Nuba people.

Third, natural resources are subject to increasing scarcity due to rapid environmental change, increasing demand, and their unequal distribution (Homer-Dixon and Blitt 1998). Environmental change may involve land and water degradation, overexploitation of wildlife and aquatic resources, extensive land clearing or drainage, or climate change. Increasing demands have multiple social and economic dimensions, including population growth, changing consumption patterns, trade liberalization, rural enterprise development, and changes in technology and land use. Natural resource scarcity may also result from the unequal distribution of resources among individuals and social groups or ambiguities in the definition of rights to common property resources. As noted by Homer-Dixon and Blitt (1998, p. 8), the effects of environmental scarcity such as "constrained agricultural output, constrained economic production, migration, social segmentation, and disrupted institutions … can, either singly or in combination, produce or exacerbate conflict among groups."

Intercommunity and interethnic conflict in the Nam Ngum watershed in the Lao People's Democratic Republic has resulted from diverse pressures causing greater natural resource scarcity (Hirsch et al., this volume). In some parts of the watershed, forced migration into areas already settled by other ethnic groups increased pressures on the forested land used in shifting cultivation systems. In other areas, the disruption of government institutions by reforms of the traditional economy led to redrawing of administrative boundaries of some villages and the creation of a "no man's land" where tenure rights are vaguely defined. Hydropower development greatly reduced the resource base of villages affected by flooding, leading to deforestation of areas critical to the conservation of upstream water resources.

Fourth, natural resources are used by people in ways that are defined symbolically. Land, forests, and waterways are not just material resources people compete over, but are also part of a particular way of life (farmer, rancher, fisher, logger), an ethnic identity, and a set of gender and age roles. These symbolic dimensions of natural resources lend themselves to ideologic, social, and political struggles that have enormous practical significance for the management of natural resources and the process of conflict management (Chevalier and Buckles 1995). Ideologic, social, and political practices are contested in most settings, making it difficult to bring to bear on natural resource problems the diverse knowledge and perspectives of resource users. The viewpoint of local Chortis in Copán, Honduras, was suppressed by landowning elites anxious to deny their indigenous heritage (Chenier et al., this volume). Local perspectives were also initially ignored by Chortis political representatives preoccupied with the national struggle for legitimacy.

Because of these dimensions of natural resource management, specific natural resource conflicts usually have multiple causes — some proximate, others underlying or contributing. A pluralistic approach that recognizes the multiple perspectives of stakeholders and the simultaneous effects of diverse causes in natural resource conflicts is needed to understand the initial situation and identify strategies for promoting change.

From conflict to collaboration

Conflicts over natural resources have many negative impacts. However, people who study conflict also recognize its value as a catalyst for positive social change. Conflict is an intense experience in communication and interaction with transformative potential. For marginal groups seeking to redress injustices or extreme inequities in resource distribution, conflict is an inherent feature of their struggle for change. Although confrontation can lead to violence, avoiding and shunning conflict can be equally dangerous, as unresolved problems may flare up with renewed vigour. Misunderstandings or confusion regarding rights to natural resources and management responsibilities can escalate into more intense conflicts as the number of people involved and the problems multiply. As Lederach (1992) noted, problems become entanglements that turn into fights.

Conflicts are only fully resolved when the underlying sources of tension between parties are removed, a state of affairs that may be antithetical to social life (Chevalier and Buckles, this volume). For those who view conflict as a normal and potentially positive feature of human societies, conflict should not be altogether eliminated through "resolution" but rather "managed" so that it does not lead to violence but can achieve change. Brown (1983, p. 9, quoted in Driscoll 1994, p. 8) goes so far as to suggest that "conflict management can require intervention to reduce conflict if there is too much, or intervention to promote conflict if there is too little."

The field of conflict management draws many of its principles from North American experiences with alternative dispute resolution (ADR). In contrast to litigation and other confrontational modes of conflict resolution, ADR refers to a variety of collaborative approaches including conciliation, negotiation, and mediation (Pendzich et al. 1994; Moore 1996). Conciliation consists of an attempt by a neutral third party to communicate separately with disputing parties to reduce tensions and reach agreement on a process for addressing a dispute. Negotiation is a voluntary process in which parties meet "face to face" to reach a mutually acceptable resolution of the issues in a conflict. Mediation involves the assistance of a neutral third party, a mediator, who helps the parties in conflict jointly reach agreement in a negotiation process but has no power to direct the parties or enforce a solution to the dispute. Through ADR, multiparty "win–win" options are sought by focusing on the problem (not the person) and by creating awareness of interdependence among stakeholders.

Although these approaches to conflict management are appealing, do the principles really work in conflicts involving natural resources? Techniques of ADR depend on both cultural and legal conditions, such as a willingness to publicly acknowledge a conflict, and administrative and financial support for negotiated solutions (Bingham 1986; Shaftoe 1993; Pendzich et al. 1994). They also depend on the voluntary participation of all relevant stakeholders. These conditions are not present in many contexts in both the North and the South. Enlightened self-interest among stakeholders may not be apparent or sufficiently urgent in situations involving the interests of national elites or others with coercive measures at their disposal. ADR may even be counterproductive if the process only manages to get certain groups together to mediate their differences when the causes of conflict and obstacles to resolution are beyond their control. Meanwhile, conflict management training based on ADR principles is promoted around the world, giving rise to a new class of development consultant — the mediator. ADR emphasis on the role of mediators in resolving problems can lead to dependence on "experts" and the neglect of processes that lead to enhanced local capacity to manage recurring conflicts. Given this trend, there is an urgent need to critically assess the approaches with a view to determining the conditions under which they lead to more stable, transparent, and inclusive decisions.

It is also critical to recognize that although negotiation, mediation, and conciliation are being promoted as "alternatives" in Western societies, they are not completely new. Castro and Ettenger (1996, p. 1) argue that "all legal orders," whether based on customary or state institutions, "rely, to varying extents, on the same basic procedural modes to handle disputes … avoidance, coercion, negotiation, mediation, arbitration, and adjudication." In addition, people in diverse societies use other "mechanisms to handle disputes at a local level, including peer pressure, gossip, ostracism, violence, public humiliation, witchcraft, and spiritual healing" (Castro and Ettenger 1996, p. 7).

These local mechanisms of conflict management are not always equitable and effective, especially in conflicts involving multiple dimensions and increasing intensity. Some may hinder equitable and sustainable development and can be legitimately challenged. Nevertheless, Western traditions of conflict management need to be balanced with the systematic study of local practices, insights, and resources used to manage conflict (Chevalier and Buckles, this volume). Cultural, symbolic, and psychological factors that emerge from this analysis can be used to strengthen the integrity of local strategies and redress inequities in local forms of conflict management. Moreover, attention to local strategies is important because the diversity they embody is needed to keep methodological debates open to alternative voices and experiences. In an homogenizing world, diverse local insights and methods are critical sources of innovation.

Multistakeholder analysis of problem areas and conflicts is a key step in catalyzing recognition of the need for change. The cases presented in this volume show that natural resource management decisions are made through complex interactions between actors and the natural resource base at various levels, from the farm and watershed to national institutions and beyond. Problems and conflicts that arise as a result of these decisions are never entirely caused by one individual or group. Understanding and real solutions usually cannot emerge if all stakeholders do not see their own role in creating and perpetuating the conflict.

Multistakeholder analysis is a general analytical framework for examining the differences in interests and power relations among stakeholders, with a view to identifying who is affected by and who can influence current patterns of natural resource management (Ramírez, this volume). Problem analysis from the points of view of all stakeholders can help separate the multiple causes of conflict and bring a wealth of knowledge to bear on the identification and development of solutions. Particular attention is paid to gender-based and class-based differences in problem identification and priority setting because in many societies these differences are systematically suppressed or ignored.

Various research methods can be adapted as part of this analytical approach, including participatory rural appraisal, participatory action research, gender analysis, and the analysis of differences in class interests and power relations. As Ramírez (this volume) points out, stakeholder analysis can be undertaken by external researchers, or it may be used by the stakeholders themselves as a participatory process in support of conflict management. When stakeholders come to recognize for themselves the common interests and strategic differences that connect them to each other, new opportunities can emerge for turning conflict into collaboration.

The limits to collaboration

Perhaps the most intractable yet critical challenge in the pursuit of collaboration in natural resource management is to engage the most powerful stakeholders in analysis of the causes and alternatives to conflict. Although in many settings marginalized groups must be empowered to undertake problem analysis and formulate strategies for negotiation, change will only come about if the powerful are moved to act on the causes of marginalization, inequity, and mismanagement. The conditions, and related pressures, needed to accomplish this movement are not well understood and rarely studied. In short, how do you get the lion to sit at the table with the lamb (Thomas et al. 1996)?

Research by Scott (1987, 1990) suggests that sources of power are nearly always available to marginal stakeholders, if only as an undercurrent or "hidden transcript." In response to a very articulate proposition, dead silence can, at times, make an equally forceful point. The challenge is to enhance the capacity of marginal groups to use their power effectively to engage the overtly powerful in meaningful negotiation. It is this challenge that tests the limits of collaborative approaches to natural resource management and shows why real collaboration is so difficult.

Several of the case studies in this volume note that a show of strength through confrontation may be needed to get the attention of key stakeholders who can redress power imbalances. In the Galapagos Islands, Ecuador (Oveido, this volume), and in Cahuita, Costa Rica (Weitzner and Fonseca Borrás, this volume), the threat of violence by local stakeholders drew in remote government and international stakeholders with the power to change the distribution of natural resource rights and responsibilities.

Violent confrontation may prove to be unproductive, however, and "is prone to generating consequences that are unanticipated, unintended, and uncontrollable" (Bush and Opp, this volume, p. 189). It usually leads to suffering when used against an opponent that uses similarly blunt tools. In a case involving bloody armed conflict in the Sudan (Suliman, this volume) change is coming about very gradually as people's perceptions of the causes and effects of conflict over natural resources change. The fragile peace that is emerging between the Nuba and the Arab Baggara is sustained by recognition that both sides are losing everything important to them (people, cattle, trade). Attention is shifting to external political and economic causes of their violent confrontations.

Contrary to the confrontational scenario, local alliances with advocacy groups, international bodies, and academics offer some scope for dealing with power imbalances more imaginatively and more productively. Widespread screening of two films on threats to an environmentally sensitive wetland in Uruguay posed by the practices of commercial rice growers was critical in swaying public opinion (Pérez Arrarte and Scarlato, this volume). The momentum created by this campaign was then used by research nongovernmental organizations (NGOs) and local governments to change patterns of public and private investment in development and conservation.

The opinions of academics can also influence key stakeholders, such as legislators and senior government officials, when based on solid experience, detailed information, and lucid analysis (Williamson 1999). In the Nusa Tenggara of eastern Indonesia, an informal network of individuals from NGOs, research institutions, government agencies, and local communities is facilitating an ongoing regional process of community consultation, research, mediation, and negotiation that engages multiple stakeholders in the management of conflicts over forest resources (Fisher et al., this volume). Through this process, the unintended impacts of national policies at the community level were brought to the attention of senior government officials, opening the way to government recognition of the need for flexible policies and the value of bringing previously excluded groups into the decision-making process. Research played a catalytic role by helping to make implicit conflicts explicit and by providing credible and detailed information needed to understand the dimensions and various levels of the conflicts and opportunities for change.

Alliances with broader social movements that articulate demands for democratization and environmental accountability can also enhance the voices of the marginal in ways that engage people in dialogue and generate popular discussion. Coalition-building between local groups and progressive social movements is critical to redefining the terms of debate over access to and use of natural resources and to creating or enhancing spaces and mechanisms for negotiating the diverse interests that separate farmers from ranchers, loggers from indigenous peoples, men from women, local officials from national policy-makers, and primary producers from financiers. To sustain and inform popular discussion, more research attention needs to be paid to how external factors (structural adjustment, trade agreements, domestic policies, etc.) are built into local conflicts. Drawing out the historical and structural relationships between communities and the broader processes affecting society opens up the possibility of identifying fundamental problems and formulating alternative social discourse.

Constructing an environment in which conflicts over natural resources can be dealt with productively will also require new structures and processes for governing natural resources management decisions (Agarwal 1997; Kothari et al. 1998). Given the multiple dimensions of natural resource management, negotiating for change can be wasted effort if policy, administrative, and financial factors at higher levels block or contradict the decisions made locally (Tyler, this volume). Changes to national policies and legal frameworks are needed to accommodate the development of relations between formal and informal institutions at various levels. As noted by Ashby (Eberlee 1999, p. 4), "The critical problem is not so much capacity at the micro level, but the incapacity of governments to provide effective public sector counterparts to community-based organizations."

Experiences from Indonesia (Fisher et al., this volume), India (Kant and Cooke, this volume), the Philippines (Talaue-McManus et al., this volume), and Costa Rica (Weitzner and Fonseca Borrás, this volume) suggest that governing structures and processes that bring previously excluded groups into decision-making offer new opportunities for improving natural resource management decisions and finding better ways to avoid, resolve, or manage conflict. The joint forest management (JFM) policy in India calls for the involvement of a wide range of stakeholders, including women, in resource management decisions. In some settings, the policy has resulted in new local mechanisms for reaching agreement on procedures, power sharing, and dispute resolution (Kant and Cooke, this volume). The policy is incomplete and inflexible, however, often leading to contradictions between formal and informal decision-making processes. For example, in some villages the regulation banning the sale of fuelwood under JFM undermines the livelihood strategy of poor caste groups who depend on this resource. Although the decision-making process of village leaders could accommodate these needs based on customary law and locally accepted behaviour, the local JFM committees lack the power to adapt the norms of the policy to local circumstances.

In Cahuita, Costa Rica, a local committee set up to handle a specific dispute over services to visitors to Cahuita National Park evolved over a few years into a management committee involving local people and government officials concerned with the management of the natural resources of the park (Weitzner and Fonseca Borrás, this volume). An executive decree outlining the mandate of the committee helped create an environment conducive to local participation in natural resource management decisions. Although the decree fell short of full devolution of administrative authority to the committee, local actors effectively exploited the legitimacy it provided. Conflict was resolved effectively, and resource management decisions were made to the satisfaction of government officials.

These successes are opening the way to the development of a comanagement regime with profound implications for the way parks are managed in Costa Rica. The experience suggests that although consensus is not always possible, governance that is more inclusive, transparent, and efficient can help groups in conflict accommodate some differences, find some common ground, and improve key decisions affecting their livelihoods.

Although the development of transparent and participatory structures for governing natural resources is an essential step, several other challenges arise. New and multiple roles for local and external stakeholders will need to be negotiated and implemented. As the familiar workings of existing institutional arrangements are replaced and the status of stakeholders is transformed, the development of social relations of trust will become even more critical (Seligman 1997). Farming women and men will need to be sincerely recognized and listened to as site experts. Local governments and organizations will need to develop new communication and training systems to enhance community capacity to generate information and knowledge relevant to stakeholders. Government officials will need to act as facilitators and implementors of decisions emerging from local systems of governance rather than as decision-makers per se (Tyler, this volume). The extent of "readiness to learn" and — because challenging and learning new roles is a risky undertaking — the "margin for learning" (Bernard and Armstrong 1997) will be critical factors affecting who participates in collaborative natural resource management and how. Our hope is that this volume points to relevant new research needed to support this process and enhance the capacity of communities to manage and transform the conflicts that affect their lives.

References

Anderson, J.; Gauthier, M; Thomas, G.; Wondolleck, J. 1996. Setting the stage. Presented at the Global e-Conference on Addressing Natural Resource Conflict Through Community Forestry, Jan–Apr 1996. Forests, Trees and People Programme of the Food and Agriculture Organization of the United Nations, Rome, Italy.

Ascerlad, H. 1992. Environment and democracy. Instituto Brasileiro de Analisis Sociais e Economicas, Rio de Janeiro, Brazil.

Agarwal, B. 1997. Environmental action, gender equity and women's participation. Development and Change, 28, 1–44.

Ayling, R.; Kelly, K. 1997. Dealing with conflict: natural resources and dispute resolution. Commonwealth Forestry Review, 76(3), 182–185.

Bernard, A.; Armstrong, G. 1997. Learning and integration: learning theory and policy integration. International Development Research Centre, Ottawa, Canada. Unpublished report.

Bingham, G. 1986. Resolving environmental disputes. a decade of experience. Donnely and Sons, Harrisonburg, VA, USA.

Brown, L.D. 1983. Managing conflict at organizational interfaces. Addison-Wesley, Reading, MA, USA.

Castro, A.P.; Ettenger, K. 1996. Indigenous knowledge and conflict management: exploring local perspectives and mechanisms for dealing with community forest disputes. Presented at the Global e-Conference on Addressing Natural Resource Conflict Through Community Forestry, Jan–Apr 1996. Forests, Trees and People Programme of the Food and Agriculture Organization of the United Nations, Rome, Italy.

Chevalier, J.; Buckles, D. 1995. A land without gods: process theory, maldevelopment and the Mexican Nahuas. Zed Books, London, UK.

Driscoll, C. 1994. Diversity, dialogue and learning: the case of the Forest Round Table on Sustainable Development. Queen's University, Kingston, ON, Canada. PhD thesis.

Eberlee, J. 1999. Alternative approaches to managing conflict over natural resources. IDRC Reports, 278, 1–5.

Homer-Dixon, T.; Blitt, J. 1998. Ecoviolence: links among environment, population, and security. Rowman & Littlefield, Lanham, MD, USA.

Kothari, A.; Anuradha, R.V.; Pathak, N. 1998. Community-based conservation: issues and prospects. *In* Kothari, A.; Anuradha, R.V.; Pathak, N.; Taneja, B., ed., Communities and conservation: natural resource management in South and Central Asia. Sage Publications, New Delhi, India.

Lederach, J.P. 1992. Enredos, pleitos y problemas: una guia practica para ayudar a resolver conflictos. Comision Central Menonita. Ediciones Clara-Semilla, Guatemala City, Guatemala.

Moore, C. 1996. The mediation process; practical stradtgies for resolving conflict. Jossey-Bass Publishers, San Francisco, CA, USA.

Ortiz, P. 1999. Apuntes teórico-conceptuales para el diseño de una propuesta metodológica de manejo de conflictos socioambientales a través de la forestería comunitoria. *In* Ortiz, P., ed., Comunidades y conflictos socioambientales: experiencias y desfíos en América Latina. Ediciones ABYA–YALA; FAO–FTPP; COMUNIDEC, Quito, Ecuador.

Peet, R.; Watts, M. 1996. Liberation ecologies: environment, development and social movements. Routledge, London, UK.

Pendzich, C.; Thomas, G.; Wohlgenant, T. 1994. The role of alternative conflict management in community forestry. Food and Agriculture Organization of the United Nations, Rome, Italy.

Scott, J. 1987. Weapons of the weak: everyday forms of peasant resistance. Yale University Press, New Haven, CT, USA.
———— 1990. Domination and the arts of existance: hidden transcripts. Yale University Press, New Haven, CT, USA.

Seligman, A. 1997. The problem of trust. Princeton University Press, Princeton, NJ, USA.

Shaftoe, D., ed. 1993. Responding to changing times: environmental mediation in Canada. Interaction for Conflict Resolution, Waterloo, ON, Canada.

Thomas, G.; Anderson, J.; Chandrasekharan, D.; Kakabadse, Y.; Matiru, V. 1996. Levelling the playing field: promoting authentic and equitable dialogue under inequitable conditions. Presented at the Global e-Conference on Addressing Natural Resource Conflict Through Community Forestry, Jan–Apr 1996. Forests, Trees and People Programme of the Food and Agriculture Organization of the United Nations, Rome, Italy.

Williamson, R. 1999. The international fur ban and public policy advocacy: the significance of Inuit cultural persistence. Practicing Anthropology, 21(1), 2–8.

Concept

Culture

Chapter 1

CONFLICT MANAGEMENT:
A HETEROCULTURAL PERSPECTIVE

Jacques M. Chevalier and Daniel Buckles

Research on community-based natural resource management (CBNRM) has paid little attention to key assumptions it uses in the analysis of conflict and conflict management. The concepts of pacifism, egalitarianism, communalism, secularism, and rationalism are built into the community-based approach to natural resource management and are often treated as universal principles. In this paper, we examine differences in cultural perspectives on these assumptions. We also invite researchers to ground their practice of conflict management in the different social and cultural settings they encounter. Through the use of a conversational style of presentation and reference to cases presented in this volume, we attempt to bring the reader closer to oral forms of community-based politics, learning, and teaching, as an alternative approach to resolving differences in perspectives on the meaning of conflict and conflict management.

Boomerang anthropology

Institute: Are you familiar with the literature and experiments in the field of CBNRM?

Anthropologist: Do you mean the community-based natural resource management approach? Sorry, I hate acronyms, especially this one. It doesn't even have a vowel! Yes, I am familiar with it.

Institute: Well, could you help us develop research questions that deal with some of the cultural dimensions of CBNRM?

Anthropologist: Sure, I'm good at asking questions. But tell me more.

Institute: We think that CBNRM is a good thing, minus the acronym perhaps. For many years, we have supported research and development on means to enhance community-based natural resource management. The basic premise of much of this work is that access to relevant knowledge about resource management options combined with more inclusive decision-making processes can contribute to more equitable and more sustainable natural resource management.

Anthropologist: Sounds fine. Where does anthropology fit in?

Institute: Our experience shows that conflicts both within and between communities over access to and use of natural resources are significant barriers to CBNRM. We've been looking at recent approaches to conflict management, such as alternative dispute resolution (ADR), for ways to avoid, resolve, or manage conflict over natural resources (Bingham 1986; Shaftoe 1993). Although these new approaches to conflict management are promising, there is a risk that they be uncritically applied to cultural contexts that may require strategies of their own. Our concern is that, in conflict management, cultural differences be taken into account. Why are you laughing?

Anthropologist: Actually, it's more ironic than funny. Yours is a boomerang question, the kind that rebounds from answers to previous questions. I am thinking of responses already provided by the ADR literature.

Institute: What do you mean?

Anthropologist: Avruch and Black (1996) wrote an interesting article on the North American trend toward alternative means of conflict resolution: rent-a-judge, neutral expert fact-finding surveys, mini- or summary jury trials, ombudsman interventions, etc. The trend comprises all paralegal forms of conciliation, facilitation, mediation, or arbitration currently applied to commercial, juvenile, and family law. Reforms to the American justice system go back to the small-claims court movement of earlier decades. They can also be traced to the turmoil of the 1960s and the Federal Mediation and Conciliation Service that came out of the *Civil Rights Act* (1964), a service designed to help communities settle racial and ethnic disputes. These first developments of an alternative justice system were followed in the 1970s by discussions of neighbourhood justice centres and multidoor courthouse options inspired by the dictum: let the forum fit the fuss.

Institute: Interesting, but what do these origins have to do with our questions regarding anthropological contributions to conflict resolution?

Anthropologist: I was getting there. Avruch and Black (1996) claim that this American "informal justice" movement was influenced by anthropology. It borrowed elements from dispute resolution models originating from tribal societies and used them to promote a peaceful, noncoercive, community-based approach to justice. Richard Danzig's (1973) article, "Toward the creation of a complementary, decentralized system of criminal justice," was particularly influential in this regard. Danzig took some of his inspiration from Gibb's (1963) classic anthropological contribution to the subject matter, "The Kpelle moot: a therapeutic model for the informal settlement of disputes."

Institute: Which means we are not the first to ask this kind of question. So much the better!

Anthropologist: Anthropology is always a risky venture, though. Danzig's reading of Gibb was not without problems. His article oversimplified the Liberian Kpelle moot system. It neglected real functions, such as assigning blame, demanding apologies, imposing sanctions, and the system's coexistence with formal adjudicative court-like institutions. Incidentally, Abel (1982) and Nader (1980) also critically address the history of the American judicial system reform.

Institute: You're saying that alternative approaches to conflict resolution have already used, if not misused, anthropology. If so, should we not try to correct this by seeking "deeper" anthropological insights into conflict resolution?

Anthropologist: Yes, of course. But I should warn you that the exercise is not without danger. As Avruch and Black (1996) remark, great caution should be used when borrowing alternative conflict resolution methods from other cultures. Having said that, where do you want to start?

Institute: Aaaa … We don't really know. Where would you start?

Anthropologist: Aaaa … I hate giving answers. What if we looked at the anthropological literature to see what it has to say about this topic?

Institute: Fine.

Ethnoenvironmental politics

Anthropologist: There is a long history of anthropological research on indigenous customary laws. The emphasis is usually on interpersonal disputes dealing with issues of land tenure, livestock ownership, inheritance, marriage, and witchcraft accusations. Most case studies are in Africa and, to a lesser extent, Asia.

Institute: Can you give us some examples of useful readings in the field?

Anthropologist: There is Gluckman's (1955) *The Judicial Process among the Barotse* and his *Politics, Law and Ritual in Tribal Society* (Gluckman 1965), especially chapter 5 which deals with issues of dispute and settlement. I should also mention Evans-Pritchard's (1940) *The Nuer*, Schapera's (1943) *Tribal Legislation among the Tswana of the Bechuanaland Protectorate*, and Paul Bohannan's (1957) *Judgement and Justice among the Tiv*, to name just a few. Barton's (1919, 1949) classic books on the Ifugao and Kalingas of the Philippines give us very good accounts of recorded cases of tribal governance as well.

Institute: Should CBNRM practitioners read this literature and see what alternative methods of natural resource conflict management they can borrow?

Anthropologist: You could always do that. But I wonder sometimes how useful literature reviews can be. They are a bit like museums. The last thing you want is a compulsory visit to a museum of conflict management practices ossified into showcases and extracted from their living contexts. Alternative methods of conflict management worth exploring are those that are found in the practitioner's research area.

Institute: You're suggesting that each CBNRM project should include questions about the particular ways in which disputes and settlements over natural resources are locally or regionally dealt with, outside the formal institutional context?

Anthropologist: That's a good way of putting it. CBNRM practitioners can also ask which local conflict management practices are likely to fit into a CBNRM approach and which are not. They could tap into local methods that seem CBNRM-friendly and leave aside those that are not. Alternatively, they could choose to revise CBNRM principles in ways that fit local cultural conditions.

Institute: Incidentally, do you know of any catchword we can use to capture this anthropological contribution to alternative, nonlegalistic methods of natural resource conflict management?

Anthropologist: Buzzwords do help, don't they? Be careful though. They are like consumer goods — things designed to be fashionable for a while only. Still, how about "ethnoenvironmental politics"? The expression evokes indigenous forms of conflict management that go beyond "official" institutions (track I) and "unofficial" settlement practices (track II) currently proliferating in North America. Ethnoenvironmental politics (EP) would be the acronym; it has a vowel in it.

Institute: Sounds a bit academic.

Anthropologist: It's not academic, it's "emic," to use Weldon and Jehn's (1996) argument. EP underscores cultural definitions of conflict and conflict resolution behaviour.

Institute: Could you give us a sense of the kind of findings that EP might generate?

Anthropologist: The list is long. Practices that may be relevant to natural resource conflict management are quite varied. As Castro and Ettenger (1996) explain, they may include peer pressure, gossip, ostracism, violence, public humiliation, theatre, rituals, witchcraft, spiritual healing, kinship alliances, the fragmentation of kin or residential groups, etc.

Institute: What about ethno-organizational mechanisms for conflict management?

Anthropologist: Here again there is considerable diversity. In Kirinyaga (Kenya), informal meetings of kinsmen might be the place to start. In northern India, the role of hamlet leaders in formal and informal *panchayat* meetings are critical in dealing with conflicts over land (Moore 1993; Wadley 1994). A case can also be made for moots among the Gwembe Tonga in Zambia and the Ndendeuli and Chagga communities in Tanzania (Moore 1986; Gulliver 1971; Colson 1995). More generally, socially organized groups that play a role in EP may comprise kinship units, neighbourhood or village councils, local authorities, age sets, religious groups, ethnic or caste associations, work-related groups, etc. (Yang and Wolfe 1996).

Institute: The EP structures you have just listed have been severely eroded by centuries of colonial history though, have they not?

Anthropologist: Definitely. For instance, in the Nusa Tenggara region of eastern Indonesia, local kings (*rajahs*), tribal councils, and clan leaders used to exercise effective authority over community land use and forest exploitation. As Fisher et al. (this volume) point out, however, these indigenous forest management systems have been affected by recent government efforts to impose national regulations on community access and determine forest boundaries and classifications based on technical considerations alone. All the same, we need to know more about traditional mediation methods. The *musyawarah* in Indonesia is a case in point; some of its elements could perhaps be incorporated into public policy related to environmental mediation issues (Moore and Santosa 1995).

CBNRM assumptions

Institute: But what about EP that don't fit in with the CBNRM approach? Should we not try to accommodate them in some way?

Anthropologist: I agree; unfriendly EP do pose a problem, but they also raise an interesting question. Could it be that CBNRM has in-built assumptions that are culturally specific and that impose limits on our choice of alternative EP?

Institute: Hmmm, doesn't sound good. Do we have to let the spectre of ethnocentrism haunt us all the time? Can't we assume that CBNRM, given its sensitivity to local conditions, will automatically adjust itself to diverse cultural expressions and adaptations? Provided, of course, that the right questions are asked when developing research and pilot projects inspired by this umbrella approach. It's not a recipe. It's a cooking pot, and the final recipe and ingredients are to be selected, weighed, and mixed locally.

Anthropologist: I like your metaphor. However, different cooking pots will add different flavours to the dish. Have you ever tasted potatoes cooked in a dirt oven, the way they do it in the Andes?

Institute: Okay, then tell us what CBNRM tastes like?

Anthropologist: Before I answer your question, I should mention that recently, while in Washington, I did some reading on the life and history of Jefferson.

Institute: What does the author of the US Declaration of Independence have to do with our discussion?

Anthropologist: Well, our conversation reminds me of some of the things evoked and narrated in the material I read. I have this nagging feeling that a Jeffersonian perspective, understood very broadly, provides what you might call the cultural spirit of CBNRM.

Institute: Hmmm. I'm starting to worry that this is going to be longwinded. Could you try to structure your questions and give us concrete examples so that we can use your comments as guidelines for applied research purposes?

Anthropologist: I take your point. Let's say we do this in five lessons, each under the rubric of a word that ends with a Jeffersonian "ism," and with illustrations taken from the CBNRM and conflict management literature and some case studies supported by institutes such as yours.

Institute: Sounds good. We're all ears.

Pacifism

Anthropologist: One set of questions CBNRM practitioners and researchers should ask themselves when looking at EP has to do with pacifism — the Jeffersonian ideal of peaceful harmony and civility, you might say. Jefferson was not a man of warlike disposition. He struggled to achieve reforms through peaceful means and objected to harsh punishment of the leaders of Shay's Rebellion (1786–87) in Massachusetts. He reduced the military budget and opposed the Alien and Sedition Acts (1798) which threatened the freedom of Americans. Last but not least, Jefferson preferred economic pressure to war in response to British and French violations of American sovereignty during the Napoleonic Wars.

Institute: How is this Jeffersonian ideal of peace built into CBNRM?

Anthropologist: Conflict management means what it means — that you want to manage conflict in a nonadversarial manner. Socioenvironmental conflict management strategies adopted by CBNRM practitioners are geared to preventing, reducing, or resolving conflicts between people. Peace is an important goal.

Institute: Is that a problem? Doesn't everyone want peace?

Anthropologist: I do. Like everyone else though, there are other things I value, and finding out how to secure all the good things in life is by no means easy. For instance, justice matters to people, as do material well-being and a healthy environment. The question is whether there might be situations where CBNRM will favour peace at the expense of justice, real improvements in livelihoods, and the conservation of nature.

Institute: It is as if CBNRM has to mediate potential conflicts between its own multiple goals.

Anthropologist: Correct. To give you an example, Kant and Cooke (this volume) note that the results of community *panchayat* meetings in Madhya Pradesh, India, are not always fair to the weaker parties. Mediators may do everything they can to secure peace but end up with settlements more beneficial to groups wielding the most power.

Institute: Peace and equity do not always go hand in hand.

Anthropologist: Right. Some leading thinkers in this field, Nader (1990) for instance, would go so far as to say that attempts to integrate informal "tribal" dispute management institutions into modern society are primarily concerned with social control. The end result of apparently well-intended reforms to the justice system is that macrostructural questions of power and inequality are covered with a thick cloak of peace and harmony. Legitimate rights are compromised in a wash of "cultural sensitivity," and plaintiffs are encouraged to consent to "personal growth" therapy through mediation. Meanwhile, profitable jobs go to a new breed of hired "have process, will travel" mediators, missionaries of United States democracy offering a menu of McMediation techniques designed to cool things down across the world (Avruch and Black 1996, pp. 52–53).

Institute: Ooof … that's a very sombre view of genuine attempts to move away from judicial forms of litigation, is it not?

Anthropologist: Yes, but given the world we live in, warnings may be in order. One illusion we should avoid lies in the notion that anthropology necessarily points to things that are external, foreign, and alien to our culture. We ourselves move between different "cultures" and related practices from within our own social environment. Sometimes and for some of us, the ethos of peace is of paramount importance and other considerations can be treated as important but nonetheless secondary. Other times and for other groups, the ethics of justice, conservation, or material well-being may be a priority instead. Differences mapped along these variable priority lines can be found within and between communities across the world and history as well.

Institute: We know of many situations where concerns of livelihood clash with CBNRM goals of sustainable development. I remember a discussion between community-sensitive eco-tourism planners and leaders of a remote Mexican indigenous community. After a trial run with Californian eco-tourists, the planners asked what people intended to do with the money harvested through eco-tourism. "Buy cattle" was the answer. "But what about the forest that would need to be cleared for pasture?," asked a dismayed planner. "Don't worry," answered the noble savages, "We'll leave enough trees along the trail so they don't notice the clearings." Enhancing income and conservation can be such alien concepts!

Anthropologist: Another example of this is reported by Fisher et al. (this volume), where the conservation agenda of provincial, regional, and national agencies in Nusa Tenggara, Indonesia, conflict with the development goals of local governments and the Livestock Division of Agriculture Service. Similar stories are legion.

Institute: Okay, peace may be at odds with other legitimate goals of CBNRM, but isn't it safe to say that CBNRM cannot be achieved in situations of chaos and war?

Anthropologist: Yes and no. The point you make requires some qualification. It may be that the use of force or the threat of force is at times the best way to go if lasting peace is to be secured. Villareal (1996) describes how conflicts over community forests in Latin America often involve large-scale marches, occupation of public buildings, hunger strikes, and alliances with international activist organizations designed to bring governments to the negotiation table. Remember the protest marches of indigenous people from Pastaza and also Beni in Bolivia that involved the detention of senior state officials. In 1995, fishers in the Galapagos Islands threatened to confine tourists and set fire to the national park following a government ban on the sea cucumber fishery (Oveido, this volume). These threats created the conditions needed to bring about a comanagement plan sanctioned by the *Law on the Special Regime for the Province of Galapagos.*

One more example, this time from Africa. We know that the government of Cameroon relies on the revenue generated by foreign logging companies to compensate for declining world prices for its major exports (oil, coffee, cocoa). Given this, can it be expected that the government will freely transfer authority over forest resources to local communities without locals using strong pressure tactics: blockading logging companies and threatening to kidnap expatriate workers (Thomas et al. 1996)?

Institute: Environmental politics in Costa Rica seem to support your argument as well. The takeover of Cahuita National Park in 1995 by community actors (Weitzner and Fonseca, this volume) was instrumental in getting the attention of central government bureaucrats in a position to convene multistakeholder negotiations, establish a representative service committee, and appoint qualified members of the community to positions in the park administration.

Anthropologist: The lesson is that situations of inequality may force weaker actors to take radical action, sometimes violent, to bring the powers that be to the negotiating table. The challenge is not simply to promote a culture of peace, but rather to ask what conditions are needed for the lion to be brought to the negotiating table with the lamb, as Thomas et al. (1996) aptly put it. It may be that the Spanish–American "ethnoconflict theory" is the right one after all: in some cases, a show of force may be the best way to get attention and real action (Arvuch and Black 1993, p. 139).

Institute: The use of force or the threat thereof, as opposed to the force of the better argument.

Anthropologist: Well put. CBNRM may foster hopes of optimal congruence between its own goals and the methods proposed to achieve them: in other words, cooperative natural resource management attained through collaborative conflict management methods. Peaceful means to achieve peaceful ends. Conflict settlement is thus pursued through the creation of committees, round tables, user groups, agencies, organizations, alliances, and networks of all sorts that will use incremental and iterative processes of social conversation and mediation to negotiate multiparty win–win options.

Institute: A bit like endless rounds of ADR training of Middle Eastern researchers and activists, when the blockage is at the political level. But what about the risk of creating a culture of violence? The Spanish–American model seems to have created the expectation that conflict must turn openly violent before it is taken seriously. The Guatemala Peace Accords following the protracted war between the government and guerilla forces have created spaces for dialogue among indigenous peoples, intellectuals, and government officials that never existed before. But what a cost in human lives and legacy of collective suffering! Furthermore, the Hispanic expectation of violence can work against some native American cultures. The Embera people of Panama have been struggling peacefully against encroachment on their lands by Mestizo settlers for decades. They've been totally ignored by the settlers and the state yet refuse to become violent. Couldn't we say that CBNRM is the ideal strategy to adopt if nonviolent options are to be identified?

Anthropologist: I would say so, but only if sensitivity is shown to local EP that may not appear to reflect overt expressions of peace. Some EP may be friendly to CBNRM despite appearances to the contrary. In some cases, getting rid of a conflict may be the last thing you should do.

Institute: A bit like political parties constantly fighting in the parliamentary arena but with certain rules and boundaries that are conducive to the exercise of democracy? Or stakeholders using the legal system to challenge positions while spelling out divergent interests and conflicting views on quarrels over natural resources? The implication is that confrontation is not necessarily negative and may be used as a springboard for positive change (Lee 1993)?

Anthropologist: Yes. And, in some situations, too much civility might be wasted, whereas a good verbal brawl or show of force will get you closer to the final settlement. Peaceful and well-intentioned CBNRM dispositions can create problems; the road to hell can be paved with good intentions. Some approaches to conflict management may seem friendly enough to all parties concerned yet end up creating new conflicts or exacerbating old ones. This may be the case with joint forest management (JFM) schemes in India, as Chandrasekharan (1996) explains. Decentralization and devolution in the area of forest management mean a transfer of power aimed at facilitating conflict management. But the entire process can have the opposite result as well: transferring conflicts to the local level (Traore and Lo 1996).

Institute: Less peaceful means may yield better results?

Anthropologist: Possibly; only research and praxis can tell. The road to heaven can be covered with stones and bricks. In their discussion of mediation in South Africa, Chan et al. (1993) suggest that coercion may play a rational and constructive role in mediation. In a similar vein, Nader and Todd (1978), Nader (1990, 1991), and Schweitzer (1996) challenge the anthropological attachment to models of social harmony, models that ignore the vital role overt disputes play in conflict management and social change. Adversarial behaviour is more in line with a realist view of the Hobbesian international order, a zero-sum game governed by the use of pressure and the deployment of threat and reward tactics.

Institute: Can you think of other examples of EP challenges to pacifism?

Anthropologist: Take the American approach to conflict management compared with how disputes are handled in the Republic of Palau, a small archipelago in the remote western Pacific. The American assumptions are that parties should leave their guns at the door, sit down, put their cards on the table (after keeping them close to their chest for a while), and treat one another as equals — if only before the law or the ADR mediator. According to Avruch and Black (1996), Palauans do things differently; theirs is a wealth-oriented culture where competition operates at all levels of the social hierarchy. The American legal system implanted in Palauan society since 1944 has been appropriated by Palauans in ways that reflect the rule of tactical politics as opposed to appeals to authority for effective conflict settlement. If not adapted to these local conditions, ADR techniques can lead to disastrous results. In the end, the best strategy may be a two-track or contingent diplomacy approach: applying some of the principles of ADR (empowering weaker parties and focusing on the problem, not the people) while being cautious of the American value system and accepting that some mediations may be guided by competitive manoeuvres and yield contingent outcomes at best.

Institute: Many roads can lead to Rome, crooked ones included.

Anthropologist: One final example. Traditional measures of land conflict resolution amongst the West Caucasian Abkhazians include child kidnapping. One group kidnaps another group's infant son and adopts it so as to make the two families relatives. The Abkhazian saying is that "blood can be washed away with mother's milk but blood and milk can never be mixed" (Garb 1996). The conflict ends automatically when enemies become relatives — a far cry from the reasonable conflict management techniques advocated in CBNRM.

Egalitarianism

Anthropologist: My second set of research questions has to do with egalitarianism. Remember Jefferson's struggle against aristocracy and his commitment to the ideals of democracy and equality before the law?

Institute: You're not going to suggest that CBNRM assumes equality between stakeholders, are you?

Anthropologist: Not really. I know that the literature is clear about this. Few researchers and practitioners are naive enough to assume that communities are homogeneous and unstratified. The world is recognized for what it is: a battlefield of conflicts of interests governed by power imbalances. A key strategy advocated in the literature is the empowerment of the weak and the poor. Some CBNRM projects may even recognize the need to exclude some stakeholders from the conflict management process. For instance, the continental fisheries industry was left out of the negotiations that led to the comanagement plan embodied in the *Law on the Special Regime for the Province of Galapagos* (Oviedo, this volume).

Institute: So in what way is egalitarianism problematic?

Anthropologist: The danger is when equality is presented as a universal imperative, an ideal that should be put into practice whenever the opportunity arises, irrespective of the cultural circumstances of CBNRM practice and variations in EP. Thomas et al. (1996) call it "levelling the playing field: promoting authentic and equitable dialogue under inequitable conditions."

Institute: There is a tendency among CBNRM practitioners to ignore or downplay the positive role of specialized knowledge and leadership, including their own, in the management of conflicts. It is as though they are too embarrassed to recognize their own power and the clarity that comes with good leadership. You think this raises important EP questions?

Anthropologist: Yes. Westerners tend to view ideal community structures as individuals with equal rights, including the right to be represented by someone of their own like. Farmers don't ask dentists to represent them, nor do Veracruzanos rely on the good services of citizens living in the State of Puebla to represent their views and interests. When CBNRM researchers and practitioners go into the field, they look for ideal groups and communities and their corresponding delegations and representatives, spokespersons usually chosen through mechanisms of collective choice — consensus, elections, nominations by legitimate authorities, procedures, etc. The anthropological question that needs to be raised here is twofold: should the principle of equality and equal representation allow for variations in its cultural expression? and can CBNRM accommodate or even require deviations from this egalitarian ethos?

Institute: Those are big questions. Could you be more specific?

Anthropologist: Take the two most important EP factors that CBNRM researchers and practitioners are constantly faced with: age and gender. Many CBNRM case studies mention the critical and legitimate role that community elders play in the management of local disputes and natural resources such as land. This is the case amongst the Abkhazians of the Caucasus and the Kpelle of Liberia. CBNRM advocates are realistic and sensitive enough to local authority structures to know that it is those who are the least representative of their communities who will be the best and most legitimate spokespersons for "their people." They typically consist of elderly men or women esteemed for their great wisdom, skills, leadership, and moral authority — qualities deemed to come with age. Respected school teachers and priests or monks may also play a key role in dispute settlement, as in India. Their role is to build, maintain, or restore consensus, as opposed to representing the interests of a particular community or a majority of voters (Nader 1990; Castro and Ettenger 1996; Chandrasekharan 1996).

Institute: Which goes to show that CBNRM can adapt to local EP.

Anthropologist: Yes, but most studies also show a concern for the widespread imbalances that exist between men and women, or between the old and the young. The implicit assumption is that wisdom of the elders is tainted with elements of patriarchy or geron-tocracy, to be reduced or attenuated through proper participatory methods (Villareal 1996). Defining the stakeholders in a dispute is considered all the more problematic, as some parties — women, youth, the poor — may not be viewed locally as interest groups entitled to be heard in the negotiation process. CBNRM may wish to empower these voices with greater equality in view, yet this may generate new conflicts, as Castro and Ettenger (1996) remark.

Institute: You find this ambivalence toward indigenous age and gender EP objectionable?

Anthropologist: No, not exactly. The problem is not that we value the role of local authority structures and are suspicious of them at the same time. My suggestion rather is that this ambivalence should be converted from mechanical assumptions into dynamic EP research questions.

Institute: How do you do that?

Anthropologist: You bracket your own cultural definitions of equality, and you ask questions about local understandings of equality and reciprocity. Unexpected findings may result. Research and practice may lead you to conclude that local forms of differentiation between age and gender and other status differentials based on occupation or kinship may not be endemically contested, socially conflictual, or environmentally maladaptive. If so, local EP may be deemed to be CBNRM friendly. They may constitute functional modes of reciprocity that are alien to Western conceptions of equality and representation but nonetheless compatible with CBNRM practice. For example, among the Aö of Nagaland in northeast India, a village council of male elders determines where community members will be allowed to clear land for cultivation. This ensures that land clearing is concentrated in the same area so that paths can be cut and guarded against raiding, fires can be con-trolled, and fallow periods can be assured long enough for the land to recover. Conditions for collective work and sustainable land management are created through this gerontoc-racy (Keitzar 1998).

Institute: So CBNRM should adjust to local EP and incorporate flexible conceptions of fairness and equity. But what if you end up concluding that local age and gender EP are CBNRM unfriendly?

Anthropologist: Then the problem would have to be researched. What matters in the end is that there be adequate understanding of how power differentials, local and institu-tional, play themselves out in particular situations of environmental conflict management. Perhaps we should emulate Gambian mediators who do take into account power differ-entials when negotiating, arbitrating, or adjudicating disputes. They are wise enough to know that there is no single negotiation strategy because "not everyone is the same" (Sheehan 1996).

Institute: I presume that not all situations will fall neatly into your CBNRM-friendly and unfriendly categories?

Anthropologist: Actually, few will. The Indian literature presents quite a challenge in this regard. Social conflicts are often prevalent in heterogeneous villages where power imbalances based on class, caste, age, gender, tribe, ethnicity, and religion intersect in ways that produce a complex hierarchy of customary and legal–administrative modes of management (Sarin 1996). The hierarchy may be such that silences from the margins will outnumber the official voices that clamour for expression and manage to be heard. Which aspects of Indian EP create favourable conditions and which are a hindrance to CBNRM and can be legitimately challenged from within or without is not a question that can be easily answered.

Institute: What would be the consequences of inadequate understanding of the role of power differentials in CBNRM practice?

Anthropologist: That's another empirical question. One possible effect is that CBNRM may forego some useful conflict management opportunities because of its out-of-hand rejection of apparently unfriendly EP. Another consequence is that equality may be prioritized and promoted to the point of creating new local conflicts that jeopardize other legitimate pursuits of CBNRM, such as sustainable land use. Conversely, insufficient research might lead some apparently friendly practices to be incorporated at great cost, that is, reinforcing power differentials and inequities. Finally, a misunderstanding of power differentials may result in CBNRM projects being merrily co-opted by the powers that be.

We know that national governments can create community-level arbitration forums of their own, sometimes under the guise of decentralization. The *salish* in Bangladesh and *gram panchayat* in India are indigenous forums that are incorporated into the state system. Research has shown that they can be dominated by local power structures favouring the wealthy and the politically connected and excluding the interests of women and the poor (Castro and Ettenger 1996; Kant and Cooke, this volume). The village development boards of Nagaland were modeled on traditional village councils of some tribes but come into conflict with governance structures of other tribes.

Communalism

Institute: You have just debunked two monumental principles: pacifism and egalitarianism. Are we heading toward yet another exposé on the virtues of cultural relativism? The kind that justifies total inaction and tolerance toward all forms of social organization, from outright machismo to extreme forms of social stratification? Isn't there a risk that CBNRM will reach total paralysis as it seeks maximum sensitivity to the diversity of value systems and cultural forms of life?

Anthropologist: Yours is an either–or, black-or-white question. My point is not that we should be willing to compromise our beliefs and commitment to a peaceful and equitable management of natural resource conflicts. Rather, the point is that researchers and practitioners working in contexts that are often multicultural should be open to complex and unexpected forms of CBNRM-compatible practices that do not conform to ready-made recipes of Western inspiration.

Institute: Fine. What's your next Jeffersonian "ism"?

Anthropologist: I call it communalism, for want of a better word. As in community-based natural resource management. Not that Jefferson advocated community-based modes of governance, the Jeffersonian parallel doesn't work all that well in this case. Mind you, Jefferson devoted a lot of his time to farm and family. Also, he was an advocate for self-governance for America under British rule and for the western territories.

Institute: Is "communalism" another problem? Is your point going to be that communalism belongs to a culturally specific value system that should not be spread around the world via CBNRM? Or, better still, are you going to say that you're not against the idea, provided that it be problematized and subjected to EP analysis?

Anthropologist: No. This time I think CBNRM is in trouble. The concept of community creates serious problems.

Institute: Pity. If you drop the concept of community, are you not jeopardizing the underlying notion that the decision-making process in the field of environmental management should be inverted from top down to bottom up? Decentralization is embedded in this concept.

Anthropologist: I understand. But could it be that social scientists have committed a grave error in fostering this "community" view of life in society? The term *community* usually assumes two things: first, a group delimited by distinctively recognizable boundaries; second, an identity constituted by what is shared between members located inside those boundaries. What if social relations worked exactly the opposite way — that is, the inside would consist essentially of two things: relations between those deemed to be different and exchanges with the outside world? What if life in society was neither monocultural (the idea that each society has a culture of its own) nor multicultural (the idea that we all live in multiethnic and pluralistic environments)? What if the rule was rather heterocultural or heterosocial — social life thrives on intercourse between those considered different?

Institute: Did you say "heterocultural"? Never heard of the word.

Anthropologist: I don't like acronyms, but I do have this habit of manufacturing words.

Institute: How does heteroculturalism work in real-life situations?

Anthropologist: Take the Sudanese Nuba. They are Nuba for several reasons. First, not because of what they have in common, but rather because of the particular ways in which they establish differences and relations between villages and lineages, the young and the old, men and women, people and land, plants and animals, humans and spirits. Second, they are Nuba because they know not who they are but rather who they are not: namely, the neighbouring Baggara who construct differences and relations differently. Nubaness points to how the Nuba do not do things the Baggara (or the Jellaba) way. Third, the Nuba are Nuba not because they don't mingle with the Baggara, but rather because of the intercourse that binds and sustains the two "communities": real commerce, intermarriages, etc. At the heart of Nuba identity lies a long history of trade and politics linking the Nuba and the Baggara, hence interdependence across the ethnic divide. To give you just one example of this, there used to be a time when each Baggara subtribe defended its respective Nuba hills and allies so as to secure supplies of grain and slaves as well (Suliman, this volume).

Institute: How does this discussion of Nubaness illustrate the idea of heteroculturalism?

Anthropologist: It means that the Nuba identity lies in a web of negotiated differences and relations, internal and external. It's as if the differential fluids exchanged and circulating within and between the two bodies, the Nuba and the Baggara, determined the shape and anatomy of each group. Note also that these fluids are in constant motion, something that the concept of identity tends to hide. The Nuba are Nuba not because of static attributes that can be assigned to them but rather because of convoluted stories moving through time: the fluids of social history.

Institute: Your notion of heterocultural identity formation sounds "sexy." Yet we know that not all zones and exchanges of the body social are erogenous. Some are covered with wounds suffered at the hands of other groups. Less metaphorically, the Nuba history of relations with other groups includes stories of slavery and repression verging on genocide.

Anthropologist: I was getting there. Notice the term I was using, *relations*, which may range from commerce and marriage to invasion and armed conflict. All such relations, be they cooperative or conflictual, play a direct role in histories of shifting identities. Without outside interaction, it is unlikely that Nubaness would have been recognized as a distinct cultural identity. The Nuba comprise more than 50 dialect groups who share most of all a common history of Turkish and British invasions, Jellaba domination, and slave-raids at the hands of the Baggara previously roaming the plains of Kordofan and Darbur. Nineteenth-century raids have forced them to retreat into the Nuba mountains; territorial identity is never a simple matter of a group choosing its habitat independent of outside forces. Without this common destiny vis-à-vis external forces, the boundaries of Nuba identity and territory would be meaningless. Even the term *Nuba* has been imposed from outside and is used mostly in reference to the non-Nuba world. Ethnicity is never merely an internal construction; it's also a response to external actions and definitions.

Institute: Hasn't this Nuba identity been severely eroded through recent population movements and increased contact with other ethnic groups through urban migration? If so, wouldn't that contradict your "heterocultural" thesis?

Anthropologist: On the contrary. Urbanization is affecting the Nuba way of life, but mostly in the sense of making constructions of ethnicity more rigid than ever. People are pigeon-holed into ethnic categories, which means that "culture" is artificially disembedded from other aspects of social life. According to Suliman (this volume), the Nuba have thus further "discovered" their Nubaness through the diaspora; life in the towns of the Sudan and expressions of northern Arab arrogance toward non-Arab Southerners and Westerners have reduced Nuba cultural diversity to a single, second-class Nuba identity.

Institute: Yours is a different way of seeing "community constructions" that may be insightful, but is this not an academic exercise?

Anthropologist: Not really. One implication of this argument is that the history of social sciences has in common with colonial and neocolonial politics a propensity to divide or reorganize populations into apparently homogeneous national, ethnic, or linguistic groups. People are slotted into island-like entities that hide the interaction and movements occurring across boundaries. Communities constructed as biological-like organisms classifiable like genera and species are partly an offshoot of an academic discourse that may feed into strategies of domination and war. The end result is a hierarchical and conflictual sort of heteroculturalism that hides under a thick cloak of "tribalism" — people fighting apparently because they cannot tolerate their differences.

Institute: Would this argument apply to official accounts of the 10-year-old war between the Nuba and the Baggara?

Anthropologist: Precisely. As you know, wars in Africa are often explained away as ethnic conflicts or wars of religion and tribal identity. As Suliman (this volume) argues, the problem is not so much that the explanation is false, which it is. Rather, the problem is that the explanation tends to make things worse, fueling the conflict as it were, and not without intent. Up until the 1980s the Nuba and the Baggara were relatively at peace with one another; since then, they have been at war. The civil war that broke out in 1983 led the Arab Jellaba government and eventually the National Islamic Front to repress the Nuba-led opposition party called the Sudan National Party and also to arm the Murahaliin militia and the Baggara nomads against Nuba communities and the Sudanese Popular Liberation Army roaming in the rebel-friendly Nuba mountains. Faced with problems of overgrazing and persistent droughts, the Baggara used this opportunity to raid Nuba communities and dispossess them of their land. However, these raids have most benefited the Jellaba government and a minority of land-hungry Jellaba farmers and absentee landlords intent on introducing large-scale mechanized farming into the region. Needless to say, the official account of the Nuba–Baggara war is quite different and revolves around issues of "difference." While they actively supported the Baggara war against the Nuba, landlords and the government have fueled the conflict by treating it as an outburst of tribalism, or a Jihad Holy War against the non-Islamic Nuba.

Institute: Couldn't we say that this case study is a good example of stakeholder analysis, which happens to be a standard tool in CBNRM and related conflict management practice?

Anthropologist: You might say that. But the case study also teaches us that stakeholder analysis is better done with an understanding of "community" that stresses its heterocultural origins and functions, be they cooperative or conflictual. By the way, the experience in Nam Ngum, Lao PDR, is another illustration of how useless the notion of a common interest and stable, long-standing community structure can be (Hirsch et al., this volume). The Nam Ngum River watershed area is the site of many social divisions, creating factional competition between regional and national livelihoods, local and external claimants to forest and water resources, subsistence and commercial producers, village residents and settlers, communities with different ethnic compositions, upland and lowland production systems, and so on.

Institute: Let's say we buy into your notion of heteroculturalism. How does it affect the research agenda dealing with environmental conflict?

Anthropologist: Three things. First, when doing stakeholder analysis, you can ask questions not only about things that members of a "community" have in common, but also what they do not share and yet binds them together through ongoing relations, cooperative or conflictual. Second, the same question applies to members of different communities and interest groups: intercourse between "communities" is as binding as resemblance and similarities. Questions regarding heterosocial movements across community boundaries, be they defined as localities or communities of interests, matter as much as straightforward community affiliations. During the last century, the Miskito drove the Sumo into the upper reaches of the great floodplain of the Atlantic coast of Nicaragua and Honduras. Interaction during the Contra war transformed this relationship, leading to the formation of a common political body seeking to establish their rights to territory in the newly declared reserve of Bosawas. Finally, social change is at the heart of identity formation.

Where people and groups wish to go matters as much as where they come from. History is full of dreams and aspirations either frustrated or partly satisfied by courses of events. Take these dreams and fears away, and you have rigid cultural identities, or the appearance thereof.

Institute: Can you think of any stakeholder terminology that captures your last point?

Anthropologist: The notion of a playing field is the closest I can think of. A playing field means people play. Games are of no interest if the players and their respective positions remain the same throughout the game. Change is all the more inevitable as people typically play many different games and occupy multiple positions that vary through time.

Institute: Could you give us other examples of the negative consequences of using more conventional notions of community?

Anthropologist: The management of gender differences offers a good example of how mechanical notions of "community boundaries" can be harmful. On one hand, CBNRM practitioners cannot simply assume that men and women belonging to the same community must share and occupy the same participatory rural appraisal forums, for the greater glory of equality without difference. On the other hand, they cannot presume that each gender forms a distinct "community of interests," to be recognized and treated as such through separate "representations." Relations and flows within and between genders will vary from one social environment to another and call for conflict management strategies that eschew "simple community" recipes.

Institute: Should we not simply trust the parties concerned to identify strategic "community" boundaries?

Anthropologist: Not necessarily. Take the Mexican Gulf Nahua battle for communal land ownership fought throughout the 1970s and early 1980s. The media treated the battle as a struggle for the preservation of cultural identity and traditional community heritage against the redistribution of parcels of land (following the *ejido* model) and the encroachment of the government-owned oil industry. In reality, however, the "native community battle" story was fed to the press by native cattle ranchers who were in control of municipal and communal land-tenure institutions (Chevalier and Buckles 1995). Observers who bought the "communal" interpretation, pitting the whole Nahua village against the expropriation or redistribution of land, played into the native cattle-rancher strategy. They fell into the trap of assuming that customary resource-allocation and conflict-settlement institutions had not been distorted by centuries of colonial and postcolonial history involving market forces, state bureaucracies, and broader national politics.

Institute: Your response is intriguing. You argue that local accounts of conflicts cannot always be taken at face value. But your evocation of colonial and postcolonial history suggests that communities might be less divided and better off if they were left on their own, without outside intervention, in keeping with CBNRM philosophy. Could it not be that natural resource conflicts stem essentially from a relative lack of community autonomy vis-à-vis outside forces?

Anthropologist: You're opening up another can of worms. Heterocultural polity is not merely a horizontal phenomenon. It also points to vertical relations between the "inside" and "outside," interactions that are constitutive of community life and history. CBNRM itself is an illustration of flows and movements across vertical boundaries. Let's face it,

CBNRM would never capture any institutional imagination were it not for some third party promoting or facilitating its practice. More often than not, the intervention occurs in response to a request for assistance or some regional, national, or international imperative to be protected, be it conservation, democracy, or structural adjustment.

The request or intervention is all the more needed as externalities are built into how localities and communities of interests are structured and come to be. The end product of this outside intervention may be a government actually taking leadership in CBNRM. This is the case with the Philippines, where an Executive Order passed in October 1997 required no less than 800 coastal municipalities to formulate comprehensive development plans to be used in designing national fishery ordinances. To be fair, the order took some of its inspiration from the experience of the Multisectoral Committee on Coastal Development Planning instituted in the municipality of Bolinao, Pangasinan (Talaue-McManus et al., this volume).

Institute: So local autonomy is a misleading concept?

Anthropologist: I would say so. Take the Indonesian case study (Fisher et al., this volume). We know that boundary disputes over agricultural lands between villages and communities in Indonesia used to be resolved at the local level, through the intervention of local leaders and without outside assistance. It is only when government and business enter the picture that a pitch has to be made, often with the support of third parties, for decentralization and community devolution entailing comanagement arrangements.

In Nepal, institutions charged with managing natural resource conflicts evolving at the community level include bilateral agencies, the Department of Forests, the Department of National Parks and Wildlife Management, legal associations such as the Nepal Bar Association, propublic and multidisciplinary groups such as Nepal Madhyashata Samuha, and nongovernmental organizations (NGOs) such as Women Acting Together for Change (Chandrasekharan 1996). When you look at the Nepalese and Indonesian experiences in CBNRM, community-based management is a bit of a misnomer.

Institute: The notion that externalities are built into community structures and histories and should be part of CBNRM practice is part of your heterosocial or heterocultural concept?

Anthropologist: Yes, and the implications are many. For one thing it means community traditions are never simple; nor are they static. Social transformations over the last two centuries are particularly significant in this regard. In Indonesia, the implementation of government policies and the growth of national bureaucracies have severely affected the authority of tribal councils and microleadership structures. Nowadays, the government appoints village administrators, imposes laws and procedures, runs an educational system of its own design, and facilitates the expansion of markets and migratory movements. All of this has generated tensions not only between local and national institutions but also between local constituencies (Fisher et al., this volume).

Institute: Given these inevitable ties between micro- and macrolevel processes, we might be better off using the term *comanagement* instead of *community-based management* (McCay 1998; Uphoff 1998).

Anthropologist: Comanagement is a useful concept, indeed. The term captures what Quebec government resource managers are attempting to do when they treat community tallymen and the Cree Trapper Association as their co-equals, in keeping with stipulations of the James Bay and Northern Quebec Agreement. Tallymen are recognized hunting leaders who rely on kinship ties, reciprocity, and personal influence to exercise authority over activities performed on their traplines and to settle disputes when they arise (Feit 1989). Take also CBNRM in India. We know that Indian community systems of forest management underwent profound transformations during British rule. More recently, JFM schemes have been created and adopted in 25 Indian states. They involve the forest department and local communities organized into forest protection committees and village forest protection committees.

Institute: You should know that institutional partnership between local and external institutions is not without difficulties, though. Local committees include all *panchayat* officials elected every 5 years. But they also comprise a resident teacher, women, and landless people, many of whom tend to be young and find themselves competing with the *panchayat's* traditional role in conflict mediation. Lack of complementarity between institutions can be a problem (Chandrasekharan 1996; Kant and Cooke, this volume).

Anthropologist: Still, comanagement goals are worth pursuing. The Indonesian experience in CBNRM offers promises of a collaborative, comanagement strategy that combines horizontal and vertical linkages. One important lesson of the Nusa Tenggara Uplands Development Consortium is that the management of forest and conservation disputes requires a multicommunity, interinstitutional approach, hence new alliances built across traditional political and cultural boundaries. The consortium comprises all stakeholders: villages adjacent to the protected areas, NGO leaders, researchers and scientists committed to conservation and community development, and district and provincial officials from key government agencies.

Institute: In short, your argument is that we should be concerned not so much with community autonomy as with real collaboration between concerned parties. Still, isn't there a danger that comanagement principles may serve to justify top-down limits on community-based management activity?

Anthropologist: Perhaps, but comanagement can also be enabling. CBNRM practitioners might wish to persuade government institutions, multinationals, and large national industries to yield to the wiser ways of community-based management of natural resources and related conflicts. A better strategy, however, would be to promote the economic and political empowerment of weaker "communities" within broader social systems, with upward links enabling communities to affect broader policies. Structurally adjusting governments may opt to transfer natural resource rights and responsibilities over fully autonomous communities but without transferring anything else — no financial resources; no credit or marketing assistance; no technical support; and no protective legislation against local merchants, landowners, lumber bosses, multinational pulp and paper companies, the oil industry, or commercial farmers. If so, autonomy and decentralization add up to pure rhetoric. CBNRM is doomed to failure if there is no real sharing of costs and benefits between micro- and macrolevels, as Uphoff (1998) suggests.

Institute: But village forest reserves and community-based management plans would never have seen the light in the Babati District of Tanzania had it not been for Tanzania's national policy of decentralization and corresponding effort to reduce government costs in forest management (Thomas et al. 1996)?

Anthropologist: Decentralization *does* create new opportunities for community management. But it can also lead to the greater weight of market forces and increased concentration in the hands of the few. In the absence of comanagement policies and structures, anything can happen.

Institute: Your research questions regarding the concept of community are most relevant. But we're not entirely convinced by your anthropologic critique of "communalism." Can there not be CBNRM-friendly adaptations of the conventional "community" rhetoric?

Anthropologist: Perhaps. After all, a good heterocultural story that produces worthwhile results doesn't have to be true, does it? Shoring up some "authentic community" story that seeks to preserve a commonly shared identity can serve a worthwhile cause. When you think of it, the Honduran Chortis gained a lot from the anthropologic documentation of their indigenousness and preservation of the Maya way of life. Rivas (1993) contradicted the Copán landowner view that the Chortis should not be recognized as a native people, given everything they have lost, including their language and other external features of "native" life (for example, traditional clothes). The landowner view was not without political motivation: the implication was that the Chortis should not be eligible to seek land ownership, in accordance with Honduras' Agreement 169 signed under the presidency of Carlos Roberto Reina (1994–97) (Chenier et al., this volume).

Who knows, fictions of well-preserved identities could bring further benefits through the expansion of tourism in Copán, an important archeological site. The Chortis could alleviate their subsistence problems by packaging themselves as interpretive commodities for the tourist industry. Landowners and merchants might gain from the growth of Copán tourism currently under their control. Peace could be restored, and some further land concessions could be secured by the Chortis. The net "Copán community" benefits would be enhanced if local cultural tourism, a heterocultural phenomenon in its own right, were done intelligently, the CBNRM way. Everything is possible.

Institute: Are you suggesting that communalism can be CBNRM friendly under conditions that need further specification? If so, it sounds like an acceptable compromise.

Anthropologist: Fiction can pay off — it's called "strategic essentialism" — as long as researchers and actors keep asking themselves whether the dream is not about to turn into a nightmare.

Institute: Point well taken.

Secularism

Anthropologist: But we're not finished, are we? Now comes the fourth "ism": secularism.

Institute: Are you referring to the separation of State and Church, as fathered by Jefferson via his bill on religious freedom introduced in Virginia?

Anthropologist: Yes. But more importantly, the extirpation of religion from economics and politics.

Institute: Are preachers of Greenpeace, animal rights, and Gaïa politics about to knock at our door?

Anthropologist: I'm afraid so. But I promise to be brief and to offer relevant CBNRM adaptations of the Gaïa research agenda.

Institute: Not to worry. Ours is a serious institution, which means we are open to alternative views of nature. We firmly believe there is a lot to be learned from indigenous attitudes toward the universe. We too are heteroculturals!

Anthropologist: Some of my questions you will therefore anticipate. It takes no great imagination to suggest that CBNRM researchers and practitioners should ask questions about how some people view other life forms as stakeholders in their own right, to be listened to in the appropriate forums and through adequate mediation. Sensitivity is to be shown to the role of religious leaders, sorcerers, healers, animals, plants, and spirits in the management of natural resource activities and related disputes between humans and between life forms.

Institute: Could you give us examples of concrete observations that can be made in the field and that pertain to the religious aspects of environmental management and related dispute settlements?

Anthropologist: Of course. In Africa, connections between natural resource management activities and Islamic laws of inheritance can be crucial to CBNRM planning (Sheehan 1996). When pursuing dispute settlements, Gambians resort not only to customary laws and legal statues, but also to Islamic laws; forum shopping crosses the divide between secular and religious institutions and belief systems (Sheehan 1996). In Tonga, Christian congregations have been shown to play a critical role in local conflict management (Olson 1993). In the Nusa Tenggara region of Indonesia there is a strong spiritual motivation for land and forest management practices; numerous forest sites are still regarded as sacred, and traditional restrictions on exploring these areas are still upheld (Fisher et al., this volume). All these examples converge in one lesson: religion and religious institutions do matter.

Institute: Given these considerations, should we not be conscious of the limitations of such terms as *natural resources* and their *management* by human beings? Should we not seek alternative, less anthropocentric terms that address the intercourse of nature and culture, terms that are less secular and may enhance the local sustainability of CBNRM?

Anthropologist: Definitely. Culture's relationship with nature is heterocultural in its own right, a playing field where CBNRM can learn from indigenous knowledge systems that speak to the complex interdependencies that tie humans to all life forms, perceived or imagined.

Institute: Do you think that research questions pertaining to "land ethic" values should be built into CBNRM, as McCay (1998) proposes? Or should we simply let local actors add whatever EP interpretation or translation they deem relevant to their CBNRM practice? The Ojibway of central Canada, for example, may include a chair at formal meetings on land issues with government officials for "the seventh generation to come" and discuss what that person might say before making decisions.

Anthropologist: There is no simple answer to that question. It's the question that matters, to be answered differently from one context to another. In some cases, outside efforts to translate everything into local cultural belief systems can result in overengineering and downright demagogy. In other cases, institutions and NGOs that neglect to ask questions about native EP rituals and cosmologies may send a clear message, wittingly or not: use our "managerial" language, scale it down to your community level if need be, forget your superstitions, or keep your idiosyncratic beliefs to yourselves. "Locals" should keep religion out of CBNRM or be discreet about it.

Institute: Can we safely assume that CBNRM concessions to some ecocentric Gaïa EP will automatically bring dividends? Sorry, we mean raise all spirits to a higher plane of environmental consciousness?

Anthropologist: Certainly not. We know too well that the playing field of humans having intercourse with gods can produce all sorts of secular alliances. Advocates of Jellaba Islam may call upon the Baggara to invade Nuba land and massacre its inhabitants. African peasants may convert to Pentecostalism and struggle against the cult of animals and forest sites. The Christian hierarchy may invite followers all over the world to renounce animism and paganism. A Mexican community leader known to offer healing ritual services may happen to be the local *cacique*, a relatively wealthy rancher, or the mayor's brother. While we're at it, mention could be made of sectarian divisions in rural communities of Northern Ireland, an issue somewhat neglected in British contributions to social anthropology (Moore and Sanders 1996). In short, spirituality is never simply neutral; nor is it always socially or environmentally enlightened.

Rationalism

Institute: Religion can be a touchy subject. Could that explain the conspicuous absence of discussions of religious matters in the CBNRM literature?

Anthropologist: That's one reason. But there is an even deeper reason: the notion that rational management strategies should be applied to natural resource activities. Which brings me to our fifth "ism": rationalism, the last assumption on my hit list. By it, I mean reason applied to natural resource management issues and deployed in ways that are predominantly utilitarian, analytic, logical, and contractual. You might call this "environmental rationalism."

Institute: That's a mouthful!

Anthropologist: Please bear with me. Let's start with the utilitarian approach, an attitude that emphasizes things and activities that are useful. Doing useful things and seeking rational, methodical ways of attaining environmental management goals are part and parcel of CBNRM. Vernooy and Ashby (this volume) put considerable emphasis on the organizational principles of CBNRM and local capacity-building for monitoring and planning resource use.

Institute: You think this assumption should be problematized, anthropologically speaking?

Anthropologist: Yes, in two different ways. First, by looking at cultural differences in perceptions of goals and related means assigned to their attainment. Second, by asking ourselves how much energy and time people are willing to devote to these rational activities, as distinct from crazier things people also engage in.

Institute: How are these assumptions embedded in CBNRM?

Anthropologist: Patience! We need to address two other facets of reason before we proceed to more concrete illustrations. Analytic logic is one of them: organizing our thoughts into discreet categories, writing, and measurements, if possible, and putting them into some sequential order. When combined with a utilitarian attitude, reasoning of this kind is conducive to cost–benefit analysis of ends and means to achieve them. Left-brain stuff.

Institute: You're not going to give us an exposé on the lessons of right-brain thinking for CBNRM and the management of related conflicts, are you?

Anthropologist: No, unless you keep interrupting me! The third and final aspect of reason is what might be called contractualism: reaching formal agreement through an exchange of logical arguments leading to some exercise of free choice by all parties concerned, usually with legalistic implications.

Institute: All of these assumptions seem so reasonable. Our view is that reason is badly needed in dealing with problems of massive destruction and pervasive conflicts in the field of natural resource management. Actually, mismanagement would a better word to describe what usually happens.

Anthropologist: I agree. But we also need to consider other cultural responses to problems of environmental degradation. Comparing such views with our own rational value system is bound to offer new insights into the cultural waters we swim in; fish are reputed to have a hard time recognizing water for what it is.

Institute: The principles you've just outlined were embedded into Jeffersonian philosophy?

Anthropologist: Yes, to the extent at least that Jefferson was both father and child of the modern era, which he was in several ways. Jefferson studied law and advocated natural rights theory. He attempted to modernize the curriculum of the College of William and Mary and to create a public library and a free system of tax-supported elementary education. Modern education was so important to him that he considered the creation of the University of Virginia to be one of his greatest accomplishments. Moreover, he supported the use of the decimal system, which led to the adoption of the dollar in 1792. On the economic side of things, Jefferson helped negotiate international commercial treaties while in Paris. Finally, the man experimented with new agricultural technologies and even built a nail factory. Although certainly not committed to a conservation or sustainable development philosophy, Jefferson had faith in the virtues and powers of education, science, and reason.

Institute: How are these premises problematic from an anthropological perspective? Doesn't utilitarianism provide us with tools essential to the management of scarce natural resources and the legitimate satisfaction of human needs, however they may be defined?

Anthropologist: Yes, assuming that you're swimming in the right waters. But what if the terms you just used did not capture the lifeworld other people live in? What if natural resources did not exist as "natural resources," that is, as objects and life forms devoid of spirituality and intentionality? Could it be that other cultures do not conceive of things and bodies that can be thrown into the "purely physical" universe we call nature? What happens to CBNRM practice when faced with African or native American cultures that speak a language of zoning and ecology alien to our "natural resource" perspective? Shouldn't the CBNRM language adjust accordingly (Henshaw Knott 1993)?

Institute: But surely words like *nature* and *resource* are no more than words, empty shells that can be filled with different contents and belief systems?

Anthropologist: Not really. Words are symptomatic of attitudes and behaviour expressed toward things that surround us. The impact of nature conceived as a vast reservoir of material means to satisfy human wants has been discussed at great length by anthropologists and ecologists and should not be underestimated. Nor should the insights offered by other cultural perspectives on "nature" be ignored in CBNRM practice. In conventional economic terms, we might say that there are real cultural costs to models that seek universal applications of rational cost–benefit analysis and the value system of capital. Paradoxically, utilitarianism is an expensive proposition (Hanna 1998).

Institute: But CBNRM is deeply committed to sustainable development goals and the preservation of nature for future generations. It takes the origins of the word *resource* most seriously, from the old French word *resourare*, to arise anew: *re-* means again, *sourdre* is to spring up as water, from Latin *surgere*, to arise. This concern with letting nature "arise anew" radically departs from all endeavours to harness the environment to our immediate needs. It is also generally compatible with other cultural perspectives on nature.

Anthropologist: Again, I beg to disagree. The goals you speak of are commendable and represent a new perspective on our relationship to Mother Nature. Still, sustainability finds its source of inspiration in reason. It elevates rational behaviour to a higher plane, so to speak, namely, entire "communities of interests" exercising "social choices," hopefully to the benefit of future generations and the whole of humanity. This is a challenge to models of unregulated individuals preoccupied with their personal well-being alone, which is what Hardin's theory of the "tragedy of [free access to] the commons" used to assume (Ostrom 1998). Nevertheless, sustainability is generally pursued without a voice being granted to spirits and other life forms dwelling in nature. The concept still evolves within the orbit of Western reason.

Institute: Your point brings us back to the issue of secularism and religion, does it not?

Anthropologist: Yes.

Institute: The utilitarian attitude also ties in directly with the imperatives of logic and analytic problem-solving, *a priori*, that are by no means culture-free (Avruch and Black 1993). CBNRM practitioners rarely ask critical questions about the managerial assumptions that underlie their work.

Anthropologist: That is unfortunate. Actually, with the utilitarian and managerial assumptions come a whole range of methodologic prescriptions that are part and parcel of CBNRM. Take prescriptions of "clarity" for instance. Logic tends to have little tolerance for ambiguity and confusion, to say the least. What if, instead of stressing maximum dissonance reduction, CBNRM were to make some concessions to chaos theory, as do many people in cultural settings other than our own? By the way, this is what Pederson (1995) suggests in his discussion of non-Western concepts of multicultural conflict management as applied to migration issues.

Institute: How would chaos theory affect CBNRM practice?

Anthropologist: For one thing the boundaries of communities and stakeholder groups might become fuzzier, with gray zones and overlaps that introduce muddles into models of social reality. Expectations that rival parties clearly define their interests and goals and focus on the task at hand, doing things step by step and leaving all other considerations aside, might have to be revisited as well.

Institute: But rational management methods do require that issues and boundaries be clearly analyzed and handled with efficiency, through proper dialogues and with definite plans and deadlines to be followed and adjusted according to needs.

Anthropologist: Don't get me wrong. The methods you describe are powerful tools and do work, given the right conditions. Setting up village forest reserves in Tanzania meant that stakeholders, representatives, and group interests (distinct or shared) had to be identified; problems and alternative solutions adequately circumscribed and prioritized from different perspectives; technical and social information gathered and distributed; risks of failure and success realistically assessed; links to national decentralization policies explored; preliminary contractual agreements recorded and later sanctioned by law; minuted meetings and follow-up activities scheduled and structured with enough time devoted to each phase; and ground rules established from the start. And everything had to be done under the neutral guidance of properly trained mediators and facilitators (Thomas et al. 1996). Practically all of these step-by-step procedures were used in the development of comanagement plans in Cahuita, Costa Rica (Weitnzer and Fonseca Borrás, this volume) and in the Galapagos as well (Oviedo, this volume).

Institute: Which goes to show that people can behave rationally and with some success!

Anthropologist: True enough. But what if cultural and historical circumstances required different strategies?

Institute: Then we would look for local codes of behaviour and try to adjust CBNRM practice accordingly.

Anthropologist: So would I. Two caveats, though. First, the notion that people follow fixed codes is a corollary of analytic logic. As Colson (1995) and Castro and Ettenger (1996) argue, the danger with studies of "other cultural codes" is that we ignore the ambiguities and dynamic chaos built into local "norms of conduct"; the risk is that we understand and apply these codes more rigidly than community members normally would. Second, what if local rules were downright CBNRM unfriendly in some important respects?

Institute: For example?

Anthropologist: Let's say people were not inclined to talk about conflicts, preferring instead to speak of gossip, fuss, imbroglios, or problems that need "fixing," as in Costa Rica (Lederach 1992). Would CBNRM work if cultural norms discouraged people from converting latent conflicts into public disputes (Uphoff 1998)? What if rival parties were practically illiterate and had no knowledge of methodic management practices and little familiarity with the legalities and administrative implications of CBNRM? Or if only young men had such skills, to the exclusion of elders customarily responsible for the settlement of disputes, as among pastoralists in Mali (Verdeld 1994)? What if people preferred to handle disputes not quickly and straightforwardly but rather slowly, obliquely, with arguments that wander off in all directions? Can rational management activities do without the use of written law and allow instead for a generous deployment of proverbial sayings, oath-taking, praying, embracing, feasting or gift-giving, as in Nusa Tenggara?

Institute: Reason would compel us to research these questions before undertaking a CBNRM project.

Anthropologist: If so, other questions would also follow. For instance, how would natural resource conflicts be managed in a context where traditional mediation strategies consist of a marathon of emotional outbursts aimed at dissipating strong feelings, as among the Malaysian Semai (Avruch and Black 1993; Robarchek and Robarchek 1993)? What if the eloquence, humour, or wisdom of an elderly Gikuyu man or Abkhazian mediator mattered more than his ability to facilitate a dialogue? Or if the mediatory abilities of a northern Zapotec compadre, a Tanzanian Ndendeuli notable, or an Indian and northern Somali lineage leader stemmed not so much from the person's impartiality as from his or her capacity to play on his or her links with the parties in conflict? How does CBNRM adjust to situations where trust is the key factor, as among the Arusha of Tanzania, who use lineage and age-set institutions to settle local disputes and court procedures for disputes with untrustworthy strangers (Gulliver 1971; Nader 1990; Colson 1995)?

Institute: We agree that methods of environmental conflict management should not be culturally disembedded (McCay 1998). Does this mean, however, that local methods of conflict management should always be preferred over standard CBNRM practices?

Anthropologist: No. Conflict management systems may be mutually friendly after all. Although employed by the government, councillors duly elected in the Simbu province of the highlands of Papua New Guinea intervene in ways that resemble the traditional "big man" institution; the two systems appear to have been syncretized into a single institution (Podolefsky 1990). Systems may also continue to coexist without synthesis. This can happen for all sorts of reasons. People may prefer to maintain the option of moving from one forum to another depending on the advantages and disadvantages of each and the gains to be obtained from multiple-forum actions. We must keep in mind that communities are heterosocial formations, which means that a plurality of forums may create checks and balances that a single conflict management system may not generate.

Institute: We know of many cases where preserving community interests will require legal action.

Anthropologist: Legal systems may be used to back up the rights of communities against external forces, as in the Costa Rican Cahuita National Park arrangement (Lindsay 1998; Weitzner and Fonseca, this volume). Laws may be needed to fight corruption and inequity at the local level. They may serve to promote the rights of immigrants or marginal groups (women, the landless) that are inadequately recognized by community structures and customary law, as in rural India (Chandrasekharan 1997). Let's face it, customary conflict management practices are not always committed to achieving consensus, equity, and ecological sustainability. Romantic views of non-Western societies are to be taken with a grain of salt and may do considerable harm to CBNRM research and practice.

Return of the boomerang

Institute: It seems we've covered all the issues you wanted to raise. It's funny when you think of it.

Anthropologist: Think of what?

Institute: *Paradoxical* might be a better word. We asked you to develop research questions dealing with the cultural aspects of natural resource conflict management. You ended up playing two tricks on us. First, you sent the question back home, just like a boomerang. You converted what was essentially an anthropological question into a commentary on the cultural spirit of CBNRM. Second, although you addressed the cultural limitations of analytical thinking, your overall exposé was highly structured. Moreover, your answers revolved around logical contrasts pitting "our own" cultural assumptions against "theirs." Logic and categorical thinking were no less embedded in your mode of critique than they were embedded in the object of your critique.

Anthropologist: Interesting points. I will have to think about it. I must confess that when pitched at a conceptual level anthropology is inevitably a "residual" form of thinking. Willy-nilly, it portrays other cultures by emphasizing their otherness. Anthropology understands other milieus by showing how they differ from our own, a strategy that is bound to bring us back home. We view our "significant others" as living beyond our own surroundings — surroundings expressed in a familiar language that we can never fully escape and that will colour our explanations of otherness.

Institute: Can we not play with and alter our own surroundings and languages to express them, though?

Anthropologist: We certainly can, and this is precisely what I attempted to do with this apparently strange notion of "heteroculturalism." But there is another level of anthropological research that I have stressed throughout this conversation, namely, grounded anthropology, the kind that immerses itself in different social and cultural settings and remains open to unexpected findings. My objective was to map out the different areas where surprising results are likely be found, using as the point of departure some CBNRM assumptions: those of peace, equality, community, secularity, and rationality. I hope you found the exercise useful. Consulting the map, however, will never be a substitute for the actual journey.

References

Abel, R., ed. 1982. The politics of informal justice. Vols. 1 and 2. Academic Press, New York, NY, USA.

Avruch, K.; Black, P.W. 1993. Conflict resolution in intercultural settings: problems and prospects. *In* Sandole, D.J.D.; van der Merwe, H., ed., Conflict resolution theory and practice: integration and application. Manchester University Press, Manchester, UK. pp. 132, 142–143.

———— 1996. ADR, Palau, and the contribution of anthropology. *In* Wolfe, A.W.; Yang, H., ed., Anthropological contributions to conflict resolution. University of Georgia Press, Athens, GA. Southern Anthropological Society Proceedings, 29, 47–63.

Barton, R.F. 1919. Ifugao law. University of California Press, Berkeley, CA, USA.

———— 1949. The Kalingas; their institutions and custom law. University of Chicago Press, Chicago, USA.

Bingham, G. 1986. Resolving environmental disputes: a decade of experience. Donnely and Sons, Harrisonburg, VA, USA.

Bohannan, P. 1957. Justice and judgment among the Tiv. Oxford University Press, New York, USA.

Castro, A.P.; Ettenger, K. 1996. Indigenous knowledge and conflict management: exploring local perspectives and mechanisms for dealing with community forest disputes. Presented at the Global e-Conference on Addressing Natural Resource Conflict Through Community Forestry, Jan–Apr

1996. Forests, Trees and People Programme of the Food and Agriculture Organization of the United Nations, Rome, Italy.

Chan, S., Jabri, V., du Pisani, A. 1993. Introduction: mediation theory and application. *In* Chan, S., Jabri, V., ed., Mediation in southern Africa. Macmillan, London, UK. Southern African Studies. p. xiv.

Chandrasekharan, D. 1996. Addressing natural resource conflicts through community forestry: the Asian perspective. Presented at the Global e-Conference on Addressing Natural Resource Conflict Through Community Forestry, Jan–Apr 1996. Forests, Trees and People Programme of the Food and Agriculture Organization of the United Nations, Rome, Italy.

Chevalier, J.M.; Buckles, D. 1995. A land without gods: process theory, maldevelopment and the Mexican Nahuas. Zed and Fernwood, London, UK; Halifax, NS, Canada.

Colson, E. 1995. The contentiousness of disputes. *In* Caplan, P., ed., Understanding disputes. Berg, Oxford, UK.

Danzig, R. 1973. Toward the creation of a complementary, decentralized system of criminal justice. Stanford Law Review, 26, 1–54.

Evans-Pritchard, E.E. 1940. The Nuer: a description of the modes of livelihood and political institutions of a Nilotic people. Clarendon Press, Oxford, UK.

Feit, H. 1989. James Bay Cree self-governance and land management. *In* Wilmsen, E.N., ed., We are here: politics of aboriginal land tenure. University of California Press, Berkeley, CA, USA. pp. 68–98.

Garb, P. 1996. Mediation in the Caucasus: Caucasian diplomacy. *In* Wolfe, A.W.; Yang, H., ed., Anthropological contributions to conflict resolution. University of Georgia Press, Athens, GA, USA. Southern Anthropological Society Proceedings, 29, 31–46.

Gibbs, J. 1963. The Kpelle moot: a therapeutic model for the informal settlement of disputes. Africa, 33, 1–11.

Gluckman, M. 1955. The judicial process among the Barotse of northern Rhodesia. Manchester University Press, Manchester, UK.

———— 1965. Politics, law and ritual in tribal society. Aldine, Chicago, IL, USA.

Gulliver, P. 1971. Neighbours and networks. University of California Press, Berkeley, CA, USA.

Hanna, S. 1998. Co-management in small-scale fisheries: creating effective links among stakeholders. Presented at the International Workshop on Community-based Natural Resource Management, 10–14 May, Washington, DC, USA. Economic Development Institute of the World Bank, Washington, DC, USA; International Development Research Centre, Ottawa, ON, Canada; Ford Foundation, New York, NY, USA.

Henshaw Knott, C. 1993. Views of the forest: local people and indigenous knowledge in the Adirondack Park land-use conflict (New York). Cornell University, NY, USA. PhD dissertation.

Keitzar, S. 1998. Farmer knowledge of shifting cultivation in Nagaland. International Development Research Centre, Ottawa, ON, Canada. Report. 108 pp.

Lederach, J.P. 1992. Enredos, pleitos y problemas. Una guia practica para ayudar a resolver conflictos. Ediciones Clara, Semilla, Guatemala.

Lee, K. 1993. Compass and gyroscope: integrating science and politics for the environment. Island Press, Covelo, CA, USA.

Lindsay, J. 1998. Designing legal space: law as an enabling tool in community-based management. Presented at the International Workshop on Community-based Natural Resource Management, 10–14 May, Washington, DC, USA. Economic Development Institute of the World Bank, Washington, DC, USA; International Development Research Centre, Ottawa, ON, Canada; Ford Foundation, New York, NY, USA.

McCay, B. 1998. Co-managing the commons. Presented at the International Workshop on Community-based Natural Resource Management, 10–14 May, Washington, DC, USA. Economic Development Institute of the World Bank, Washington, DC, USA; International Development Research Centre, Ottawa, ON, Canada; Ford Foundation, New York, NY, USA.

Moore, C.; Santosa, M. 1995. Developing appropriate environmental conflict management procedures in Indonesia: integrating traditional and modern approaches. Cultural Survival Quarterly, 19, 23–29.

Moore, E. 1993. Gender, power and legal pluralism: Rajasthan, India. American Ethnologist, 20, 522–542.

Moore, R.; Sanders, A. 1996. The limits of an anthropology of conflict: loyalist and republican paramilitary organizations in Northern Ireland. In Wolfe, A.W.; Yang, H., ed., Anthropological contributions to conflict resolution. University of Georgia Press, Athens, GA, USA. Southern Anthropological Society Proceedings, 29, 131–143.

Moore, S. 1986. Social facts and fabrications. Cambridge University Press, Cambridge, UK.

Nader, L., ed., 1980. No access to law: alternatives to the American judicial system. Academic Press, New York, NY, USA.

———— 1990. Harmony ideology. Stanford University Press, Stanford, CA, USA.

———— 1991. Harmony models and the construction of law. In Avruch, K.; Black, P.W.; Scimecca, J.A., ed., Conflict resolution: cross-cultural perspectives. Greenwood Press, Westport, CT, USA. pp. 41–59.

Nader, L.; Todd, H.F., ed., 1978. The disputing process — law in ten societies. Columbia University Press, New York, NY, USA.

Olson, E.G. 1993. Conflict management in congregation and community in Tonga. University of Arizona, Phoenix, AZ, USA. PhD dissertation.

Ostrom, E. 1998. Self-governance and forest resources. Presented at the International Workshop on Community-based Natural Resource Management, 10–14 May, Washington, DC, USA. Economic Development Institute of the World Bank, Washington, DC, USA; International Development Research Centre, Ottawa, ON, Canada; Ford Foundation, New York, NY, USA.

Pederson, P. 1995. Non-Western concepts of multicultural conflict management applied to migration issues. Communication and Cognition, 28(4), 3987–3408.

Podolefsky, A. 1990. Mediator roles in Simbu conflict management. Ethnology, 29(1), 67–81.

Rivas, R. 1993. Pueblos indigenas y garifunas de Honduras: una caracterización. Editorial Guaymuras, Tegucigalpa, Honduras.

Robarchek, C.A.; Robarchek, C.J. 1993. Waging peace: the psychological and sociocultural dynamics of positive peace. In Avruch, K.; Black, P.W.; Scimecca, J.A., ed., Conflict resolution: cross-cultural perspectives. Greenwood Press, Westport, CT, USA. pp. 64–80.

Sarin, N. 1996. Actions of the voiceless: the challenge of addressing subterranean conflicts related to marginalised groups and women in community forestry. Presented at the Global e-Conference on Addressing Natural Resource Conflict Through Community Forestry, Jan–Apr 1996. Forests, Trees and People Programme of the Food and Agriculture Organization of the United Nations, Rome, Italy.

Schapera, I. 1943. Tribal legislation among the Tswana of the Bechuanaland Protectorate. London School of Economics and Political Science, London, UK.

Schweitzer, M. 1996. Harmony ideology works at the mill. In Wolfe, A.W.; Yang, H., ed., Anthropological contributions to conflict resolution. University of Georgia Press, Athens, GA, USA. Southern Anthropological Society Proceedings, 29, 119–130.

Shaftoe, D., ed., 1993. Responding to changing times: environmental mediation in Canada. Interaction for Conflict Resolution, Waterloo, ON, Canada.

Sheehan, N.A. 1996. Opening statement for West/Central Africa paper. Presented at the Global e-Conference on Addressing Natural Resource Conflict Through Community Forestry, Jan–Apr 1996. Forests, Trees and People Programme of the Food and Agriculture Organization of the United Nations, Rome, Italy.

Thomas, G.; Anderson, J.; Chandrasekharan, D.; Kakabadse, Y.; Matiru, V. 1996. Levelling the playing field: promoting authentic and equitable dialogue under inequitable conditions. Presented at the Global e-Conference on Addressing Natural Resource Conflict Through Community Forestry, Jan–Apr 1996. Forests, Trees and People Programme of the Food and Agriculture Organization of the United Nations, Rome, Italy.

Traore, S.; Lo, H. 1996. Natural resource conflicts and community forestry: a West African perspective. Presented at the Global e-Conference on Addressing Natural Resource Conflict Through Community Forestry, Jan–Apr 1996. Forests, Trees and People Programme of the Food and Agriculture Organization of the United Nations, Rome, Italy.

Uphoff, N. 1998. Community-based natural resource management: connecting micro and macro processes and people with their environments. Presented at the International Workshop on Community-based Natural Resource Management, 10–14 May, Washington, DC, USA. Economic Development Institute of the World Bank, Washington, DC, USA; International Development Research Centre, Ottawa, ON, Canada; Ford Foundation, New York, NY, USA.

Verdeld, T. 1994. The state and rangeland management. Dryland Networks Programme, International Institute for Environment and Development, London, UK. Paper 46.

Villareal, C. 1996. Socio-environmental and community forest conflicts in Latin America. Presented at the Global e-Conference on Addressing Natural Resource Conflict Through Community Forestry, Jan–Apr 1996. Forests, Trees and People Programme of the Food and Agriculture Organization of the United Nations, Rome, Italy.

Wadley, S. 1994. Struggling with destiny in Karimpur, 1925–1984. University of California Press, Berkeley, CA, USA.

Weldon, E.; Jehn, K.A. 1996. Examining cross-cultural differences in conflict management behavior: a strategy for future research. International Journal of Conflict Management, 6(4), 387–403.

Yang, H.; Wolfe, A.W. 1996. Epilogue: agenda for applied research in conflict resolution. In Wolfe, A.W.; Yang, H., ed., Anthropological contributions to conflict resolution. University of Georgia Press, Athens, GA, USA. Southern Anthropological Society Proceedings, 29, 144–149.

Part 1
Forestry

Chapter 2

Nam Ngum, Lao PDR:
Community-based natural resource management and conflicts over watershed resources

Philip Hirsch, Khamla Phanvilay, and Kaneungnit Tubtim

Nam Ngum watershed is of vital importance to Lao PDR. Its resources provide a subsistence livelihood to about 80 000 lowland and upland cultivators from diverse ethnic groups. Over the past two decades, Nam Ngum Dam has provided about one-quarter of the country's foreign-exchange earnings and most grid-linked electricity. Timber cut from the watershed also generates a sizeable foreign-exchange income. However, these demands have heightened competition for resources and conflict. This case study describes the types of conflicts experienced at a local level in four main localities in Nam Ngum watershed and document the ways in which the conflicts are being managed. Some limited project interventions are discussed and evaluated.

Alternative approaches to resolving conflicts over resource use can be examined using a basic diagnostic approach that works backward and forward from the point of conflict. Working backward usually involves seeing conflict as an outcome of resource competition among different actors. These may be similar actors, each of whom exerts more pressure on a resource to which all lay claim, or different types of actors making a combination of direct and indirect claims on a resource for various uses. The next stage backward is, thus, to examine resource competition in terms of intensified or changed use of a particular resource. Ultimately, this requires examining a starting point of existing resource-use patterns by different actors in a particular context, and the forces for change that led to pressure. Thus, resource use, change, competition, and conflict are examined in sequence.

The forward-looking stages include developing cooperative solutions as a means of resolving conflicts, and this implies a combination of biophysical and social analysis of the resource conflict in question.

Understanding conflict is a prerequisite to developing approaches to resolving it through cooperative means, whether via community-based natural resource management or otherwise. This requires both a material analysis of the basis for resource use and a social analysis of the stakeholders involved. The implication here is that conflicts and their resolution need to be examined in their ecological, sociocultural, economic, political, and policy contexts. Broadly speaking, the analysis thus works within a political-ecology theoretical paradigm (Blaikie and Brookfield 1987; Bryant 1998).

With context in mind, a key problem in developing alternative approaches is the balance or tension between national policy and local implementation, that is, between generalized approaches and catering to specific instances, between top-down technocratic implementation and bottom-up participatory design, between new institutions and modification of existing institutional means of dealing with conflict. Even a single medium-scale watershed may have diverse local settings in which application of policy, however progressive, needs to be adapted to local circumstances for successful and equitable resolution of resource conflicts (Khamla et al. 1994; Hirsch et al. 1997).

The Nam Ngum case

This case study deals with intensified resource use conflicts and institutional approaches to dealing with them in the Nam Ngum watershed, Lao PDR (Figure 1). The Nam Ngum River is one of the major tributaries of the Mekong. The watershed is defined as the area draining into the Nam Ngum Dam. Its significance to the issue of conflict management arises from the multiple use of watershed resources (land, water, forests, fish) for subsistence and commercial production in the context of rapid change. The watershed is important nationally for electricity production, and locally its resources are the main source of livelihood for about 80 000 mainly subsistence cultivators from diverse ethnic groups living above the dam.

The natural resources of Nam Ngum watershed are significant in a number of ways. Over the past two decades, the sale of electricity generated at the Nam Ngum Dam to Thailand has contributed on average one-quarter of the country's foreign exchange income. The dam has also generated most of the country's own grid-linked electricity. The watershed's lowland paddies and upland swiddens are the principal source of livelihood to farmers from numerous ethnic groups including Thai Phuan, Hmong, and Khamu in more than 200 villages of three provinces. In addition, the watershed has played a disproportionately significant role as source of commercial forest products due to the scale of logging operations at and above the Nam Ngum reservoir. Timber and nontimber forest products are also highly significant for subsistence uses. Fish from the Nam Ngum reservoir form a large proportion of the catch entering the Vientiane markets and the most significant contribution of animal protein in the diets of people in numerous villages situated adjacent to the reservoir.

There are several dimensions to resource competition and actual or potential conflict in Nam Ngum watershed (Kaneungnit et al. 1996). Most immediately for many communities, competition between people of different ethnic groups in neighbouring villages arises from different traditional production systems and the proximity of communities

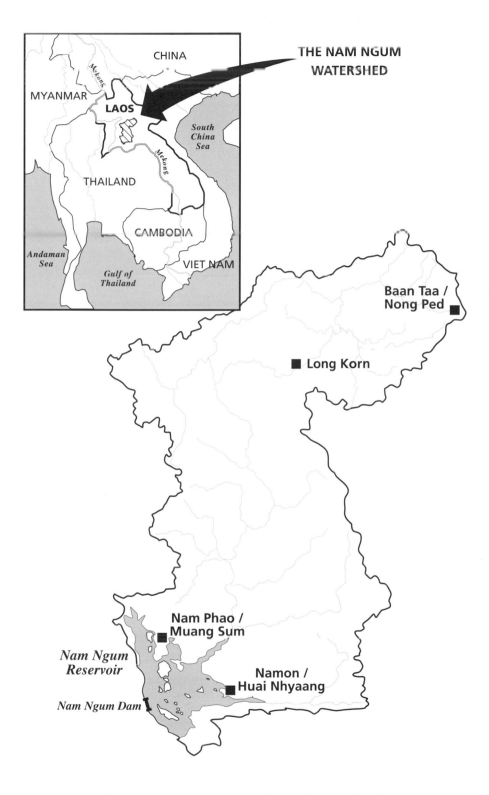

Figure 1. Nam Ngum watershed and the study sites.

resulting from a high rate of population movement within the watershed, attributable, in part, to the aftermath of wartime devastation. As in any watershed, upstream–downstream conflicts arise, both directly from extraction of water for upstream agriculture and, less directly, as upstream forest clearance affects downstream agriculturalists. Resource competition between subsistence and commercial resource uses is also increasing. Yet another dimension is competition between uses for national development and for local livelihoods, as existing and proposed hydropower developments encroach on land and water resources.

The main political–economic contextual factors relevant to the Nam Ngum case arise from the reforms of Lao PDR's transitional economy since the mid-1980s. Domestically, these reforms involve a move away from collective production within a socialist central planning system, toward a market economy. The market reforms are particularly significant in encouraging intensified resource use instead of subsistence-based production. The reforms also involve an outward orientation of macroeconomic policy, based on attracting foreign investment to develop the country's natural resources for export; within this, hydropower has received particular attention. The Nam Ngum case thus provides something of a microcosm and a baseline for anticipation of the local implications of such policies.

Significant policy reforms in the natural resources sector have accompanied the wider economic reorientation (AusAID 1996). Notably for the purposes of this case study, decree 169 dealing with allocation of forest land was seen to have potentially far-reaching implications when it was issued in late 1993. The decree involves allocation of rights and responsibilities over forest management to local communities, partly in recognition of the limited ability and effectiveness of the Department of Forestry to administer all state lands under its jurisdiction and partly in recognition of the traditional role of communities in governing local land and forest resources.

Between 1992 and 1996, we led an applied research project that investigated the changing resource use, intensified competition, emerging conflict, and cooperative solutions to resource management within Nam Ngum watershed. The study was carried out in two phases. The first involved investigating socioeconomic conditions and resource management systems in the watershed at the community level through an extensive survey of all villages and an intensive participatory study of two adjacent villages (one lowland Lao, one Hmong) on the northeastern edge of the reservoir. Phase II involved intensive study and limited interventions in four pilot areas (see Figure 1), each of which represented a particular resource conflict and management challenge. The application of decree 169 at the local level in diverse agroecological, sociocultural, and politicohistorical circumstances within the watershed was a primary focus of the second phase of study.

The situation requiring institutional change

The overall situation prompting institutional change has been the intensification of resource use among the many users of Nam Ngum watershed resources. The competition over a limited resource base has resulted in degradation and unsustainable use of increasingly scarce land, forests, water, and fish. This scarcity necessitates some formalization of allocation procedures, dispute resolution, and devolution of management authority at various levels.

As indicated above, it is necessary to refer to local contexts to understand and find points of intervention to deal with particular instances of conflict. The four areas subjected to intensive study were selected according to key aspects of intensified resource use and competition within and between communities in the locality and with reference to external policies or resource demands affecting local natural resource use. Long Korn is in a resource-rich area that has suffered from the aftermath of geopolitical conflict, but where ethnic minority farmers at last have the potential to reestablish their livelihoods. The Nong Ped and Ban Taa area was selected, because potential conflicts have emerged there due to the forced return of land from an ethnic minority community to a neighbouring Lao community as geopolitical conditions have "stabilized." Nam Phao and Muang Sum were chosen because conflict has emerged as this stable, long-established community has had to cope with demands on its resource base from more transient neighbouring villages and official resettlement programs. The Namon and Huai Nhyaang area was selected as a microcosm of conflicts between lowland and upland ethnic groups, with different cultivation systems, which have been exacerbated or brought to a crisis point by external demands on the resource base.

Long Korn

Long Korn village in Phukood District of Xieng Khouang Province is a recently reestablished village; it has been at its present location since 1994. Settlement in the area has been affected by periodic insecurity and displacement — first as a result of bombing by the United States and deliberate depopulation of Xieng Khouang during the early 1970s, later by remnants of right-wing Hmong forces previously led by the ex-CIA supported Vang Pao. The insecurity and associated high rate of population movement reflects one of the key background problems that have historically constrained the livelihoods of most communities in Nam Ngum watershed. The Khamu villagers of Long Korn are at an early stage in terms of securing their livelihoods in an area of relative abundance, but isolated. Because of the loss of livestock to wartime destruction and difficulty in reestablishing herds during recent moves, a major constraint to sedentary farming is a shortage of draught animals and thus also natural fertilizer. This problem is quite general to communities on the Plain of Jars. Long Korn and surrounding areas are eyed by the district as potential sites for resettlement of communities from elsewhere, lending particular significance to a participatory approach to establishing the limits of sustainability in agricultural production.

Nong Ped and Baan Taa

Nong Ped in Paek District of Xieng Khouang Province is an established Lao Loum village in the upper part of Nam Ngum watershed. The village was destroyed during the 1960s by aerial bombardment; thus, it has experienced major upheaval like other communities in the area. Baan Taa is a neighbouring upstream Hmong village that was established shortly after the end of the war in 1975. Some of the rice terraces at Baan Taa include old fields previously worked by Nong Ped villagers. The Hmong newcomers also cleared and established new rice terraces higher up the stream system. Baan Taa is one of many Hmong communities that have resettled in line with government policy but face pressure as their cultivation demands place them in competition with adjacent and longer established lowland communities.

For the first few years after both communities resettled, land was farmed cooperatively and no claims were made on the older fields that had been rehabilitated by the
Hmong newcomers. However, in the mid-1980s, individual Nong Ped farmers began to
claim their former family plots. In 1994, after several years of negotiation involving district
and provincial authorities, the older rice terraces at Baan Taa were returned by Hmong
farmers to their original owners from Nong Ped.

This marked the culmination of not only the settlement changes in the area, but also
changing tenure conditions accompanying a move from cooperative to household production and landholding. The changed conditions have prompted renewed encroachment on
upper-watershed forests, causing problems for both communities, as Nong Ped rice fields
are irrigated by streams whose sources are in the upper parts of Baan Taa.

Nam Phao and Muang Sum

Muang Sum village (until recently located in Vangvieng District of Vientiane Province) is
an old community with a well-established and hitherto sustainable resource management
system. Livelihoods are based on wet rice farming with supplementary rotational shifting
cultivation. Forested areas on surrounding slopes have long been protected by a village
custom prohibiting cutting and clearing in several areas. Recently, Muang Sum has been
targeted as a resettlement site for Hmong returnees from Thailand. It has also been designated to receive mainly Khamu villagers evacuated from surrounding upland communities
and lowland Lao villagers from reservoir-edge and island communities. There is thus a
sharp increase in demands on the resource base.

Nam Phao is a more recently established adjacent community, with a mix of settlers
from diverse geographic and ethnic origins. The factionalism of the village is symptomatic
of many problems with the "community-based" approach that often assumes a common
interest and stable, long-standing community structure. Problems of forest clearance and
degradation at Nam Phao have spilled over into forests traditionally managed and protected by Muang Sum villagers.

Management of this issue has become very difficult with the redrawing of administrative boundaries that has left Nam Phao in Vangvieng District but placed Muang Sum in
the new special administrative zone of Saisomboun. Not only does this complicate the district role in dealing with local resource competition and conflict; it also involves a redrawing of village boundaries between Nam Phao and Muang Sum, so that a partly forested "no
man's land" is open to uncontrolled exploitation. Maintaining sustainable management of
Muang Sum forests and lands requires appropriate action in neighbouring communities,
notably Nam Phao. This area thus presents a complex management challenge within and
between communities and involving multiple state authorities.

Namon and Huai Nhyaang

Namon village, in Long San District, Saisomboun Special Administrative Zone, used to lie
in the area that is now flooded by the Nam Ngum reservoir. Villagers have reestablished
their livelihoods close to their original area of settlement, but with a considerably constrained resource base. This community's resource base has been greatly affected by
hydropower development, and its situation is indicative of the more widespread challenges
faced by relocated communities relying on the more efficient use of increasingly scarce
land, forest, and water endowments.

During the 1980s, a Hmong settlement was established at neighbouring Huai Nhyaang, reflecting the more general situation arising from the government policy of resettling shifting cultivators. One outcome of such resettlement is that upland shifting cultivators now live closer to lowland cultivators, potentially exacerbating the scope and immediacy of conflict. Since the early 1990s, prohibition of reservoir fishing in the Kaeng Noi area close to where the Nam Ngum River flows into the reservoir has led to the establishment of two more communities close to Namon: Don Samphan and Don Seua. This has created a further incremental increase in pressure on local forest resources as upper slopes have been cleared by villagers from these communities. Most recently, raised reservoir levels have flooded about 20% of the two villages' wet rice lands since 1994 and have reduced the drawdown area available for grazing. As a result, there is increased reliance on the remaining forest area for shifting cultivation. This situation is perpetuated by the Nam Song diversion, which increases energy output at the Nam Ngum Dam by raising water levels and throughput. Competition for forest and land resources has intensified as a result of this combination of pressures. Competition is most evident in a rapid and clearly observable loss of natural forests on the slopes immediately above the villages, particularly in the headwater areas of streams that are used to irrigate the remaining wet rice fields.

The change process: policy environment, local responses, and intervention

Just as competition for resources in Nam Ngum watershed must be understood at different levels, so the change process involves interaction between the national-level policy environment and reform process, on one hand, and local responses and adaptation to rapidly changing circumstances, on the other. Inserted into this dynamic of change are limited project interventions, based on analysis of the key local resource management challenges summarized above. Key actors include villagers from diverse community situations, environmental circumstances, and ethnic groups; staff of each of the four districts; and project staff from the Department of Forestry.

Institutional and policy environment

In many cases, policy supportive of community-based approaches to conflict resolution may be part of a wider policy environment that simultaneously creates difficulties and uncertainties. Some difficulties are due to lack of institutional capacity, whereas others are related to incompatible policies. The following discussion concentrates on the latter issue. In the case of Nam Ngum watershed, several areas of national policy and its provincial interpretation are relevant.

Resettlement

Vientiane Province has periodically developed plans to move people who are settled on the edge of the Nam Ngum reservoir to areas on the other side of Phou Khao Khouay protected area (that is, out of the watershed altogether). This includes communities settled on the islands and those in Namon and Huai Nhyaang who do not have permanent cultivated land (paddy). However, this plan has been cancelled due to the shortage of suitable areas for settlement and a lack of funds for development of infrastructure. Nevertheless, population movement into and out of the area is considerable, partly as a result of government policy. Most of the movement is based on voluntary settlement and usually is based on family relationships and the search for new permanent cultivable land. However, in the case of Namon and Huai Nhyaang, the movement of fishers from Kaeng Noi has created considerable problems.

Decree 169

The Management of Forest and Forest Land Decree (3 November 1993) aimed to provide guidelines for districts and villages to demarcate their forest resources for management, protection, and conservation (forest zoning). Some detailed guidelines on forest demarcation were included in this decree. In principle, therefore, it is supportive of community-based natural resource management. However, outside limited pilot areas, the implementation of decree 169 was mostly based on dissemination of the document to the district level; this was passed on to the village level in a short verbal or written missive. Implementation of the decree thus depended mainly on the capability and competence of the district staff, notably those at the District Agriculture and Forestry Office.

Namon, Houai Nhyaang, and adjacent communities failed to implement the decree fully due to the lack of staff at the district level and weakness in communication between district and village. There was a significant difference between the expressed desires of Namon and Huai Nhyaang villagers, on one hand, who wanted to maintain collective management of the remaining natural forest between the two villages, and the district authorities on the other, who wanted to divide the natural forest area for individual village allocation, including two new communities resettled from Kaeng Noi.

Forest Law No. 125/PO

The Forest Law was issued on 2 November 1996 to replace decree 169 on the management of forest and forest land and decree 186 on the allocation of land and forest land for tree plantation and forest protection (issued 12 October 1994). Article 1 states the purpose of the Forest Law is to define basic principles, regulations, and measures on the management, conservation and use of forest resources and forest land. The law is meant to promote forest generation and plantation in Lao PDR to improve people's livelihoods as well as to sustain the natural environment and maintain equilibrium of the ecosystem. According to Article 16, the forest is divided into five categories: (1) protection forest; (2) conservation forest; (3) production forest; (4) regeneration forest; and (5) degraded forest or bare land.

Article 18 defines conservation forest as forest and forest land designated to reserve the historical, cultural, tourist, environmental, educational, and research values of wildlife and plant species and the ecosystems of which they are part. The tenure rights to forest and forest land can be obtained by transfer, allocation, and inheritance (Article 48). However, customary rights to use of forest and forest land are recognized. Customary use includes the collection of nonprohibited wood for fences and fuel, the collection of forest products, hunting and fishing of nonprohibited species for household consumption, and other uses following custom (Article 30). Village authorities are accorded significant rights and duties to organize and develop local regulations on the use and allocation of forest and forest land to individuals for management, protection, and conservation of forests, watersheds, wildlife, and natural environment appropriate to the actual conditions of the village (Article 63). In practice, the new forestry law has not yet been translated into bylaws or regulations for detailed enforcement. The old decree 169, in some circumstances, is still valid and to be used as the guideline for legal enforcement, such as in land allocation and land-use zoning at the village level.

At the Nam Ngum watershed and project level, although all actors shared a perception that change was necessary to overcome a deteriorating resource base, there were quite different perspectives on what constituted the main reasons for such deterioration. At the national policy level, a standard explanation for deforestation in Lao PDR is vegetation clearance and burning by shifting cultivators. However, the situation becomes much more complex at the local level, particularly where forests that have been managed by communities of long-standing come under pressure either from within the community itself or from recent settlers who have been displaced from elsewhere as a result of a range of extraneous pressures and policy measures.

Local responses: dealing with conflict at the local level

Although project interventions reveal the potential and limitations of applied and participatory research in terms of material inputs and collaborative approaches to conflict management, an equally important aspect of the research process was the documentation of means of dealing with conflict at the local level. Attention was paid to aspects of conflict and its resolution, avoidance or exacerbation within and between communities, and between local villagers and district authorities. The following observations summarize aspects of conflict management in the four pilot localities.

Namon and Huai Nhyaang

Villagers in Namon and Houai Nhyaang are keenly aware of the potential for conflict within and between their communities over occasional encroachment on nearby natural forest areas. Conflict avoidance has taken a number of forms. In one case of encroachment into forest for shifting cultivation by a local Huai Nhyaang villager, other villagers initially issued a warning to the offender. When this proved insufficient, rather than impose penalties themselves, the villagers reported this case to the village head, who in turn reported it to the district for consideration and judgment. When there was no response from the district, the villagers who had petitioned and the head man perceived that the higher authority could not make any judgment. Rather than alienate themselves from other villagers, they decided to keep quiet. In general, there is a reluctance to risk social tension by reporting such offences.

Some farmers in Huai Nhyaang tried to avoid conflict with neighbours by grazing their livestock far from other villagers' fields. A few used to graze their cattle seasonally in the Phou Khao Khouai Protected Area, but this is now prohibited by protected-area managers. This creates tension between these farmers and other villages close to the new grazing areas, exacerbated by the loss of grazing land near the reservoir because of the increased capacity of Nam Ngum Dam.

The limited supply of water for paddy cultivation has resulted in conflicts between Namon rice farmers who need to irrigate their fields and paddy cultivators in the newer neighbouring communities of Don Seua and Don Samphan. However, this type of conflict had been resolved through the discussion between village committees and among beneficiary groups who share the same weirs and canals. This type of traditional system for water allocation has involved defining the date and time to irrigate water along the weir and canal systems shared by each group. To complete the work within the constrained planting period, cooperative labour sharing is still practiced.

In some cases, to avoid conflict between villages, people have simply asked authorities to deal with disputes. For example, when villagers from Don Samphan illegally cut trees in Namon's forest area, people from Namon reported the case to subdistrict authorities to avoid direct confrontation and conflict with their neighbours. However, the authorities prefer communities to solve conflicts themselves as they have their own difficulties in dealing with such problems, such as, lack of money for travel and extension and lack of established mechanisms to deal with conflict.

An external source of conflict between villagers was a small timber mill, which was seen by some as contributing to local economic development and making use of forest resources by extracting abandoned timber cut by a former logging company and by shifting cultivators at the local level. However, this type of activity only benefited a minority of households and, at the same time, it encouraged local people to fell trees to sell to the sawmill. The mill created conflict within both communities, in part because of the highly uneven distribution of benefits when the mill was using the entire community's forest resources. It also created conflict between local people and outsiders because of the unfair distribution of benefits from the business. Ultimately, the collapse of the sawmill eliminated this source of conflict.

An instructive dispute arose when a Namon villager marked a tree for cutting, then left it too long. A Huai Nhyaang villager cut the tree without telling the person who marked it, resulting in conflict over who had the right to that particular tree. This experience led the two village committees to establish a new rule: if anyone in the two communities wants to use wood, marking is prohibited and the person must make a request to, and consult with, both village committees.

Nam Phao and Muang Sum

People from different ethnic groups came to Nam Phao at different times, resulting in five main groups in the village. For the most part, people try to avoid both confronting others and bringing cases out into the open. In principle, ethnic conflict should be resolved by the village committee, but due to the weakness of decision-making and enforcement at the village level, sources of conflict have not been addressed and tension has continued to grow.

Even more serious is the deteriorating relationship with the neighbouring village of Muang Sum. In the case of Hmong returnees at Muang Sum, The United Nations High Commission for Refugees (UNHCR) is supposed to make temporary settlement provisions for Hmong returnees within Muang Sum boundaries. It proposed to provide paddy fields for every family, but there is no water supply for the vacant land. Although UNHCR planned to build a weir to divert water from the present source used by Muang Sum villagers, this proved unsuccessful. Enough water could not be supplied to the newcomers without affecting existing users in Muang Sum downstream. Although this "managed" the potential conflict over water, Hmong families have been left with little option but to clear upland slopes, threatening to create disputes over areas of forest hitherto protected by lowlanders in Muang Sum.

In addition to pressures from neighbouring Nam Phao and the resettlement of refugees into their area, Muang Sum villagers faced another unexpected problem when the neighbouring communities of Lak 18, Lak 24, and Nam Paad started clearing land within Muang Sum boundaries. To control such encroachment, Muang Sum decided to divide some land for them on the condition that they would not encroach further on the village's protected area.

Nong Ped and Baan Taa

Villagers in Baan Taa whose land was claimed by the original owners from Nong Ped were keen to maintain paddy land, both because of the cultivation opportunities it gave them and because farming paddy land gives villagers security that they will not be resettled by the authorities because they are encroaching on forest. Because of the limits on paddy land for permanent settlement and cultivation and to avoid being moved, Hmong people in Baan Taa tried to buy paddy land from the owners in Nong Ped. However, Nong Ped people also need paddy fields and were thus unwilling to sell.

Forest encroachment by Baan Taa people caused villagers in Nong Ped to take the case to the district. However, there was no response, because the district did not want to exacerbate the conflict and tried to calm down Nong Ped villagers, encouraging them to negotiate. Part of this quiet response was due to fact that the district had no alternatives. Resettlement was not an option because of lack of appropriate sites. One site earmarked for resettlement was found to be too barren and infertile, with no trees or infrastructure.

Some Baan Taa families who lost land were threatened with eviction on the grounds of protecting the forest at the head of the watersheds in Nong Ped. Some of these villagers issued a counterthreat that they would burn forest if they had to move. This is another example of the constraints on district authorities to use external measures, such as resettlement, to deal with problems without reference to community preferences and preparedness to compromise.

Long Korn

Long Korn is particularly remote, and most of the returned villagers have previously lived in the area. Land allocation to individual households was based on available household labour, and allocation procedures were based on community consultation and perception of what was fair. The village committee is quite strong and the village is small, so achieving consensus is less difficult than elsewhere. Fair land allocation has enabled the community to preempt the type of conflict that has arisen in other areas.

Clear understanding between district and villagers over land use and zoning has also resulted in reduction in the potential for conflict. However, district plans for future resettlement in the area are still not clear to the community. It is not known whether newcomers will settle in the village voluntarily or be selected by the district.

Project interventions

Project interventions worked broadly within the framework of the forest-land-allocation policy. However, they were based on the hypothesis that different local circumstances require different measures and need to be developed by the local communities concerned in consultation with district-level authorities. In all cases, interventions were associated with, and contingent on, a process of participatory land-use planning through the use of three-dimensional terrain models.

At Long Korn, stabilization of wet-rice-based permanent agriculture was hindered primarily by a shortage of livestock; thus, intervention took the form of a revolving fund to purchase buffalo. Twelve buffalo were contributed to the village for distribution to families without their own livestock. A buffalo bank was established to maintain these as community property with a revolving fund. Linked to this scheme was a process of participatory land-use planning to protect the watershed area of streams irrigating the rice fields.

In Baan Taa, stabilization of livelihoods among the Hmong families whose land had been redeemed by neighbouring Nong Ped farmers was seen as a priority. Although the project was intended to help seek small-scale alternative opportunities for the group of 22 households at the core of local tensions, this was initially hindered by uncertainty over the status of these households and their right to continue to live in the area. Subsequently, a German-funded participatory watershed management project selected Baan Taa as a target village and further project intervention here was deemed unwarranted.

At Nam Phao, assistance with the construction of a weir was deemed the best way to reduce pressure on the remaining forest within the village boundaries and in neighbouring Muang Sum. The weir was constructed at the site of a previous structure that had twice been washed away in floods. The original idea was to revitalize the production potential of the low-lying rice fields of Nam Phao by dividing land from those producing a surplus among those without their own wet rice fields. However, there was no certainty that the weir would live up to its promise. In fact, the potential of the weir was considerably overestimated by the villagers, possibly as a way to ensure support from the project and from the district. It is now doubtful that land division will take effect. In any case, this is well beyond the scope of outside project intervention to influence.

In the case of Namon and Huai Nhyaang, the main emphasis was on cooperative management of the common forest area of the two villages. The project intervention consisted of facilitation of meetings between the villages and the district, which otherwise has had little direct and detailed involvement with land-use planning in this remote part of Long San. A significant aspect of negotiation was over the different models of forest-land allocation between the villages, one of which (Namon) wished to maintain common management of the natural forest area between the two villages, and the district that wished to divide up the area according to its interpretation of the decree 169 procedure.

Outcomes and lessons learned

The salient findings of Phase I of the project were used to guide the next stage of activities during Phase II. The findings can be summarized as follows:

◆ Contrary to common assumption, there is substantial pressure on natural resources and food production systems in the Nam Ngum watershed area. *Implication — significant changes in land, forest, and water use and management are required to achieve a sustainable pattern of production.*

◆ The nature of resource degradation and resource conflicts varies significantly from one part of the watershed to another, based on a range of social, historical, and ecological parameters. *Implication — an overly generalized approach to watershed management should be avoided in favour of one based on local knowledge and participation of communities and local authorities in each area.*

✦ Community management of forest, land, and water resources is longstanding and widespread throughout the watershed. *Implication — local and traditional practices and arrangements should be seen as the starting point for resource management initiatives and planning.*

✦ Resource competition and conflicts can be identified at a number of levels: within communities, between communities, between local people and external claimants (notably forestry and hydropower), and between ethnic groups with different agroecological practices, or, differently stated, between upland and lowland production systems. *Implication — there is a need to develop conflict preemption and resolution procedures at a number of levels, including more participatory impact assessment procedures for externally conceived projects.*

✦ Ambiguity of both individual and community resource tenure is a basic source of competition, conflict, and resource degradation. *Implication — demarcation and definition of resource tenure at the village level must be backed up at the district and other levels.*

✦ At the district level, division of duties is often unclear; district-level staff lack technical and organizational experience; and district staff tend to be involved in village-level activities, relying more often on written directives. *Implication — district level staff need support, including technical and organizational training and experience in community liaison, in combination with more clearly defined duties in the field of forest, land, and water management.*

✦ From a local perspective, there are ambiguities in government policy regarding rights and duties of village, district, provincial, and national authorities. *Implication — the rights and duties regarding resource management, planning, and enforcement need to be clarified.*

At this stage, it is difficult to quantify outcomes of Phase II project interventions in terms of reducing forest clearance, assisting the poorest within each community, or reducing tensions along each axis of conflict. Because the learning process among national-, district-, and village-level staff was integral to the process, the lessons learned are part of the project outcome. In this regard, heightened awareness of the importance of community dynamics among district and Department of Forestry staff was probably a more significant outcome than any immediate and mensurable improvement in environment or human welfare, although, in the case of Long Korn, significant improvements in livelihoods were observed as direct project outcomes.

Less positive lessons learned from the Nam Phao case include the extreme difficulty in ensuring any linkage between project intervention and reduction of land clearance, particularly in a village with many factions and weak leadership. The weir project might well allow for an increase in rice production, although this still awaits evaluation. In any case, outcomes are likely to be less impressive than anticipated because of the overestimation referred to above. However, it is unlikely that those without immediate access to the limited area irrigated by the weir will be helped to move away from their unsustainable pattern of shifting cultivation in and around the village. Realistic appraisals of water yields and of the limited extent of beneficiary groups are thus key to the success of such interventions.

The involvement of local staff (villagers) in the implementation of the project, through training, data collection, workshops, and a study tour, created more confidence among local people in official recognition of their role in decision-making over resource management in their village territory. This influence allowed villagers to take on the joint management of forest between Namon and Houai Nhyaang, where the two villages preferred to share the forest, land, and water resources. This case also reflects on land allocation and zoning policy, wherein the community itself has rights to decide how local resources should be managed and conserved, as well as the right to protect them from outside claimants. This is an improvement on the more widespread situation, in which villagers are unaware of their rights as governed by national policy.

A small revolving fund provided by the project to develop local livelihoods in Namon, Houai Nhyaang, and adjacent villages still awaits full evaluation and assessment. Lessons learned from Namon and Huai Nhyaang at a wider level had some influence on the Centre for Protected Area and Watershed Management (CPAWM), the national level agency within the Department of Forestry that was directly responsible for project implementation. At a practical level, running a project with such intensive local involvement from a central agency presented many logistical limitations that restricted the effectiveness of comanagement, particularly in Long San District where the intermediary local government authorities were less responsive than in other districts, notably Phukood. However, feedback and experiences from Phase I of the project had a direct influence on national policy in the development of decree 169, especially over the issue of community-level implementation, such as the establishment of village committees for land allocation and control and monitoring of forest resources. At that time, the Nam Ngum Watershed Community Resource Management Study was the only Department of Forestry project that tackled issues dealing with social aspects of forest, land, and water resources management at the village level.

The results from Phase I and Phase II of the study also provided input into CPAWM in promoting more community involvement in protected-area management. Data and information from the study have been used by other projects working in the Nam Ngum watershed, such as the large Nam Ngum Watershed Conservation Project, supported by the German Gesellschaft für Technische Zusammenarbeit (agency for technical cooperation), Nam Ngum Watershed Management and Reforestation, supported by the Japanese International Cooperation Agency, and Nam Ngum Watershed Strategic Management Planning, supported by the Asian Development Bank, to prepare a strategic plan for Nam Ngum watershed. This plan is expected to be used as a model for preparing management plans for other watersheds in Laos, including ways to return value generated by watershed resources in the form of hydropower to other watershed stakeholders.

At the district level, awareness of the complexities of community-level management was built by compiling baseline information, presented through maps and tables as a tool for resource monitoring during training courses for district staff in Phase II of the project. The districts also developed awareness of the time-consuming nature of work with communities and the need for experienced staff and proper organizational structuring. However, districts paid different levels of attention to such lessons, and Long San District was one of those in which less importance was attached to community consultation.

For the project itself — and, therefore, CPAWM and the Department of Forestry more widely — the important outcomes were that project staff had a chance to learn about applied research. Since project completion most of the staff have used the experience gained to work with other projects and local consultancy firms in the field of community development and natural resource management.

References

AusAID (Australian Agency for International Development). 1996. Country environmental profile of Lao PDR. AusAID, Canberra, Australia.

Blaikie, P.; Brookfield, H., ed. 1987. Land degradation and society. Methuen, London, UK.

Bryant, R. 1998. Power, knowledge and political ecology in the third world: a review. Progress in Physical Geography, 22(1), 79–94.

Hirsch, P.; Khamla Phanvilay; Kaneungnit Tubtim. 1997. Resource management in Nam Ngum watershed, Lao PDR: lessons and experience. Final report. International Development Research Centre, Ottawa, ON, Canada. Internal document.

Kaneungnit Tubtim; Khamla Phanvilay; Hirsch, P. 1996. Decentralisation, watersheds and ethnicity in Laos. In Howitt, R.; Connell, J.; Hirsch, P., ed., Resources, nations and indigenous peoples: case studies from Australia, Melanesia and Southeast Asia. Oxford University Press, Melbourne, Australia. pp. 265–276.

Khamla Phanvilay; Kaneungnit Tubtim; Hirsch, P. 1994. Resource management in Nam Ngum watershed, Lao PDR. Centre for Protected Area and Watershed Management, Department of Forestry, Ministry of Agriculture and Forestry, Vientiane, Lao PDR.

Chapter 3

THE NUSA TENGGARA UPLANDS, INDONESIA:
MULTIPLE-SITE LESSONS IN
CONFLICT MANAGEMENT

Larry Fisher, Ilya Moeliono, and Stefan Wodicka

Increasing demands on Indonesia's forests have resulted in resource management con-
flicts. Rural communities in and around these protected areas have been excluded from
decisions about and access to important forest resources. Ministry of Forestry policies and
programs have attempted to reconcile growing conflicts over forest management through
integrated conservation and development programs, and international agencies have pro-
moted these approaches in a number of sites with mixed results. Assessments have
pointed out the need for a regional approach, securing benefits for local people, infor-
mation gathering, consensus-building, and collaboration. This case study presents the
experience of the Nusa Tenggara Community Development Consortium's Conservation
Working Group in mitigating conflicts and building collaborative approaches to forest
management.

During the past three decades, Indonesia's forests have been mapped, classified, and subjected to increasing demands for commercial exploitation, watershed protection, recreation, and biodiversity conservation. Throughout the archipelago, previously isolated forest
areas have been opened up through rapid construction of roads and the extension of government administrative units. Shifting demographic and economic trends have hastened
the pace of change and heightened interest in these forest areas, intensifying resource
management conflicts. Rural communities in and around these protected areas have been
gradually marginalized from decision-making processes and disenfranchised from important forest resources.

Recent Ministry of Forestry policies and programs have attempted to reconcile grow-ing conflicts over forest management through a variety of approaches (Kartasubrata et al. 1994). These efforts have extended to establishing conservation areas, with emphasis on approaches that can broadly be identified as integrated conservation and development pro-grams (Brown and Wyckoff-Baird 1992; Wells et al. 1992). International agencies, such as the World Wide Fund for Nature (WWF), the World Bank, and the Asian Development Bank, have promoted these approaches in a variety of sites in Indonesia and throughout the region with mixed results (Wells 1997). Assessments of the programs have pointed out the need for an ecoregional approach and an emphasis on securing economic benefits for local people, the importance of information-gathering and adaptive management strate-gies, and the value of consensus-building and collaboration (Larson et al. 1997).

In this paper, we draw on the experiences of the Nusa Tenggara Community Development Consortium (NTCDC), an interagency network that seeks to address key technical, institutional, and policy issues related to poverty alleviation and environmental conservation in the Nusa Tenggara region of eastern Indonesia. In the past 3 years, the consortium's Conservation Working Group has catalyzed and monitored the emergence of new collaborative alliances addressing the challenges of forest and conservation manage-ment at several priority conservation sites across the region. We discuss the evolution of this network and the lessons learned in mitigating conflicts and building collaborative approaches to forest management. Key interventions developed to facilitate these multi-stakeholder approaches to forest management have included the following: community organizing, coalition-building, participatory research, training, and capacity-building, along with a variety of innovative strategies for convening diverse stakeholder groups at both the local and the regional level.

The setting

The Indonesian islands southeast of Bali and northwest of Australia are known as the Lesser Sundas or Nusa Tenggara (Figure 1). Administratively, the region is divided into three provinces, Nusa Tenggara Barat, Nusa Tenggara Timur, and the former Portuguese colony of East Timor. The geology of the area is based on extremely rugged mixed volcanic and limestone rock. The climate is semi-arid — about 1 500 mm of rain falls within a 3–5 month period.

The 8.12 million people living in these three provinces are ethnically diverse, as Nusa Tenggara lies at the transition point between the Malayan and Papuan racial groups. More than 50 distinct languages are spoken in the area.

Nusa Tenggara is one of the poorest and least developed regions in Indonesia, because of the combined effects of physical isolation, inadequate infrastructure, and lim-ited natural resources (Corner 1989). Local incomes are approximately one-third the national average; infant mortality rates and illiteracy figures are among the highest in Indonesia. The province of East Timor has experienced protracted civil unrest since it achieved independence from Portugal in 1975.

The rural economy is based on agriculture, and shifting cultivation is still practiced throughout the islands of Nusa Tenggara. Although paddy rice is cultivated in some low-land areas, less than 2% of the arable land is suitable for irrigation. Farming systems are largely based on maize and cassava as the staple crops. In drier areas, maize is replaced with sorghum or millet as the principal grain. Extensive grazing of livestock (cattle, water

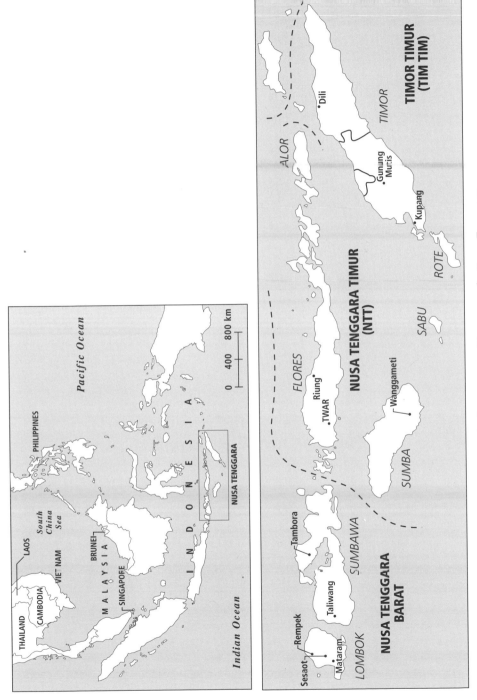

Figure 1. Priority conservation areas in Nusa Tenggara.

buffalo, horses, goats, and sheep) is practiced throughout the region. A variety of forestry and horticultural species (tamarind, candlenut, coffee, cacao, etc.) are an important source of income, particularly during the frequent famines and crop shortfalls, which occur during long periods of drought. Coastal fisheries, small industries (food processing, weaving, leather, etc.), and tourism are increasingly important sectors of the economy.

Conservation and forest management

Conservation in Nusa Tenggara has only recently received attention from the central government and from local and international conservation agencies. In the early 1980s, surveys by the Food and Agriculture Organization of the United Nations, in collaboration with the Department of Forestry's Directorate General of Forest Protection and Nature Conservation identified priority areas for conservation (MacKinnon et al. 1982). More recently, international conservation agencies, such as the WWF, Birdlife International, the Wildlife Conservation Society, and the Nature Conservancy, have become actively involved in the region, sponsoring field programs at selected sites, as well as biodiversity research, conservation education, and the development of regional biodiversity conservation plans (WWF 1993; Jepson et al. 1996).

The contrast between the rich biological and cultural diversity and the chronic poverty of the area presents obvious challenges to those making decisions about natural resource management. Settlements are found within and around all forests and designated conservation areas in the region, making land-use conflicts a routine problem. These communities are frequently isolated and retain strong traditional values and practices, often strongly linked to land and forest (or coastal) resources.

The Nusa Tenggara Community Development Consortium

The importance of conservation in regional development strategies emerged through a lengthy process of analysis sponsored by the NTCDC (before 1997, the Nusa Tenggara Uplands Development Consortium). The consortium is an interagency network comprising representatives from government agencies, nongovernmental organizations (NGOs), research institutions, and local communities. It seeks to address key technical, institutional, and policy issues related to poverty and environmental problems in Nusa Tenggara by strengthening successful grass-roots programs, enhancing local organizational capacity, increasing collaborative working relations, and expanding the impact of successful upland development programs (Khan and Suryanata 1994; World Neighbors 1994).

The consortium's Working Group on Natural Resource Management (or Conservation Working Group [CWG]), established in 1991, addresses concerns about the management of critical conservation areas, as well as the social and economic impacts of forest exploitation and conservation programs. The CWG has outlined a series of individual and collective activities to address these concerns and identified eight priority sites in which these activities can be carried out and monitored on a sustained basis (Figure 1).

The sites represent the ecological and socioeconomic diversity in the region. They are located on several islands in different ecosystems and have diverse official classification

Table 1. Eight priority sites chosen by the CWG.

Site	Designation	Perceived threats	Key institutions
Rempek, Lombok, NTB	Protected forest	Boundary and land disputes, jurisdictional conflicts, encroachment, migrants, logging	Ministry of Forestry, Land Bureau, local government, LP3ES, LBHR
Sesaot, Lombok, NTB	Protected forest	Change in forest status, population pressure, coffee taxes, illegal wood collection	Ministry of Forestry, local government, LP3ES
Bangkat Monteh, Sumbawa, NTB	Protected forest	Enclave community, land use, forest boundaries	Ministry of Forestry, local government, LP3ES
Tambora, Sumbawa, NTB	Protected forest, nature reserve	Boundary and land use disputes, encroachment by migrants, logging	Ministry of Forestry, local government
Ruteng, Flores, NTT	Recreation forest	Boundary and land use disputes, encroachment, logging	Ministry of Forestry, local government, ADB
Riung, Flores, NTT	Protected forest, nature reserve	Boundary and land tenure disputes, migration, settlement	Ministry of Forestry, local government, Yayasan Sanusa
Wanggameti, Sumba, NTT	Protected forest, nature reserve (proposed national park)	Boundary and tenure disputes, livestock grazing, fire management, illegal logging	Ministry of Forestry, local government, Yayasan Tananua, Birdlife International, Wildlife Conservation Society, WWF
Gunung Mutis, West Timor, NTT	Nature reserve	Boundary and land disputes, livestock grazing, wood collection	Ministry of Forestry, Dept of Public Works, Tourism, local government, WWF

Note: ADB, Asian Development Bank; LBHR, People's Legal Aid Institute; LP3ES, Institute for Economic and Social Research, Education and Information; NTB, Nusa Tenggara Barat; NTT, Nusa Tenggara Timur; WWF, World Wide Fund for Nature.

and management objectives, perceived threats, and institutional settings (Table 1). The "priority" designation was not based purely on ecological or biodiversity considerations; the CWG sought to indicate the importance of these sites from the perspective of each of the principal participating agencies and, therefore, made the choices with the understanding that long-term institutional commitment was the most important factor in developing effective programs and in monitoring and assessing impacts over time.

Although forest and conservation management activities continue at many other sites, these eight locations have provided opportunities for more in-depth analysis and monitoring over the past 3 years. The following short case studies give us a perspective on key management issues at four of the priority sites: Gunung Mutis, Wanggameti, Sesaot, and Rempek.

Gunung Mutis Nature Reserve, West Timor

The nature reserve surrounding Gunung (Mount) Mutis is considered to be one of the few remaining pure stands of *Eucalyptus urophylla* in Indonesia (Robinson and Supriadi 1981). Gunung Mutis lies within the central mountains of Timor and is the source of all major river systems in the western part of the island. Although faunal surveys have yet to be completed, Gunung Mutis is believed to provide habitat for most of the native Timorese mammals and its 217 bird species (Petocz 1991). The proposed total area of the reserve is 12 000 ha; however, this includes two communities within its boundaries.

Fourteen villages surround the reserve; their total population is 25 486. The two villages within the reserve (Nenas and Nuapen) and several along its border share land with the reserve. The relatively fertile soils, moderate rainfall (2 000–3 000 mm/year), and mountainous terrain make this a good region for agriculture, and the reserve covers some of the most productive land.

Local farmers cultivate corn and cassava as staple foods but have also diversified into vegetables and other cash crops, including onions, garlic, potatoes, and fruit trees. Livestock-raising is another important component of the rural economy and tradition and represents one of the most divisive and challenging aspects of conservation management. A recent animal census conducted by the WWF reported that more than 14 000 large animals (horses, cattle, water buffalo) are allowed free range within the boundaries of the reserve; an additional 4 000 are stall-fed in border communities but are occasionally released to graze within the reserve (BKSDA 1998). Conservationists have suggested that these animals suppress understorey growth and development of young seedlings for forest regeneration, and the WWF and the Department of Forestry's Centre for Natural Resource Conservation (BKSDA) have proposed that the livestock be removed from the reserve area.

BKSDA and the local forest service are attempting to engage local communities in forest conservation. These efforts have included education and extension events, community development programs, and reforestation projects. The WWF selected Gunung Mutis as its primary program site in Nusa Tenggara and has been active in the area since 1994. It has conducted biodiversity and socioeconomic surveys, mapped boundaries and land use, monitored forest fires, and organized communities (including the training of conservation cadres).

The challenges to effective management of the Gunung Mutis Nature Reserve are both institutional and practical: conflicting policies and jurisdictions among the key agencies vested with management decisions, the issue of free-ranging cattle within the reserve, and lingering questions over the placement of community–reserve boundaries (Lentz, Mallo, and Bowe 1998). The growing number of immigrant settlers has created additional tension over land use and trade within communities.

A comprehensive management plan has yet to be developed for the reserve, and there is limited collaboration among key local government agencies, NGOs, and local communities. There is obvious conflict between the development agenda of local government and the conservation priorities of provincial, regional, and national agencies. The livestock issue exemplifies these competing agendas: whereas local government and the agriculture service (particularly the livestock division) continue to promote cattle as a source of revenue, conservationists have pressed for the removal of livestock from the reserve.

A proposed collaborative study of livestock management (BKSDA 1998) represents a renewed attempt to integrate land use and interinstitutional decision-making over these complex issues. WWF has already conducted a participatory mapping process in several communities along the boundaries of the reserve, although substantial disagreement remains over boundaries and procedures for reconciling disputes. The broader study of livestock and land use, scheduled for late 1998, will be an opportunity to engage all key agencies and local communities in a more systematic and inclusive discourse on future management of the reserve.

Wanggameti Conservation Area, East Sumba

Sumba exhibits one of the driest climatic regimes in the Indonesian archipelago: average rainfall is only 1 000–1 500 mm annually. The island consists primarily of uplifted lime stone terraces, now covered with range grasses extensively grazed by cattle, horses, and goats. The Sumbanese regularly use fire to manage these rangelands, which has reduced forest cover on the island to less than 10% of the total area (Petocz 1991; Jepson et al. 1996). Natural protection has preserved gallery forests in deep gorges and ravines in the lowlands and moist, closed-canopy evergreen forests in the Massu hills in the southern portion of the island. The Gunung Wanggameti–Laiwangga forest complex is the largest and most diverse extant forested area on Sumba, covering an estimated 45 000 ha. It is the most critical in terms of its biodiversity and role in water catchment for the extensive northeastern plains.

The Wanggameti Conservation Area (WCA) encompasses 42 567 ha. The area was formerly classified as "protection forest" (*hutan lindung*) but has recently been designated as a national park. It contains diverse forest types and has been highlighted for its special importance as habitat for birds. According to recent surveys, the area is home to 176 avian species, including 25 national endemic species and at least nine found only on Sumba (Jepson et al. 1996). These reports also confirm that several of the important indigenous bird species (most notably the yellow-crested cockatoo, *Cacatua sulfurea*, subgenus *citrinocristata*) are seriously threatened by habitat destruction, hunting, and trade (Petocz 1991).

The proposed national park contains two settlements and 15 villages surround it. Farmers continue to practice varied forms of shifting cultivation throughout the area and also use the forest as a source of fuelwood, construction material, and nontimber products such as dyes and medicinal plants for trade in Sumba's markets (Lentz, Fisher, and Mulyana 1998). Grazing of livestock is largely carried out along the periphery of the reserve. In Sumbanese religious myths, the major clan groups originated in the mountains of Wanggameti: numerous sites within the forest are regarded as sacred, and traditional restrictions on exploiting these areas are still widely respected.

Although the area has remarkable scenic beauty and cultural distinction, the lack of infrastructure restricts access. Nevertheless, improved roads and communications on Sumba and the increasing emphasis on tourism (and ecotourism) in Nusa Tenggara indi-cate that visitors to the area will be an important aspect of future development of the national park.

In short, the WCA is regarded as a priority protected area for its rich biodiversity, importance in watershed protection, and its potential for recreational tourism. The forest service has undertaken a number of reforestation projects along the periphery of the reserve with limited success. Poor technical management, difficult site conditions (poor soils and drought), range fires, and outright sabotage have been cited as reasons for fail-ure. In response to concerns over continued encroachment and failure to implement key project activities, local government moved to relocate the communities along the forest margins. In 1993, residents of Katikutana were forcibly evicted from their village. This stirred strong reactions in neighbouring communities and on the part of local and interna-tional NGOs working for conservation and community development in the WCA.

Fear of escalating conflict and concern over the lack of a comprehensive manage-ment plan for the WCA led to the organization of a series of participatory surveys and col-laborative planning measures. From June 1996 to July 1997, key public and private agencies conducted village studies and public discussions in 10 villages surrounding the WCA. These studies present the most complete picture to date of local actions and perspectives on the management of the forest zone. They were facilitated by the consortium's Research Coordination Team for Natural Resources Management (KOPPESDA) and undertaken by teams of researchers from key participating government agencies and NGOs. They included public meetings in each of the communities, as well as the first multicommunity dialogues on the state of the forest, involving representatives from the villages surrounding the WCA. These community dialogues offered important opportunities for villagers to identify and negotiate their own common agenda for forest management.

The information and recommendations from these studies and dialogues were reported to all participating agencies and later discussed in a large multistakeholder regional meeting in July 1997. This meeting led to the creation of a broad-based coalition of agency and stakeholder representatives, the Wanggameti Conservation Area Forum, and to the adoption of several key recommendations related to land-use management, conservation activities, and coordination among government agencies.

Rinjani National Park, West Lombok

The Gunung Rinjani complex on Lombok Island is one of the largest volcanic mountains in Indonesia, reaching an altitude of 3 726 m and covering an area of about 125 000 ha (Petocz 1991). The dramatic beauty of the area, which includes a shallow lake within the caldera, and its proximity to the neighbouring island of Bali are two key factors in its increasing attraction for tourists.

The volcanic complex also contains a broad range of floral communities (tropical and semievergreen to upper montane rainforest types). Zoological studies by the Western Australian Museum and the Indonesian National Museum in Bogor will likely add to the number of identified species — 33 mammals and 136 birds — reported in the area.

In addition, this area is the major watershed for irrigation in the lowlands of the northern part of the island. The forest areas surrounding Gunung Rinjani provide the basis for the economy in the communities within and adjacent to the boundaries of the protected area (LP3ES 1993). Local farmers continue to clear forest patches for their mixed agroforestry gardens (the main crops include coffee, candlenut, vanilla, and a variety of fruit trees) and harvest the forest for fuelwood, timber, and fodder.

Since 1993 the Institute for Economic and Social Research, Education and Information (LP3ES), a national NGO with a regional office in Lombok, has worked in selected forest margin communities surrounding the Rinjani complex. A series of participatory appraisals and in-depth socioeconomic studies have documented community–forest interactions in several communities along the forest boundaries. The studies, conducted in collaboration with the local forest service, the University of Indonesia, and Cornell University, have provided important new insights into conflicts over land use and forest exploitation in these varied settings. Recommendations based on these studies have resulted in new initiatives for resolving these disputes. Two of the communities along the periphery of the Rinjani complex are described below.

Sesaot, Narmada District

The village of Sesaot (population 11 000) is located along the southern boundary of the Rinjani complex, just 20 km from the provincial capital of Mataram. Current conflicts over forest management in Sesaot date from the change of status of the forest zone from restricted production forest to protection forest in 1983 (Suhardi and Fisher 1996). The local government viewed this reclassification as a necessary step in protecting the upper watershed for the large High-level Diversion Project, which was designed to transport water for irrigation from the northern foothills of Rinjani to the marginal drylands of southern Lombok.

However, the change in classification resulted in the immediate loss of access and income for residents of Sesaot, most of whom were initially attracted to the area by employment opportunities in local logging operations. The change in forest status was also accompanied by significant new regulations and policies restricting local access to its resources. For example, restrictions were placed on cultivation of agroforestry gardens within the forest zone; the government planted mahogany as the main forest species, resulting in a more closed canopy and loss of opportunities to cultivate and harvest understorey species; a 50% tax was imposed on coffee yields from gardens within an identified "buffer zone," a major disincentive to local farmers; and restrictions were placed on the collection of all forest products, including fuelwood, fodder, and construction materials.

In April 1993, LP3ES began working in Sesaot, carrying out an initial participatory appraisal to gain a sense of priority issues and begin developing working relations with village leaders. The appraisal resulted in a number of community development activities, including the construction of an irrigation system, the formation of farmer working groups and consumer cooperatives, and, subsequently, the development of the Partnership for Forest Protection (Kelompok Mitra Pengaman Hutan).

This community-based partnership was formed to limit forest theft and assist the forest service in more effective management of the forest zone. It has also addressed issues of corruption and harassment by public officials. The partnership has sought (to date, unsuccessfully) to gain legitimacy for fuelwood collection (the primary source of income for the community) and to obtain access to degraded sites within the forest for community reforestation efforts.

LP3ES has continued to play an important liaison role between the community and government officials (district, provincial, and regional), facilitating public meetings, village studies, training workshops, and conducting regular shuttle diplomacy among the parties in Sesaot and Mataram.

Rempek, Gangga District

The village of Rempek, located along the northern slopes of Gunung Rinjani, presents an entirely different set of issues. Rempek has become a high-profile and highly politicized case, certainly one of the most vexing and intractable land-use disputes in Lombok. As in Sesaot, the settling of Rempek has been rather recent — the village was established in the 1930s, with much of the growth occurring in the 1960s and 1970s. Conflicts over forest access are linked to disagreements over the placement of the forest boundary and subsequent decisions over land use within and immediately adjacent to the forest zone.

In the early 1950s, following independence and the transfer of authority from local government units, the forest service moved the boundaries, established during the Dutch colonial administration, 3 km closer to community settlements. Disputes over these boundaries and over government tree-planting within this designated forest zone resulted in eviction of Rempek farmers in the late 1970s. In subsequent reforestation efforts (1982–83), the forest service employed migrant settlers from the neighbouring communities of Monggal and Gondang. These settlers planted more than 100 ha of agroforestry gardens within the forest zone, and when the government retracted its policy of coffee planting within designated forest areas (in 1989), the farmer cultivators refused to leave their gardens.

The forest boundary dispute is further complicated by jurisdictional disagreement between the forest service and the Land Registration Board (BPN). The latter, apparently recognizing the previous Dutch and local-government boundaries, issued land certificates within the forest zone, which seemed to validate local residents' claims regarding the "correct" forest boundary. In addition, this action strengthened the resolve of Monggal and Gondang settlers to remain in the area and to seek formal ownership of their garden plots.

In summary, the dispute over forest boundaries in Rempek involves contradictory policies of the forest service and the BPN. It has enhanced tensions within the community and created conflicts between local residents and new migrants encouraged to settle in the area. The various parties have maintained hard-line positions on these issues, and there have been few formal initiatives to resolve the issue of the boundary and related tenurial questions. There have been incidents of public demonstrations and localized violence, and encroachment on the forest zone continues.

In September 1995, the forest service asked LP3ES to help mediate the conflict in Rempek. LP3ES conducted a participatory rural appraisal, followed by more in-depth research that outlined many of the issues described above (LP3ES 1996). These findings were presented to the forest service, which has incorporated many of the study's recommendations into a large social forestry project aimed at Rempek and other villages on the northern boundary of the Gunung Rinjani protected area. A regional workshop on Community Participation in Forest and Conservation Management (November 1996) also highlighted the forest management dispute in Rempek. Nevertheless, the social forestry program, implemented largely as a conventional tree-planting project, failed to address the boundary issues. The project nursery and field site became targets for acts of sabotage, and the project was subsequently discontinued in Rempek and moved to neighbouring villages.

Analysis of cases

Collectively, the eight priority sites provide a sense of the complexity of forest and conservation management in Nusa Tenggara (Table 1). The diversity of sites and issues is perhaps their most significant feature, and this can be seen in their varied ecological features, agricultural and land-use systems, ethnic populations, and settlement histories. It is also important to note the differences in forest classification, conservation and institutional priorities, perceived management threats, and varied intervention strategies.

Although diversity is a conspicuous feature of these protected areas, analysis also reveals themes common to all the sites, and these have formed the basis for much of the NTCDC's collaborative action to date. Community surveys and interdisciplinary studies in selected program areas have yielded important insights into issues of community participation, access, rights, and jurisdiction over forest resources.

In general, forest management disputes in Nusa Tenggara fall into four broad categories:

✦ *Legal, regulatory, and procedural issues* — There is a dizzying array of rules, procedures, and jurisdictions regarding the management of forest and conservation areas. Although the Ministry of Forestry has general authority over planning and management of forest lands, the interests of other important national line agencies — agriculture, tourism, public works, and rural development, among others — result in considerable challenges to integration, both in planning and implementation, through local government units at provincial, regency, and sub-regency levels. The considerable overlap among agencies makes coordination and effective decision-making difficult. The most prominent problems are in setting boundaries and classifying forest zones, land-use planning, and establishing mechanisms for forest management and conservation. All of the sites present disturbing examples of how competing administrative jurisdictions and interests have tended to undermine sound management practice. It is also apparent that local communities, NGO program leaders, and indeed many public officials are unaware of, or confused by, the many regulations and procedures that guide management interventions.

✦ *Policy and program implementation* — The centralized nature of policy-making and project development has been one of the main constraints on sound local forest management. A number of enlightened policies guide the development of social or community forestry programs, environmental impact assessment, and general rural development. Nevertheless, the implementation of these projects is often based on plans developed with little knowledge of local conditions or the participation of local actors. At the local level, individuals who are most directly involved in forest management and exploitation are often poorly informed and have limited influence in the planning process. Government and NGO programs are frequently designed with narrow institutional or program objectives, often neglecting the critical elements of integration and coordination. Local government units represent the administrative nexus for this coordination, yet in reality they have mixed authority, limited experience and implementation capacity, and are frequently overwhelmed. The conspicuous failure of reforestation, social forestry, and forest protection initiatives has been reported in Wanggameti, Sesaot, Riung, and Rempek.

✦ *Economic and livelihood issues* — Widespread exploitation of forest land and forest-based products continues in all of the program sites. Agricultural encroachment, logging, the gathering of nontimber forest products, and the grazing of livestock have, in many cases, intensified despite regulatory policies, education and extension programs, and enforcement efforts. In the WCA, the capture of valuable bird species, such as the yellow-crested cockatoo, is seriously diminishing already threatened or endangered species. In Riung, several communities that had been resettled in coastal areas have returned to establish extensive garden areas in the upland forest zone.

✦ *Social and cultural factors* — In several of the sites (for example, Gunung Mutis, Wanggameti, and Riung) strong cultural traditions continue to guide local community attitudes and practices regarding land use and forest exploitation. In these areas, the division, classification, and the laws and regulations regarding access to forest areas have been a primary concern of local rulers (*rajahs*) or tribal councils, often reinforced by clan and kinship alliances.

In Gunung Mutis, for example, the indigenous classification includes "sacred forests," "restricted forests" where hunting is prohibited, "clan forests" for the gathering of forest products, and forests for cultivating gardens (Mallo 1996). The designated rajah and clan leaders have traditionally controlled access to these lands, both for practical and spiritual purposes, and they have broad authority for decision-making and the imposition of sanctions or punishments. Similarly, in East Sumba, the kinship unit exercises strong control over village and forest lands.

These indigenous forest management systems are often based on intimate knowledge of local landscape and ecology and steeped in social and historical tradition. They stand in stark contrast to more recent government efforts to determine forest boundaries, classify forest zones (based primarily on technical considerations), and impose national laws and regulations on community access. The implementation of national government policies and programs is thus often viewed as a direct attack on existing traditions, values, institutions, and leaders.

Lessons learned and confirmed

The diversity of sites, issues, history, and institutional settings has necessitated the use of a variety of interventions to resolve forest management disputes and seek more collaborative and sustainable approaches to forest and conservation management. Although there is considerable local experience in mediation and conflict resolution, there are still few procedures or protocols for effectively managing complex public policy or environmental disputes. Formal mediation of environmental disputes has been introduced into Indonesia only recently (Moore and Santosa 1995). NTCDC participants are quick to recognize the problems of competing interests, poor coordination among agencies, and ineffective programs and policies. However, they are often reluctant to characterize these situations as conflicts and less comfortable about intervening in official efforts at mediation, particularly when the issues are beyond their station or jurisdiction. In each case, interventions aimed at resolving conflicts have been subtle, oblique, responsive, and multi-faceted. Many of the intervening agencies have used indirect means to convene parties, including community organizing, coalition-building, joint fact-finding and collaborative research, training and capacity-building, and a range of strategies to improve dialogue and working relations among stakeholders.

Over the past 3 years, there has been continuous monitoring of interventions in these priority sites through the CWG. Regular meetings have been called to review the case studies, highlight site-based activities, and identify common lessons in this diverse experience. Cross visits among sites by practitioners, policymakers, and community leaders have stimulated important learning and comparisons of key issues. Research in several of the sites has helped in the analysis and documentation of local realities and the assessment of emerging strategies for addressing land-use and forest management conflicts. Annual evaluation meetings have been convened to synthesize lessons learned, chart new initiatives at each site, and seek recommendations for activities that enhance regional collaboration. The collective analysis of regional experience in Nusa Tenggara has yielded the following general lessons for forest and conservation management programs.

Regional, multisite approach

Working in several sites simultaneously is an important strength that provides

- ✦ Opportunities to compare and learn from successes and failures across sites;
- ✦ The ability to extrapolate common themes and use them to address broad policy and program challenges;

✦ An opportunity to use the regional forum as a mirror to reinforce the benefits and the tools for collaboration;

✦ Access to a range of technical knowledge, program experience, local insight, and wider networks of interests;

✦ Opportunities for "leap-frogging" from local to higher jurisdictions by involving officials and policymakers in field visits and field-level discussions.

As a larger coalition, the NTCDC offers stronger legitimacy and political standing than individual member agencies. It also represents a structure for accountability, with regularly scheduled meetings, milestone events, reunions, and evaluations. The revolving meetings held at each of the sites provide an important impetus for local groups to come together within the framework of this regional working group to discuss problems and potential solutions.

Unit of analysis

Many research and intervention programs have been undertaken at individual sites within large protected areas or watershed zones. These studies and projects provide important insights into the dynamics of natural resource management at the local level. Nevertheless, single-site studies or project initiatives cannot address the wider issues of scale and policy that are critical to effective management of large ecosystems. In the WCA, for example, one member of the recently established Forest Protection Committee complained that their isolated efforts to stop forest theft were like "locking the front door of the house against burglars, while the back door and the windows are left wide open." Effective management of protected areas necessitates a broad systems perspective and analysis — and this must be addressed in both ecological and institutional terms. The resolution of forest and conservation management disputes requires a multicommunity, interagency, and ecosystem-based approach to analysis and decision-making.

Concept of "community"

Widespread concern over the limited participation of local communities in environmental decision-making has resulted in recent shifts toward community-based approaches to natural resource management (Wright et al. 1994; Borrini-Feyerabend 1996). Engaging and empowering local communities is an essential, although insufficient step in seeking more inclusive and sustainable approaches to the management of protected areas. Ultimately, community-based approaches must involve all active stakeholders — villages adjacent to the protected area; government officials at district, provincial, and regional levels; researchers and scientists; and NGOs actively engaged in conservation and community development programs. The cattle dispute in Gunung Mutis is a case in point, as it involves informed decision-making and coordinated management by many communities and public agencies. The newly created WCA Forum is a unique example of a new alliance of community representatives, public officials, and NGO leaders working together to forge a common vision and management plan for the reserve.

Importance of an interinstitutional network

The NTCDC has provided the organizational setting that has catalyzed multiparty collaboration. Through the NTCDC, community leaders, public officials, NGO leaders, researchers, etc., have come to know and understand each other's perspectives. Cooperation and initial trust at this regional level have helped build personal relationships that have led to the rejection of stereotypes and prejudices and the development of new collaborative working relationships. Interaction has helped participants put faces to policies and practices; for example, important connections have been made between government officials and NGO leaders. The broader network of the consortium enabled connections with other resources. For example, the Working Group on Participatory Research provided much of the guidance and training for field studies in Sumba and Timor; and participants from the Agroforestry Working Group offered technical support to programs in Wanggameti and Sesaot.

The consortium has also provided an important mechanism for funding these initiatives. Although the Ford Foundation has offered sustained funding of regional activities, regional efforts have often been supported jointly by several public and private agencies.

Links to the policy apparatus

Many forest-management conflicts are rooted in policy decisions that are made at great distances from the location of the management activity — at the district, regency, provincial, or national level. Therefore, local-level disputes are difficult to resolve because the appropriate decision-makers are unaware of the implications of their policies or are unwilling or unable to participate in the process of finding creative solutions. Local-level officials often do not have the authority or may be reluctant to officially sanction innovative approaches. They may also be using these policies, however flawed, for their own personal or institutional advantage. The result is often seen in various informal accommodations where local officials "look the other way," avoiding the problems altogether; officials may even use these opportunities to extort bribes or develop private enterprises within forest conservation areas.

In some cases the consortium's CWG has been effective in engaging high-level officials from the regency, provincial, and regional levels. Forest service, BPN, and local-government officials have been invited to site-based and regional meetings, and these interactions have resulted in relationships that have produced occasional breakthroughs in local impasses. For example, the experimental community-based reforestation effort in Sesaot came about through dialogue encouraged at a series of workshops involving community leaders and district- and provincial-level forest service officials.

"Leapfrogging" over intransigent (or timid) low-level officials is often the most effective strategy in seeking binding decisions for more creative approaches to forest management. However, links to central government, where many forest management policies originate, remain weak. The CWG has occasionally invited national-level officials to attend workshops, and this has allowed personal contacts that can be followed up in Jakarta. Still, the cost of this networking remains high, and the distance and low priority of the Nusa Tenggara region to the national government present serious challenges to future efforts.

Collaboration, mediation, and advocacy

Many conflict management interventions have been initiated by NGOs (both national and international), that have struggled with determining the most effective strategy for mediating fractious and often long-standing disputes. Many have found themselves moving from traditional advocacy approaches (regarding both community and environmental concerns) to more responsive, dynamic roles of facilitating more inclusive processes. In program discussions, practitioners have often emphasized the distinctions between these approaches, speaking of the occasional necessity of playing the confrontational watchdog (jokingly referred to as "ninja turtles" after the heroic cartoon characters who champion truth and justice) in contrast to the more flexible and responsive role of the mediator–facilitator (also referred to as "chameleon" mediators).

Although practitioners have recognized that advocacy is a critical part of the process of leveling the playing field and focusing the issues, many have come to understand the compromises they must make in opting for a more collaborative, convening role. In Lombok, for example, LP3ES has often struggled to play several roles simultaneously (advocate, convenor, and mediator), often finding itself compromised in its relations with both local communities and government agencies. In contrast, the WWF initially defined its role in Nusa Tenggara as one of the lone agencies "speaking for the environment." Over time, WWF has moved toward a more active role of convenor of community representatives and public officials, recognizing the importance of collaborative approaches in achieving broader management objectives for Gunung Mutis.

Research as mediation

Much of the literature on mediation underscores the importance of information-gathering in achieving sound agreements (McCreery 1995). At the four sites discussed above, the research process itself has been used to engage widespread participation of stakeholder groups, both in the field studies and subsequent workshops presenting research findings for public discussion. At each of these sites, mid-level government officials, NGO leaders, and village representatives have been actively involved in the studies, and this has encouraged more applied, systems-oriented analysis and interagency (and interpersonal) sharing. The result has been a more comprehensive understanding of forest management dynamics and more integrated solutions to existing disputes. Most important, these leaders have helped "socialize" the research findings within their respective organizations, so that by the time the key participants have reached the planning and negotiation phase (often in the form of a workshop discussing the findings of the research), the issues are better understood and less threatening to those in a position to decide (including agency directors and village leaders).

Because research is often viewed as "neutral," focusing on analysis of research results helps move stakeholders from entrenched and occasionally poorly informed positions to new understandings of the complex, integrated nature of these disputes. This approach often mitigates some of the potential uneasiness of direct negotiation, opening the dialogue for more creative solutions (Fisher and Ury 1981). The objective validation of information from several perspectives has encouraged more rational, systemic, and collaborative thinking about appropriate action.

Opportunities for community involvement

Conventional government planning processes in Nusa Tenggara have been ineffective in engaging local communities in the planning of forest and conservation management programs. In Rempek, during the height of a dispute over the accepted boundary of the forest zone, the village head commented that he "often felt like a spectator in a volley-ball match," watching government agencies compete to implement their separate, often contradictory programs, with no active community engagement in the process.

A major outcome of the site-based research in Nusa Tenggara has been a common understanding that this limited local involvement is often the source of many ill-conceived programs. Many CWG members are now seeking new opportunities to involve local communities in constructive, nonthreatening, and often unobtrusive ways. In Nusa Tenggara, this has been achieved through participatory research efforts, public meetings at the community (and multicommunity) level, and carefully considered, progressive interaction with public officials. The approaches have also involved extensive shuttle diplomacy and "socialization" between government officials and local communities, facilitated by researchers, NGO staff, or mixed teams.

Process and continuity

The consortium and the CWG have provided both context and continuity for collaborative problem-solving. As programs have expanded and faced a new generation of challenges, there has been growing recognition of the stronger institutional base. Over time, the CWG has worked to form a distinct unit to maintain the momentum of these activities, provide logistical support, and retain the institutional memory and network of contacts needed to facilitate these initiatives. This unit, KOPPESDA, now consists of six staff members working simultaneously at several of the sites. KOPPESDA provides the technical and logistical support (research methods, process design, facilitation), the initiative and leadership, and the experience across sites that is needed to meet many of the difficult challenges of addressing more contentious situations. The team also organizes and helps document site-based and regional workshops.

Because KOPPESDA is perceived to be institutionally independent and generally neutral (compared with other stakeholder groups), it has frequently been called on to convene stakeholder groups in nonbureaucratic and nonconfrontational settings. In short, although not necessarily identified as such, KOPPESDA has quickly become a rapid-deployment mediation–facilitation team for many of the settings where historical relationships and conventions have not allowed for open public discourse on forest and conservation management.

Although this unit has become highly valued within the region (and beyond), requests for assistance have rapidly overburdened its capacity. In each case, KOPPESDA must seek a balanced approach between outside intervention and local capacity-building to sustain the process of resolving disputes and developing new alliances for effective management of the forest and conservation areas.

The larger context: economic and political realities

The regular monitoring and evaluation of site-based interventions has also provided a sobering sense of the constraints of undertaking these relatively new, often protracted approaches to collaborative decision-making. In economic terms, both direct and opportunity costs constrain agency and community participation. This is particularly true for the rural poor, who often must leave farm and community to participate in discussions that may have limited immediate results. At the institutional level, inflexible policies, hierarchical organizational structures, a command-and-rule culture, and limited budgets must often be addressed higher up within the administrative system. The frequent transfer of public officials presents a major challenge, in terms of the considerable investment in education and relationship-building required, and innovative agreements are often informal, nonbinding, and based on personal trust. The investment can prove disappointing when a supportive official is replaced with someone less informed and less than sympathetic to these approaches. Access to sustained and flexible funding is another critical factor in encouraging agency participation and in encouraging more dynamic responses at the local level.

Finally, recent political and economic upheaval in Indonesia has had both direct and subtle impacts on the programs in Nusa Tenggara. The political turmoil of the past year, combined with protracted drought and economic crises have conspired to affect the dynamics of forest exploitation, perceptions of NGO participation, and the ability and willingness of various parties to participate in these processes. Current activities take place in a climate of tremendous uncertainty about future policies related to forest management and community development. A national policy dialogue is currently being encouraged by the newly restructured Ministry of Forestry and Plantations, and the consortium has been asked to host a series of regional meetings to discuss these issues. However, it is too early to tell whether the current government will be able to follow through on proposed new initiatives and policy reforms.

Conclusions

The experience in Nusa Tenggara provides insights into the current state of forest and conservation management and offers important lessons on effective intervention strategies. Each case is unique and presents an example of cultures and livelihoods under new pressures from inevitable economic and social change. The forest sites currently under review by the consortium's CWG are threatened by increased exploitation, flawed policies, and weak coordination and implementation. Collectively, they provide a fairly accurate view of the challenges of reconciling local realities with wider conservation and development objectives.

The interventions described above have been subjected to regular and intense scrutiny over the past 3 years. The approaches have been adapted and refined through collective assessment at each of the sites and comparative evaluation across the Nusa Tenggara region. The CWG has provided a unique structure and forum for this analysis, bringing together community leaders, researchers, government officials, and NGO field staff.

However, these program initiatives are still considered to be in a rather rudimentary stage of development. Progress is varied and success uncertain. Although there are important lessons here for researchers and practitioners engaged in conservation and sustainable development programs, predictive measures remain tentative and imperfect. For example, the convening process in Sesaot initially appeared to be making excellent progress but later stalled and became sidetracked by other issues and priorities. Work in Wanggameti has progressed steadily and has achieved significant agreement on a new structure for coordination in managing the WCA; however, implementation of key program recommendations remains questionable. In Rempek, perhaps the most fractious of all the settings, recent overtures from the government provide at least a glimpse of the simplicity of reconciliation; yet there are no guarantees that these initiatives will achieve lasting resolution.

The activities described in this paper are based on the assumption that the two primary elements for effective decision-making are accurate information and the inclusive participation of stakeholders (Lee 1993). Site-based interventions have emphasized the role of strategic research in providing accurate information on land-use and forest management conflicts. The collaborative nature of this research, which involved communities and public agencies, has, where implemented, led to the most conspicuous progress in mitigating conflicts over management and policy.

At each of the sites, research and field surveys have led to sound recommendations, and diverse structures are emerging to address the challenges of coordinating and integrating development and conservation agendas. These local coalitions are rather recent and still fragile alliances of individuals and groups that are beginning to work together, trust one other, and understand their cultural and institutional differences. Nevertheless, they are inspiring examples that are transforming thinking about environmental management, governance, and participation in Indonesia.

References

BKSDA (Centre for Natural Resource Conservation, Indonesian Department of Forestry). 1998. Pengkajian Sosial, Ekonomi, dan Budaya Ternak Lepas di Sekitar Kawasan Cagar Alam Gunung Mutis (Usulan Kegiatan) [Socioeconomic and cultural research on livestock managmeent in the Gunung Mutis Nature Reserve (proposed activities)]. BKSDA, Balai Konservasi Sumberdaya Alam VII Kupang, Kupang, Indonesia.

Borrini-Feyerabend, G. 1996. Collaborative management of protected areas: tailoring the approach to the context, issues in social policy. International Union for the Conservation of Nature, Gland, Switzerland.

Brown, M.; Wyckoff-Baird, B. 1992. Designing integrated conservation and development projects. Biodiversity Support Program, World Wildlife Fund; World Resources Institute; The Nature Conservancy, Washington, DC, USA.

Corner, L. 1989. East and west Nusa Tenggara: isolation and poverty. *In* Hill, H., ed., Unity in diversity: regional economic development in Indonesia since 1970. Oxford University Press, New York, NY, USA.

Fisher, R.; Ury, W. 1981. Getting to yes: negotiating without giving in. Houghton Mifflin, New York, NY, USA.

Jepson, P.; Suparman Rais; Ora, A.; Raharjaningtrah, W. 1996. Evaluation of protected area network for the conservation of forest values on Sumba Island, East Nusa Tenggara. Birdlife International; Directorate General of Forest Protection and Nature Conservation, Department of Forestry, Jakarta, Indonesia.

Kartasubrata, J.; Sunito, S.; Suharjito, D. 1994. A state of the art report of the social forestry programme in Java. Center for Development Studies, Bogor Agricultural University, Bogor, Indonesia.

Khan, M.A.; Suryanata, K. 1994. A review of participatory research techniques for natural resources management. Ford Foundation, Jakarta, Indonesia.

Larson, P.; Freudenberger, M.; Wyckoff-Baird, B. 1997. Lessons from the field: a review of World Wildlife Fund's experience with integrated conservation and development programs. World Wildlife Fund, Washington, DC, USA.

Lee, K. 1993. Compass and gyroscope: integrating science and politics for the environment. Island Press, Covelo, CA, USA.

Lentz, C.; Fisher, L.; Mulyana, A. 1998. Natural resources decision-making in Wanggameti: a collaborative research and convening process. Presented at the International Association for the Study of Common Property, 10–14 June 1998, Vancouver, BC, Canada.

Lentz, C.; Mallo, M.; Bowe, M. 1998. Environmental management in Gunung Mutis: a case study from Nusa Tenggara, Indonesia. Presented at the International Association for the Study of Common Property, 10–14 June 1998, Vancouver, BC, Canada.

LP3ES (Institute for Economic and Social Research, Education and Information). 1993. Laporan Penjajagan Kebutuhan Masyarakat Kawasan Hutan Lindung Lombok Barat, Nusa Tenggara Barat [report of needs assessment study in the protection forest of Sesaot, West Lombok, Nusa Tenggara Barat]. LP3ES, Mataram, Lombok, Indonesia.

———— 1996. Laporan Pelaksanaan PRA Dalam Program Hutan Kemasyarakatan Rempek, Lombok Barat [report on the implementation of PRA for the social forestry Program in Rempek, West Lombok]. LP3ES, Mataram, Lombok.

MacKinnon, J.; Beudels, R.; Robinson, A.; Artha, M.B. 1982. Feasibility studies of potential reserves of Sumba Island (Food and Agriculture Organization/United Nations Development Programme field report). Directorate of Nature Conservation, Bogor, Indonesia.

Mallo, M. 1996. Kearifan Tradisional Dalam Pengelolaan Sumberdaya Alam pada Masyarakat di Kawasan Hutan Mutis [Traditional knowledge in natural resource management in the Mutis Conservation Forest]. Presented to the Annual Meeting of the Nusa Tenggara Uplands Development Consortium, 21–25 April 1996, Dili, East Timor, Indonesia.

McCreery, S. 1995. Independent fact-finding as a catalyst for cross-cultural dialogue. Cultural Survival Quarterly, Fall.

Moore, C.; Santosa, M.A. 1995. Developing appropriate environmental conflict management procedures in Indonesia. Cultural Survival Quarterly, Fall.

Petocz, R. 1991. General summary profile for Nusa Tenggara. World Wide Fund for Nature, Jakarta, Indonesia. Unpublished report.

Robinson, A.H.; Supriadi, D. 1981. West Timor nature conservation areas: trip report and recommendations. United Nations Development Programme/Food and Agriculture Organization, Directorate of Nature Conservation, Bogor, Indonesia.

Suhardi, S.; Fisher, L. 1996. On boundaries and access: resource management conflicts in forest areas of west Nusa Tenggara, Indonesia. Presented at the Conference of the International Association for the Study of Common Property, Berkeley, CA, USA.

Wells, M. 1997. Indonesia ICDP study: interim report of findings. World Bank, Jakarta, Indonesia.

Wells, M.; Brandon, K.; Hannah, D. 1992. People and parks: linking protected area management with local communities. World Bank; World Wildlife Fund; United States Agency for International Development, Washington, DC, USA.

World Neighbors. 1994. Nusa Tenggara Uplands Development Consortium: annual report, 1993/1994. World Neighbors, Southeast Asia Regional Office, Ubud, Bali, Indonesia.

Wright, R.M.; Western, D.; Strum, S., ed. 1994. Natural connections: perspectives in community-based conservation. Island Press, Covelo, CA, USA.

WWF (World Wide Fund for Nature). 1993. Integration of conservation and development in Nusa Tenggara. WWF, Jakarta, Indonesia. Unpublished report.

Chapter 4

Jabalpur District, Madhya Pradesh, India: Minimizing Conflict in Joint Forest Management

Shashi Kant and Roshan Cooke

Joint forest management (JFM) is a system in which forestry departments and local communities share both responsibilities related to forest management and benefits in terms of the proceeds. The critical factor in its success is the resolution of conflicts between state (forest manager) and local communities and of conflicts within and between communities. In this chapter, JFM institutions in four villages are examined, and the conditions needed to minimize conflicts are identified. These conditions are complementarity among formal institutions and between formal and informal institutions: transparency of institutions, accountability of change agents, a shift in the custodial paradigm of forest managers, and absence of uncertainty.

Only few countries in the world have adopted community-based natural resource management systems on a national scale. India belongs to this select group and is at the forefront of the movement. On 1 June 1990, India's Ministry of Environment and Forests issued a circular requesting all states to adopt joint forest management (JFM) (SPWD 1993). By mid-1996, 16 of the 25 states had done so with varied degrees of success (Saigal et al. 1996).

JFM is an attempt to forge a partnership between the forestry department and local communities based on common management objectives. Under JFM, communities share both responsibilities related to forest management and benefits in terms of the proceeds.

The critical factor in the success of JFM is the resolution of conflicts between state (forest manager) and local communities and of conflicts within and between communities.

In this chapter, JFM institutions in four villages located in Jabalpur district in Madhya Pradesh (Figure 1) are examined, and the conditions needed to minimize conflicts are identified. A case study approach was used, and data were collected using participatory rural appraisal (PRA) techniques.

The short period in which JFM has been in existence in these four villages has been insufficient for the causes of conflict to have developed into identifiable effects. As a result, many of our observations are focused on identifying what villagers perceive to be inequitable, unjust, and discriminatory. By assessing the various aspects of JFM against the values of various user groups in the village, we were able to identify potential areas of conflict. We conclude that if JFM is to be successful in the long term, it is critical that a conflict resolution mechanism be built into the program so that conflicts generated from different sources, such as the lack of transparency, accountability, and equity can be dealt with in a timely fashion.

Joint forest management in India

India's forests have played an integral role in sustaining its people over many millennia. In addition to an abundance of nutritional, medicinal, and subsistence goods, wilderness areas have provided the environment for the spiritual and cultural expression of the Indian people. In the pre-British period, the forests were owned by the rulers of the various kingdoms across India. Forest management was geared toward minimizing social conflicts through a fair, although not necessarily equal, distribution of returns to all sectors of society. For example, the Maurayan empire (324–180 BC) aimed to satisfy the requirements of all social strata through a classification of forests based on use requirements: forests reserved for the king or the state, forests donated to eminent Brahmans, and forests for the public (Dwivedi 1980). There are no records of classification-based forest management in the post-Maurayan period.

With few exceptions, access to forests was largely unrestricted throughout the pre-British period (Guha 1983). The focus of forest "management" continued to be fair distribution of returns. At the village level, the use of all natural resources was managed by a local community institution known as the *Panchayat*, composed of five village elders who managed all village affairs. A significant part of their duties revolved around settling disputes over land, access to water, and mediating conflicts among villagers. These *Panchayats* were the institutional expression of village solidarity (Guha 1989).

Some well-documented examples of community-based management systems are the Kans of Uttar Kanada, the scared groves in the Himalayas, the Orans in Rajasthan, and the Shamilat forests in Punjab (Sarin 1993). In the nonconsumerist Eastern cultures, a distribution perceived to be fair by local communities, but not necessarily equal, was sufficient to prevent serious conflicts that would have hampered forest management decisions. Hence, fair distribution of forest resources helped reduce conflicts among communities and between ruler and communities.

During the British period, the sole purpose of forest management became to redistribute economic resources in favour of the empire. This was achieved by large-scale deforestation, commercialization of timber, and restriction of the rights of local people. Restrictions on people's access to forests were accompanied by an increase in reserve areas

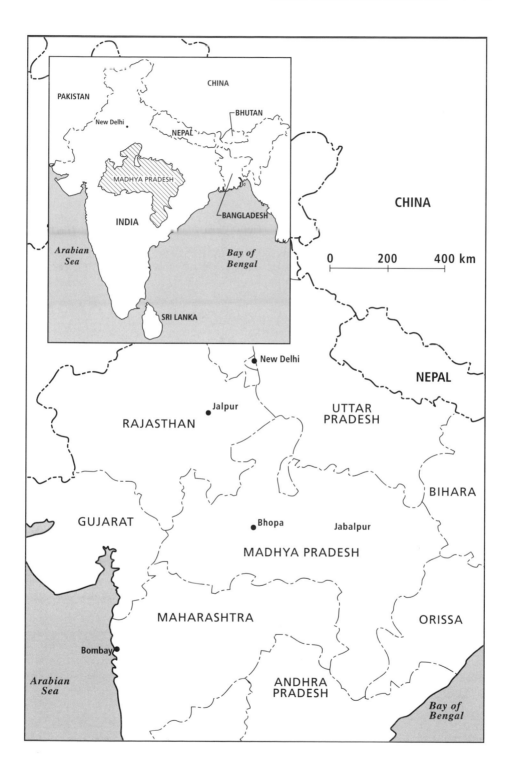

Figure 1. Jabalpur district, Madhya Pradesh, India.

Restrictions on people's access to forests were accompanied by an increase in reserve areas (Guha and Gadgil 1989).

The exclusion of local people from forest resources led to conflicts between the empire and local people. The local people searched for a solution through various nonviolent movements, although some eventually turned to violent means. Their success was sporadic and limited: for example, the British agreed to community-based forest management for some forests in the Himalayas — *Van Panchayats* in Uttar Pradesh and forest cooperatives in Himachal Pradesh (Guha 1983). Thus, the British period created large-scale conflicts between forest managers and local people and marked the beginning of the breakdown of a symbiotic relationship between many communities and the forests in which they were situated (Shah 1996). In the process, traditional communal systems of forest management began to disintegrate.

After independence, from 1947 to 1987, the Government of India tried to redefine social-utility and social-welfare functions, but the emphasis of forest management regimes continued to be on commercial timber exploitation and the exclusion of local people. This further distanced forest-dependent communities from essential resources and fostered conflicts between them and forest managers over rights of access and use.

The continuation of forest regimes geared toward revenue maximization was a result of several factors (Kant 1998):

- ◆ Inertia in the attitudes of forest managers who were trained during the colonial period;

- ◆ The expectation of increasing returns from heavy investments in the establishment of reserves and the training of forest managers;

- ◆ The effects of the attitude of the "old guard" on new forest service personnel; and

- ◆ The expectations of the government, based on the scientific training of forest managers.

Postindependence forest regimes led to the alteration of forest ecosystems and to the devastation of vast tracts of forest (Biswas 1988; Palit 1996; Poffenberger et al. 1996). In addition, the increase in population began to exert strong pressure to convert forest lands to agriculture. Furthermore, after independence the *Panchayat* was transformed from a system of local governance to one of a state regulated "representative democracy" (Sarin 1993). The former legitimacy of local leadership and the tradition of collective decision-making were abolished; in their place, a new institution, which continued to be referred to as the *Panchayat*, took over (Sarin 1993).

In the late 1970s and early 1980s, forest protection initiatives by local communities emerged across India in response to growing scarcities of forest products and threats of exploitation by outside groups. These community actions were an indication of conflict between formal and informal institutions involved in forest management and inefficiencies in existing forest regimes. In isolated cases, some innovative and daring forest officers attempted to resolve conflicts by supporting local forest protection initiatives, thus violating normal practices and the legislated policies of the forest department.

By the mid-1980s, both government and environmental circles began to admit the failure of exclusion-based forest regimes and their corollary affect of generating conflict between local people and forest managers. As a result, the *National Forest Policy 1988* was tabled in parliament; it sought popular participation as a means for resolving conflicts between local and national goals of forest conservation and for restoring wastelands. The issuance of a circular on 1 June 1990 requesting that all states adopt JFM was the first tangible attempt by the government to engage local communities in a partnership for managing and protecting India's forests. The most crucial aspect of this circular, which marks a radical departure from past policies, was the decision to place people's needs above those of commercial interests (SPWD 1993).

As a result of these steps by the national government, in 1991 the government of Madhya Pradesh issued an order specifying details of JFM and the method of establishment of this program in the state. It stipulated that Forest Protection Committees (FPCs) should be set up in "sensitive areas" (areas in which forest cover is over 40%) and that they should receive 20% of net income derived from the forest areas they protect. In degraded areas (canopy cover less than 40%), Village Forest Protection Committees (VFPCs) would be established, and forest regeneration activities would be undertaken. VFPCs were allocated 30% of the final timber produce, 30% of income obtained from nationalized nontimber forest products (NTFPs) and unrestricted access to nonnationalized NTFPs. In addition, VFPCs were entitled to 100% of revenues from intermediate yields, such as from thinning and clearing (SPWD 1993).

In 1995, the state government amended many provisions of the 1991 order. One of the major changes was that FPCs were no longer entitled to a percentage of the final timber harvest — only access to traditional rights were guaranteed. The provision guaranteeing VFPCs 30% of income from nationalized forest products was also revoked, and the forest department's working plans were replaced with 10-year microplans developed in consultation with the villages. In addition, all FPCs and VFPCs are to be constituted in villages or clusters of villages located within 5 km of the forest boundary, and provisions were made to engage *Gram Panchayats* (local governing institutions), women, and the landless in the JFM process (GOMP 1995). Although the 1995 amendment clarifies and further develops several components of JFM, the revoking of financial and other benefits narrows the scope of the program.

In response to these government orders, the Madhya Pradesh Forest Department started the JFM process by establishing FPCs and VFPCs. Four villages selected for this case study are Kundwara, Tikaria, Roriya, and Jamuniya (Table 1) from the Kundwara region of Kundam Development Block in Madhya Pradesh. Kundwara, a forest village (established by the forest department in the early 1900s for its labourers) and the smallest of the four, comprises primarily people of the Gond tribe. Tikaria, the largest village, is inhabited mainly by Baigas tribals, and has a significant population of caste members. Several houses have TVs, and a tower has been built to install a telephone line to the village. Tikaria is the only one of the four villages that has a small store cum tea stand.

Table 1. Comparison of the populations and areas of the four study villages.

	Kundwara	Tikaria	Roriya	Jamuniya
Population	248	624	312	286
Ethnic groups	Gond tribe (except 7 people)	Baigas tribe (125 caste members)	Gond tribe (9 people belong to various castes)	Kol tribe (20% of population are members of various castes and other tribes)
Forest area	303 ha	300 ha	70 ha	303 ha
Agricultural area	88 ha	383 ha	182 ha	93 ha

Although Roriya is the second largest village, it has the smallest forest area. The four villages, which are all within 15 km of each other, come under one *Gram Panchayat* with the head of the *Panchayat* (*Sarpanch*) and five other councilors (*Panchs*) residing in Tikaria.

The main economic activity in this area is agriculture; one rain-fed crop is grown each year. Because grain and other stored crops are sufficient for only 6–8 months, the majority of the villagers are dependent on forest products to meet their nutritional and economic needs. As a result, NTFP collection, primarily by women, is a widespread activity in this area. The few employment opportunities are obtained through the forest department and other farmers. A significant number of youth, as well as landed villagers, migrate to other areas in search of employment for several months of the year. Overall, the Kundwara region is economically impoverished, which in turn increases the dependency of the villagers on the forest for survival.

The initial situation

The four villages are only 60 km away from Jabalpur (one of the major cities of Madhya Pradesh), and Bagaraji — a large town and commercial centre — is only a few kilometres away from Jamuniya. Demands for fuelwood and timber from these two cities are the main cause of many problems faced in the four villages. As the city limits of Jabalpur expanded with its population, villages surrounding the city became the suppliers of wood to meet the growing needs of the metropolis. As nearby forests were denuded, pressure shifted to those further away, and the Kundwara region became one of the primary suppliers of these products. This situation was compounded by population increases within the villages themselves. Throughout the 1970s and 1980s, illicit cutting of timber was common in the Kundwara area, and the forests suffered significant deforestation and degradation. Furthermore, in the late 1980s a fire swept through the Roriya forest leaving it devastated.

Rather than purchasing wood from forest department depots, merchants from Jabalpur recruited Kol tribals as suppliers of cheap illegal timber. Kol tribals, who are adapt at cutting timber, responded to this new economic activity with enthusiasm. Similarly, Baigas tribals — traditional collectors of fuelwood — became the primary suppliers of firewood for visiting merchants. Gond tribals on the other hand have traditionally farmed the land and have relied on forests for soil nutrients and maintenance of groundwater supplies, as well as for augmenting their nutritional needs during lean periods. Thus, activities of the Kol and Baigas tribals were viewed with disfavour by the Gonds in the area. Furthermore, conflict between the forest department and Kol and Baigas tribals began to intensify as forests under the protection of the department began to disappear at a rapid pace.

The majority of caste members in the villages are landed farmers and are economically better off. They are less dependent on the forest, using it primarily as grazing grounds for their livestock. Because the felling of trees by Kol and Baigas tribals led to the opening of the canopy cover and the subsequent formation of grasslands within the forest, caste groups had minimal objection to this activity as it increased the supply of fodder. In addition, several of the influential households that belong to caste groups became intermediaries between timber merchants and loggers and were able to benefit significantly from this illegal activity.

Thus, although the forest resources were under state control, in practice they were being used as an open resource. There were no considerations of economic efficiency, equity, or sustainability in resource use. From about the mid-1980s, the problem was apparent to the villagers as well as to the forest department officials. If the rate of timber and fuelwood extraction had continued at the same rate, forest cover would likely have disappeared and conversion of the land to other uses would have been complete.

The transition to joint management

In 1989, acute resource shortages, caused by the fire in Roriya, brought together village elders to confer on the problem, and out of this came a "self-initiated" forest protection committee. Visiting forest officers using the department's guest house in Kundwara became aware of Roriya's protection activities, and, after the state government's order of 1991, this informal protection committee worked as a catalyst for initiating JFM in this area.

In 1992, as a result of the degraded conditions of forests in the area, the local forest officer approached the elders of Tikaria and explained the objectives of the JFM program. The villagers agreed, and the first official VFPC was established. However, Tikaria's VFPC was dissolved a year later by the forest department, on the grounds that the villagers were not conducting forest protection activities adequately. The villagers contested this, saying that they did not see the necessity of conducting protection activities when the forest department still had a forest guard in its service. According to informal JFM agreements between the forest department and villages, forest guards' services were to be discontinued, and their wages were to be deposited in the FPC–VFPC collective fund.

In 1994, World Environment Day, organized in Tikaria by the State Forest Research Institute, brought most of the villagers and forest department officials into close contact and provided an opportunity for sharing views and understanding each other's perspectives. At the request of the villagers, the forest department reinstated their VFPC soon afterward. Concurrently, after discussion between local forest officials and village leaders, a FPC was also formed in Jamuniya.

The establishment of the Madhya Pradesh Forestry Project in 1995 — funded by the World Bank and other bilateral donor agencies — provided impetus to the JFM program and motivated the forest department to form other forest protection committees in the area. As a result, discussions were initiated with the local people of Kundwara and Roriya, the self-initiated committee of Roriya was formalized as a VFPC, and an FPC was established in Kundwara.

The process by which the forest department formed FPCs and VFPCs was the same for all villages. Initially, individuals and groups were informed of the JFM program, and these people discussed the program with others in the village. Subsequently, the deputy ranger and the local forest officer — in the presence of the *Sarpanch* (head of the local *Panchayat*) — would convene a general meeting in the village. According to the 1995 JFM amendment, a minimum of 50% of the adult population had to be present at this meeting; with their agreement, a forest protection committee could be formed.

No more than 40 villagers were present at these meetings. However, there was representation from both categories of local stakeholders: tribal as well as nontribal groups. The forest department does not recognize timber traders from nearby towns as stakeholders, as they get their returns only through illegal activities and, thus, have no claim over the forests. Hence, they were not asked to attend the meetings. Women were also absent, due to local customs, which usually prohibit their interaction with outsiders. However, decisions were made known to female members of households.

The organizational structure of the FPCs and VFPCs was established by the government order. They have an "executive committee" comprising a president, vice president, secretary (the local forest officer), at least two women and landless people, all elected *Panchayat* officials, and a resident teacher. The officers and members of the executive committee are elected annually. The executive committee is expected to meet monthly to carry out its responsibilities. The executive committee is responsible for enforcing all rules and implementing decisions made at the monthly meetings. The main management rules include

- ✦ Prohibition of timber felling;

- ✦ Protection of forests from fire;

- ✦ Prohibition of fuelwood extraction for commercial sale (only one headload per family is permitted for domestic use);

- ✦ Prohibition of livestock grazing in the forest; and

- ✦ Sustainable harvest of NTFPs.

An FPC or VFPC has the power to prohibit people in neighbouring communities from access to their forest patch. Although NTFP harvesting is still allowed, the FPC or VFPC can prevent people, including its own members, from collecting certain types of NTFPs within specific areas in the forest and can ensure that all collection activities are conducted sustainably.

Most of the management rules are similar across the committees because broad guidelines were specified in the 1995 government order. However, FPC and VFPC members can develop situation-specific and innovative rules to deal with their own problems. In Jamuniya, for example, the committee does not enforce a ban on the commercial harvest of fuelwood. The process of sitting together and drafting a rule about forest use that is acceptable to almost everyone, facilitates the understanding of different perspectives and contributes to the evolution of a mechanism to reduce conflicts. Thus, these new institutions play an important role in managing local conflicts over forest use.

To meet JFM objectives, villagers are required to patrol the forest to ensure that rules are not being broken and to check for fires. Initially, two male members of different families carried out this responsibility on a rotational basis. Problems arose because villagers could not patrol during busy periods of the farming cycle. Currently, patrolling is conducted by a specific watcher hired by the FPC or VFPC. Watchers are paid a monthly salary of 500–600 INR (in 1999, 43.255 Indian rupees [INR] = 1 United States dollar [USD]) from the FPC–VFPC collective fund. Other management rules require that degraded areas be reforested and that resources resulting from forest protection be distributed equitably among villagers.

The FPC or VFPC has the authority to levy fines against anyone who breaks the rules. Penalties for illegal timber cutting are determined by the local forest officer in consultation with the committee and the offender; they are calculated according to the species, size, shape, and volume of the felled tree. Offenders have been eager to settle their debt by this process, rather than being taken to court, which could be time-consuming and costly. At the discretion of the local forest officer, part of the fine is deposited in the collective fund and the remainder is deposited in the forest department's account. This is an example of an open consultative process for resolving conflicts between three parties; because the offender is usually from the same or a neighbouring village, this process contributes to the resolution of conflicts in and between villages.

The FPCs and VFPCs acquire financial resources through membership fees, contributions from the forest department for their protection activities, fines, and interest from loans. Two other sources of funding arose through innovations of FPCs and VFPCs regarding NTFPs. Previously, NTFP collectors were at the mercy of visiting traders, who usually paid rates far below market prices. Now protection committees facilitate transactions between traders and collectors and are able to demand higher returns. For every 10 INR that a collector receives, 2 INR are deducted as commission. In the second initiative, FPCs and VFPCs purchased *mahua* flowers (*Madhuca longifolia*), which are stored for sale at a higher price during the off season. The profits accruing from these schemes are deposited in the collective fund, which is banked in a joint account with the forest department. The president of the committee and the local forest officer have authority for signing cheques.

Use of the collective fund is determined by consensus. FPC and VFPC members present their views at a general meeting. Each idea is assessed by the general membership in terms of its utility for the entire village. A short list is drawn up and, depending on available resources, one or several of the proposals are selected. This process further strengthens understanding of others' views about the common interest of the village.

Outcomes at the village level

State of the forests

In all four villages, the quality of the forests has improved significantly since the inception of forest protection activities. Natural regeneration and other ecological processes are proceeding remarkably well now that pressure on the forest resources has been reduced. Afforestation efforts in 1993–94 in Tikaria and in 1995 in Roriya are reclaiming several wasteland areas. As a result of early protection activities in Roriya, water retention capacity has increased in several areas of the forest; several streams and ponds that had dried up during the early 1980s are now filled with water.

Kundwara has become a model for forestry management activities, because of the special attention it has received as a consequence of its proximity to the forest department's guest house. The village has benefited from projects in the area. A research project funded by the Ford Foundation is seeking to develop better methods of drying, storing, and marketing NTFPs. A plot to grow medicinal plants has also been established. Roriya is also involved in this project, which is attempting to establish three valuable medicinal plant species (*Withania somnifera*, *Abelmoschus moschatus*, and *Asparagus racemosus*) in degraded areas in the forest.

The forest department has trained several Kundwara FPC members in PRA methods. These people, in turn, are to train other villagers. The forest department also coordinated the sale of 200 quintals of grass, collected from Kundwara and two other villages outside the area, to the Lucknow army. Unfortunately, in Kundwara the sale has put pressure on grazing resources needed at the end of summer and created a situation that contributes to forest degradation. Although the initiatives launched by the forest department are praiseworthy, neighbouring villages feel that it is neglecting them in favour of Kundwara.

Jamuniya has the only FPC that does not officially ban the sale of fuelwood; about 65% of its families engage in the sale of this resource. Because Jamuniya's forest is adjacent to Bagaraji, it is the most vulnerable to illegal timber extraction. Nevertheless, since the inception of the FPC there has been a reduction in illegal harvesting and the rate of deforestation has decreased.

Community development

In June 1997, the collective funds of the four villages were 37 495 INR (Kundwara), 10 280 INR (Tikaria), 19 582 INR (Roriya), and 8 420 INR (Jamuniya). In all four villages, musical instruments were the first purchases made with the funds. Villagers take pride in the fact that they own their own *harmonium* (wind driven keyboard), *dholak* and *tabla* (percussion instruments), *majiras*, (shakers), and, in the case of Kundwara, microphones and amplifiers. Furthermore, to enliven the atmosphere at community gatherings, cooking utensils, a mat for the community gathering area, and petromax lamps have been purchased. The villagers feel that this money has been well spent, and it appears that these purchases are fostering better community relations.

The collective fund has also been used for other development activities. For example, a 3-hp motor was purchased for irrigation in Kundwara, and electric grain-milling machines were purchased for Kundwara and Roriya. A religious shrine was constructed in Jamuniya.

Financial assistance

The collective fund serves as a source of credit for villagers. Small loans at interest rates that are 2–5% lower than those offered by village moneylenders (10%) are provided to those in need. These loans are usually used for emergencies, marriages, medical treatment, and the purchase of agricultural inputs. The amount of the loan is determined by the earning capacity of the borrower and the ability of that person to repay it. These terms put poorer members of the community at a disadvantage; however, the service is being used extensively.

Welfare of the poor

Many of the NTFP collectors belong to the lowest economic group in the village and comprise mainly women. The NTFP value-added projects have substantially enhanced their economic status. Collectors of *mahua* flowers in Tikaria have been selling their produce at higher prices to the Kundwara FPC, which is storing it for sale during the off-season.

The Roriya VFPC has devised an innovative scheme for reducing competition among NTFP collectors and for distributing resources equitably. Depending on its size, each family has been assigned 2–4 *mahua* trees for harvesting flowers. Also, group collection is encouraged to ensure that no family's allocated resources are infringed upon. This scheme is a very good example of local innovations for reducing possible conflicts. However, as a result of the ban on the commercial sale of fuelwood, an important source of income for many families has been denied. These families are now shifting toward collection of other products.

Community health

The purchase of community assets from the collective fund is fostering better relations in all villages. In many ways, the collective fund has become a source of pride and has helped galvanize the communities. FPCs and VFPCs have gained legitimacy because they manage the collective fund, and this has led villagers to look to them to resolve conflicts. FPC and VFPC meetings have become a forum for discussing various issues unrelated to forest protection, such as religious festivals and social activities. As a result, since the inception of the VFPC in Tikaria drunken disorderliness and fighting among villagers has decreased; thus, the VFPC has begun to play the role of a controlling force, normally reserved for the *Panchayat*. This situation could lead to conflict with the *Panchayat*, where rumblings of discontentment are evident among those who think their authority has been usurped.

Comparison of outcomes among the villages

It is clear that Kundwara and Roriya are functioning relatively better than Tikaria and Jamuniya. Kundwara's accomplishments illustrate the level of success that can be achieved under the proper guidance and with the resources available to the forest department. Their ability to capitalize on the NTFP value-added initiatives organized by the forest department has benefited individual collectors and the community as a whole. The homogeneous composition of Roriya and Kundwara has also allowed them to pursue forest protection activities more easily than the other two villages. Furthermore, the populations of these villages are predominantly Gond tribals, who have traditionally depended on farming and are aware of the natural resources that forests can provide for maintaining agricultural productivity. As a result, they have taken to the idea of forest protection more readily. Roriya's success is linked to the community's resolute capacity to respond to circumstances of resource scarcity. In Roriya, there is an enthusiasm for, and greater knowledge of, JFM practices. This is facilitated by the age composition of the executive committee, as most members are in their 20s or early 30s. VFPC meetings are held fairly regularly and are well attended.

In Tikaria and Jamuniya, the dominant tribal groups are Baigas and Kol, who have traditionally lived through the harvest and sale of forest products. Regulations restricting their access to these resources, thus, meet with greater resistance. Also, the presence of an appreciable number of caste groups in these two villages tends to confound forest protection efforts, as the economic situation of these villagers makes them less dependent on the maintaining the forest. Population pressures in Tikaria and the proximity of Jamuniya to Bagaraji raise additional obstacles.

The lessons learned

Considering the short period in which JFM has been practiced in the four villages, the success achieved illustrates the abilities of the rural populace to be partners in conservation, even in the face of many challenges. The villagers dependence on and proximity to the forest make them ideally suited for managing and conserving forest resources. However, to ensure the long-term sustainability of the JFM system, attention must be directed toward minimizing conflicts among local people and between local people and forest managers. A number of potential sources of conflict have been identified over the course of the project and will be elaborated upon below. In order to deal with these problems in a timely manner, conflict resolution mechanisms that specifically address them should be built into JFM.

Lack of complementarity of institutions

Forest management regimes are the rules that shape human interaction with respect to forest resources. Such a regime is a combination of both informal and formal institutions. Informal institutions are endogenous to user groups — in this case, the villagers — and cannot be changed rapidly because of their inherent inertia. Formal institutions — for example, those established by JFM — are, normally, exogenous and should complement existing informal ones. If formal and informal institutions are incompatible, conflict will arise between forest managers and local people. Likewise, if formal institutions for forest management are linked, either horizontally or vertically, to other formal institutions, they should be complementary. If not, the objectives of JFM will be undermined and conflict among local peoples will be increased.

A number of conflicts have been observed between informal village and formal JFM institutions. The executive committee at the heart of each FPC or VFPC is one such source of incompatibility. According to the 1995 JFM amendment, executive committees should include all *Panchayat* members, a resident teacher, and at least two landless persons. All members of the executive committee must be elected annually by the general membership. However, *Panchayat* elections are held every 5 years, and the elected officials thus remain on the FPC or VFPC for this period. Also, in a village where there is only one teacher, as is the case in Kundwara, that person becomes a semipermanent member of the committee. Thus, the annual elections will not have much effect on the composition of the executive committee. This situation can lead to conflict among FPC or VFPC executive committee members, as certain groups become entrenched and monopolize resources; for example, in the four villages, the paid position of watcher has been seized by *Panchayat* officials.

Although, legally, the authority of the *Panchayat* supersedes that of FPCs or VFPCs, their overlapping jurisdictions make them competitive, rather than complementary. This could lead to tension between the two institutions, which would be counterproductive to the goals of JFM. Initial signs of discontent have already been observed in Tikaria, as a result of feelings within the *Panchayat* that their authority is being usurped by the VFPC. Other potential problems have also manifested themselves. For example, previously, a transit pass issued by the district forest officer was required to transport any type of timber. In 1997, this regulation was relaxed, and the *Panchayat* was granted the authority to provide transit passes for 10 tree species. This arrangement could lead to conflict if the *Panchayat* acted counter to the goals of forest protection. However, the formal institutions of FPCs and VFPCs do not always come into conflict with the informal village practices. As has been shown, when the two work together through the FPC or VFPC to draft rules about forest use that satisfy everyone, they begin to develop their own conflict resolution mechanisms. These mechanisms can then become essential components of the management of local conflicts.

The ban on the sale of fuelwood is another instance in which formal institutions are incompatible with informal ones. The regulation banning the sale of fuelwood under JFM denies poorer groups an economic activity that has been widely practiced by many families in Jamuniya and Tikaria. It has had a less pronounced effect on Kunwara and Roriya, however, as their principal tribal groups have traditionally avoided engaging in this activity. In Roriya especially, this greater awareness of environmental issues has resulted in more enthusiasm and commitment to JFM as a whole. Thus, in Kunwara and Roriya, formal and informal institutions have been complementary, whereas in Jamuniya and Tikaria they have not. This difference partially explains the greater success of the projects in Kunwara and Roriya, as compared with Jamuniya and Tikaria. Changes in the practices of these households cannot be brought about abruptly by creating new institutions. A mechanism has to be developed to change informal institutions gradually or better adapt formal institutions to them. At the same time, it is important to pay close attention to the sociocultural dimensions of village life, such as the number of caste groups or the traditional tribal practices. These factors clearly impact on the success of the project and the potential level of conflict.

In the collection of fines for illegal cutting of timber, the formal and informal institutions are again at odds. Having expended little effort, the forest department appropriates a percentage of the financial penalty in addition to the seized timber. However, the villagers are the ones who have expended the energy to apprehend the illegal timber loggers. Whereas it has not yet resulted in any serious threat, this incompatibility of institutions is certainly felt by the villagers.

JFM has also been troubled by conflicts between formal institutions. The Watershed Development Program (WDP) is another formal institution that operates in this area. The objectives of the JFM and the WDP are similar in that they both attempt to restore the ecology of the watershed. However, the fact that these institutions are under the guidance of different government departments (the forest department and the rural development department) makes them work independently and at odds with each other. The formation of different local institutions for the delivery of the WDP is also straining the human resources of the villages and is weakening both programs. In many cases, as a result of conflicts between the members of these two organizations, one program has come to overshadow the other. Linking them and making them complementary would reduce the conflict among people involved in these programs and would enhance their efficiency.

Full transparency of institutions

In order to minimize conflict, it is important that institutions be transparent and that lines of communication remain open. Partial transparency of institutions transmits varied signals to different members of the community and can become a major source of conflict among community members, as well as between the communities and the state. When protection committees were established, essential details contained in the 1995 JFM order were not disclosed. This lack of transparency does not allow for the development of relationships based on trust. The importance of such a relationship was made clear in the early days of JFM in Tikaria. Their VFPC program was reinstituted only after villagers and forest department officials were able to share their views and gain an understanding of each other's perspectives. Clearly, increased interaction, openness, and access to information by stakeholders diminishes conflict and positively impacts on JFM.

Furthermore, documentation, such as a memorandum of understanding, is needed to specify the formal and informal details of the agreement between the forest department and FPCs or VFPCs. In the absence of such documentation, inaccurate information has filtered down to the communities, and, as a result, confusion among the villagers is acting as a barrier to the proper functioning and implementation of JFM. For example, for a long period, people in Tikaria believed that they were entitled to 50% of the final timber harvest and were unaware of their entitlement to 100% of intermediate timber yields. When they learned of the actual provisions contained in the 1995 JFM order, their mistrust of forest officials was consolidated. Such situations lead to conflicts and the failure of the program.

Accountability of change agents

The situation at the field level indicates that change agents (government officials, committees, etc.) are not clearly accountable either to the government or to the public for their actions. For example, except for Roriya's, the protection committees meet sporadically. As a result, conflicts that emerge are not dealt with in a timely manner and can snowball into complicated issues that require sophisticated mediation. In Jamuniya, the lack of regular meetings has allowed the local forest officer to bypass democratic processes and appoint an influential member of the community as president of the FPC. The FPC president, in turn, has appointed himself and a Kol tribal to the paid post of watcher. These actions have caused discontent among the villagers and are fostering a sense of disillusionment with JFM. This example reflects how the lack of accountability of forest department officials influences others to follow suit.

Panchs in the other villages have used their positions to become the president or watcher for their FPC or VFPC. Not only are they attempting to enhance their power within the village, but they have also snared the only paid job related to forest protection. These nonaccountable actions of change agents have created new conflicts within the village, and, if this situation continues, they may become unmanageable.

According to the 1995 JFM order, 10-year microplans were to replace the forest department's working plans. However, the forest department continues to harvest mature trees from 10-ha plots in the Tikaria forest. The Tikaria VFPC has not been given a percentage of these harvests, nor have they been granted the 100% of intermediate yields from thinning operations that have been conducted since the inception of the VFPC. These actions of the forest department violate the provisions of the 1995 order and are contributing to conflict between the state's representatives and the local community. Although this has not resulted in uncooperative outcomes yet, the villagers' feelings of mistrust signal a deficiency in the system. It is evident that there is a need for stronger accountability of forest officials and *Panchayat* members as a means to prevent these self-created conflicts.

Paradigm shift

Under the new JFM environment, forest officials have to be open to a paradigm shift that requires a change from a policy emphasizing commercial returns and management by exclusion to one concerned with the needs of local peoples and management in partnership with them. This will require a change on the part of forest officials from being conflict generators to conflict managers. There is evidence that many higher-ranking forest department officers have made this shift. However, the unwillingness of those in the lower ranks to give up power and its corollary benefits establishes a major obstacle in the way of realizing the objectives of a participatory management regime. Many of the activities of the forest department — such as the nondisclosure of entitlements under the government order, the appointment of the FPC president by the local forest officer, and the dissolution of the Tikaria FPC without consulting the villagers — are all indicators of the department's inertia. Thus, a participatory and conflict-minimizing management regime will require forest officials to adopt a new paradigm.

Uncertainties

One of the objectives of forest management systems is to reduce uncertainty and provide stability by offering an institutional structure to all stakeholders in the resource. A certain and stable environment is also conducive to conflict resolution. However, rapid changes in formal institutions (amendment of the 1991 order in 1995) and the failure to implement formal institutions fully (by not divulging essential details nor replacing working plans with microplans) create an environment of uncertainty that facilitates the emergence of new conflicts. The frequent transfers of forest officers can also give rise to new conflicts; for example, a new officer may overturn an informal agreement between the villagers and the previous officer. Varying attitudes and conflicting views of forest officers regarding the provisions of the government's order also create an environment of uncertainty. This uncertainty, in turn, discourages the community from embracing the program and fuels the pessimistic view of villagers that government programs are transient and unreliable.

Gender equity

Although Indian cultural traditions are diverse, in most of these traditions women rarely play a role in decision-making related to community affairs and are normally absent from community forums (Sarin 1993). In the case of forest use, the critical role women play in collecting and processing forest products and the contribution of their activities to the household economy make them vulnerable to decisions regarding JFM. Hence, their participation in JFM is critical not only from a gender-equity but also from a forest management perspective.

The government of Madhya Pradesh has made provisions for women's representation on executive committees. In our four villages, even though FPCs and VFPCs have taken the initiative in promoting household equity and increasing returns to the poor, gender equity is still a low priority. Women are largely uninformed about JFM, and little has been done to include them in the process.

Many of the activities under JFM actually operate against women. As mentioned earlier, most NTFP collection is conducted by women. Thus, the 2-INR commission for the services provided by the FPC or VFPC in facilitating the sale of NTFPs disproportionately taxes the efforts of women. As yet, the collective fund has not provided any specific benefits to women, and the purchase of cooking utensils for providing meals for community gatherings has in fact increased their workload.

Although gender inequity may not endanger the JFM process in the short term, if the concerns of women are not addressed, this could lead to disproportionate costs being shouldered by this segment of the community and, consequently, the creation of a dynamic that facilitates the rejection of both conservation and equity goals.

Conclusions

Because of a lack of resources, communities cannot manage large areas of forests independently. Thus, partnerships like JFM are critical. Local JFM institutions are evolving all across India and in other parts of the world. The communities of the four villages we studied have demonstrated ingenuity in adapting and designing innovative local institutions for the welfare of local people. These will contribute to the evolution of JFM. Given the presence of many barriers, the successes achieved in relation to improvement of forest quality and the welfare of local people are remarkable. It is evident, therefore, that there is great potential for establishing JFM on a large scale.

However, for the long-term sustainability of JFM, conflict resolution mechanisms must be built into its institutions and processes. Continuation of the program in the presence of dissatisfaction among local people, resulting from conflicts in peoples' perceptions, should be carefully evaluated. The continuation of conflicts over a long period may lead to the failure of the program. Thus, potential sources of conflict should be identified and dealt with. The complementarity of institutions, transparency of agreements, accountability of change agents, equitable distribution, and a certain and stable environment will help reduce the emergence of conflicts between community members and forest managers and among community members. Likewise, a paradigm shift in the attitude of forest managers will help resolve existing conflicts. Efforts should, therefore, be made to address these issues, which have emerged during this study.

Acknowledgments

We are extremely thankful to the Society for Promotion of Wasteland Development, New Delhi, for its support during data collection. We especially thank Sushil Saigal (senior program officer, Society for Promotion of Wasteland Development), local forest officials, and villagers who extended their whole-hearted support during fieldwork. We are also indebted to the participants at the international workshop (Washington, 10–14 May 1998), for their comments and suggestions, and to the World Bank Institute and the International Development Research Centre, for financial support to attend the workshop.

References

Biswas, S.K. 1988. Forest administration in India. Chugh Publications, Allahabad, India. Chapter 1.

Dwivedi, A.P. 1980. Forestry in India. Jugal Kishore and Co., Dehradun, India.

GOMP (Government of Madhya Pradesh). 1995. Madhya Pradesh Raj Patra (JFM State Order). GOMP, Bhopal, India. [Translation by Amit Bararia].

Guha, R. 1983. Forestry in British and post-British India: a historical analysis. Economic and Political Weekly, 29 October, 1882–1896.

———— 1989. The unquiet woods. Oxford University Press, New Delhi, India.

Guha, R.; Gadgil, M. 1989. State forests and social conflicts in British India past and present. Journal of Historical Studies, 123, 143–177.

Kant, S. 1998. Socio-economic factors and the dynamics of forest regimes. Presented at the International Symposium on Institutional Aspects of Managerial Economics and Accounting in Forestry, organized by the International Union of Forestry Research Organization, Rome, Italy, 16–18 April 1998.

Palit, S. 1996. Indian forest departments in transition. In Poffenberger, M.; McGean, B., ed., Village voices, forest choices: joint forest management in India. Oxford University Press, New Delhi, India.

Poffenberger, M.; McGean, B.; Khare, A. 1996. Communities sustaining India's forests in the twenty-first century. In Poffenberger, M.; McGean, B., ed., Village voices, forest choices: joint forest management in India. Oxford University Press, New Delhi, India.

Saigal, S.; Agarwal, C.; Campbell, J.Y. 1996. Sustaining joint forest management: the role of non timber forest products. Working Paper, Society for Promotion of Wasteland Development, New Delhi, India.

Sarin, M. 1993. From conflicts to collaboration local institutions in joint forest management. Society for Promotion of Wasteland Development; Ford Foundation, New Delhi, India.

Shah, S.A. 1996. Status of Indian forestry. Wasteland News, Nov. 1995–January 1996, 14–31.

SPWD (Society for Promotion of Wasteland Development). 1993. Joint forest management update 1993. SPWD, New Delhi, India.

Concept

Society

Chapter 5

STAKEHOLDER ANALYSIS AND CONFLICT MANAGEMENT

Ricardo Ramírez

This chapter seeks to support community-based natural resource management by providing a framework for analysis and understanding of two closely interrelated themes: stakeholder analysis and conflict management. The origin and meaning of stakeholders and of stakeholder analysis are sketched. A conceptual framework is proposed as a template to relate two common situations: those in which stakeholders share enough consensus around an issue to collaborate and those stressful situations in which conflict is a given reality and stakeholders may not be certain about the value of joint decision-making or negotiation. Further, this chapter mentions some general principles fundamental in stakeholder negotiations, namely, voice (participation) and procedural justice (agreement on the fairness of rules for collaboration).

Stakeholders and stakeholder analysis

Origins and definitions

The word "stakeholder" was first recorded in 1708 as "a person who holds the stake or stakes in a bet"; the current definition is "a person with an interest or concern in something" (Bisset, personal communication, 1998[1]). Freeman (1984, p. vi) defines a stakeholder as "any group or individual who can affect, or is affected by, the achievement of a corporation's purpose." In the context of natural resource management, however, Röling

---

[1] A. Bisset, personal communication, 1998.

and Wagemakers (1998, p. 7) offer a more appropriate definition: "Stakeholders are ... natural resource users and managers."

Other terms are used interchangeably with stakeholder in colloquial language, but with slightly different connotations. For example, systems analysts refer to an "actor" as "a person who carries out one or more of the activities in the system" (Checkland 1981, p. 312); sociologists talk about "social actors" as individuals or social entities who are knowledgeable and capable (Long 1992) and can thus formulate and defend decisions (Hindess 1986). One recent article (Mitchell et al. 1997) lists 27 definitions of "stakeholder" in the business literature, and many more are proposed in natural resource management fields. What is relevant here is that modern uses of the term are not synonymous with persons or individuals only but also refer to groups and organizations that have an interest or are active players in a system.

Stakeholder analysis refers to a range of tools for the identification and description of stakeholders on the basis of their attributes, interrelationships, and interests related to a given issue or resource. The term transcends several fields of study, including business management, international relations, policy development, participatory research, ecology, and natural resource management. It is rather vague as it is often mentioned loosely without specific indication of the context.

To clarify the meaning of the term, it is useful to ask why stakeholder analysis is used. There are several reasons for carrying out stakeholder analysis (Grimble and Wellard 1996; Engel 1997; Röling and Wagemakers 1998):

✦ Empirically to discover existing patterns of interaction;

✦ Analytically to improve interventions;

✦ As a management tool in policy-making; and

✦ As a tool to predict conflict.

"Stakeholder analysis can be defined as an approach for understanding a system by identifying the key actors or stakeholders in the system, and assessing their respective interest in that system" (Grimble et al. 1995, pp. 3–4). This definition is useful in that it defines stakeholder analysis as a natural resource management approach and acknowledges its limits — it cannot be expected to solve all problems or guarantee representation (Grimble and Wellard 1996).

Grimble and Wellard (1996) underline the usefulness of stakeholder analysis in understanding complexity and compatibility problems between objectives and stakeholders. Likewise, Freeman and Gilbert (1987) propose the concept of "stakeholder management" as a framework to help managers understand the turbulent and complex business environment. Hence the term "stakeholder" is often associated with corporate management. A central assumption in Freeman's writing is the manager's ability to manage stakeholder relationships. This is difficult to transport to other fields, such as natural resource management, where the power to control the system is at the heart of many debates.

A thorough description of stakeholder analysis as a qualitative method in organizational research is provided by Burgoyne (1994). Grimble and Wellard (1996) trace several other origins of stakeholder analysis, including political economy, namely through the notion of how to combine numerous individual preferences by applying cost–benefit analyses. Stakeholder analysis is also derived from participatory methods of project design, such as rapid and participatory rural appraisal (PRA), that seek to integrate the interests and perspectives of disadvantaged and less powerful groups (Pretty et al. 1995; Chambers 1997).

The questions of who is a stakeholder and under what circumstances the opinions or knowledge of stakeholders count are common to both participatory research and business literature, in both instances, power is described as a central attribute of knowledge (Chambers 1997; Mitchell et al. 1997). Furthermore, stakeholder analysis is also a central theme in conflict management and dispute resolution and has important roots in the social actor perspective in the sociology of development (Long 1992).

Stakeholder analysis: steps and tools

Stakeholder analysis seeks to differentiate and study stakeholders on the basis of their attributes and the criteria of the analyst or convenor appropriate to the specific situation. These may include

+ The relative power and interest of each stakeholder (Freeman 1984);

+ The importance and influence they have (Grimble and Wellard 1996);

+ The multiple "hats" they wear; and

+ The networks and coalitions to which they belong (Freeman and Gilbert 1987).

For example, in conflict assessment, four types of stakeholders are expected: those with claims to legal protection, those with political clout, those with power to block negotiated agreements, and those with moral claims to public sympathy (Susskind and Cruikshank 1987).

It follows then, that in the natural resource management literature we find a range of terms such as

+ Primary, secondary, and key stakeholders (ODA 1995);

+ Internal or external to the organization (Gass et al. 1997);

+ Stakeholders, clients, beneficiaries (ASIP 1998); and

+ Stakeholder typologies on a macro- to microcontinuum and on the basis of their relative importance and influence (Grimble et al. 1995).

Although differentiation among stakeholders is a necessary step in stakeholder analysis, the distinction is often based on qualitative criteria that are difficult to generalize. The use of matrices is a common tool in stakeholder analysis, in which stakeholder groups appear on one axis and a list of criteria or attributes appears on the other. For each overlapping area, a qualitative description or quantitative rating is given (see Annex 1).

Grimble et al. (1995, p. 7) list a flexible set of steps for conducting stakeholder analysis:

+ Identify the main purpose of the analysis;

+ Develop an understanding of the system and decision-makers in the system;

+ Identify principal stakeholders;

+ Investigate stakeholder interests, characteristics, and circumstances;

+ Identify patterns and contexts of interaction between stakeholders; and

+ Define options for management.

Three major phases are involved: defining the problem, analyzing constraints and opportunities, and agreeing on an action plan. These phases are common to several methods that seek to engage multiple stakeholders in joint analysis and action in natural resource management:

* Rapid appraisal of agricultural knowledge systems (Engel and Salomon 1997) (see Annex 2);

* Collaborative management (Borrini-Feyerabend 1996); and

* Collaborative learning (Daniels and Walker 1996).

A logical question arises: Who decides on the purpose of the analysis and who counts most? In other words, who is a stakeholder? The question refers ultimately to the relationship both between the stakeholder and the problem and between the stakeholder and the analyst or convener. For the convener, it has to do with having the power, legitimacy or resources to convene others, the power to choose the criteria for inclusion or exclusion of stakeholders, and the authority to define the reason or theme around which stakeholder analysis takes place (Grimble and Wellard 1996). On the side of the stakeholder, it has to do with "being noticed" or having a "voice," which in turn is the result of having attributes such as power, legitimacy, and urgency in relation to an issue (Mitchell et al. 1997).

For corporate managers the question of power is often taken for granted: the corporation decides what the problem situation is and who the stakeholders are. In natural resource management, however, the use of power to convene and select stakeholders may not be agreeable to all. Moreover, unless there is agreement on the boundaries around a resource problem, there may not be enough parameters around which to decide who the stakeholders are in a system. In fact, the stakeholders in all likelihood do not form a system unless they expressly agree to see themselves as belonging to one (Röling and Jiggins 1998). For this to happen, stakeholders must agree on a problem domain, that is, a problem conceptualized by the stakeholders (Trist 1983).

Stakeholders are part of a management strategy, an arbitrary concept that exists only to the extent that people can agree on its goals, boundaries, membership, and usefulness (Röling and Wagemakers 1998). Stakeholder analysis tools tend to be straightforward: matrices or lists of criteria or attributes. Complex and ever changing, however, are the challenges of establishing commonly agreeable definitions of issues or problem situations, defining the boundaries, and identifying the relevant stakeholders.

Conceptual framework

The conceptual framework as a guide to inquiry

The conceptual framework presented below (Figure 1) is based on a number of propositions and is accompanied by examples. It is intended as a map to guide inquiry; its aim is to help readers situate their experience and compare it with other situations where multiple stakeholders interact. The framework is made up of propositions derived from a review of the literature across many fields of study. These include organizational management; knowledge systems and systems thinking; stakeholder salience theory; sociology of development; negotiation and social conflict; "common-pool" and natural resource

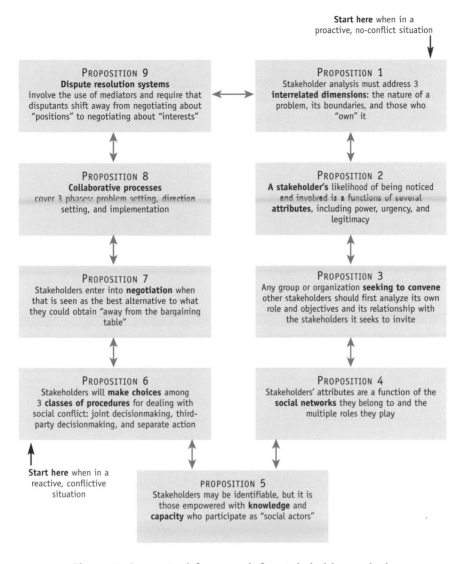

Start here when in a
proactive, no-conflict situation

PROPOSITION 9
Dispute resolution systems
involve the use of mediators and require that
disputants shift away from negotiating about
"positions" to negotiating about "interests"

PROPOSITION 1
Stakeholder analysis must address 3
interrelated dimensions: the nature of a
problem, its boundaries, and those who
"own" it

PROPOSITION 8
Collaborative processes
cover 3 phases: problem setting, direction
setting, and implementation

PROPOSITION 2
A stakeholder's likelihood of being noticed
and involved is a function of several
attributes, including power, urgency, and
legitimacy

PROPOSITION 7
Stakeholders enter into **negotiation** when
that is seen as the best alternative to what
they could obtain "away from the bargaining
table"

PROPOSITION 3
Any group or organization **seeking to convene**
other stakeholders should first analyze its own
role and objectives and its relationship with
the stakeholders it seeks to invite

PROPOSITION 6
Stakeholders will **make choices** among
3 **classes of procedures** for dealing with
social conflict: joint decisionmaking, third-
party decisionmaking, and separate action

PROPOSITION 4
Stakeholders' attributes are a function of the
social networks they belong to and the
multiple roles they play

Start here when in a
reactive, conflictive
situation

PROPOSITION 5
Stakeholders may be identifiable, but it is
those empowered with **knowledge** and
capacity who participate as "social actors"

**Figure 1. Conceptual framework for stakeholder analysis
and conflict managment.**

management; sustainable development and regenerative agriculture; adult education and communication; interactive policy-making; and organizational learning.

The first set of propositions (from 1 to 5, inclusive) is particularly relevant to situations in which there is no crisis, but rather where one party is seeking to understand the dynamics of a natural resource management issue or to intervene in it. Propositions 6 to 9 are more specific to decision-making behaviour by groups faced with social conflict. Almost all propositions relate to each other; hence, the conceptual framework in Figure 1 can be read beginning anywhere. The case studies in this volume are used as examples to test the propositions; in turn, the framework serves as an instrument to explore the case studies.

Proposition 1: Stakeholder analysis must address three interrelated dimensions: the nature of a problem, its boundaries, and those who "own the problem"

This proposition is one of the most challenging to comprehend because of the seemingly never-ending interplay between these three dimensions. The arenas in which this interplay evolves are many; they are dynamic, complex, and subject to many interpretations. A brief discussion on the global context in which multiple stakeholder situations arise is, therefore, necessary.

On one hand, there is a global trend toward increasing decentralization of power from state agencies to local government; this is evident in the increasing responsibilities transferred to local authorities and the growing number and importance of civil-society organizations. On the other hand, investment and the globalization of the economy and information concentrate decision-making power in the hands of multinational corporations, around financial centres of power, and in multilateral trade agreements. The literature is rich with debates about the negative impacts and promising opportunities for various sectors arising from the forces of globalization and from decentralization (Kooiman 1993; Hirst 1997). Reconciling the different opinions lies beyond the scope of this paper, but reference to the complexity and dynamic nature of these arenas is necessary to locate this proposition in a controversial, real world.

Although the global trend toward decentralization is recent, the notion of *pluralism* that often accompanies it is not. Pluralism emerged from political theory and philosophy (Kekes 1993; Rescher 1993; Hirst 1997). In simple terms, pluralism represents an acknowledgement of multistakeholder situations. However, there are widely differing interpretations of the philosophical, political, or sociological ramifications of pluralism. Much debate surrounds the issue of whether pluralism is a "slippery middle ground" between relativism and monism (absolutism) (Kekes 1993; Daniels and Walker 1997). In forestry and rural development, "pluralism refers to situations where a number of autonomous and independent groups with fundamentally different values, perceptions, and objectives demand a role in decision-making about natural resource management outcomes" (Anderson et al. 1998).

"Systems thinking" provides a complementary approach for learning about complex situations in that it analyzes, in a systematic manner, the nature of the relationship between stakeholders and what is to be studied. "A system consists of a number of elements and the relationships between the elements" (Flood and Jackson 1991, p. 5). One derivation of systems thinking is "soft systems methodology" that follows a sequence of steps to study the nature of a problem, its boundaries, and the actors who are affected or "own the problem" (Checkland 1981; Naughton 1984; Checkland and Schöles 1990). The approach acknowledges that the different dimensions are interrelated in that the nature of a problem is influenced by the characteristics of the boundaries, which in turn define the actors involved, who in turn have opinions on the attributes of the boundaries. Each dimension changes the other. Systems thinking is useful to interdisciplinary research (Ackoff 1969).

When the boundaries of an issue are ill-defined, they will become a source of conflict, which in turn will spread to disagreements over the definition of relevant stakeholders. In Matagalpa, Nicaragua downstream communities believe that upstream communities should be forced to manage and protect water sources more carefully, as both depend on them for their drinking water (Vernooy and Ashby, this volume). They don't share, however, a common notion of the watershed as a management unit. Elsewhere in the watershed the legal status of lands turned over to farmers during the revolution is contested by their former owners. Both parties deny that the other is a legitimate stakeholder. These disagreements about the boundaries of a problem and whose problem it is can lead to a spiral of conflict that becomes increasingly difficult to manage (Carpenter and Kennedy 1988). At the heart of such conflicts lie disagreements over the three dimensions of this proposition: Who is a stakeholder? What is the problem? and What are the boundaries? There are no simple answers because there are numerous interactions involved.

This proposition suggests that "systems thinking" and soft systems methods provide relevant ways of studying complex situations. The proposition further suggests that the institutions and the rules that deal with these situations need to evolve toward more flexible, resilient, and adaptive ways of responding to situations in which definitions of stakeholders, boundaries, and the problem need to be agreed on as a first step. In a context as conflictive as the Honduran case, the proposition serves as a lens through which to examine the dimensions of the problem.

Proposition 2: A stakeholder's likelihood of being noticed and involved is a function of several attributes including power, urgency, and legitimacy

The "theory of stakeholder identification and salience" proposed by Mitchell et al. (1997) highlights three stakeholder attributes that merit attention:

- ✦ The stakeholder's power to influence the firm;

- ✦ The legitimacy of a stakeholder's relationship to the firm; and

- ✦ The urgency of the stakeholder's claim on the firm.[2]

On the basis of these attributes, the theory proposes a typology of stakeholders "to whom management should pay attention" (Mitchell et al. 1997). It follows that stakeholders with two or more attributes are likely to be noticed and participate; those without them will tend to be ignored. In the context of this paper, I refer to the issue or problem situation, rather than the "firm."

When local groups lack power and legitimacy in the eyes of public authorities, they may be unable to participate or even take advantage of new laws expressly drafted to delegate authority to them. Others may have to intervene on their behalf. In Lao, the Management of Forest and Forest Land Decree supported community-based natural resource management (Hirsch et al., this volume). However, outside limited pilot areas, implementation of the decree was mostly based on dissemination of the document to the district level, and this was passed on to the village level through a short verbal or written missive. Thus, implementation of this decree depended mainly on the capability and competence of the district staff, not on demand capacity of the beneficiaries. Had the beneficiaries enjoyed some power, or some legitimacy, in combination with some urgency, they would have been less at the mercy of well-intended district staff.

Power remains a key attribute, and this point provides a direct link to the first proposition: in situations where power is concentrated in the hands of an elite, the process of stakeholder identification and boundary and problem definition will be distorted and manipulative. Power is a recurring theme that accompanies many of the propositions in this paper and deserves some additional attention.

---

[2] In this context, "power" is defined as "a relationship among social actors in which one social actor, A, can get another social actor, B, to do something that B would not have otherwise done"; "legitimacy" as "a generalized perception or assumption that the actions of an entity are desirable, proper, or appropriate within some socially constructed system of norms, values, beliefs, definitions"; and "urgency" as "the degree to which stakeholder claims call for immediate attention" (Mitchell et al. 1997, p. 869).

"Power is the capacity to achieve outcomes … . Power is not, as such, an obstacle to freedom or emancipation but its very medium … . The existence of power presumes structures of domination whereby power … operates" (Giddens 1984, p. 257). When looking at power, we see struggle, negotiation, and compromise; understanding power also involves personal abilities to perceive "edges" that can be taken advantage of, and social networks are the context within which these processes evolve (Villarreal 1992). In other words, the dynamics of power are fluid and complex.

Another broader interpretation of power suggests four "modes": (1) power as attributed to a person, an endowment; (2) the ability of one ego to impose its will on an alter, in social action or interpersonal relations (as was used by Mitchell et al. 1997) and also referred to as "influence" (ODA 1995); (3) "tactical" or "organizational" power that controls the setting for interaction; and (4) "structural power," which is based on Michel Foucault's (1984, p. 428) notion of power as an "ability to structure the possible field of action of others." This fourth notion refers to governing power: "Structural power shapes the social field of action so as to render some kinds of behaviour possible, while making other less possible or impossible" (Wolf 1990, p. 587).

Joint forest management (JFM) was introduced in India by government order in an attempt to forge a partnership between the forestry department and local communities. (Kant and Cooke, this volume). In JFM, communities share both responsibilities and proceeds. When Village Forest Committees (VFCs) and Village Forest Protection Committees (VFPCs) were formed, the officials from the forest department did not inform the communities that they would also have a share in the final timber harvest. Instead, future shortages of forest products were emphasized. The power held by the forest department officials was tactical, in that they controlled the bulk of information reaching the communities, which is indicative of their resistance to giving up control over their interactions with villagers. For instance, no memorandum of understanding was drafted to specify the details of the agreement between the forest department and FPCs and VFPCs, largely because the forestry staff wanted to remain unaccountable. Although the JFM order may have sought a more democratic use of common-property forests, the plan was stalled because the forest department had little incentive to implement the new regime.

Proposition 3: Any group or organization seeking to convene other stakeholders should first analyze its own roles and objectives and its relationship with the stakeholders it seeks to invite

According to Freeman (1984, p. 64), the challenge of stakeholder identification is further complicated by what he calls the "congruence problem." "Analyzing stakeholders in terms of an organization's perception of their power and stake is not enough. When these perceptions are out of line with the perceptions of the stakeholders, all the brilliant strategic thinking in the world will not work." The congruence problem has to do with the assumptions an organization makes about its stakeholders, about how it interacts with them, and on what basis it is willing to negotiate with them.

Stakeholders' attributes, such as power and legitimacy, help explain the odds of a stakeholder becoming a "convener" or a facilitator. With regard to the time element, or *urgency*, some authors suggest that avoidance of urgency on the side of the facilitator is a key component of successful conflict management (Thomas et al. 1996). An organization may be able to convene others temporarily; thereafter, however, the stakeholders will decide on the role and desired attributes of the convener and on specific functions for other neutral parties, such as facilitators, who may become providers of expert information.

This proposition merits the attention of agencies and projects that assume they have the power and legitimacy to convene and intervene in a rural setting. Much of the literature on stakeholder analysis fails to question this assumption and seems to be directed predominantly at those groups or agencies who seek to convene and assume they will control a project (Warner and Jones 1998). The result is often the imposition of urgency, as a result of administrative deadlines imposed by a distant head office. It is argued here that a convening organization can gain legitimacy by openly acknowledging its own limitations as a convener.

The ability to convene a wide range of stakeholders requires a convener with widespread recognition and neutrality. The Nusa Tenggara Uplands Development Consortium in Indonesia is an interagency network comprising representatives from government agencies, nongovernmental organizations (NGOs), research institutions, and local communities (Fisher et al., this volume). Over time it has acquired power and legitimacy through its members and responded to the time frame or degree of urgency they have agreed on. The Indonesia case study suggests that the government organizations have realized that they need a third-party convener with a reputation as a legitimate, neutral multiactor organization, even though the government organizations may have had the power and urgency to convene on their own.

Proposition 4: Stakeholders' attributes are a function of the social networks they belong to and the multiple roles they play

There is a need to understand how stakeholders interrelate, what multiple "hats" they wear, and what networks and other groups they belong to. Social network theory seeks to understand actors' behaviour by analyzing the types of relationships they experience and the structure of those relationships (Rowley 1997).

Social network analysis is used by authors across many fields of study in a number of ways:

- ✦ The review of networks in agricultural research systems (Shrum and Beggs 1995; Shrum 1997);

- ✦ Stakeholder networks as sources of innovation in agriculture (Engel 1997) and in business (Wheatley 1992; Wicks et al. 1994);

- ✦ Social networks in relation to the notion of "social capital" (Ostrom 1995; Coleman 1966);

- ✦ The influence of social networks on stakeholders' relations to natural resources, especially forests (Colfer 1985; Grimble et al. 1994, 1995; Grimble and Chan 1995; Hobley 1996; Grimble and Wellard 1996);

- ✦ Policy renewal emerging from social networks (Röling 1997); and

- ✦ The study of the spread of infectious diseases in epidemiological studies (Morris 1994).

Recent developments in negotiations research attribute great importance to social context in determining the preference for different procedures to negotiate social conflict (Pruitt and Carnevale 1993). Social context also influences what coalitions stakeholders join, where coalitions are defined as "subgroups whose purpose is to influence the decision of a larger group" (Polzer et al. 1995, p. 135), as well as different behaviours on the part of mediators (Pruitt and Carnevale 1993).

A social network is "a set of actors and the set of ties representing some relationship — or lack of relationship — between the actors" (Brass et al. 1998). Management writers suggest the need to analyze "the complex array of multiple and interdependent relationships existing in stakeholder environments" (Rowley 1997, p. 890). To do this, they propose two dimensions: "density," as a measure of interconnectedness, and "centrality," referring to an actor's relative position in a network. Of significance here is the notion of understanding stakeholders in the context of the web of relationships within which they are embedded (Granovetter 1985). Among the issues that influence negotiation attitudes, interdependence is of central importance, as actors' attitudes and behaviour are shaped by the fact that they will need to coexist after the period of negotiation (Susskind and Cruikshank 1987).

Proposition 4 suggests that stakeholders are likely to form alliances, or use alliance-forming opportunities, both as bargaining tools and as a means of striking new institutional arrangements. Having options and having a number of agendas can help empower a group. At the same time, switching from a rival to a collaborative mode may be the result of stakeholders' perceptions of future opportunities and interdependencies that merit attention. These decisions are made, modified, and reviewed constantly by stakeholders as they sense the odds of advancing their objectives via different alliances.

Research by Ostrom (1998) suggests that local groups of resource users, sometimes alone and sometimes with outside institutional assistance, have managed to create a wide diversity of institutional arrangements for coping with common-pool resources when they have not been prevented from doing so by central authorities (Ostrom 1998). She notes that they must be in direct communication for this process to develop. When individuals are held apart and unable to communicate face-to-face, they may overuse common-pool resources. This proposition complements proposition 2 in that it focuses on the decision-making behaviour of stakeholders based on their analysis of opportunities and costs in a social context. For a convener, this means that stakeholder behaviour cannot be fully explained on the basis of their attributes.

The social networks surrounding a natural resource may, through time and interaction, create trust among parties with seemingly opposed positions. In the Laguna Merin watershed in Uruguay (Pérez Arrarte and Scarlato, this volume), agreements on innovative natural resource management practices were achieved at the local level among stakeholders with very divergent interests (commercial rice producers, local authorities, and environmentalists). In contrast, the distant central-government agencies and technical institute personnel not part of the social networks were the least willing to modify their positions.

Proposition 5: Stakeholders may be identifiable, but it is those empowered with knowledge and capacity who participate as "social actors"

"Social actors" are those with the capacity to make decisions and act on them; thus, the concept of social actor may be distinct from that of stakeholder (Long 1992). The notion of "human agency" is central to the concept of a social actor: "In general terms, the notion of agency attributes to the individual actor the capacity to process social experience and to devise ways of coping with life ... social actors are 'knowledgeable' and 'capable.'" (Long 1992, pp. 22–23). Ostrom (1995, p. 126) refers to "human capital" in similar terms:

"Human capital is the knowledge and skill that individuals bring to the solution of any problem." Social actors seek to solve problems, learn how to intervene in social events, and continuously monitor their own actions (Giddens 1984). From Long's perspective, the environment cannot be described as a social actor, whereas there is mention of it as a stakeholder in the business literature (Mitchell et al. 1997). As noted by Chevalier and Buckles (this volume), in some cultures ancestors or forest spirits may be considered stakeholders.

This discussion suggests that marginalized actors who may be easily identified as stakeholders will need support through information provision and training to enable them to negotiate and defend positions. Stakeholders who do not have the capacity to make decisions and act on them are unlikely to become part of a collaborative decision-making process. Helping a group become a social actor is one strategy for "leveling a playing field," as it gives legitimacy to a disempowered group, however, unless such a group also gets some sort of political endorsement, its involvement in a negotiation is not guaranteed.

This statement supports proposition 2 regarding a stakeholder's salience. It can be argued that stakeholders are likely to become social actors through the process of becoming involved in separate action, be it political lobbying or civil disobedience. By gaining political clout, community groups may level the playing field, forcing the more powerful stakeholders to negotiate. If the community groups also acquire the skills to prepare proposals and defend them in multistakeholder meetings, then they are in a position to participate at the table as empowered stakeholders.

Proposition 5 is also closely related to proposition 6 on the different procedures available to stakeholders faced with social conflict. The Honduras case (Chenier et al., this volume) describes how the conflict in Copán, which had simmered for many years, came to a head as a result of the ratification of Agreement 169 by the government. If the conflict had not come to a head, the locals would probably never have developed the skills to handle it." The case study provides insight into how delicate this process can be. External material and moral support can be of great value in helping to assure a "level playing-field" for the different actors involved but needs to be planned and implemented with care in order to avoid risking damaging the credibility of the local actors by leading to accusations of external political manipulation. Another example is from the Philippines (Talaue-McManus et al., this volume). In the process of developing the Coastal Development Plan for Bolinao, direct resource users (subsistence fishers, fish vendors) were mobilized, oriented, and empowered through knowledge and skills to participate in a collective process.

Situations like these illustrate the switch from stakeholder analysis in a proactive, nonconflict situation, to stakeholder analysis as part of a range of procedures for dealing with social conflict. The remaining propositions describe common situations where conflict is a given starting point. Daniels and Walker (1996) argue that conflict in natural resource management is not only unavoidable, but also desirable to the extent that it can lead to negotiated, innovative agreements among stakeholders.

Proposition 6: Stakeholders will make choices among three different classes of procedures for dealing with social conflict: joint decision-making, third-party decision-making, and separate action

In natural resource management, conflict is often inevitable (Daniels and Walker 1997; Hildyard et al. 1997, 1998). The growing demand for finite or renewable natural resources to satisfy the needs of different stakeholders is a common source of conflict. As resources become scarce, the competing interests cannot be fully met. Faced with such situations, stakeholders will make choices about how best to act to pursue their own interests. Stakeholder negotiation will inevitably involve conflicts of interest and trade-offs (Grimble et al. 1995; Grimble and Wellard 1996).

Procedures for dealing with social conflict can be grouped into three classes along a continuum (Pruitt and Carnevale 1993). Numerous factors influence why stakeholders (or "disputants" in negotiation terminology) will opt for one over another, depending on the nature of the conflict, the stage of the negotiation, and the attributes of the stakeholders:

- ✦ Joint decision-making
  - ✧ Negotiation
  - ✧ Mediation

- ✦ Third-party decision-making
  - ✧ Adjudication
  - ✧ Arbitration
  - ✧ Autocratic decision-making

- ✦ Separate action
  - ✧ Retreat
  - ✧ Struggle
  - ✧ Tacit coordination

The following hypothetical example is used to describe these procedures, using actors from the case study by Oviedo on the Galapagos Islands (this volume).

A tourism operator and local fishers are in a dispute: the first wants to bring tourists to view the aquatic life in a coastal natural reserve; the other makes a living from fishing in those very waters. Negotiation would mean discussing these issues, and mediation would involve the help of a third party. Adjudication would mean going to court, whereas arbitration would involve a hearing and a decision by an official of lesser rank than a judge. Autocratic decision-making occurs when the third party gathers the information directly rather than inviting testimony at a hearing. If one of the disputants gives in — if the tourism operator were to close the business or the fishers stop fishing — it would be yielding or retreating. Struggle occurs if one or both disputants employed harassing moves, such as damaging touring vessels or cutting up fishing nets. Finally, tacit coordination would involve both parties trying to work out an exchange of concessions without talking, such as if the first reduced the number of visits to the site, and the other stopped fishing a particular species.

In this classification, struggle is the only procedure in which the disputants do not collaborate. At any point in the process, disputants will differ in their preference for these various procedures, but with the exception of retreat, they almost always end up using the same procedure.

The choice of any one class of procedure (for example, joint decision-making) will be made when the other classes (third-party decision-making and separate action) do not seem cost-effective or strategic in achieving an objective. Moreover, one type of procedure may give a stakeholder new recognition or additional legal leverage, forcing other stakeholders to consider negotiations.

A problem situation will evolve from struggle and confrontation to a stage of negotiations in which power differences are overcome and the issue at stake is open to modification. In the Cahuita National Park, Costa Rica, a Committee of Struggle was struck in 1995 to oppose a unilateral decision by the state to triple park fees for foreigners, as this move was expected to reduce tourism significantly (Weitzner and Fonseca Borrás, this volume). The committee represented several stakeholders: the Cahuita tourist industry, community members whose lands had been expropriated without compensation, and the community at large. These groups formed a coalition to protest (separate action) and confront the ministry. Subsequently, the government assigned an ombudsperson as a mediator, which is indicative of recognition by the state of the committee's power and legitimacy.

In contrast, after the signing of the 1997 agreement, the dynamics of the new Management Committee were radically different. This committee includes representatives from different factions and seeks to negotiate around complex issues to do with uncertain property rights and the lack of a management plan for a national park and seafront area. In other words, the situation evolved from separate action to joint decision-making.

The decision of stakeholders to engage in negotiation is influenced by many factors, not simply self-interest. Pruitt and Carnevale (1993) suggest that, beyond self-interest, preference for different conflict management procedures is a function of

- ✦ Other interests beyond self;

- ✦ Norms;

- ✦ Relationships, group process, and networks;

- ✦ Coalitions;

- ✦ Power to negotiate;

- ✦ Mediation; and

- ✦ Internal organizational dynamics.

Most disputants have some degree of concern for the other party's welfare, especially if they will continue to interact in future. Norms, including principles of fairness, encourage efforts to achieve equal outcomes and concessions. Past and future relationships will shape positions, especially when stakeholders know they will have to continue interacting with opposing groups on a regular basis. Furthermore, coalitions form within organizations to influence positions; coalitions are common in multistakeholder negotiations where groups of stakeholders may coalesce to build support for a position.

This proposition is closely related to proposition 5 on social actors and to the discussion on the role of power. The major contribution in this proposition is the notion that different procedures exist to deal with social conflict and that stakeholders will choose among them on an ongoing basis.

Proposition 7: Stakeholders enter into negotiation when that is seen as the best alternative to what they could obtain "away from the bargaining table"

BATNA stands for "best alternative to a negotiated agreement." Negotiations hinge on this concept. No group will choose to be part of a negotiation if what it can obtain "away from the bargaining table" is better than it is likely to get by negotiating (Susskind and Cruikshank 1987, p. 81).

The three major procedures for addressing problematic situations are individual action (which also includes unilateral action and no action), going to court (including a continuum of other less costly methods of arbitration, all of which require that the disputant give up control over the decision), or negotiation. All stakeholders will make choices among the procedures on the basis of perceived odds of advancing their objectives and minimizing costs. Many issues will influence choices (see proposition 6), but all stake-holders will likely address the following questions (often implicitly) when deciding to enter into a joint-decision or negotiation process (Susskind and Cruikshank 1987):

+ Can the key stakeholders be identified, and, if so, can they be persuaded to come to the table?

+ Are the power relationships sufficiently balanced?

+ Can a legitimate spokesperson be found for each group?

+ Are there realistic deadlines?

+ Can the negotiations steer away from positions and values, toward specific interests?

These questions are strategically important for a convener in deciding whether the right conditions exist for a collaborative process to take place. (For a checklist of conditions that constitute blockages to negotiation, see Annex 3.) Susskind and Cruikshank (1987) further suggest that each major type of stakeholder should ask several additional questions before negotiating. The major stakeholder groups they discuss are public officials, citizen groups, and the private sector.[3]

The public official needs to ask

+ Can I participate in a consensus-building process without violating my terms of office?

This may not always be straightforward, given the rules and regulations of public ser-vants and may require the identification of an outside convener and, later, a mediator.

The citizen group needs to ask

+ Do we have the resources to participate effectively?

+ Can we present a united front?

+ Will it help our organization to participate?

The private-sector representative needs to ask

+ Do I have the mandate to proceed?

+ Is there someone with relevant negotiating experience to represent the organization?

+ Do we intend to continue doing business in the same community?

The above list of questions suggests that parties collaborate only if they believe they have something to gain from it (Gray 1989) or when they have no better option than to negotiate (Lee 1993).

---

[3] Susskind and Cruikshank's (1987) grouping of "for-profit" and "non-profit" organizations may raise some confusion. In their analysis, they are bulked together when they behave in such a manner to "maximize their return on investment" (p. 187). It follows then that, when an NGO behaves differently, it is best described as a citizen group.

To avoid a national decree defining the Galapagos Islands, Ecuador, as a national park, the local population focused on achieving provincial status for their archipelago to gain more legal autonomy (Oviedo, this volume). In parallel, local "separate action" and protest ensued until the more powerful actors (national government, tourism operators from the mainland) came to realize that there was no solution without a genuine involvement of local groups. In other words, initially it was a process of unilateral balancing of power that subsequently led national authorities to seek a negotiated agreement with local stakeholders.

Although multiparty negotiations are common in natural resource management situations (Gray 1989), this proposition underlines the fact that negotiation is sought when no better alternative can be achieved by the stakeholders separately. This suggests that negotiation has costs associated with it and represents a commitment of resources and time that is often made only when other procedures for managing social conflict appear less promising. A sobering example from the Horn of Africa illustrates this proposition (Suliman, this volume).

The armed conflict between the Nuba people (cultivators) and the Arab Baggara groups (nomadic pastoralists) in southern Kordofan, Sudan, arose when the Khartoum government placed the best lands in the hands of Sudanese (Jellaba) absentee landlords, who have introduced mechanized cotton farming. The Baggara and the Nuba had enjoyed peaceful relations for centuries. However, the Baggara began fighting the Nuba after the government persuaded them to join its crusade against the Nuba by giving the Baggara arms and promising them Nuba lands after a quick victory. Not only has this not happened, but misery and great loss of human and animal life has been the outcome for both groups.

Three peace agreements between the Nuba and the Baggara (1993, 1995, and 1996) have been sabotaged by the government by violent means. In other words, the only party gaining from the war has been actively stopping any form of negotiation between the two groups that have most to gain from collaboration. This tragic example describes a national disaster that is comparable, at a smaller scale, to the abuse and unequal distribution of power and land in many rural situations elsewhere in developing countries.

Proposition 8: Collaborative processes follow three major phases: problem setting, direction setting, and implementation

Although conflict in natural resource management is unavoidable, some argue that it can be a source of innovation from which progress often emerges (Daniels and Walker 1996). When parties do choose to negotiate, there are a number of stages common both to collaborative negotiation (Gray 1989) and to consensus-building processes (Annex 4). First, problem setting is the stage in which parties get to know each other and agree on a problem definition. In direction setting, parties agree on the rules of negotiation, define agendas, seek information, assign tasks, and seek an agreement. Implementation of the agreement centres on monitoring and compliance. This last phase commonly includes an agreement on a mechanism for renegotiation.

Stakeholder analysis is a set of tools used most often during the first phase:

◆ In the identification of stakeholders;

◆ In the analysis of their legitimacy;

- ✦ In gaining an understanding of how stakeholders will relate and what coalitions are likely; and

- ✦ In appreciating what trade-offs they may be willing to consider during negotiation and what differing levels of participation can be expected, etc.

The stakeholder groups in Copán, Honduras, identified and described by Chenier et al. (this volume) are the indigenous Chortis, plantation owners, local and national government officials, NGOs, and the tourism industry. Identification of the problems as perceived by the various stakeholders was an important initial step undertaken by the authors that brought to light not only the tensions among the groups but also pointed to a priority problem the Chortis felt they could address. The Chortis had received some land from the government as part of a land reform process but they had no clear idea on how to distribute it among themselves and make it productive. By turning to this problem, they consolidated their position within the community as responsible members and gained support from the municipal government and tourism stakeholders keen to restore peace. This strategy has provided the Chortis with a stronger alliance with which to continue their land claims.

The major phases of Gray's (1989) collaborative process are mirrored by comparable experiences in natural resource management, with modifications with regard to the steps within each process (Table 1).

This proposition is well substantiated by a growing number of operational methods used in natural resource management, many of which have emerged from systems thinking and business management (Daniels and Walker 1997). Field practitioners and researchers who seek to facilitate stakeholder negotiations using these methods can benefit from an appreciation of how this proposition relates to the earlier ones in the conceptual framework. This should help them recognize situations where power differentials are so large that collaborative processes are unlikely to yield result or where the impact of the operational methods will be limited or, at worst, manipulated by the existing powers that dominate.

Table 1. The similarities between the major phases in three collaborative methods.

Collaborative management of protected areas[a]	RAAKS[b]	Collaborative learning for recreation area management[c]
Preparing for the partnership	Problem definition and system identification	Inform stakeholder groups and involve them in process design
Developing the agreement	Analysis of constraints and opportunities	Provide a common base of knowledge about major issues, identify concerns about management of the resource area, generate suggested improvements
Implementing and reviewing the agreement	Policy articulation and intervention planning	Organize the improvements based on different strategic visions for the resource area, debate the improvement sets

[a] Borrini-Feyerabend 1996, p. 29.
[b] Rapid appraisal of agricultural knowledge systems (Engel 1997, p. 166).
[c] Daniels and Walker 1996, p. 86.

Proposition 9: Dispute resolution systems involve the use of mediators and require that disputants shift away from negotiating about "positions" to negotiating about "interests"

In parallel with a collaborative process, there is a notion of designing dispute resolution systems. Pruitt and Carnevale (1993) propose the design of dispute resolution systems as a forward-looking application of negotiation research.

Two central ideals in this perspective are also voice and procedural justice (Pruitt and Carnevale 1993): the first refers to a disputant's need for the opportunity to state a case; the second refers to the importance of agreement between disputants about the fairness of the procedure and some degree of process control. If voice — or participation — of all interested parties is not possible or not allowed, then a process of stakeholder collaboration will be faulty, or worse, used to cover up a consolidation of existing power structures (Hildyard et al. 1997, 1998). This proposition is directly linked to proposition 6, which describes the various procedures stakeholders choose from when they are engaged in social conflict. The typical case of natural resource disputes, in which one group is unilaterally dominating, be it a corporation or government, comes to mind. In such circumstances, it may be more realistic to prepare the ground for dispute resolution. The design of dispute resolution systems is based on a number of principles that are similar to those mentioned in the collaborative management literature examples above (Annex 5).

What is important in this proposition is the move from negotiating about positions (rights) to negotiating about concrete interests. Another, practical way of looking at this is: it is less costly and more rewarding to focus on interests than on rights, which in turn is less costly and more rewarding than focusing on power (Ury et al. 1989). Whether the process originates from conflict or trade-offs (Grimble and Wellard 1996), the thrust is a shift toward a negotiated accommodation of interests and on social learning of new shared perspectives (Röling and Jiggins 1998).

The case study from Uruguay (Pérez Arrarte and Scarlato, this volume) concludes that there is a need for integrated action research to address key issues in the dispute — research that might generate options for consideration by different stakeholders and that remains neutral and trustworthy to all stakeholders involved, including the most marginalized groups. A key challenge in the Uruguay case is the development of a dispute resolution system — one that can be kept on stand-by in the event that the process of action research loses legitimacy in the eyes of the less flexible stakeholders.

The conceptual framework in perspective

The conceptual framework can be summarized as follows: stakeholder analysis is used primarily to analyze and plan around a complex situation and as part of conflict management and negotiation procedures. A systems approach is a natural starting point (proposition 1) for situations that do not require an immediate response to a crisis. In such situations there is a need to

✦ Embrace the dynamic interrelations between a problem definition, its boundaries, and the stakeholders affected;

✦ Assess an organization's potential to convene others;

✦ Describe the attributes of stakeholders and the social context they are embedded in; and

◆ Seek out and provide support to those actors who will otherwise not be able to become involved in a multistakeholder process.

Where a conflictive situation already exists, a strategic starting point is an understanding of stakeholder preferences for different procedures for dealing with social conflict (proposition 6). In Figure 1, the propositions on the right side (1–5) refer to stakeholder and convenor attributes, to the context that shapes their attributes, and to some mechanisms for engaging disenfranchised stakeholders (proposition 5). On the left side of Figure 1 lie the propositions that deal with procedural choices, behaviour, collaboration, and dispute resolution or management. As several of the case studies in this volume demonstrate, the propositions are interrelated.[4]

Both the Costa Rica (Weitzner and Borrás, this volume) and Ecuador (Oviedo, this volume) examples describe a situation in which a local community stakeholder group was affected by a "decide–announce–defend" (DAD) situation in which a national government agency unilaterally changed the rules of access to a common-pool resource. The stakeholder groups, who made a living directly from that resource, were not invited to a negotiation process, which is symptomatic of the large power imbalance (demonstrated by the DAD situation itself). The stakeholder group chose unilateral action (struggle), gained power by acting in coalition with others, and gained some prominence through acts of civil disobedience. This unilateral action made the stakeholder groups salient enough in the eyes of more powerful stakeholders, who saw their chances of unilateral action becoming less cost-effective. It was at this stage that they invited the community groups to negotiate; in other words, they realized that they had no BATNA. Hence, choices about procedures changed as the crisis escalated and stakeholders sought to even out large power differences.

Conclusion

The above discussion "tests" the applicability of the conceptual framework to the case studies included in this volume. However, several questions deserve consideration.

Question 1: Had a more structured stakeholder analysis been done by the stakeholders, would conflict management have been more successful?

Although all of the case studies in this volume include some stakeholder analysis, there are few accounts of explicit use of stakeholder analysis tools during the negotiation process among stakeholders. One can only speculate that a systematic use of stakeholder analysis tools would have improved the process of negotiation by making relationships more transparent and would thereby have provided tools to all parties for negotiation about more specific issues. A point of caution is necessary here: the terminology and the underlying theoretical foundations presented in this framework are predominantly Western. Indeed, the terminology itself is awkward to translate into other languages. Hence, the lack of reference to stakeholders and to stakeholder analysis is not necessarily an adequate measure of the extent to which the social actors embraced these propositions or some of the tools of analysis associated with them. Furthermore, it is evident that all the case studies in this

---

[4] In "soft systems methodology," Figure 1 could be described as a "rich picture" in that it seeks to illustrate interrelated propositions that come together to form a conceptual framework (Checkland 1981; Checkland and Schöles 1990).

volume emerged out of existing conflict situations. Hence, it can be argued that a systematic understanding of conflict management situations and options would have been more useful (starting with proposition 6) relative to further attention on stakeholders per se.

Question 2: What type of stakeholder analysis tool would have yielded best results?

This question cannot be answered in a generalized manner, as each context and case study situation would have called for specific criteria and attributes through which to analyze stakeholders. Annex 2 describes the method of "rapid appraisal of agricultural knowledge systems" (RAAKS), which includes 16 steps; at each step, users are asked to choose from a range of tools to analyze their situation according to its specific circumstances. In other words, there are no recipes in stakeholder analysis, only major common phases of inquiry (see Table 1).

Question 3: Who benefits most from participating in stakeholder analysis and negotiation in community-based natural resource management situations?

The case studies suggest that in many situations, multistakeholder negotiation is neither possible nor desirable for powerless groups. Weak, disenfranchised stakeholders stand to lose much from negotiations where power differences are too acute to enable collaboration. Nevertheless, all stakeholders stand to benefit when the negotiation playing field is transparent, so that the decision to venture into a negotiation is based on reliable information.

Stakeholder analysis can also be a stepping stone toward agreements on collaborative management of natural resources. "Comanagement" provides negotiated options to move forward in the context of conflicting interests, in an age of pluralism and new patterns of local governance. Collaborative management seeks to build on locally agreed-to approaches in an adaptive, progressive manner. One desirable outcome of collaboration is that it yields agreements on ways to move forward that emerge from interaction among stakeholders, rather than being imposed from outside (Engel 1997; Holling et al. 1998; Röling and Jiggins 1998).

Stakeholder analysis is a tool, or set of tools, commonly used within most collaborative planning processes. In such instances, it is best described as a set of analytical tools embedded in collaborative or negotiation methods. On the other hand, stakeholder analysis moves to centre stage as a method when it is used to plan an intervention or to understand and analyze a complex situation (Burgoyne 1994; Grimble et al. 1995; ODA 1995; Grimble and Wellard 1996) In such cases, it is common to find stakeholder analysis combined with other planning and appraisal methods that are based on systems thinking and that seek to embrace complexity and the interrelated parts, such as collaborative learning (Daniels and Walker 1997), RAAKS (Engel and Salomon 1997), collaborative management (Borrini-Feyerabend 1996), and PRA (Ramírez 1997).

It is worth returning to the global arena to situate the contribution of this conceptual framework in a broader context. Keohane and Ostrom (1995) argue that neither modern states nor small farmers in remote areas of poor countries can any longer appeal to authoritative hierarchies to enforce rules governing their relations with one another. The "politics of ecology" are a matter of which stakeholders, local and global, gain decision-making authority and enter into negotiations with shared long-term goals (Wyckoff-Baird 1998).

The patterns of power, governance, and governing are shifting toward an interactive "social–political governance" where new forms of interaction occur in policy-making (Kooiman 1993; Bernard and Armstrong 1997; Röling 1997). Heterogeneity and cooperation are the hallmarks of emerging interdependence. Public management today operates in a pluralistic context in which goal consensus cannot be assumed, in which authority is dispersed, in which conflict is legitimate, and in which the various constituents are interdependent and have common interests, however dimly perceived (Metcalfe 1993). In this dynamic and complex context, conceptual and operational frameworks should be built and modified through iterative processes; they should be put to work to assist social actors in understanding the process of negotiation and the opportunities for crafting new relationships.

Annex 1. Examples of analytical tools used in stakeholder analysis

✦ A typology of tree resource stakeholders in Thailand on a macro- to micro-continuum (Grimble et al. 1995), followed by another matrix classifying the trade-offs and conflicts at each level (Grimble et al. 1995);

✦ A listing of stakeholder types, coupled with a description of their composition and sensitivities to changes in forestry projects (Hobley 1996);

✦ Checklists for identifying stakeholders and for drawing out interests, followed by a summary of stakeholders, interests, and the potential of a project impact on each (ODA 1995);

✦ Stakeholders and a scored ranking on several dimensions: proximity to forest, preexisting rights, dependency, indigenous knowledge, culture–forest integration, power deficit (Colfer 1985);

✦ Matrices showing stakeholders vis-à-vis the "4R framework" referring to responsibilities, rights, revenues, and relationships (Dubois 1998); and

✦ Predicting actor behaviour on the basis of actors' preferences assigned to actions and outcomes; how they acquire, process, and apply information; the criteria they use in deciding what course of action to follow; and the resources each actor brings to a situation (Ostrom et al. 1994).

Annex 2: The major phases of RAAKS

An actor-oriented method has been developed for appraising stakeholders and their networks in a systematic and participatory manner: RAAKS (Engel and Salomon 1997). The RAAKS method is relevant in that stakeholder analysis is done systematically and from a number of perspectives. RAAKS covers three phases and 16 steps, as summarized below.

For each step, several tools or "windows" are proposed: some are analytical, some help in synthesis, others are useful in designing options and making choices. The choice of windows or tools for each step is discussed and agreed upon by the group involved in implementing the RAAKS exercise. RAAKS (Engel and Salomon 1997) is perhaps the most innovative stakeholder analysis tool in the literature in that it requires stakeholder participation in its implementation and it calls for choices of analytical tools to suit the local context at each step:

Phase A: Defining the problem
    1. Appraise objective(s)
    2. Identify relevant actors
    3. Diverse missions
    4. Define environment
    5. Clarify–redefine the problem

Phase B: Analysis of constraints and opportunities
    1. Impact
    2. Actors
    3. Knowledge networks
    4. Integration
    5. Tasks
    6. Coordination
    7. Communication
    8. Understanding the social organization for innovation

Phase C: Strategy–action planning
    1. Knowledge management
    2. Actor potential — who can do what?
    3. Strategic commitments to an action plan

Annex 3: Conditions suggesting that the odds of a successful collaboration are poor

+ The conflict is rooted in basic ideological differences;

+ One stakeholder has power to take unilateral action;

+ Constitutional issues are involved, or legal precedents are sought;

+ A legitimate convenor cannot be found;

+ Substantial power differences exist, or one of more groups of stakeholders cannot establish representation;

+ The issues are too threatening because of historical antagonisms;

+ Past interventions have been repeatedly ineffective;

+ Parties are experiencing perceptual or informational overload and need to withdraw from the conflict; and

+ Maintenance of interorganizational relationships represents substantial costs to the partners.

Source: Whetten and Bozeman (1984, p. 31, cited in Gray 1989, pp. 255–256).

Annex 4: Phases of collaboration

Phase 1: Problem setting

- ✦ Common definition of a problem

- ✦ Commitment to collaborate
  1. Will the present situation fail to serve my interest?
  2. Will collaboration produce positive results?
  3. Is it possible to reach a fair agreement?
  4. Is there parity among the stakeholders?
  5. Will the other side agree to collaborate?

- ✦ Identification of stakeholders

- ✦ Legitimacy of stakeholders

- ✦ Disputes over legitimacy

- ✦ Necessary trade-offs

- ✦ Differing levels of participation

- ✦ Legitimacy within stakeholder groups

- ✦ Convenor characteristics

- ✦ Insider or outsider

- ✦ Convening power

- ✦ Legitimate authority

- ✦ Skills — capacity to propose a process, identifying additional stakeholders, often by bringing in a third party; having a sense of timing

- ✦ Identification of resources

Phase 2: Direction setting

- ✦ Establishing ground rules, namely roles of representatives, deadlines, handling confidential information, handling media and publicity, reimbursement for expenses incurred, record of proceedings, determining consensus

- ✦ Agenda setting

- ✦ Organizing subgroups

- ✦ Joint information search

- ✦ Searching for "the facts"

- ✦ Managing complex and controversial data

- ✦ Role of third parties in information search

- ✦ Exploring options

- ✦ Reaching agreement and closing the deal

Phase 3: Implementation

+ Dealing with constituencies

+ Building external support

+ Structuring, depending on
  ◇ Whether the collaboration leads to information exchange or decision-making
  ◇ How much organizational change is required
  ◇ Who has the resources to accomplish the change
  ◇ Whether the agreements are self-structuring or not

+ Monitoring the agreement and ensuring compliance

Source: Gray (1989).

Annex 5: Principles for dispute resolution systems

1. Provide for early discussion of differences;

2. Include several negotiation parties on each side, in the hope that at least one channel will become operational during a crisis;

3. Provide for a multistep negotiation process in which "a dispute that is not resolved at one level of the organizational hierarchy moves to progressively higher levels, with different negotiators involved at each step" (Ury et al. 1989);

4. Give potential negotiators enough authority that people on the other side will find it worthwhile dealing with them;

5. Provide easy access to intermediaries (for example, ombudspeople, mediators) who can encourage negotiation or coordinate the development of a consensus;

6. Teach the disputants problem-solving skills — how to listen, probe for interest, explore creative options;

7. Build in "loop-backs" to negotiation, which move disputants from a right or a power orientation to an interest orientation; and

8. Start with low-cost procedures and move to high-cost ones only if the low-cost ones do not work.

Source: Summarized from Pruitt and Carnevale (1993).

References

Ackoff, R. 1969. Systems, organizations, and interdisciplinary research. *In* Emery, F., ed., Systems thinking. Penguin Books, Middlesex, UK.

Anderson, J.; Clement, J.; Crowder, L. 1998. Accommodating conflicting interests in forestry — emerging concepts from pluralism. Unasylva, 49(194), 3–10.

ASIP (Agricultural Sector Investment Programme). 1998. Systematic stakeholder participation and consultation (draft dated 2 April 1998). ASIP, Ministry of Agriculture, Nairobi, Kenya.

Bernard, A.; Armstrong, G. 1997. Learning and integration: learning theory and policy integration. International Development Research Centre, Ottawa, ON, Canada. Unpublished report.

Borrini-Feyerabend, G. 1996. Collaborative management of protected areas: tailoring the approach to the context. International Union for the Conservation of Nature, Gland, Switzerland.

Brass, D.; Butterfield, K.; Skaggs, B. 1998. Relationships and unethical behaviour: a social network perspective. Academy of Management Review, 23(1), 14–31.

Burgoyne, J.G. 1994. Stakeholder analysis. *In* Cassell, C.; Symon, G., ed., Qualitative methods in organizational research: a practical quide. Sage Publications, New Delhi, India. pp. 187–207.

Carpenter, S.L.; Kennedy, W. 1988. Managing public disputes. Jossey-Bass, San Francisco, CA, USA.

Chambers, R. 1997. Whose reality counts? Putting the first last. ITP, London, UK.

Checkland, P. 1981. Systems thinking, systems practice. John Wiley & Sons, Chichester, UK.

Checkland, P.; Schöles, J. 1990. Soft systems methodology in action. John Wiley & Sons, Chichester, UK.

Coleman, J.S. 1966. Equality of educational opportunity. US Government Printing Office, Washington, DC, USA.

Colfer, C. 1985. Who counts most in sustainable forest management? Center for International Forestry Research, Bogor, Indonesia.

Daniels, D.; Walker, G. 1996. Collaborative learning: improving public deliberation in ecosystem-based management. Environmental Impact Assessment Review, 16, 71–102.

Daniels, S.; Walker, G. 1997. Rethinking public participation in natural resource management: concepts from pluralism and five emerging approaches. Paper presented at the FAO Workshop on Pluralism and Sustainable Forestry and Rural Development, 9–12 Dec 1997, Rome, Italy.

Dubois, O. 1998. Capacity to manage role changes in forestry: introducing the "4Rs" framework. International Institute for Environment and Development, London, UK. Forest Participation Series 11.

Engel, P. 1997. The social organization of innovation: a focus on stakeholder interaction. Royal Tropical Institute, Amsterdam, Netherlands.

Engel, P.; Salomon, M. 1997. Facilitating innovation for development. Royal Tropical Institute, Amsterdam, Netherlands.

Flood, R.; Jackson, M. 1991. Creative problem solving: total systems intervention. John Wiley & Sons, Chichester, UK.

Foucault, M. 1984. The subject and power. *In* Wallis, B., ed., Art after modernism: rethinking representation. New Museum of Contemporary Art, Boston, MA, USA. pp. 417–432.

Freeman, R.E. 1984. Strategic management: a stakeholder approach. Pitman, Boston, MA, USA.

Freeman, R.; Gilbert, D., Jr 1987. Managing stakeholder relations. *In* Prakash, S.; Falbe, C., ed., Business and society: dimensions of conflict and cooperation. Lexington Books, Toronto, Canada. pp. 397–422.

Gass, G.; Biggs, S.; Kelly, A. 1997. Stakeholders, science and decision making for poverty-focused rural mechanization research and development. World Development, 25(1), 115–126.

Giddens, A. 1984. The constitution of society: outline of the theory of structuration. University of California Press, Berkeley, CA, USA.

Granovetter, M. 1985. Economic action and social structure: the problem of embeddedness. American Journal of Sociology, 91, 481–510.

Gray, B. 1989. Collaborating: finding common ground in multiparty problems. Jossey-Bass, San Francisco, CA, USA.

Grimble, R.; Aglionby, J.; Quan, J. 1994. Tree resources and environmental policy: a stakeholder approach. Natural Resources Institute, London, UK. Socio-Economic Series 7.

Grimble, R.; Chan, M.K. 1995. Stakeholder analysis for natural resource management in developing countries. Natural Resources Forum, 19(2), 113–124.

Grimble, R.; Chan, M.K.; Aglionby, J.; Quan, J. 1995. Trees and trade-offs: a stakeholder approach to natural resource management. International Institute for Environment and Development, London, UK. Gatekeeper Series 52.

Grimble, R.; Wellard, K. 1996. Stakeholder methodologies in natural resource management: a review of principles, contexts, experiences and opportunities. Paper presented at the ODA NRSP Socioeconomic Methodologies Workshop, 29–30 Apr, 1996, London, UK.

Hardin, G. 1968. The tragedy of the commons. Science, 162, 1243–1248.

Hildyard, N.; Hedge, P.; Wolverkamp, P.; Reddy, S. 1997. Same platform: different train. Pluralism, participation and power. Paper presented at the FAO Workshop on Pluralism and Sustainable Forestry and Rural Development, 9–12 Dec 1997, Rome, Italy.

———— 1998. Pluralism, participation and power. Forests, Trees and People Newsletter, 35 (Mar), 31–35.

Hindess, B. 1986. Actors and social relations. In Wardell, M.; Turner, S., ed., Sociological theory in transition. Allen & Unwin, Boston, MA, USA. pp. 113–126.

Hirst, P. 1997. From statism to pluralism: democracy, civil society and global politics. UCL Press, London, UK.

Hobley, M. 1996. Participatory forestry: the process of change in India and Nepal. ODI, London, UK.

Holling, C.; Berkes, F.; Folke, C. 1998. Science, sustainability and resource management. In Berkes, F.; Folke, C., ed., Linking social and ecological systems: management practices and social mechanisms for building resilience. Cambridge University Press, Cambridge, UK. pp. 342–362.

Kekes, J. 1993. The morality of pluralism. Princeton University Press, Princeton, NJ, USA.

Keohane, R.; Ostrom, E. 1995. Introduction. In Keohane, R.; Ostrom, E., ed., Local commons and global interdependence: heterogeneity and cooperation in two domains. Sage Publications, London, UK. pp. 1–26.

Kooiman, J., ed. 1993. Modern governance: new government–society interactions. Sage Publications, London, UK.

Lee, K. 1993. Compass and gyroscope: integrating science and politics for the environment. Island Press, Washington, DC, USA.

Long, N. 1992. From paradigm lost to paradigm regained? In Long, N.; Long, A., ed., Battlefields of knowledge: the interlocking of theory and practice in social research and development. Routledge, London, UK. pp. 16–43.

Metcalfe, L. 1993. Public management: from imitation to innovation. In Kooiman, J., ed., Modern governance: new government-society interactions. Sage Publications, London, UK. pp. 173–189.

Mitchell, R.; Agle, B.; Wood, D. 1997. Towards a theory of stakeholder identification: defining the principle of who and what really counts. Academy of Management Review, 22(4), 853–886.

Morris, M. 1994. Epidemiology and social networks: modeling structured diffusion. In Wasserman, S.; Galaskiewicz, J., ed., Advances in social network analysis: research in the social and behavioral sciences. Sage Publications, Thousand Oaks, CA, USA. pp. 26–52.

Naughton, J. 1984. The soft systems analysis: an introductory guide. Complexity, management and change: applying a systems approach. The Open University Press, Milton Keynes, UK.

ODA (Overseas Development Administration). 1995. Guidance note on how to do stakeholder analysis of aid projects and programmes. ODA, London, UK.

Ostrom, E. 1995. Constituting social capital and collective action. In Keohane, R.O.; Ostrom, E., ed., Local commons and global interdependence. Sage Publication, London, UK. pp. 126–160.

———— 1998. Coping with tragedies of the commons. Paper presented at the 1998 Annual Meeting of the Association for Politics and the Life Sciences, 3–6 Sep 1998, Boston, MA, USA; Directorate Guest Lecture at the International Institute for Applied Systems Analysis, Vienna, Austria.

Ostrom, E.; Gardner, R.; Walker, J. 1994. Rules, games, and common-pool resources. University of Michigan Press, Ann Arbor, MI, USA.

Polzer, J.; Mannix, E.; Neale, M. 1995. Multiparty negotiation in its social context. In Kramer, R.; Messick, D., ed., Negotiation as a social process. Sage Publications, London, UK. pp.123–142.

Pretty, J.; Guijt, I.; Scoones, I.; Thompson, J. 1995. A trainer's guide for participatory learning and action. International Institute for Environment and Development, London, UK.

Pruitt, D.; Carnevale, P. 1993. Negotiation in social conflict. Brooks/Cole Publishing, Pacific Grove, CA, USA.

Ramírez, R. 1997. Understanding farmers' communication networks: combining PRA with agricultural knowledge systems analysis. International Institute for Environment and Development, London, UK. Gatekeeper Series 66.

Rescher, N. 1993. Pluralism: against the demand for consensus. Clarendon; Oxford University Press, Oxford, UK.

Rowley, T. 1997. Moving beyond dyadic ties: a network theory of stakeholder influences. Academy of Management Review, 22(4), 887–910.

Röling, N. 1997. Emerging knowledge systems thinking: the renewal of policy theory for facilitating agricultural innovation. *In* The role of research in agricultural policy-making in sub-Saharan Africa. Feldafing, Germany, 7–11 April, 1997. Bundesministerium fur wirtschaftliche Zusammenarbeit und Entwicklung, Agricultural Division, Bonn, Germany; Deutsche Gesellschaft für Technische Zusammenarbeit, Eschborn, Germany; and Technical Center for Agricultural and Rural Cooperation, Wageningen, Netherlands.

Röling, N.; Jiggins, J. 1998. The ecological knowledge system. *In* Röling, N.; Wagemakers, M., ed., Facilitating sustainable agriculture: participatory learning and adaptive management in times of environmental uncertainty. Cambridge University Press, Cambridge, UK. pp. 283–311.

Röling, N.; Wagemakers, M., ed. 1998. Facilitating sustainable agriculture: participatory learning and adaptive management in times of environmental uncertainty. Cambridge University Press, Cambridge, UK.

Shrum, W. 1997. A social network approach to analyzing research systems: a study of Kenya, Ghana and Kerala (India). International Service for National Agricultural Research, The Hague, Netherlands.

Shrum, W.; Beggs, J. 1995. Methodology for studying research networks the developing world: generating information for science and technology policy. Unpublished report to Advisory Council for Scientific Research in Development Problems, Ministry of Development Coorperation, The Netherlands.

Susskind, L.; Cruikshank, J. 1987. Breaking the impasse. Basic Books, New York, NY, USA.

Thomas, G.; Anderson, J.; Chandrasekharan, D.; Kakabadse, Y.; Matiru, V. 1996. Levelling the playing field: promoting authentic and equitable dialogue under inequitable conditions. *In* Forests, trees and people II. Community Forestry Unit. E-Conference on addressing natural resource conflicts through community forestry, Food and Agriculture Organization, Rome, Italy. Conflict Management Series. pp. 165–180.

Trist, E.L. 1983. Referent organizations and the development of interorganizational domains. Human Relations, 36(3), 269–284.

Ury, W.; Brett, J.; Goldberg, S. 1989. Getting disputes resolved. Jossey-Bass Publishers, San Francisco, CA, USA.

Villarreal, M. 1992. The poverty of practice: power, gender and intervention from an actor-oriented perspective. *In* Long, N.; Long, A., ed., Battlefields of knowledge: the interlocking of theory and practice in social research and development. Routledge, London, UK. pp. 247–267.

Warner, M.; Jones, P. 1998. Assessing the need to manage conflict in community-based natural resource projects. ODI Natural Resouce Perspectives, 35 (Aug).

Wheatley, M. 1992. Leadership and the new science: learning about organizations for an orderly universe. Berret-Koehler, San Francisco, CA, USA.

Whetten, D.A.; Bozeman, B. 1984. Policy coordination and interorganizational relations: some guidelines for sharing power. Presented at the Conference on sharing power. Humphrey Institute and School of Management, University of Minnesota, 10 May.

Wicks, A.; Gilbert Jr, D.; Freeman, R. 1994. A feminist reinterpretation of the stakeholder concept. Business Ethics Quarterly, 4(4), 475–497.

Wolf, E. 1990. Facing power: old insights, new questions. American Anthropologist, 92(3), 586–596.

Wyckoff-Baird, B. 1998. The power of nature: negotiating decentralization processes for biodiversity conservation. Analysis and Adaptive Management Program, Biodiversity Support Program, Washington, DC, USA.

Part 2

Coastal Areas

Chapter 6

CAHUITA, LIMÓN, COSTA RICA:
FROM CONFLICT TO COLLABORATION

Viviane Weitzner and Marvin Fonseca Borrás

Since the 1970s Costa Rica has designated more than 25% of its territory as conservation areas; however, to do this, the government expropriated land, forced the relocation of communities, and denied them access to their land and resources. Although the establishment of Cahuita National Park on the southern Caribbean coast of Costa Rica had a significant impact on local residents, the community has used innovative tactics to manage conflicts with the state over the last 30 years, and a collaborative management institution has emerged. This precedent-setting case has caught the attention of many players in the Central American conservation community. Moreover, Cahuita's experience in moving from conflict with the state to collaboration mirrors a policy shift within the government from a top-down approach to natural resource management toward a more decentralized, democratic system, and conservationists are looking to the management arrangement established in Cahuita National Park as a possible approach to be adopted in other conservation areas.

Costa Rica is known for two things: its history of peace and democracy and its ambitious conservation agenda. Since 1948 Costa Rica has not had a national army. And since the 1970s it has established protected areas in more than 25% of its territory. These two factors appear to go hand in hand in what many regard as a progressive vision espoused by the government of Costa Rica.

Alpheus Buchanan, prominent community leader and member of the Committee of Struggle, has remarked that

> If the government is really concerned about protecting the area, there is nobody more
> capable of preserving it than those who preserved and protected it for more than a

hundred years. They can come and enjoy it with us as long as they respect our rights and our property ... .

If they are intelligent they would realize that you can't function a park in an area where people are going to be hostile. If you take away our rights, the people are going to be hostile, and the tourists are not going to want to come, and the park is not going to be effective.

(see Palmer 1977)

Buchanan's words shed light on the fact that it does not take an external threat to disrupt the peace in Costa Rica. In fact, some of the most insidious conflicts have arisen from the government's centralized, "fences-and-fines" approach to conservation policy of the 1970s (Wells and Brandon 1992; Solórzano 1997). The establishment of parks led to the expropriation of lands and the forced relocation of communities that were denied subsequent access to their lands and resources. Clearly, this approach was a recipe for conflict.

This case study examines the impact of the establishment of Cahuita National Park on Cahuita, a largely Afro-Caribbean community located on the southern Caribbean coast of Costa Rica. Although the establishment of the park has had a significant impact on local residents, the community has used innovative tactics to manage conflicts with the state over the last 30 years, and a collaborative management institution has emerged. This case has caught the attention of many players in the Central American conservation community. Although interesting management arrangements have been established in Costa Rica for less protectionist categories of conservation area, such as wildlife refuges, the arrangement in Cahuita National Park is precedent setting in that it involves a national park intended strictly for conservation and recreation.

Moreover, Cahuita's experience in moving from conflict with the state to collaboration mirrors a policy shift within the government from centralized, top-down natural resource management toward a process of "deconcentration, decentralization and democratization" (Solórzano 1997). This process was catalyzed by international commitments, such as those made at the United Nations Conference on the Environment and Development, which led to a series of legislative and policy changes to decentralize natural resource management and to increase the participation of civil society in environmental decision-making.

In 1995, the government introduced the Sistema Nacional de Áreas de Conservación (SINAC; National System of Conservation Areas) to take over the administration of more than 100 protected areas initially managed by a central office in San José. The result has been the establishment of 11 conservation areas covering the whole country; these are broken down into even smaller management areas. Today SINAC is searching for new models for involving local communities in decision-making, for two reasons: government cutbacks and a lack of personnel to care for Costa Rica's large protected-areas system; and SINAC's belief that the principal economic beneficiaries of parks should be the local communities (Solórzano 1997). Conservationists are looking to the management arrangement established in Cahuita National Park, in the Amistad Caribe Conservation Area, as a possible approach to be adopted in other conservation areas.

In light of this policy context, an in-depth evaluation of the Cahuita experience is essential. The case has already been cited by Costa Rican policymakers as a success, making close analysis even more urgent. The Cahuita experience provides valuable lessons on key elements required for managing conflict situations effectively, negotiating collaborative agreements, and moving collaborative processes forward so they become more appropriate to the local context. As such, it is important not only to policymakers but also to local people throughout the country and region who want to assert greater control over the resources on which they depend.

This case study is based on field research conducted between February and May 1998, using three principal methods for gathering information: direct observation, particularly within local decision-making forums; informal and formal interviews with members of the joint management committee, representatives of local organizations, leaders, key informants, and community members at large; and participatory land-use mapping with user groups both in Cahuita and in the neighbouring communities of Hone Creek and Punta Riel. The tools used to evaluate the collaborative management process include Arnstein's (1969) ladder of citizen participation and Borrini-Feyerabend's (1996) adaptation for protected areas; Ostrom's (1990) eight design principles for a rigorous institution; and Berkes' (1997) hypotheses on the four conditions required for successful comanagement. A group of community members, together with the director of the Amistad Caribe Conservation Area, helped guide the project process.

The context: from cocoa and coconuts to conservation and catering

Natural and cultural diversity

Cahuita is located on Costa Rica's southern Caribbean coast in the canton of Talamanca, province of Limón (Figure 1). The province is of vital importance to the national economy and ecology: it boasts the largest port in the country and contains a variety of the country's most ecologically important and diverse tropical forest ecosystems. These two factors, together with the province's beautiful coconut-tree-lined beaches, have made Limón a haven for investment. There is ongoing exploitation by transnational banana and logging companies, and since the 1980s the tourism industry has been an important economic force, particularly in coastal communities. Despite its natural richness, the region is one of the most economically depressed in the country (Mora 1998), which puts increased pressure on natural resources.

The area is also culturally diverse. Talamanca is home to 85% of Costa Rica's indigenous peoples (Bribri and Cabecar, who live mainly in or near Talamanca's mountain range), a large population of Afro-Caribbeans (who live along the coast), mestizo farmers, primarily from the central valley or Pacific region (who live mostly in the southern valley of Talamanca), and foreigners, primarily from Asia and, to a lesser extent, Europe and North America (who are dispersed throughout the canton) (Calderón 1998).

A brief history of Cahuita

The first historical record to describe Cahuita (Pittier 1895) notes that the site was a favourite fishing and turtle-hunting ground of the Miskito Indians from Nicaragua and Panama. They traveled to the site every year, following the migration of turtles. In fact, the community was named by these hunters and fishers "Cahuita," which means "point of blood trees" in Miskito and refers to the vast number of blood trees growing on the promontory known as Cahuita Point.

It wasn't until 1828 that the site was permanently settled. That year, William Smith, an English-speaking Afro-Caribbean who came from Panama every year to hunt green and

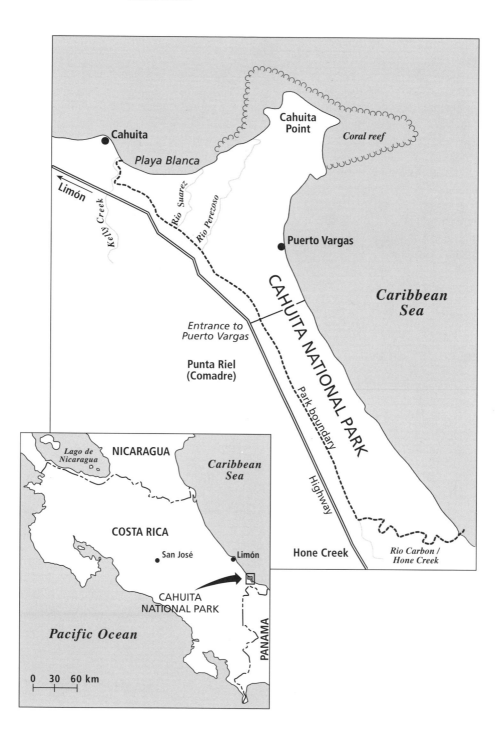

**Figure 1. Cahuita National Park and
neighbouring communities on the Caribbean coast of Costa Rica.**
Source: Adapted from MINAE's information pamphlet on
Cahuita National Park (MINAE 1997).

hawksback turtles, decided to make Cahuita his permanent home (Palmer 1977). By the end of the 1800s, the settlement had grown to a conglomeration of 20 houses located on the point (Pittier 1895), as a result largely of the migration of Jamaicans to the area. These settlers came at first to build the railway to transport coffee from the central valley to the port city of Limón, 42 km north of Cahuita. Later, more were recruited by the United Fruit Company to help build railways to transport bananas along the Caribbean coast and to work on the plantations (Palmer 1977). Shortly after 1914, the town of Cahuita was moved from the point to its present site at the other end of the beach. The land was purchased from William Smith and donated to the townspeople by the president of Costa Rica in gratitude for their having rescued him from a sinking ship (Orthello 1972).

In addition to working on the United Fruit Company's banana plantations, the settlers undertook small-scale coconut and cocoa production and engaged in subsistence farming, hunting, and fishing. Women participated in many of these activities and were primarily responsible for cocoa drying and taking care of the coconut walks; they contributed to the economy of the household by selling coconut oil and baked goods (Grant, personal communication, 1998[1]). These coastal people had a reputation for being self-sufficient; many traded their goods with the Bribri and Cabecar and sold their produce in Limón. Their way of life was preserved for many decades, largely because the community was not accessible by road until 1976 (Palmer 1977).

Conservation hits Cahuita

The 1970s brought about a sea change for the community of Cahuita. In 1970, the coral reef that lines Cahuita Point was declared a national monument — without any consultation with the community — because the state wanted to protect the flora and fauna of the area, the coral reefs, the historical artefacts in the area, and the various marine ecosystems (Figure 1).

The reef contains 35 species of corals, 140 species of molluscs, 44 types of crustaceans, 128 varieties of algae, and 123 types of fish (Bermudez and Yadira 1993). The terrestrial portion includes a variety of animal species, including howler monkeys, three-toed sloths, crab-eating raccoons, and white-nosed coatis, as well as important ecosystems, such as swamp mangroves (Boza and Cevo 1998). Executive Decree 1236-A, establishing the national park, declared that the terrestrial portion would cover 1 067.9 ha; the marine portion, 22 400 ha, including 600 ha of reef. It strictly forbade forestry activities, hunting and trapping, turtle hunting and turtle-egg gathering, extraction of corals, and commercial, agricultural, industrial, and other activities detrimental to the resources of the national monument. Commercial and sports fishing would be subject to restrictions deemed necessary to protect the natural resources of the protected area.

For the community, this declaration meant the end of a way of life that had endured since the turn of the century. Coconut farmers were told they could no longer manage their coconut walks, and fishers were told their activities would be restricted. When officials informed those who lived inside the national-monument boundaries that they would have to sell their lands, the community objected. Resistance grew when the community heard that the state was contemplating changing the category of protected area to national park, which would mean even greater restrictions.

---

[1] L. Grant, community member and President of the Association of Craftswomen of Cahuita, Cahuita, Costa Rica, personal communication, 1998.

Cahuita fights back

Spurred by growing community concerns, an ad hoc commission of government officials and community leaders was established in 1974 to review the community's needs and propose amendments for consideration by the Legislative Assembly during its legal review of the change in protected area category. Although Cahuita took the lead, neighbouring communities were also consulted and asked for input. In 1977, the commission presented its report — an agreement between the community of Cahuita and the government — to President Oduber.

The agreement recognized that the local people were a "favourable factor" in terms of conserving the natural and cultural resources of the area. It stated that people living within the boundaries of the proposed park should continue to reside on their property and engage in subsistence activities "as long as they do not extend beyond their currently occupied areas nor change their traditional methods of work." The report also recommended that a socioeconomic study be conducted on land tenure in the park. A 1977 study revealed that 87% of the land was owned by small-scale farmers, and, of these, 93% did not want to sell their land (Ramírez 1977). Therefore, the community had a large stake in ensuring that the government pay heed to its proposed amendments.

But the government disregarded these amendments when the national park was established in 1978. Instead, it forced those within the park boundary to relocate and denied them access to their coconut walks and farms. The government agreed to offer compensation to those affected. However, because of lack of funds (resulting from Costa Rica's debt crisis in the 1980s) and the fact that many owners did not have the necessary papers to show title or possession, only a few people have actually received compensation. Documents were available for only 25 of the 71 affected plots of land; 10 of the owners have never been paid. Problems were further compounded by passage of the beachfront law (Ley Marítimo-Terrestre) in 1977, which eliminated private-property rights within the first 200 m of the seashore, affecting all coastal residents.

It should be noted, however, that although the government's official position was to relocate community members and deny them access to their lands and resources, in practice many still continued using their lands. When the *Monilia* fungus hit the region in the late 1970s and early 1980s, destroying 95% of the cocoa crops, many farmers decided to give up cocoa farming (Kutay 1984). Those with crops within the park boundaries were more disposed to sell their land to the state, and many who were previously against changing the sources of their livelihood to one of tourism turned to this expanding industry as the only feasible alternative.

In short, in the space of 15 years, the community of Cahuita was forced to change its source of livelihood from subsistence agriculture and fishing to tourism because of the establishment of the national park, the decimation of the area's cocoa crops, and the development of tourism.

Today, tourism is the number-one source of income for Cahuita. The population in the district has grown to 3 983, including the town of Cahuita and surrounding settlements (MINEH 1997). The 1 091 people living in the town are English-speaking Afro-Caribbeans, Spanish-speaking mestizos, people of Chinese origin, and a growing population of North American and European foreigners investing in the tourism industry.[2] There are about 70 businesses in the town, ranging from tour agencies and hotels to

---

[2] Equipos Básicos de Atención Integral en Salud. 1998. Población del Área de Salud Atracción. Cahuita. Unpublished survey.

restaurants and bakeries (Cruz 1996), all of which depend on tourism directly or indirectly.

Clearly, the impact of this change has been large: several Cahuitans claim their culture is being eroded and link this erosion to growing social problems in the town, such as drugs and alcoholism. A number of community organizations have cropped up to help target these social problems, and other organizations are working to strengthen Cahuitans' cultural identity and cohesion: a theatre group stages the plays of Claudio Reid, a Cahuitan playwright and community leader; a women's group aims to empower Afro-Caribbean women; and a band plays calypso.

Perhaps the greatest impact of the change from a subsistence economy has been that on women. Women no longer have the social space in which to meet, and engaging in small-scale cottage industries is becoming more difficult (Grant, personal communication, 1998[3]). Moreover, many women do not attend events and meetings held for them, because they fear reprimands from their husbands. Despite these obstacles, there are three women's groups in Cahuita whose members are working hard to gain self-empowerment and find new ways to support their families.

Although the service sector has increased, a small number of Cahuitans and people from neighbouring communities still engage in traditional resource-based activities. Cahuita's 15 or so fishers sell their catch — primarily lobster and a variety of fish — to local restaurants and families and supplement their income by taking tourists on sports-fishing and snorkeling outings (Maerena, personal communication, 1998[4]). Resource users in the neighbouring communities of Punta Riel (Comadre) and Hone Creek are unable to diversify their sources of income, as 100% of their income depends on subsistence activities in and around the park, according to informal interviews. Tourism has not caught on in these communities, primarily because they are not on the beachfront, as is Cahuita. Many residents continue farming their land in the park, catching turtles and gathering their eggs, fishing, and hunting iguanas and small mammals. As community representative Noel McLeod has remarked (see Palmer 1977), "I know hotel is good business, but I'm not going to build a hotel in Cahuita because we don't want tourist business. We want our own way of life."

The conflict: price increase threatens Cahuitans' livelihood

Things came to a head on 1 September 1994 when the state imposed a nation-wide increase in park entrance fees for foreigners from 200 CRC to 2 400 CRC, an increase of more than 1 000% (nationals would still pay 200 CRC) (in 1999, 282.5 Costa Rican colon [CRC] = 1 United States dollar [USD]). If the government had its way, a foreign family of four would have to pay 60 USD/day to visit Cahuita's beach; this would most certainly mean the death of the tourism industry in Cahuita. There were two main issues at stake for Cahuita: economic survival (the state was once again threatening Cahuitans' livelihood) and sovereignty (the community felt strongly that Playa Blanca, the beach adjacent to the community, was its own beach).

[3] L. Grant, personal communication, 1998.
[4] M. Maerena, Cahuita, Costa Rica, personal communication, 1998.

In reaction to the price hike, the community organized a Committee of Struggle (Comité de Lucha), comprising three community leaders and the president of Cahuita's Development Association (the local elected government), and staged a peaceful takeover of the park. One of the members of the Committee of Struggle describes the takeover:

> When the problem emerged, the people took the park. We took it in a pacific way. What we did was to sit next to the entrance of the park and play dominoes. When a tourist arrived, we said: "Sir, don't pay. The community of Cahuita invites you to enter the park free of charge." *We knew we were in our just right, because we knew that the law backed us given that many of us were still owed compensation for our lands.*
> (Joseph, personal communication, 1998[5]; emphasis added)

Park officials left their posts at the entrance of the park near the town of Cahuita (Playa Blanca), as well as at the entrance in Puerto Vargas (Mora, personal communication, 1998[6]). There were some incidents of vandalism of park officials' vehicles, but no open violence. The Ministry of Resources, Energy and Mines — now known as the Ministry of Environment and Energy (MINAE) — published advertisements in the major national newspapers (*El República* and *La Nación*) (MIRENEM 1994a, b) warning tourists about the conflict situation and cautioning them not to visit Cahuita National Park. According to community representatives, this had a disastrous impact on tourism. It also compounded the resentment that community members felt toward park officials.

Toward a negotiated solution

Intense negotiations between the Committee of Struggle and MINAE ensued. The Committee of Struggle maintained two initial positions: that the community of Cahuita should control the entire park and that the state should pay the remaining compensation for expropriated lands. Both of these positions went beyond the expectations of the community negotiators, but they took advantage of the situation to try to get as much out of the negotiations as possible. In the words of Alpheus Buchanan, "We knew that we couldn't get everything ... but, hey, in a negotiation you have to ask for more than you want so that in the end you get what you really need."

In counterproposals, the community negotiating team argued for 5 km of beach front inside the park, from Kelly Creek to Rio Perezoso (Figure 1). This was a strategic move, because if the government agreed, the community would have free access to the reef, which, they argued, they had the capacity to manage. However, the government countered that the community did not possess the required capacity and hired a biologist who wrote a report supporting the government's position (Cyrus, personal communication, 1998[7]).

The bottom line for the community — their primary interest — was free access from Kelly Creek to Rio Suarez, the 2 km of beach adjacent to Cahuita. Without free access to this beach, "we will die of hunger," according to Alpheus Buchanan, a prominent community leader and member of the Committee of Struggle; he noted that tourists would look for other vacationing spots (Tovar 1994). The condition regarding compensation for lands was far less urgent, as evidenced by the fact that 20 years had gone by without any collective action or uprising to tackle the situation.

---

[5] E. Joseph, Cahuita, Costa Rica, personal communication, 1998.
[6] A. Mora, Cahuita, Costa Rica, personal communication, 1998.
[7] E. Cyrus, Limón, Costa Rica, personal communication, 1998.

On the other side, the government needed to strengthen the infrastructure, services, and conservation in national parks, and it wanted foreigners to pay a higher entrance fee than nationals. By increasing the entrance fees for tourists in all of Costa Rica's parks, the government could generate more income while ensuring the self-sufficiency of protected areas. But its immediate interest was to remain in control of Cahuita National Park. For this reason, it was open to negotiations with Cahuita.

In the negotiation process, the Committee of Struggle represented Cahuita's tourism interests, the position of community members whose lands had been expropriated without compensation, and the interests of the community at large (Table 1). MINAE represented the interests of the state. The Defensoría de los Habitantes de la República, Costa Rica's ombudsperson, acted as mediator. Both parties trusted the mediator, and she played a key role in opening the dialogue that eventually led to the Agreement of Cooperation (Figure 2).

Edwin Cyrus appropriately described the negotiations as follows:

> It was a very, very, very difficult negotiation … [the community representatives] didn't want to negotiate with MINAE until they received compensation for their lands. That resulted in a situation where all the participants — the minister, vice-minister, director, all the various levels that came to the meetings — always came face-to-face with very rigid positions.

An agreement is signed

On 13 February 1997, MINAE, René Castro Salazar, and the president of the Cahuita Development Association, Rolando Shirley Brooks, signed an Agreement of Cooperation. Among the highlights, it

✦ Prohibits charging entrance fees to people who use the portion of the park between Kelly Creek and the Rio Suarez (Playa Blanca);

✦ Reconfirms the government's commitment to compensate landowners whose lots were expropriated; and

✦ Creates a services commission made up of community representatives and government officials to coadminister park services.

Table 1. Analysis of the conflict arising from the increase in park entry fees.

	Community of Cahuita	Government
Stakeholders	Development association Chamber of Tourism Landowners Businesspeople	Ministry of Environment and Energy National Conservation Areas System Amistad Caribe Conservation Area Cahuita National Park Administrator
Negotiators	Committee of Struggle ✦ 3 community leaders ✦ President of Cahuita Development Association	Director of Amistad Caribe Conservation Area Senior government officials Cahuita National Park Administrator
Positions	✦ Compensation for land ✦ Control of entire park	✦ Strengthen infrastructure, services, and conservation in national parks ✦ Establish different fee rates for foreigners and nationals
Interests	✦ Free access to Playa Blanca for tourists	✦ Generate more income for national parks ✦ Ensure self-sufficiency of protected areas

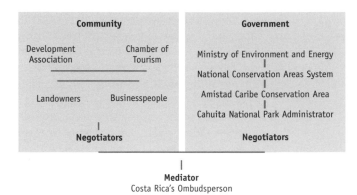

Figure 2. Stakeholders in the conflict, Cahuita, Costa Rica.

In addition, the community was given the go ahead to accept and administer dona-tions from tourists entering Playa Blanca and to reinvest these funds for the upkeep of the beach area. The community had in fact been operating on this principle since July 1995 (Joseph 1995).

The change process: from coadministration to comanagement

Since its establishment in February 1997 the collaborative management institution that emerged from negotiations has gone through an important transition, from being a Services Committee that coadministered part of the park under an "agreement of will" between the parties to being a Management Committee that comanages the entire park under legal sanction (Figure 3).

The Services Committee

The Agreement of Cooperation, dated 13 February 1997, stipulated that the Services Committee should be made up of two government representatives and three community representatives, including the director of the Amistad Caribe Conservation Area or a rep-resentative; the administrator of Cahuita National Park; two representatives of the Cahuita Development Association (Cahuita's elected local government); and one representative of Cahuita's Chamber of Tourism (an elected body representing Cahuita's business interests).

The functions of the committee were to ensure the adequate functioning and qual-ity of new services to park visitors (washrooms, camping areas, a locker room, first-aid ser-vices, and information about the park and its biodiversity), establish fees for these services, and develop guidelines for the operations and administration of the committee.

The agreement had a 5-year term, starting from the date of validation by the Contraloría General de la República, Costa Rica's Treasury Board. However, this validation was never carried out, so in effect the Services Committee was operating *de facto* rather than *de jure* for 1 year.

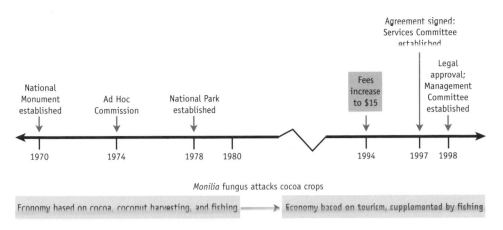

Figure 3. Milestones in the course of the conflict and its resolution, Cahuita, Costa Rica.

The Management Committee

In January 1998, the Services Committee changed its name to the Management Committee, reflecting a shift in vision from the collaborative administration of Playa Blanca only to the collaborative management of the entire park. It received legal recognition when the rules of use for Cahuita National Park were published on 20 May 1998. Outlining the rules of use, Executive Decree 26 929 (MINAE 1998)

- ✦ Refers to the Organic Law of the Environment, calling for the involvement of civil society in the planning and development of Cahuita National Park;

- ✦ Officially establishes the Committee for the Management of Resources and Services (the Management Committee), outlining its structure, administration, and process (essentially the same as those in the Services Committee);

- ✦ Describes the functions of the Management Committee: to ensure the adequate functioning and quality of services offered in Cahuita National Park; to establish fees for these services; to take the administrative measures necessary to ensure that the park is functioning well; to ensure the fulfilment of the public use rules outlined in the document, as well as those entrenched in Costa Rican environmental law; and to modify the rules of use as stipulated in the executive decree;

- ✦ Notes that the role of the Management Committee is to recommend to the Director of the Amistad Caribe Conservation Area actions needed to ensure that the park is functioning well;

- ✦ States that if the services offered to the public are not carried out satisfactorily, MINAE will assume temporary responsibility;

- ✦ Describes public-use rules, public-use zones, carrying capacity of the park, and subsistence fishing rules. Only 20 local licenced fishers can use the park, and of these no more than 5 will be licenced to fish lobster (outside the reef area only) (turtle hunting and egg gathering are prohibited); and

- ✦ Does not include a termination date.

According to MINAE's regional lawyer (González, personal communication, 1998[8]), an executive decree is a unilateral administrative decision; if there is a change of government, the decree can easily be modified. Executive decrees, agreements, etc., do not have the status of national laws within the Costa Rican legal framework.

Analysis of the collaborative process

During the year that the Services Committee operated, it expanded its mandate from coadministering Playa Blanca to managing the entire park, *even if it did not have legal backing*. This shows the willingness of the various actors to work together. The Services Committee focused on park services for visitors, and the community's role was essentially one of sharing decision-making with regard to these services. It was the solution to a conflict situation and was intended to address the immediate demands of the community.

The committee has gone a long way toward solidifying the relationship between MINAE and the community and establishing trust among its members. According to a government member, a year ago he would sit at one end of the table, and the community representatives would sit at the other. Today, the situation is much improved. According to Alpheus Buchanan, "Relations between MINAE and us are 100%. It's hard to get better than 100%."

When the committee changed its name to Management Committee in January 1998, it was in recognition of the fact that the initial terms of reference had been fulfilled; that is, the services for visitors were more or less in order. With this immediate need satisfied, members have started to broaden their vision to include issues outside of Playa Blanca and the services sector. The committee has stated that one of its first steps will be to develop a management plan for the park.

In short, the Management Committee has begun to take on a new role with a new scope. The move is a natural one, as the community demands more control over what is happening in the park. The May 1998 executive decree that gives legal recognition to the committee strengthens the community's control over the park and allows the committee the flexibility to modify the rules of use specified in the decree, including the structure of the committee itself. Moreover, MINAE has the political will and enthusiasm to move forward with this new vision of park management. But the evolution of the Services Committee into the Management Committee occurred extremely quickly and was accompanied by growing pains.

Growing pains: a brief evaluation of the change process

In-depth evaluations of resource management institutions and systems usually touch on three primary criteria: efficiency, equity, and effectiveness (or sustainability) (Oakerson 1992; Folke and Berkes 1995; Hanna 1995). However, because the Cahuita institution is relatively new and its mandate has not yet centred on resource management, such an in-depth analysis is not feasible or appropriate at this point. What is possible is an analysis of the committee's structure and process, the power relations among the members, information-sharing and feedback mechanisms, and the representativeness and legitimacy of the committee in the eyes of the community.

---

[8] C. González, Limón, Costa Rica, personal communication, 1998.

Structure and process

The committee is made up of five official members and an "adjunct treasurer" who does not have voting powers: two other members are government officials, and three are community representatives. The adjunct treasurer is also a community representative. Except for one community representative who is mestizo, all members are Afro-Caribbeans, including the government representatives.

The park administrator and the representative of the director of the conservation area are permanent members, whereas the community members rotate — they are elected by the Chamber of Tourism and the Development Association and are usually the presidents or members of these organizations' boards of directors. Each committee member is elected for a 1-year term, with the possibility of reelection. The committee meets once a week and makes its decisions based on a majority vote.

Meetings are convened by the president; the secretary is in charge of recording decisions made by the committee. Usually one of the two chairs the meeting. A meeting can take place if a minimum of three members are in attendance. In theory, then, decisions could be made with two government officials and one community member.

Power relations and decision-making

At the time of the study, the president and secretary are two MINAE officials, the park administrator and a representative of the Director of the Conservation Area, who are, respectively, responsible for chairing the meetings and managing the agenda and minutes. There is, however, ample opportunity for input from the community members who bring their concerns to the table and add items to the agenda.

Although the 1-year mark has passed, there have been no signs of an impending election; in fact, at one meeting a comment was made that the current president and secretary would probably fill their roles on a permanent basis. In other words, the reins of the operation are in the hands of the government, and electoral procedures are not being followed. If not addressed, this situation may undermine the long-term legitimacy of the Management Committee, which will in turn hamper effective comanagement.

In-depth interviews with the committee's three community representatives revealed that although one of them feels that the meetings are "very democratic" and that the government officials are not "authoritarian or negative," the other two think that relations are unbalanced. In the words of one community member,

> MINAE representatives feel they have supremacy over us community people … . For the time being we're at an impasse … because the MINAE representatives think that their ideas should prevail. The best thing about the arrangement will come when the criteria and ideas of the community prevail, because we community people will live here our whole lives.

The word "manipulation" has come up in informal conversation to describe the power relations in the committee.

Decision-making procedures are also shaky. In March 1998, a hand-written pamphlet was circulated to community businesses indicating that there would be a charge of 6 USD/person for tourists visiting the coral reef. It was signed by the Park Administration and the Management Committee. However, the decision to distribute this pamphlet was not discussed at a committee meeting: the two government officials in conjunction with the adjunct treasurer — who, although he has no vote, wields a lot of power as a respected community leader — decided to distribute the pamphlet. Other committee members were caught unaware and put in an awkward position, when community members questioned them about the decision. According to two of the community members, most decisions are in fact made by three people: the two government officials and the adjunct treasurer. Clearly, the decision-making procedures need to be more democratic.

Information-sharing and feedback mechanisms

There are no formal mechanisms by which the Management Committee disseminates information about its activities or decisions. The representatives of the Chamber of Tourism and the Cahuita Development Association inform their boards of directors. Other than this, no communication vehicles exist.

Likewise, there are no formal mechanisms for obtaining community feedback. The community representatives tend to bring to the table the concerns of the constituents of their organizations. Community members who are not represented by the Chamber of Tourism or the Cahuita Development Association can bring their concerns directly to the Management Committee. However, informal interviews and our community survey show that the vast majority do not know about the committee or who sits on it.

Representation and legitimacy in the eyes of the community

All representatives of Cahuita's user groups, fishers, and tour guides interviewed stated that their concerns are not adequately represented by the Management Committee. Informal interviews with community members at large indicated that many people do not know about the committee, its objectives, or its members, which questions its legitimacy.

Ironically, it took a potential conflict — the proposal for a 6-USD fee for each visitor to the coral reef — for the community to become aware of the committee and for the committee to take on a more legitimate role. After a series of open meetings, to which all community members were invited, the Management Committee arrived at a solution agreeable to all parties, based on the majority view expressed by community members. It should be noted that three of Cahuita's most influential leaders played a major role in the negotiations: Alpheus Buchanan (the committee's adjunct treasurer) acted as the "instigator" on the part of the Management Committee, that is, the proponent of the 6-USD fee; Enrique Joseph (Chamber of Commerce representative on the committee) played a mediating role; and Tony Mora represented the interests of his tour business primarily and those of the Chamber of Tourism generally. Other tour operators voiced their opinions as well.

After community members presented their various points of view, the final decision on how much to charge tourists for visiting the coral reef was left up to the Management Committee. The fact that the potential conflict was resolved in a 2-week period and that the community gave the committee authority to make the final decision showed that the committee is able to resolve conflicts successfully and that the community respects its decisions. However, it also showed that the committee has much to learn about how to communicate more effectively with the community and prevent such conflicts in the first place.

With the change in the committee's mandate, its membership and representation must be reviewed. At present, the community members represent development interests only; there are no user groups on board. As one member of the committee emphasized, in the future it will be critical for the resource users who know the park intimately to be represented, such as fishers and guides. More technical support will also be needed, and several people have suggested the possibility of including a biologist to this end, or else ensuring that there are strong links with universities and other institutions. Including representatives from neighbouring communities that use the park will also be critical. Dexter Lewis, community representative on the Management Committee, has stated that

> We need a biologist, a good biologist, to start with… from the community, we need various people, the fishers and the divers, for example, in order to maintain the reef. In other words, we need to involve the people that really live from the resources…. They have lots of knowledge, because they have spent many years living with the reef and in the water. They are people who know and have seen the changes that occur after each flood, for example, which is a common occurrence here.

Table 2 lists the local, regional, and national stakeholders in the park. At the local level it shows those who are currently represented, as well as those whose participation could be considered in the future.

Outcomes: addressing institutional weaknesses and managing latent conflicts

The Management Committee faces several challenges in the future, related, first, to structural and operational weaknesses and, second, to latent conflicts.

Strengths and weaknesses

Although the scope of this paper does not allow for an in-depth analysis of the committee from the perspective of the emerging theory of comanagement, it is clear that the Cahuita arrangement does not meet many of the key criteria for successful comanagement, as outlined by Ostrom (1990), Berkes (1997), and Borrini-Feyerabend (1996). The committee's weaknesses include

+ *Unbalanced power-relations* — The decision-making process reflects the status quo.

+ *Lack of clarity in terms of mandate, roles, and responsibilities and poor information-sharing* — Committee members are uncertain as to their roles and

Table 2. Local, national, and regional stakeholders in Cahuita National Park.

Local	Regional	National
+ Cahuita National Park administration	+ Amistad Caribe Conservation Area	+ Ministry of Environment and Energy (National Conservation Areas System)
+ Management Committee (Chamber of Tourism; Development Association; representatives of the La Amistad Caribe Conservation Area)	+ Municipality of Talamanca	
	+ Nongovernmental organizations (e.g., Namasol [a Dutch NGO] and Biological Corridor [a regional NGO attempting to link Costa Rica to the Central American biological corridor])	+ Ministry of Health
+ Community groups–users not currently represented by the Management Committee:		+ Ministry of Water and Aqueducts
◇ Businesspeople not directly involved in the tourism industry		+ Universities and scientific institutions
◇ Guides	+ Banana plantations, logging companies, and hydro-electric projects (do not have a stake in the park, but their activities affect the environmental health of its resources)	
◇ Resource users: fishers, turtle hunters and egg gatherers; iguana and paca hunters; coconut pickers; driftwood gatherers		
◇ Neighbouring communities: Punta Riel and Hone Creek		

responsibilities, primarily because of lack of articulation and development of these within the committee structure.

✦ *Lack of representation of user groups both from Cahuita and neighbouring communities* — The only community interests currently represented are Cahuita's development sector, that is, people who have a direct stake in tourism. These interests sometimes run counter to those of the resource users, particularly those in neighbouring communities who do not benefit from tourism. Ensuring that the interests of the various stakeholders are heard is of vital importance to the success of the Management Committee in managing the entire park.

✦ *Lack of a management plan, technical support, and resources* — The committee has no access to technical support and resources on an ongoing basis.

✦ *Lack of appropriate communication vehicles and feedback mechanisms* — To date, there no formal vehicles for disseminating information about the committee's activities and decisions or for getting feedback and input from the community at large. This is having a serious impact on the committee's legitimacy and credibility in the eyes of the community.

Quite simply, if there is no natural resource management in the park — a situation which is endemic to all Costa Rica's national parks (Polimeni, personal communication, 1999[9]) — it is difficult to say it is comanagement, "the sharing of power and responsibility between the government and local resource users" (Berkes et al. 1991) in making and implementing natural resource management decisions. However, the Management Committee is in transition; it is evolving from an institution born of a conflict situation to a solid institution that can address natural resource management issues. It will be critical for the committee to address weaknesses listed above if it is to be successful in the long term. And it will be important for the community at large to realize the importance of strengthening and taking full advantage of the committee.

The participation of respected leaders and the efforts of committee members to see through past crises bode well for the committee's future. Other strengths include

✦ *Legal recognition, as of May 1998* — Legal recognition means that the committee can now make decisions with confidence and authority. Legal backing is a key requisite for any comanagement institution.

✦ *Flexibility* — The May 1998 executive decree gives the committee the power to change its structure and modify the rules of use specified in the decree. This flexibility provides an opportunity for the committee to become a far more appropriate and effective institution.

✦ *Political will to try to do things differently* — Edwin Cyrus, the director of the Amistad Caribe Conservation Area, in which Cahuita National Park is located, has invested a great deal of energy in trying to make the Cahuita experience successful, as has the administrator of the park, Gina Cuza Jones, although other MINAE officials have shown resistance to change. The community has also displayed the political will to engage in a new relationship with MINAE.

---

[9] J. Polimeni, Director of Civil Society Participation, MINAE, San José, Costa Rica, personal communication, 1999.

✦ *Potential in managing conflicts* — This is an important foundation on which to build a stronger institution.

✦ *Trust between parties* — The trust that has been built over the last year between MINAE and the community of Cahuita is vital to strengthening ongoing collaboration. However, if and when resource users from neighbouring communities start participating on the committee, it will be important to emphasize building and maintaining trust, particularly as these users are seen as "poachers" by people in Cahuita and in MINAE.

Latent conflicts

Besides institutional weaknesses, the Management Committee will need to address several latent conflicts, including

✦ *Access to resources in the park* — Most fishers in Cahuita combine their subsistence activities with tourism and do not depend solely on fishing for a living. But people in neighbouring communities, who use a wider variety of resources, have a large economic stake in access to the park's natural resources, as many depend on these as their sole source of income. Restrictions on number of users and use, as specified in the 1998 rules, will lead to tense situations, not only between the park administration and users, but also among the users themselves. The Management Committee could play a key role in managing this situation, particularly as it has the power to change the rules of use in the park.

✦ *Balancing conservationists' and users' interests* — The interests of resource users clash with those who are primarily concerned with conservation. One ongoing conflict between park officials and people who catch turtles and gather their eggs has escalated to violence. According to turtle-egg gatherers from the community of Punta Riel, a number of incidents have occurred in which park rangers have fired warning shots at them. In 1994, park rangers shot 63 bullets in one incident (Huertas, personal communication, 1998[10]). In 1998, one turtle-egg gatherer was shot. This increase in violence is largely due to the fact that Cahuitan guides have started to take an active interest in protecting and monitoring turtle-nesting areas in the park, not only for the sake of conservation, but for economic reasons: they take tourists to see the nesting sites. There is a potential for this conflict to escalate even further, causing tension not only between two groups, but also between the two communities.

✦ *The ongoing issue of compensation for expropriated lands* — As was noted earlier, only 15 of the 71 claims for compensation have been paid (MINAE 1997). When Alpheus Buchanan, one of the landowners expecting compensation, heard that the government was planning to take another 5 years to make these payments, he retaliated by "deeply pruning" his land within the park. Instead of taking his problem to the Management Committee, of which he is an unofficial member, Buchanan contacted both the Director of the Amistad Conservation Area and the incoming Minister of Environment and Energy. As a result, he was promised compensation within a period of days. This action sets a dangerous

---

[10] E. Huertas, Punta Riel, Costa Rica, personal communication, 1998.

precedent, in that others may take to the park and start engaging in destructive behaviour. The Management Committee will need to play a role to prevent damage to the park while supporting landowners' requests.

✦ *Security within the park and Cahuita* — Security has become a central issue within the park and the community. In response to reports of robberies, possibly linked to the drug economy in Cahuita, more security guards have been hired to patrol the area. Incidents ranging from petty theft to armed robbery have had a negative effect on Cahuita's image, which in turn affects tourism.

✦ *Contamination and erosion of the reef by banana companies, loggers, and hydroelectric developments* — These are very large issues that resource users, particularly fishers, and other local people talk about, but have not begun to address. Although many are aware that the principal attraction of Cahuita National Park is its reef and that it is fragile (Cortés 1995), no local initiatives have been taken to stop its degradation.

In short, the biggest challenge facing the Management Committee is balancing power relations and interests between the government and local stakeholders; tourism representatives, conservationists, and resource users; and the "have" community (Cahuita) and the "have not" communities neighbouring the park (Hone Creek and Punta Riel). In the long term, it will be critical to address the issue of contamination and erosion of the reef.

Lessons learned

Although there are numerous instances of public participation in the management of protected areas in Costa Rica and regionally, the idea of comanagement is still very new. The Cahuita case is the first instance of collaborative management within the country's parks system and provides valuable lessons regarding the elements required to enhance these processes (Table 3).

Important lessons can be drawn from an examination of the various elements at the community level that contributed to successful negotiations with the government following the state's 1994 unilateral declaration that the national park's entrance fees would be increased for foreigners. Cahuita was the only community in the country to adamantly and successfully oppose the price hike; the outcome of its actions had a positive impact on all communities with a stake in park tourism, as the entrance fee for foreigners was soon reduced throughout Costa Rica.

Table 3. Key elements that enhanced the collaborative management process in Cahuita.

Community	Conflict management and negotiations	Collaboration
Leadership	Timing — Knowledge of when to lobby, for how long, and when to sit at the negotiating table	Legal backing
Political ties and know-how		Trust between the parties
Access to education	Mediation — The presence of a mediator trusted by both parties	Openness to listen to new positions
Organizational capacity		Mechanisms for conflict management
Flexibility and ability to adapt to new situations	Pressure tactics	Political will
	"Ask for more than you want so in the end you get what you need"	

Some of the elements that contributed to Cahuita's success include

✦ *Community leadership* — A number of "natural" community leaders were involved in the negotiations, including Alpheus Buchanan, Tony Mora, and Rolando Brooks. These people are respected in the community. Buchanan and Mora have businesses related to tourism, which means that although they have a stake in anything to do with the community as Cahuitans, they are also motivated by economic interests. They have ample experience in community mobilization and organization, largely on account of the important roles they played organizing cocoa cooperatives in the 1960s and 1970s (Palmer 1977). Other community members have become leaders through access to higher education, such as Enrique Joseph, who also played an important role in the negotiations. These three formed the Committee of Struggle, which has come together on several occasions to fight for the interests of Cahuita (Buchanan, personal communication, 1998[11]).

✦ *Political ties and know-how* — The political know-how of the Committee of Struggle shone through, not only in its ability to mobilize the community in a united front, regardless of the differences that usually prevail among community players, but also in the pressure tactics it used throughout the negotiations. Asking for more than the community needed and demanding that the Supreme Court declare the two-tariff entrance fee to the park unconstitutional pressured the state at the right time and with the right effect (GJE 1994). Moreover, several community leaders have close links to influential politicians and appealed to them to expedite the process (cf. Joseph 1995).

✦ *Organizational capacity* — Cahuita has more than eight organized groups, including the Chamber of Tourism, the Development Association of Cahuita, the Association of Naturalist Guides, and women's and cultural groups. Although some of these groups work better than others, their presence makes mobilizing the community an easier task.

Although Cahuita's leaders have become veterans in fighting for their community's interests, the Management Committee is a first in providing the opportunity for community members to work together with government officials on an ongoing basis. To date, the role of this committee has been to put out fires and to deal with the provision of services to tourists in the park. It cannot yet be characterized as a comanagement institution in which there is "sharing of power and responsibility between the government and local resource users" in making and implementing decisions about natural resource management (Berkes et al. 1991). However, the process is still very young and is a new way of doing things for both the government and the community. On one hand, government officials need to learn how to "relinquish control" and enable communities to have a sense of proprietorship, which is a rare event regardless of the global trend toward decentralization (Murphree 1994; Ghimire and Pimbert 1997); on the other hand, local people need to be empowered to take an active role in managing the park.

If the community's vision becomes a reality, local people will have more control over park management in the future, with MINAE's role relegated to one of technical support. Community representative, Mario Calderón, states that he wants "Cahuita to be an example for other conservation areas. In 10 years I see the community managing the park,

[11] A. Buchanan, Cahuita, Costa Rica, personal communication, 1998.

and MINAE giving us technical support." Likewise, community representative, Enrique Joseph, states that he sees "the future management of the park in an 80/20 split: the community would control 80% and MINAE 20%." With the passage of the 1998 rules of use, giving the committee legal power to change both this structure and the rules governing use in the park, the committee can start working on making its vision a reality. But this will not take place overnight. Many critics have noted that successful community-based or collaborative management regimes are a long-term endeavour that require much patience and trials and errors before they can begin to operate efficiently, effectively, and equitably (Ostrom 1987, 1997).

There is no doubt that Cahuita represents an opportunity for the government of Costa Rica to do things differently in terms of protecting its natural resource heritage and involving local people. However, to seize this opportunity and develop a precedent-setting arrangement, two things must happen: the government must accord the committee the autonomy and authority to make natural resource management decisions geared toward the situation on the ground, without being tied totally to national parks legislation; and local resource users from both Cahuita and neighbouring communities must be directly involved in the development of a management plan and decisions about how the resources are used.

Many have discussed the possibility of changing Cahuita's category of protected area to allow for more extensive subsistence use. But maintaining Cahuita as a national park while recognizing the autonomy and authority of the Management Committee in making resource management decisions that may go beyond national parks legislation would be a far more progressive move on the part of the government.

Acknowledgments

The authors gratefully acknowledge Pascal O. Girot, School of Geography, University of Costa Rica, and Fikret Berkes, Natural Resources Institute, University of Manitoba, for supervising this project; Edwin Cyrus, Alpheus Buchanan, Tony Mora, Enrique Joseph and Dexter Lewis, for providing guidance and feedback; the staff of La Amistad Caribe Conservation Area, particularly Gina Cuza Jones, Eduardo Pearson, and Carlos Gonzales; Elvin Huertas and Lucia Chavarría, for their field assistance; International Development Research Centre, for funding Viviane Weitzner's research; the Fundación para el Desarrollo Urbano and the Mesoamerican Conflict Resolution Network, for supporting Marvin Fonseca Borrás's work; and, most important, the people of Cahuita, for sharing their stories and way of life with us for the 4 months we were part of the community.

References

Arnstein, S.R. 1969. A ladder of citizen participation. Journal of the American Institute of Planners, 35 (4), 216–224.

Berkes, F. 1997. New and not-so-new directions in the use of the commons: co-management. Common Property Resource Digest, Jul, 5–7.

Berkes, F.; George, P.; Preston, R.J. 1991. Co-management: the evolution in theory and practice of the joint administration of living resources. Alternatives, 18(2), 12–18.

Bermudez, A.; Bazo, R. 1979. Plan estructural para el desarrollo de la conservación y la Recreación del Parque Nacional Cahuita. University of Costa Rica, San José, Costa Rica. MSc thesis.

Bermudez, F.; Yadira, M. 1993. Parques nacionales de Costa Rica. Ministerio de Ambiente y Energía, Depto de planificación y servicios tecnicos, sección turismo, San José, Costa Rica.

Borrini-Feyerabend, G. 1996. Collaborative management of protected areas: tailoring the approach to the context. International Union for the Conservation of Nature, Gland, Switzerland.

Boza, M.A.; Cevo, J.H. 1998. Parques nacionales y otras áreas protegidas Costa Rica national parks and other protected areas. Incafo Costa Rica, San José, Costa Rica.

Calderón, A.L. 1998. Caracterización del cantón de Talamanca. Fundación para el desarrollo urbano, San José, Costa Rica.

Cortés, J.N. 1995. El arrecife coralino del Parque Nacional Cahuita: un arrecife con problemas ambientales. Biocenosis, 11(2), 23–24.

Cruz, J.C.B. 1996. El nuevo monocultivo: ¿Qué pasará si el turismo se va de Cahuita? La Ecologia, 19 Jun, 6.

Folke, C.; Berkes, F. 1995. Mechanisms that link property rights to ecological systems. *In* Hanna, S.; Munasinghe, M., ed., Property rights and the environment: social and economic issues. Beijer International Institute of Ecological Economics; the World Bank, Washington, DC, USA. pp. 121–137.

Ghimire, K.B.; Pimbert, M. 1997. Social change and conservation: environmental politics and impacts of national parks and protected areas. Earthscan Publications, London, UK.

GJE (Grupo Juridico Especializado). 1994. Recurso de Amparo Rodrigo Antonio Mora Picado contra Ministerio de Recursos Naturales Energía y Minas y Director del Servicio de Parques Nacionales. 8 de septiembre. San José, Costa Rica.

Hanna, S. 1995. Efficiencies of user participation in natural resource management. *In* Hanna, S.; Munasinghe, M., ed., Property rights and the environment: social and economic issues. Beijer International Institute of Ecological Economics; the World Bank, Washington, DC, USA. pp. 59–67.

Joseph, E. 1995. Letter to José Luis Velasquez, Diputado, Provincia de Limón, Aug 30.

Kutay, K.N. 1984. Cahuita National Park, Costa Rica: a case study in living cultures and national park management. University of Michigan, Ann Arbor, MI, USA. MSc thesis.

MINAE (Ministerio de Ambiente y Energía). 1997. Parque Nacional Cahuita Tenencia de Tierra. Agosto. Subregion Siquirres-Matina. MINAE, San José, Costa Rica.
———— 1998. Reglamento Para El Manejo de Recursos y Servicios en el Parque Nacional Cahuita. La Gaceta, 20 May, p. 96. Decreto ejecutivo no. 26929-MINAE.

MINEH (Ministerio de Economía y Hacienda). 1997. Censo de población de Costa Rica. Dirección de Estadística y Censos. San José, Costa Rica. Jul.

MIRENEM (Ministerio de Recursos Naturales, Energía y Minas), Servicio de Parques Nacionales. 1994a. Advertisement. La Nación, 12 Sep, p. 32.
———— 1994b. Advertisement. La República, 11 Sep, p. 3.

Mora, J. 1998. Proyecto de investigacion y construcción de nuevos modelos de gestión ambiental en las Áreas de Conservación, Versión borrador. Fundación para el Desarrollo Urbano y Programa Frontera Agricola, San José, Costa Rica.

Murphree, M.W. 1994. The role of institutions in community-based conservation. *In* Western, D.; Write, R.M., ed., Natural connections: perspectives in community-based conservation. Island Press, Washington, DC, USA. pp. 403–447.

Oakerson, R.J. 1992. Analyzing the commons: a framework. *In* Bromley, D., ed., Making the commons work. ICS Press, San Francisco, CA, USA.

Orthello, W. 1972. The significance of Cahuita National Monument, Costa Rica: an evaluation report of the present and plans for the future. United Nations Educational, Scientific and Cultural Organization, Paris, France. Mission Report.

Ostrom, E. 1987. Institutional arrangements for resolving the commons dilemma: some contending approaches. *In* McCay, B.J.; Acheson, J.M., ed., The question of the commons: the culture and ecology of communal resources. University of Arizona Press, Tucson, AZ, USA.

———— 1990. Governing the commons: the evolution of institutions for collective action. Cambridge University Press, New York, NY, USA.

———— 1997. Local institutions for resource management. *In* Borrini-Feyerabend, G., ed., Beyond fences: seeking social sustainability in conservation. Vol. 2. International Union for the Conservation of Nature, Gland, Switzerland. pp. 14–16.

Palmer, P. 1977. What happen': a folk history of Costa Rica's Talamanca Coast. Publications in English, San José, Costa Rica.

Pittier, H. 1895. Nombres geograficos de Costa Rica. I. Talamanca. Típografía Nacional, San José, Costa Rica.

Ramírez, C. 1977. Estudio Ocupación Parque Nacional Cahuita. San José, Costa Rica.

Solórzano, R. 1997. La administración de las Areas Silvestres Protegidas mejora con la participación privada no comercial. Ambien-Tico, 55, 1–7.

Tovar, E. 1994. Ritmo de cocos, corales y caracoles. Al Día, 5 Nov, p. 8.

Wells, M.; Brandon, K. 1992. People and parks: linking protected area managment with local communities. World Bank; World Wildlife Fund; US Agency for International Development, Washington DC, USA.

Chapter 7

Bolinao, Northern Philippines:
Participatory Planning for Coastal Development

Liana Talaue-McManus, Alexis C. Yambao,
Severino G. Salmo III, and Porfirio M. Aliño

A participatory process for planning coastal development in Bolinao, northern Philippines, was integral in empowering marginal fishers and other community members and involving them in decision-making. Empowerment was effected through transfer of knowledge about their environment and natural resources, the laws that determined access to them, and the institutional mechanisms through which they could meaningfully participate. Throughout this process, resolution of conflicting interests occurred in parallel and allowed community members to achieve a consensus on appropriate management options for their coastal waters. Forging a partnership between a community and its leaders, the Coastal Development Plan embodied a collective vision for the long-term feasibility of Bolinao's living coastal resources.

Bolinao is a municipality in the province of Pangasinan on the northwest coast of Luzon, Philippines (McManus et al. 1990). One of 18 towns bordering the Lingayen Gulf, Bolinao has one of the most extensively developed reef systems and associated habitats in northern Luzon (McManus et al. 1992). Demersal fish, shellfish, and seaweeds living in reef and seagrass areas dominate the fisheries of the town. In 1993, the Lingayen Gulf was declared an environmentally critical area under Proclamation 156. The Bolinao–Anda reefs — the only coralline section of the gulf — are the spawning and feeding grounds for a significant number of fish and invertebrate species.

From an environmental perspective, significant indicators of unsustainable levels of resource extraction were evident in the late 1980s. Talaue-McManus and Kesner (1995) documented the collapse of the valuable sea-urchin fishery in 1992, despite the existence of town resolutions limiting the fishing season and establishing a minimum harvestable size. Data gathered over a 4-year period (1988–91) revealed evidence of overharvesting of reef fish: a decrease in adult-fish density and species diversity, as well as in the size of reproductively mature fish (McManus et al. 1992). A survey of the coral reefs of the Lingayen Gulf conducted during 1987 and 1988 showed that sites in the Bolinao–Anda system had 30–51% live coral cover; siltation and the use of dynamite and poison posed the major threats to the reef (Meñez et al. 1991).

This paper examines the conflicts that occurred over the coastal waters of Bolinao and the multistakeholder consultations that sought to address them. Lessons are identified regarding the role of local organizations, environmental education, and the contributions of science to the development of a collective and long-term vision of Bolinao's coastal resources.

The initial situation: resource degradation and inequities in access rights

Balingasay River and the milkfish fry concession system

Milkfish fry are found from April to September in the Balingasay River (Salmo III, personal communication, 1998[1]) (Figure 1). Currently, fishers bid on the right to collect fry, with the local government granting them a concession in return for a fee. However, the bidding process may be modified by the mayor, with support from the municipal council (the Sangguniang Bayan). For example, the mayor may enter into negotiated contracts with favoured business partners, a discretionary practice subject to many irregularities and corruption. Since postwar years the municipality of Bolinao has received significant funding in tariffs from the milkfish fry concession.

The subsistence collectors are forced to sell their catch to those holding the concession at prices usually below those dictated by market demand. The concession holder makes a large profit, and fry collectors earn a minimum income. This situation of short-term monopoly on access and distribution marginalizes the subsistence fry gatherers and leaves few incentives to regulate the harvest of fry or of spawning fish. It has also led to illegal fishing, which is widespread.

The use of the Balingasay River for tourism, navigation, and sand-quarrying further exacerbates the conflict. Resort owners want shorefronts to be open and free from any activity; however, both subsistence and deep-sea fishers living near the river must use the area for navigation and docking. Overcrowding of houses on the beach and sand quarrying activity create further tensions.

Siganid fishery in the Santiago Island reef system

Reef flats and slopes are most extensive around Santiago Island (Figure 1), making this the richest and most diverse fishing grounds of Bolinao. Each year, this area is allocated to the highest bidder as Fishery Lot 1. Forty percent of the catch obtained from this zone is made

---

[1] S.G. Salmo III, Marine Science Institute, University of the Philippines, Diliman, Quezon City, Philippines, personal communication, 1998.

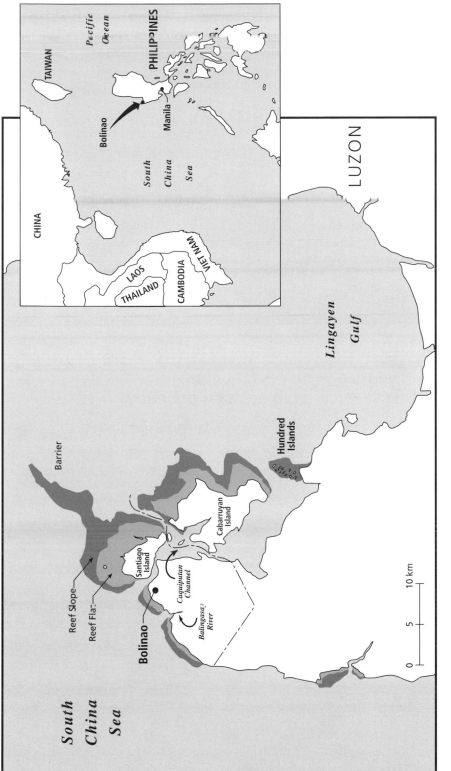

Figure 1. Lingayen Gulf and its reef areas, Philippines.

up of siganid fish, which migrate beyond the reef flats to spawn (McManus et al. 1992). Newly settled juveniles migrate back to the seagrass meadows on the reef flats to feed and grow. Siganid fish are harvested at all stages: juveniles are used in various grades of fish sauce, and adult fish are sold dried or fresh as a preferred food species.

The system for granting concessions in the siganid fisheries of Bolinao has been in place for a long time and is an important feature of the local economy (Rodriguez 1997). Concession holders, or occasionally a negotiated contractor, build fish corrals in which they catch the siganids. They may also sublease the right to set up corrals to others, provided all of the catch is sold back to the concessionaire.

Like the milkfish concession, exclusive fishing privileges for the siganid fisheries create inequitable access to a rich resource and result in a disparate distribution of economic benefits. Marginal fishers are prohibited from fishing near the fish corrals, the open arms of which collectively form a formidable trap for migrating fish coming from or leaving the reef flats. These constraints interfere with navigation and promote illegal fishing. Although the local government earns revenues from the sale of concessions, it has not been able to ensure the long-term feasibility of the siganid fisheries. Studies of the reef fisheries by McManus et al. (1992) indicate that the size of reproducing siganids is decreasing (fish 3 cm long were already gravid), a sign of overexploitation. Loss of habitat (as a result of the destruction of coral reefs) and the deterioration of seagrass beds further undermine the sustainability of the resource.

The change process: people's organizations and multisectoral planning

In July 1992, the need to take action in light of declining catches, inequity of access to resources and to benefits accruing from their use, and degradation of the coastal environment was publicly articulated. A meeting (Coastal Management Forum I) of the coastal community and agencies active in Bolinao was called by concerned scientists and environmentalists to collectively air environmental issues and begin to identify possible courses of action (Rodriguez et al. 1992). Testimonies from fishers and other stakeholders (fish vendors, shell craftspeople, etc.) echoed the findings of scientific studies showing the deterioration of the living coastal resources and the decline in fishing as a feasible livelihood and mainstay of the town's economy. The forum resolved to coordinate development work in Bolinao through an integrated coastal management approach involving citizens' groups, regional and national governmental organizations, and university-based environmental organizations.

Two years later, concerns about the sustainability of the fisheries raised during the first public meeting were intensified by a proposal of the national government to industrialize the "Northwestern Luzon Growth Quadrangle" (Executive Order 175, 30 April 1994). The first major initiative was to build a cement plant complex, including a quarry site, power plant, cement factory, and wharf to facilitate shipment of bulk cement to Taiwan. In response to this plan, concerned environmental groups called a second public meeting (Coastal Management Forum II) to discuss the potential environmental impact of the project on the fisheries and the need for a municipal development strategy to weigh the costs and benefits that municipal government support for the plan would entail.

Establishing people's organizations

Although the *Local Government Code*[2] had been in effect since October 1991, town lead ers and the community at large realized that they did not have the information and technical advice they needed to make crucial decisions regarding the direction of development and the management of the coastal resources. A University of the Philippines project called the Community-based Coastal Resources Management (CBCRM) in Bolinao, Northern Philippines was initiated in 1993 to respond to this need. (This project was supported by the International Development Research Centre [IDRC]).

The approach of the project was to focus first on community mobilization and environmental education (McManus 1995). Previously nonaligned sectors of the community were mobilized to form local groups and learn about environmental issues. The hope was that once organized and empowered with knowledge and skills, the groups would embark on their own resource management initiatives, including the development of environmentally friendly livelihood options and networking with other like-minded groups. An environmental education and information campaign was conducted in 11 of the 14 coastal villages (*barangays*) of Bolinao. Data indicated that the direct users of coastal resources — 3 000 families of marginal fishers or 30% of the town's population — could lose their resource base if it was not appropriately managed.

By early 1996, people's organizations had been set up in four coastal villages (Arendo and Balingasay on the mainland and Binabalian and Pilar on Santiago Island). A second-generation organization was established in the mainland village of Ilog Malino, with the help of the Balingasay organization (Figure 1). Among the first proposals of these organizations was the establishment of protected marine areas in the waters next to the villages of Balingasay, Arnedo, and Binabalian. They also proposed a mangrove rehabilitation area in Pilar to increase aquatic spawning habitat.

The CBCRM project held a number of internal meetings to build on these resolutions. A zoning plan for Bolinao, first conceived in 1994 (Yambao and Salmo 1998), was broadened into a coastal development planning exercise to include multiple stakeholders. The project developed strategies for facilitating the creation of new roles and functions for the local government (both the executive and legislative branches) and for the fledgling people's organizations. These included taking all possible steps to build the appropriate knowledge and skills needed to ensure the active participation of all community sectors and the local government. The team also developed first drafts of a resource map indicating the location of the proposed protected marine areas, the mangrove rehabilitation area, the watershed management area, and potential mariculture sites.

Enhancing the role of people's organizations and working toward conflict management

In May 1996, an orientation session on coastal development planning was conducted for the leaders and members of the four people's organizations collaborating with the CBCRM project. The participants defined uses in the major divisions of the coastal areas; identified fishery and coastal management issues, problems, and concerns; and described a range of management options for each area. The draft resource map developed by the project was

[2] The *Local Government Code* is a statute passed by the Philippine Congress, which provides for the devolution of governance from the central government to province, city, municipality, and village levels. It includes management of municipal waters up to 15 km from shore.

used to prepare village-level maps, and management activities for several villages were proposed.

After further discussion within the organizations and several community workshops on resource management, the four people's organizations integrated their resource maps into a regional map. Technical studies and the wide dissemination of their results were crucial steps in formulating alternative management options with the potential to resolve ongoing conflicts. For example, during community workshops and meetings, the CBCRM project widely disseminated the results of ongoing monitoring of the siganid fisheries of Bolinao by the University of the Philippines' Marine Science Institute (UPMSI). During the meetings, fishers and traders corroborated the trend toward diminishing catches and decreasing size of reproducing adults. This enhanced the credibility of the information collected by the CBCRM project and the UPMSI and led to a common understanding of the resource problems. It also provided a basis for discussion of possible solutions and local participation in data collection in some areas.

The community meetings and workshops helped clarify local perceptions of the living coastal resources, the legal and social mechanisms that govern access to them, and the problems and possible solutions associated with their use. The active participation of stakeholders in the process deepened their sense of involvement and commitment to achieving prospective solutions to the problems they had identified. Recognition of their common concerns also led to the federation of the four organizations under the name of the Municipcal-wide Federation of People's Organizations for Coastal Resource Management (KAISAKA) to promote the development of a Coastal Development Plan (CDP) for Bolinao.

Eliciting the support and participation of the local government

In August 1996, the Department of Environment and Natural Resources refused to issue an environmental compliance certificate for the cement plant complex, bringing to an end a controversy that had mobilized local and national groups concerned about its environmental impact. One of the main reasons cited for denial of the certificate was the absence of a municipal land-use plan. The CBCRM project had proposed such a plan to the municipal government sometime earlier, but the idea had been rejected by the mayor and other officials. However, after it became apparent that the absence of a plan had frustrated a significant industrial development initiative, the municipal government asked the CBCRM project to provide assistance in coastal development planning. Key officials of the Municipal Development Council (the executive branch of the local government), the mayor, the municipal planning and development coordinator, and the local government operations officer met with project personnel to discuss the CDP already developed by the KAISAKA federation. The mayor later agreed to sponsor a multisectoral consultation on the development of Bolinao to build on the existing plan and finalize it for consideration by the municipal government.

A workshop was held to present the federation's plan to other community stakeholders, including representatives of the village governments, local organizations, and other concerned groups. The results of a study on land use that was conducted by the CBCRM project were also presented. Drawing on this study and the CDP, four management zones were identified: ecotourism, multiple use (milkfish pens and fish cages), fishery management (reef fisheries), and special management (trade and navigation) (Figure 1).

In December 1998, the first Multi-sectoral Consultation on the Development of Bolinao was coordinated by the office of municipal planning and development and the CBCRM project. The meeting was attended by about 120 people, most of whom were *barangay* leaders, heads of village-based organizations, the media, and representatives of the provincial government and other government agencies and community sectors. The consolidated development plan was presented, and the need to form a drafting committee was discussed. The mayor later issued an executive order (No. 6, Series 1996) to create a Multi-sectoral Committee on Coastal Development Planning for Bolinao (MCDB), composed of 21 members representing 11 community sectors, including the four people's organizations and five members of the Municipal Development Council. The executive order also stipulated that the CBCRM project would provide technical assistance to the committee and allocated a budget of 100 000 PHP for the preparation of the plan (in 1999, 38.44 Philippine pesos [PHP] = 1 United States dollar [USD].

New conflicts emerge

Although progress was being made in the development of local capacity to manage coastal resources, new conflicts were also emerging. Throughout 1996, fish pens and cages proliferated in the Caquiputan Channel between the Bolinao mainland and the islands of Santiago and Cabarruyan (Figure 1). According to a survey by the Lingayen Gulf Coastal Area Management Commission, the number increased from about 330 in December 1996 to 3 100 in July 1997. These aquaculture facilities are used to raise the estuarine milkfish *Chanos chanos*, using fry gathered from the Balingasay River. Leases of 3 to 5 years were granted by the municipal government, but officials were not prepared to determine the optimal number of structures, locations, or the distance between them needed to sustain healthy waters.

As noted above, the economic and political elite of Bolinao controlled access to the milkfish fry of the Balingasay River and had a monopoly on feed and other supplies for aquaculture operations and the milkfish trade. When the number of pens and cages first began to increase, conflicts arose because they reduced the area of the fishing grounds and navigable waters for subsistence fishers, thereby exacerbating an already inequitable situation.

The conflict was further intensified because water quality in the channel quickly deteriorated. The rate at which water flushed through the system, naturally cleaning the channel, was reduced because the density of the pens obstructed water flow. Residues from the large amounts of feed used in the aquaculture operations built up in the channel, causing a decline in the amount of dissolved oxygen in the water. During the warm months of 1997, this reached a level that was lethal to milkfish; fish mortality increased, and growth rates declined, leading to significant economic losses. The number of pens and cages dropped the following year to 1 200 because of this.

In 1996, the CBCRM project initiated a technical study on which to base specific guidelines for coastal aquaculture operations. Using basic physical and chemical parameters, such as bathometry, water residence times, and tidal velocities, a zoning scheme and the optimal number and size of fish pens and cages were determined (MCDB 1997). This study was incorporated into the planning process for Bolinao's CDP and was also presented to the adjacent municipality of Anda, which shares the waters of Caquiputan Channel with Bolinao and was beset by the same conflict.

Preparing the Coastal Development Plan

The economic losses sustained by the milkfish aquaculture system in 1997 provided additional incentive to support the planning process. A team-building and planning workshop was held to articulate the vision, mission, and goal of the MCDB and to provide a venue to renew the commitment of its members to pursuing the planning exercise to completion. A workplan for the committee was developed and regular monthly meetings were scheduled, including community consultations in all coastal villages (Yambao and Salmo 1998). By the second meeting, the committee had adopted the proposal to divide the municipal waters into four zones, and by mid-1997 community consultations were completed and all inputs and amendments were recorded.

The committee then held a series of meetings to finish drafting the text of the plan. The draft went through a parliamentary procedure of being read and scrutinized three times while the committee sat *en banc*. The plan was assembled by the CBCRM project and revised and amended by all members of the committee. To ensure that all the concerns raised during the public consultations were addressed, all documents and the minutes of meetings were reviewed by the committee.

After the draft CDP was approved on its third and final reading in October 1997, the committee submitted it to the mayor and members of the Municipal Development Council, which included five people who were also members of the drafting committee. The mayor endorsed the plan and asked the Municipal Council (the body with legislative authority) for approval. By mid-January 1998, the Municipal Council approved the CDP.

The active participation of key municipal authorities in the development of the plan was key to securing final endorsement. However, the timing of the planning exercise and its submission to the Municipal Council was also fortuitous and instrumental in its acceptance. Just weeks before submission to the Municipal Council, the president of the Philippines issued an executive order (No. 450, Series 1997) requiring all 800 coastal municipalities of the country to formulate comprehensive coastal development plans that would form the basis for the passage of fishery ordinances. Bolinao was the first to fulfill this requirement.

The outcome: providing a practical framework for conflict management and participatory planning for coastal development

The events leading up to the development of the CDP were characterized by polarization in the Bolinao community because of inequities in access to resources and threats to livelihoods posed by the cement plant complex and resource degradation. These conflicts animated a process of community organization, demand-driven research, and multisectoral planning.

The impact of the CDP exercise on the sustainable and equitable use of coastal resources in Bolinao cannot be fully assessed, and the implementation process is still uncertain. The people's organizations supported by the CBCRM project are still too weak to spearhead implementation on their own. Partnership with nonaligned sectors of the community, such as the UPMSI and with the local government, is necessary to begin realizing key management interventions contained in the plan. Members of the people's organizations are active environmental advocates, whose level of awareness and commitment help sustain the momentum of collective efforts, but time, skill, and organizational constraints hamper their functional role in implementing the plan.

The process seems to have provided an effective venue for channeling conflicts and building consensus by articulating a development vision and formulating action plans to achieve it. Although among sectors of the communities, there were various degrees of involvement, commitment, and active participation in the drafting committee, a sense of collective ownership of the plan emerged. The Municipal Council formally acknowledged in a public meeting that the consultative and participatory process used in the CDP was positive and should be used in the formulation and passage of other forms of municipal legislation.

Key government agencies, such as the Lingayen Gulf Coastal Area Management Commission (LGCAMC) and the National Economic Development Authority (NEDA, Region 1), have also taken note of the process. During a workshop on community development plans with municipal officials from all the coastal towns of the Lingayen Gulf, the LGCAMC and NEDA presented the Bolinao plan as a model for member municipalities. Other government organizations and nongovernmental organizations working in coastal areas around the country have also used the Bolinao CDP as a reference in their planning exercises.

Lessons learned

The Bolinao experience in participatory coastal development planning is a strategy for institutionalizing collective management practices from the community level through the hierarchy of governance (local, regional, and national). Various lessons can be gleaned from this experience. These include the importance of environmental education, community mobilization, and the active participation of all stakeholders in the process.

Environmental education plays an important role in organizing and empowering communities, and so encouraging community-led resource management initiatives. Prevailing conflicts (for example, the cement plant, fish pens) that divided sectors provided potent venues for information campaigns that were conducted outside partisan politics but well within a transparent framework for coastal resources management. The wide dissemination of the results of technical studies, corroborated, whenever possible, by the observations of local fishers, further served to increase understanding of the resource issues at hand. The technical studies conducted by the CBCRM project and others at the UPMSI were widely accepted as credible sources of information and were used to help settle conflicting interests. To achieve these results, the project struck a balance between providing information and expertise and facilitating local decision-making among feasible options. This ensured credibility, even during very divisive times, a role academic institutions are well suited to play because of their accepted mandate to teach, conduct research, and provide extension services.

Two principal groups of stakeholders need to be actively involved and supportive of the planning process in order to manage conflict in the region. The first group is the direct resource users (for example, subsistence fishers, and fish vendors). In addition to being educated about environmental issues, they must be mobilized and empowered through knowledge and capacity-building. This allows them to participate effectively in a collective process, and their active participation increases their sense of commitment to finding solutions to the problems identified. In the case of the CBCRM project, such mobilization led to the formation of people's organizations. This strengthened the position of marginalized fishers, who had no other vehicle through which to participate meaningfully in larger planning processes. The contribution of plans for protected marine areas from the people's organizations in Bolinao was a major turning point in the development of the CDP. It crystallized what a grass-roots initiative could achieve when focused action was taken. It also spurred the local leaders to become involved in an exercise that had the potential to provide a much-needed blueprint for the town's development.

The second group of stakeholders that needs to be actively involved is the local government. The active involvement of the executive and legislative branches of the local government in the design and public consultation greatly enhances the institutionalization of a planning process for coastal resources management. In the early stages of the plan's evolution, elected leaders felt insecure because the people's organizations had taken the initiative in the form of a proposal for integrated protected marine areas. This insecurity was overcome when a leadership role for the municipal authorities was defined through sponsorship of the multisectoral forum. National leadership through the *Local Government Code* and the requirement that municipal governments develop coastal resource management plans also provided a direct incentive to participate. Participation led to the development among local leaders of a sense of ownership, as well as of accountability, in formulating and implementing the plan. This may be a good indicator of its future success. It also showed the representatives of the municipal government and others that public consultation and sectoral representation were effective means to develop consensus for collective action.

The experience of the CBCRM project in Bolinao demonstrates the importance of participatory planning for conflict resolution in coastal development. Environmental education, coupled with community mobilization and the active participation of all stakeholders, facilitated the participatory process. This process channeled conflict and built consensus, ensuring a collective sense of ownership for the final plan.

References

MCDB (Multi-sectoral Committee on Coastal Development Planning for Bolinao). 1997. Bolinao Coastal Development Plan (1997–2007). Municipality of Bolinao, Philippines. 76 pp.

McManus, J.W.; Nañola, C.L., Jr; Reyes, R.B., Jr; Kesner, K.N. 1992. Resource ecology of the Bolinao coral reef system. International Center for Living Aquatic Resources Management, Manila, Philippines. Studies and Reviews, 22, 117.

McManus, L.T. 1995. Community-based coastal resources management, Bolinao, Philippines: an evolving partnership among academe, NGOs and local communities. Coastal Management in Tropical Asia, 5, 6–8.

McManus, L.T.; Luna, C.Z.; Guarin, F.Y. 1990. Introduction. *In:* McManus, L.T.; Chua, T.E., ed., The coastal environmental profile of Lingayen Gulf, Philippines. International Center for Living Aquatic Resources Management, Manila, Philippines. Technical report 22. 69 pp.

Meñez, L.A.B.; McManus, L.T.; Metra, N.M.; Jimenez, J.F.; Rivera, C.A.; Concepcion, J.M.; Luna, C.Z. 1991. Survey of the coral reef resources of Western Lingayen Gulf, Philippines. International Center for Living Aquatic Resources Management, Manila, Philippines. Conference Proceedings 22. pp. 77–82.

Rodriguez, S.F. 1997. The barangen fishing concession in Bolinao: an ethnographic study of a customary marine tenure system. Department of Anthropology, University of the Philippines, Manila, Philippines. MSc thesis. 150 pp.

Rodriguez, S.F.; Ferrer, E.; Magno, A.L.R.; de la Cruz, L.P. 1992. Proceedings of the Coastal Resources Management Forum (31 July – 1 August 1992). University of the Philippines College of Social Work and Community Development, Manila, Philippines. 36 pp.

Talaue-McManus, L.; Kesner, K.P.N. 1995. Valuation of a Philippine municipal sea urchin fishery and implications of its collapse. *In* Juinio-Meñez, A.; Newkirk, G.F., ed., Philippine coastal resources under stress. Selected papers from the Fourth Annual Common Property Conference, Manila, Philippines, 16–19 June 1993.

Yambao, A.; Salmo, S. III. 1998. A preliminary assessment of the coastal development planning in the municipal waters of Bolinao, Pangasinan. Out of the Shell, 6(2), 1–6.

Chapter 8

THE GALAPAGOS ISLANDS:
CONFLICT MANAGEMENT IN CONSERVATION AND SUSTAINABLE RESOURCE MANAGEMENT

Paola Oviedo

This case study of a fishing community in the Galapagos Islands, Ecuador, describes a successful experience in protecting a valuable natural area, a prolonged conflict over the use of marine resources by various sectors, and recent efforts to manage the conflict through a participatory process. The Galapagos experience shows that, even in extremely complex situations where there is growing conflict of interests and antagonism among groups, it is possible to bring about changes that will reconcile the economic aspirations and social welfare of various groups with conservation and the sustainable use of natural resources.

This study of a fishing community in Ecuador's Galapagos Islands combines a number of elements: long-standing and successful protection of an exceptionally valuable natural area, a prolonged conflict of interest among various users, and a recent initiative to manage that conflict through a process that began with adoption of a special law, drafted through a participatory process.

From the early 1970s to the 1990s, a number of powerful interests were focused on defending their various positions without making sufficient effort to understand the needs, interests, and concerns of the weaker stakeholders, represented, among others, by the local community of small-scale fishers. For a long time, no attempt was made to manage the conflict, in part because no one was available who could serve as an effective mediator. Part of the problem was the conservationist focus and the lack of participation by important interest groups during two key periods: when the national park was created and when the marine reserve was declared. The conservationist focus was inspired by the text of the *Convention on the Protection of the Flora, Fauna and Natural Scenic Treasures of the Countries of the Americas*, which was adopted to protect designated wildlife areas but was poorly equipped to deal with the fact that most of the protected areas of Latin America are inhabited or surrounded by human settlements, usually low-income rural communities.

Although the orientation of policies on protected areas has evolved substantially to the point where traditional human settlements are considered part of the ecosystems to be protected, in practice many countries still apply the earlier, exclusive model, which insists on establishing frontiers, installing surveillance and patrol mechanisms, eliminating or reducing free access by local inhabitants, and ignoring demands for compensation or alternative measures. Under these circumstances, the local community usually suffers the greatest cost, and there is no assurance that the resources will be managed on a sustainable basis, because regulations are defied and a permanent atmosphere of conflict prevails.

The United Nations Conference on the Environment and Development and the emergence of new approaches, such as sustainable development, the equitable distribution of benefits, and local participation in decision-making, have revitalized the debate and have led to the adoption of new instruments to promote change through national legislation. The Galapagos experience shows that, even in extremely complex situations, it is possible to bring about change directed at reconciling people's economic aspirations and social welfare with action to promote the conservation and sustainable use of natural resources.

The Galapagos Islands

The islands and their inhabitants

The Galapagos Islands are located in the Pacific Ocean, some 1 000 km off the coast of the Republic of Ecuador (Figure 1). They have a land surface area of 8 000 km^2 and a marine area of more than 70 000 km^2. Because they are relatively young islands of volcanic origin and their climate is determined, to a large extent, by the interplay of ocean currents, they are a point of convergence for species of both the tropical and temperate zones.

The flora and fauna of the islands are of great value in terms of their endemism and intraspecific diversity. The wealth and peculiarities of the marine environment are less well known but are equally interesting and special. Because of oceanographic conditions and the variety of coastal habitats, there is wide ecological and biological diversity. The islands constitute a refuge for threatened animal species, especially whales and green turtles. Charles Darwin conceived some of the key ideas of his theory of evolution on the basis of his observations of the islands' fauna. Currently, the archipelago is regarded as one of the outstanding sites for the study of adaptive radiation and divergent evolution.

The Galapagos has no indigenous human population, partly because most of the islands are lacking in fresh water and cultivable soil. Human settlement occurred slowly on four of the largest islands, as a result of successive migrations that began in the mid-19th century. Currently, 3% of the islands' surface area is occupied. The 1990 census reported some 10 000 inhabitants, 80% of whom are urban dwellers.

Each inhabited island has its own port and a farming area on the edges of wetlands beginning at an elevation of 300 m above sea level. People are engaged primarily in

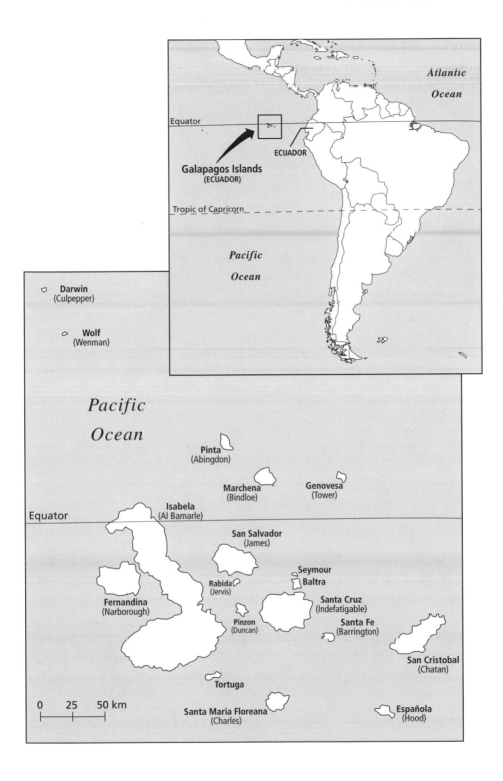

Figure 1. The Galapagos Islands.

tourism, fishing, conservation work, and public administration. Two of every three economically active people are now employed either directly or indirectly in tourism-related activities, although this proportion may vary sharply from one island to the next. Small-scale fishing is a very important traditional activity and employs 13% of the economically active population; on some islands, this figure is as high as 30%.

Land and marine resources

The Galapagos constitute a site of global importance and are protected by a number of national and international legal instruments. Some 97% of the land area was declared a national park in 1959; in 1974, it was included on the United Nations Educational, Scientific and Cultural Organization's (UNESCO's) list of World Heritage Sites, and in 1984 it became part of the network of World Biosphere Reserves under UNESCO's Man and the Biosphere program. This special situation has been key to the success of the national park, but it has brought with it a number of problems for the local inhabitants.

The land and marine resources of the islands are important in terms of

- ◆ Information for scientific research and study of species evolution and adaptation;
- ◆ Conservation of biodiversity in its natural setting;
- ◆ Tourism revenues; and
- ◆ Major source of supply of *langosta* (tropical lobster) for the international fisheries market and an important source of other products for the domestic and international markets (codfish and yellowfin tuna, respectively).

The islands' fisheries and tourism resources are both under pressure from the domestic and international markets. The relative success of these industries in the Galapagos, combined with a high rate of unemployment and underemployment in mainland Ecuador, has turned the islands into a magnet for migration.

Tourism activities generate some 60 million United States dollars (USD) a year — one-quarter of the foreign exchange receipts from tourism for the country as a whole. Although the number of visitors increased fivefold between 1972 and 1996, in general, tourism resources are being managed in a way that controls use and keeps the impact low. Nevertheless, some tourism attractions and sites infringe on traditional fishing grounds, and this has led to conflicts between the two sectors.

The fisheries resources are very important for the sustainable development of the local population but are also of interest to the national and international fishing industry. Although reliable statistics are not available, the total catch of tuna is estimated to be worth 60 million USD a year to the Ecuardorian economy; 15 million USD of this comes from island waters (Coello 1996; El Comercio 1998). Of the 12 types of fisheries, traditional and nontraditional, the most controversial are the nontraditional fisheries for sharks and sea cucumbers: the former because of the implications for the conservation of ecosystems and submarine tourism, and the latter because of its extractionist characteristics and its collateral effects on the land areas in the park. Small-scale fishing has been concentrated in the shallow inshore waters, because of limits on the operations of the fishing fleet. A further problem arises with respect to some species, such as lobster and cod, where the catch has been localized at a few sites; this has affected the reproductive capacity of those resources.

The commercial fishing fleet consists of some 30 vessels, both national and foreign. The latter are allowed to operate under contracts of association with domestic companies. The most frequently fished zones are the *bajos* to the south and southeast of the archipelago, where oceanographic conditions are especially favourable for marine life. This fleet is in competition for resources with local small-scale fishers, the tourism business, and conservation interests.

The current conflict

The establishment of the Galapagos National Park, especially the delimitation of its boundaries, provoked the first major conflict with the local populace. Declaration of the marine reserve in 1986 and approval of the management plan in 1992 (PDR–CPIG 1992) produced a second conflict, essentially over the move from a system of free access to one of restricted access, without any effort to provide information, use persuasion, or negotiate with key users of the marine resources.

Creation of the national park

In 1959, when the government of Ecuador decided to protect the region by declaring the Galapagos a national park — at the initiative of a group of experts and conservationists from the international science and education communities — little attention was paid to the needs and interests of the local population and other groups. Moreover, because there was no legal or administrative framework to back up the provisions of the decree establishing the park, the state delegated the initial task of delimiting the boundaries in parts of the park to the international conservation movement. This decision was protested and in the end was reversed, but not without creating a climate of mistrust and anticonservation sentiment among the local populace, a feeling that persists strongly even today on some islands.

Creation of the national park ended free public access to uninhabited islands and the parts of inhabited islands contained within the park boundaries. The local populace, poorly informed and excluded from the decision process, adopted a generally reactive position. In 1973, they persuaded the government to create the Province of Galapagos. The park–province duality gave rise to destructive competition in terms of authority and mission, as the mandate of the national park, intended to prevent human intrusion, was seen as blocking the ability of the provincial leaders to promote economic development on an equal footing with those in other parts of the country.

The unclear relation between the national park and the province blocked efforts to strike cooperative agreements and resolve common issues. The constant tug of war between the two sectors obstructed objective appreciation of the indirect benefits of the park in people's lives. Although local people lost access to the park and use of its resources, the national park gave rise to completely new economic activities. Two major changes resulted from the park's creation: tourism replaced the fishing business as the main economic activity, and there was a mass movement of people from the wet uplands to the port areas.

Creation of the marine reserve

Changes in the islands' economy and the increasing numbers of users of marine resources led national park authorities and the conservation sector to extend protection to marine resources through the creation of a reserve in 1986. The standard of living on the islands had improved to the point where they were now attractive to residents from the mainland. Whether this was a good thing depended on one's point of view. Although it was a positive development in social terms, it created a number of problems, such as increased immigration and expanded economic activity, especially in the fisheries, which were deemed incompatible with the goals of low environmental impact, ecotourism, sustainable use of fishing resources, etc.

The creation of the marine reserve by special decree and the subsequent approval of a management plan that attempted to establish strict fishing zones were challenged and defied in various ways and to varying degrees by the affected sectors, especially the fishing interests. (This was a unilateral decision made by the executive to avoid controversy in Congress.) As a result, between 1992 and 1995, the management plan was under attack from nearly all sectors involved, and it could not be put into effect for the following reasons (GOPA 1996):

 ✦ Lack of participation by major resource users;

 ✦ Conflicts among institutions and interest groups;

 ✦ Confusion over the administrative structure;

 ✦ Lack of funds to establish an effective patrol system; and

 ✦ A complicated and unworkable zoning system.

The major interest groups

The term "interest group" is used here to indicate a set of people or corporations, who are involved, directly as users or indirectly as managers or controllers, in the marine and fishery resources of the Galapagos Marine Reserve. These groups may be locally based, from the mainland, or from foreign countries. Their strength and negotiating power varies.

Conservation, science, and education sector

This sector has evolved from the group that promoted the creation of the Galapagos National Park. Currently, it consists primarily of individuals and national and international scientific and environmental organizations.

In general, the group's relations with the local populace have been cool and marked by mutual mistrust. For many years, local people have perceived this sector as defending the interests of an international scientific and conservationist community that is remote and in many respects abstract. Because of its contacts with an emerging local economic and social elite on the islands, some other groups, such as the fishers, regard this sector as being in alliance with the new elite. The group's standpoint is essentially conservationist, in the sense of promoting the nonextractive use of resources to avoid interfering in the evolution of land and sea life. Its members produce valuable scientific information. They have direct access to senior authorities and the national and international news media, and they have considerable financial resources. Since 1996 the sector has been seeking a participatory solution to its conflicts with the local populace, especially with the fishers.

The local fishing sector

This group is heterogeneous: its size, composition, and attitudes may change from one island to the next, depending on the importance of fishing in the local economy.

An estimated 600 families are engaged in fishing. In absolute terms, the number of fishers quadrupled between 1971 and 1996. The growing size of this community coincided with the significant rise in lobster exports during the 1980s, which led directly to the virtual exhaustion of the resource by the early 1990s. In 1992, the sudden emergence of the sea cucumber fishery, which is highly profitable by the standards of small-scale fishers, completely changed the behaviourial patterns of the island populace and provoked a wave of immigration reminiscent of a "gold rush" (Figure 2).

On Isabel Island, where 30% of the population makes a living from fishing, fishers have become more aggressive and have generally refused to comply with the rules laid down by the authorities for the national park and the marine reserve. Given its relative physical isolation and its proximity to abundant fishing grounds, this island tends to be used as a base for illegal fishing operations. The presence of "new," recently arrived fishers is making the situation worse.

Normally, there are marked differences in attitude between the traditional fishing population and more recent arrivals. The latter see their interest as extracting the maximum possible profit from the resource, then moving on. The traditional populace, on the other hand, live on the islands permanently, and because they have been exposed for at least a generation to efforts to conserve the island ecosystem and to promote environmental education, they tend to be more sensitive to initiatives aimed at sustainable use of the resource and to be ready to make a long-term commitment to this end.

Some 70% of the fishers are affiliated with a cooperative, although cooperatives are a recent phenomenon. Before 1993, the only cooperative was in San Cristobal; since then cooperatives have been set up on the other three populated islands. Initially these bodies were created to support fishers' claims and to focus protests against the decisions of the conservation authorities, who sought to prohibit or impose catch seasons on the most profitable fisheries. The present situation is rather different, but the cooperatives are still in a process of consolidation.

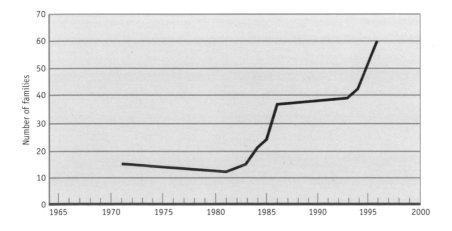

Figure 2. Number of families engaged in small-scale fisheries.

In the last 2 years, the cooperatives have been changing and have gained strength as interest groups. Their leaders have shown themselves to be effective negotiators, and in May 1997 they reached an important agreement with the government authorities in the lead-up to promulgation of the special law. Currently there is an agreement between the conservation sector and the cooperatives to create a Chamber of Fisheries that will bring all of the existing cooperatives under a single entity.

The local institutional sector

This sector is divided among the conservation authorities and the civilian and military authorities. The civilian group is made up of the autonomous authority (popularly elected) and the dependent one (appointed by the executive power).

Authority over marine resources is shared among at least seven bodies, each of which has a different degree of autonomy with respect to the national authorities on the mainland. Despite this rather confusing picture of overlap and interinstitutional squabbling, the national park has gradually been able to assert itself as the lead entity for matters relating to conservation and management of land and marine resources. Although the institution has established something of *modus vivendi* — marked by a mixture of mistrust and respect — with the island inhabitants, it has become involved in some sharp disputes, especially with those representing the fishing development sector, in part because of the lack of harmonization among the various institutional mandates.

The national institutional sector

The ministries and other high-level bodies determine the legal framework, make final decisions, and administer economic resources. In 1991, a permanent commission, with headquarters in Quito, was set up for the Galapagos Islands by executive order. Its role as a high-level advisory body and interinstitutional coordinator of programs, projects, and working groups has been subject to constant criticism by Galapagos residents because it is not seen as representing local interests.

The mainland-based business sector

This sector has been growing steadily since the 1980s. It consists of two clearly differentiated groups: the tourism industry and the commercial fishery.

The tourism industry

This is the prime generator of income in the Galapagos and contributes a quarter of the nation's entire foreign-exchange earnings. It is a very complex sector, composed of a number of powerful mainland-based companies, some with foreign capital, and small and medium-sized local operators. As mentioned, two out of every three economically active people in the Galapagos work either directly or indirectly in tourism, although the proportions may vary considerably from one island to another.

The first local operators were former fishers who shifted into tourism during the 1970s. Some of these succeeded in establishing medium-sized enterprises, whereas others were less fortunate and, unable to compete in an industry where quality is a prime consideration, sold their rights to mainland business people, who promptly became engaged in competition with local firms. Eighty percent of tourism activity and infrastructure is concentrated on just one of the islands, where location and other special attractions are most favourable. This leads to frustration and rivalry between the authorities and the inhabitants of the less-privileged islands, where economic opportunities and jobs are less attractive and varied.

There are no significant economic links between tourism and fishing, a fact that is resented by the fishers. The local populace accuse the mainlanders of taking no interest in developing the outlying economies by creating lasting and economically significant links, and blame them for spreading negative publicity that affects local small businesses and crafts. In the wake of the strikes and threatened boycotts that occurred in 1995, the mainland business sector has launched a strategy of cooperating with local people. Over the last 2 years, this sector has shown itself to be sensitive to the recession that has been afflicting the kind of tourism that happens to be the main source of clientele for the local small-scale hotel operators.

The commercial fishing sector

Operating in island waters, this sector is based in the second-largest port in the country. The strength of its ties with the island fishing populace has depended on type of product and its commercial destination. In the case of shark and sea cucumber catches, for example, which are shipped to the Asian market, the local small-scale fishers have become important suppliers.

The commercial fishery is economically important in terms of its foreign-exchange earnings and the jobs it generates in several coastal regions of the country. It is well connected with the national fishing authorities and has traditionally been able to lobby successfully for favourable legal treatment, through provincial deputies and local politicians. The financial contributions that the industry has made to fund studies by the national fisheries research institute have, however, been damaging to the latter's credibility and prestige.

This sector tends to spark conflicts with small-scale fishers over competition for resources, but the major source of opposition to its presence comes from the tourism industry, because of the way fishing activities overlap and interfere with tourism sites and conservation efforts and because of the incidental damage to native fauna (dolphins, sharks, etc.). There is also friction with the national park authorities over the fishing industry's disregard for established zoning regulations and frustration over the authorities' limited means for enforcement and supervision.

Since 1994 national park authorities and conservation officers have succeeded in having commercial fishing operations excluded from the waters of the marine reserve and in having the reserve's territorial water limits extended from 15 to 40 nautical miles from the baseline (1 nautical mile = 1 853.2 m). The attempt of the commercial fishing industry to fight this exclusion failed to garner support, either from the public or from a sufficient number of congressional deputies. Since 1994 the industry has been associated both directly and indirectly with illegal fishing activities in the Galapagos Marine Reserve, and this has damaged both its negotiating position and its public image.

Sources of conflict

The zoning of the marine reserve by executive decree, without the support of law, high-lighted at least five areas of conflict among the various interest groups (Coello 1996):

✦ Conservation interests versus small-scale and commercial fishers;

✦ Local fishers versus mainland fishers;

✦ Small-scale fishers versus tourism;

✦ Commercial fishing versus small-scale fishers, the authorities, and tourism; and

✦ Conservation authorities versus fishing authorities versus military and police authorities.

After 1990, progressively more severe restrictions were placed on free access to certain fishing resources, but no thought was given to providing compensation or finding alternative solutions. The following activities were either prohibited outright or subject to seasonal restrictions:

✦ Catching bivalve molluscs;

✦ Lobster fishing (a 7-year ban was subsequently changed to a 7-month closed season each year);

✦ Shark fishing;

✦ Extraction of black coral; and

✦ Harvesting of sea cucumbers.

By mid-1994, fishing interests were complaining that they had been without work for 14 months, thanks to the various prohibitions or closed seasons that blocked them from their primary fishing sources and the fact that a freeze had been placed on permits for expanding the size and capacity of their fleets.

The sea cucumber fishery, in which high profit margins led to flagrant violations of national park rules, was the flashpoint for disputes between local fishers, especially those of Isabel Island, and the authorities for the protected area. This activity, which had arisen as a substitute for lobster trapping during the closed season, was legally open for only a few months in 1992 and between October and December of 1994, because of the following problems:

✦ Disregard for the zoning established in the management plan for the marine reserve;

✦ Encroachment on national park lands for processing and drying the catch;

✦ Uncontrolled extraction of the resource; and

✦ Uncontrolled increase in the numbers of fishers, both local and immigrant.

The closing of this fishery provoked a series of violent reactions: illegal fishing became the number-one problem in the region (Figure 3). In 1995, a popular uprising saw the active involvement of fishers, who went as far as to threaten to kidnap tourists and to burn areas of the national park. The national park authorities confiscated large volumes of sea cucumbers, and the fishers suffered losses amounting to thousands of dollars.

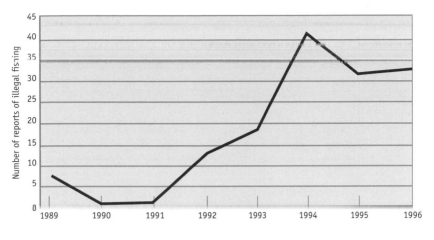

Figure 3. Extent of illegal fishing in the region.

The root causes of this upheaval were more complex and long standing, however. Warnings had been raised about the potential for conflict as a result of the large role played by the private sector and the lack of opportunities for local people to organize and participate in local government (Rodríguez 1993). Tensions existed between different types of entrepreneurs (developers and conservationist) because of unbalanced access to local resources (de Miras 1995) and between competing interests of the private sector and local population (Epler 1996). Recently, it has been suggested that there is "a clash between local interests and state-imposed policies and rules" (MacDonald 1997, p. 3), combined with structural power asymmetry between the various concerned groups (Heylings and Cruz 1998).

With respect to fishers, there was a general feeling of exclusion brought about by the systematic increase in restrictions on access to fishing resources without any process of consultation or direct or indirect measures of compensation. The underlying causes also included tensions arising from

- ✦ The perception of a tacit alliance between the conservationist forces and mainland tourism companies to displace fishers from coastal areas (the intertidal and lagoon zones) that had been their traditional fishing grounds but were now coveted by tourist interests as areas of great biological diversity and as favoured waters for recreational diving;

- ✦ The growing crisis among local tourism operators, who had invested heavily in infrastructure that was now underoccupied;

- ✦ The lack of local government funds to meet the needs of rapidly growing human settlements;

- ✦ The inequitable distribution among the islands of the benefits of tourism, which had been concentrated primarily on one island; and

- ✦ The influx of new fishers from the mainland, the increase in illegal fishing in the marine reserve, and the fines and penalties exacted against violators.

However, public opinion, both in Ecuador and abroad, was against violence as a means to solve the problems. At one point the islanders, who depended directly and indirectly on tourism and conservation activities and who had, through inaction, tacitly condoned the protest movement, finally reacted, turning against the instigators and calling publicly for peace. Paradoxically, the situation of extreme social conflict led to conditions under which negotiations became feasible. The most powerful interest groups finally recognized that there would be no winners without the genuine involvement of the local population in any decisions and that any solution would have to be arrived at through a sincere effort to demonstrate openness and a degree of flexibility.

The process of change

The process of change began in early 1996, partly as a result of the prevailing environment that demanded resolution of the conflict and partly in response to rumours that UNESCO had decided to include the Galapagos in the list of world heritage sites at risk. Local groups and national officials undertook a great many initiatives, but one key element was the change of attitude on the part of the more influential groups with respect to the weaker groups.

The national park authorities and conservation officials decided to open a dialogue aimed at overcoming the conflict and to encourage a participatory process intended to revise the marine reserve's management plan. At the same time, local associations mobilized to discuss various aspects of new special legislation, which was in draft form. A special commission created to look into the Galapagos affair also undertook a number of steps to establish points of contact with local fishers.

At the risk of oversimplification, there were three key points in the process: preparing a frame of reference for addressing the problem and defining strategies; establishing a participatory process to revise the management plan of the marine reserve; and preparing the special legislation.

A frame of reference and strategies

For the first time, expertise in conflict resolution was engaged. The resulting document, presented as a narrative analysis, diagnosed a feeling of exclusion among the local population, as a result of government policies perceived as "alien, imposed and inappropriate" (MacDonald 1997). Two broad areas of action were recommended: first, a process of strengthening local participation through new "working relations," local "rule-making," and gradual recognition of informal organizations as a formal civic body; second, the adoption of a joint problem-solving scheme based on negotiation of "needs," rather than "interests," among groups and institutions resident in the islands to shift discussion toward common "problems."

The first step included

- ✦ Identification of stakeholders;

- ✦ Recognition of the need to discuss stakeholders' interests, needs, and concerns;

- ✦ Identification of gaps, notably the absence of a strong local structure, and possible measures to strengthen it; and

- ✦ Acknowledgment of conflicts between local interests and government-imposed rules and policies.

A participatory process for revising the management plan

Once the issue of the marine reserve was accepted as a priority and the national park was designated as coordinator for revising the management plan, the park authorities — with the help of the conservation interests — were able to establish a participatory process for discussions with the various interest groups and users of marine resources.

The process was organized as a "third-party consultation–facilitation" to create the basis for long-term, joint problem-solving among conflicting groups (Heylings and Cruz 1998). A forum was created for regular discussion between involved local parties. It adapted some participatory research methods to allow participants to visualize complex issues through the use of simple techniques such as Venn diagrams, seasonal calendars, mapping, etc. (Heylings and Cruz 1998). The process began with an "interactive problem-solving workshop" that differed from previous ones in a number of important respects. For example, Puerto Ayora, on the island of Santa Cruz, was selected as the primary site for the meetings, instead of Quito. This raised the status of the local region with respect to the mainland, empowering and enhancing the profile of the weaker players — in this case, the local fishers.

Those involved in the process were classified into three categories:

+ *Participants* — Direct users, such as the fishing cooperatives, sea product merchants, representatives of the tourism industry, the conservation sector, the port and military authorities, etc.;

+ *Local observers* — Local authorities who were not directly involved (the mayors, the prefects, the governor, etc.); and

+ *National observers* — the most senior government authorities responsible for the island region: Ministry of the Environment, plus a few nongovernmental organizations.

This strategy allowed the various stakeholders to make their points of view known. There were a number of reasons behind the creation of "observer" status. In the case of the national authorities, it helped to strengthen the message of decentralization; in the case of the local authorities, it was an attempt to maintain the focus on the issues at hand. In both cases, this mechanism was seen as a way to place the authorities in a position to listen to the people. All participants and local users of the marine reserve had the same level of importance. The mainland fishing interests were excluded, because their activities were seen as incompatible with the objectives of conservation and limited use of marine resources, and to remain consistent with the proposal of extending the area of the reserve from 15 to 40 nautical miles from the baseline.

Careful preparatory work was carried out to help groups participate more effectively. This work consisted of ensuring advance distribution of documents and guidelines; making technical support available; preparing comments, proposals, and recommendations in advance; and making sure they were clear and concrete. A number of professional facilitators were appointed to provide objective help to all parties involved in revising and rewriting the management plan. These facilitators also assisted in drawing up a clear work timetable, with specific goals and outcomes. A short, clearly focused and technically oriented event was organized, aimed at reaching general consensus on the central points of the plan.

To continue the process of revising the plan, a core group of 11 people was formed: 3 representatives of the national park; 2 each from the conservation, tourism, and fishing sectors; 1 from the fisheries division; and 1 from the Merchant Marine Office. The group's mandate was to convene meetings and local discussion groups and to hold regular plenary sessions to ensure the preparation of a consensus-based document. They were given 3 months to prepare their final report.

The final product was a consensus document in three parts: (1) the principles that should govern management of the protected marine zone; (2) the points that should be included in the revised management plan (IEFANVS–SPNG 1995); and (3) aspects that should be included within a new legal framework for carrying out that plan. The document was ready on time and served as input to the work of a new government commission responsible for preparing and drafting the special law for the Galapagos National Park Service and Charles Darwin Research Station (SPNG–CHDRS 1997).

Drafting the special legislation

At the end of April 1997, after a number of false starts and in the midst of a national political crisis, the acting president issued an executive decree setting a time limit of 60 days on submission of the final draft of the special law for the Galapagos. He also broadened the inter-institutional make-up of the government commission charged with preparing that draft, inviting representatives of the local fishing, tourism, and conservation interests and of municipal governments on the islands to take part in the commission's work, and appointing the Ministry of the Environment as coordinator.

This last move was one of strategic importance because that ministry was more readily acceptable as a mediator by the parties, which allowed it to overcome the impasse created by the disputes over jurisdiction of the marine reserve between the Ministries of Agriculture and Industry. It shifted the debate to more neutral terrain and one that was more appropriate from the legal standpoint.

The commission held 12 working sessions over a period of 24 days. It organized discussions on both the islands and the mainland, based on eight drafts of the law. It delivered its final proposal 6 months after the process was launched (Ospina 1997). The proposal was handled as follows:

- ✦ Submission to the Executive for review (October 1997);

- ✦ Transmittal to Congress for discussion and approval (October 1997);

- ✦ Approval by Congress (January 1998);

- ✦ Partial veto applied by the Executive to allow commercial fishing within the 40-mile limit until approval of the new management plan, that is, for a period of 12 months (February 1998); and

- ✦ Overriding of the presidential veto, following pressure from the islanders, rendering the partial veto provision ineffective (March 1998).

The outcomes

The major outcome of the process was legal and political reform manifested in the preparation, negotiation, and adoption of the *Law on the Special Regime for the Province of Galapagos* (Congreso Nacional 1998). The principal implication of approval of this legislation has been to clarify the legal regime governing the entire island territory. This will put an end to jurisdictional disputes between the provincial and the conservation authorities, set limits on the scope of each entity's authority and action, and clearly establish the manner in which available economic resources are to be distributed.

Even more significant, it will set a precedent for the sustainable management of natural resources by local communities by defining the principles that are to govern policies and activities in the national park, the marine reserve, and the various human settlements. These principles represent an unprecedented advance; they incorporate the concepts of conservation and sustainable development into Ecuadorian legislation, in line with the international instruments adopted during the Rio Summit and in keeping with regional decentralization schemes, respect for traditional user rights, and the recognition of local management capabilities.

Specifically, the following principles have been recognized:

+ Conservation of ecological systems and biodiversity;

+ Sustainable and controlled development as a function of the carrying capacity of local ecosystems;

+ Preferential involvement of the local community, through the inclusion of special models of production, education, training, and employment;

+ Raising standards of living for the islands' inhabitants;

+ Integrated resource management; and

+ Application of the precautionary principle.

The new law has important implications for the local fishers:

+ It introduces the principles of conservation, adaptive management, and sustainable use, as well as a zoning structure for fishing activities;

+ It creates the category of marine reserve, with multiple uses and integrated administration, for protecting marine resources;

+ It confines the extraction of marine resources to the local, small-scale fishery;

+ It empowers the national park authorities to collect, administer, and distribute tax revenues to finance the marine reserve's management plan; and

+ It creates a participatory management body.

The concept of adaptive management introduces an element of flexibility that is very important for the sustainable management of resources, as it leaves open the possibility of making changes and adjusting the process as conditions evolve.

The provisions relating to residency and the exclusion of the mainland commercial fishing industry will also facilitate the move from a regime of "open access" to marine resources to one of "controlled common management," thus making it possible to define a specific number of users, give preference to local people, reduce the level of internal conflict, and facilitate long-term alliances involving commitment to, and responsibility for, the management and conservation of those resources.

One result that reflects the complexity of the negotiations and the interests at stake is the fact that the law does not make any single entity responsible for enforcement. The national park retains full jurisdiction over all of the protected land, but it must now share the mandate for the marine area with the fishery and military authorities and must respect decisions on development activities made by the appropriate regulatory body.

Introduction of this legal and political reform is expected to have the following impacts:

- ✦ Definition of general policies for conservation and sustainable development, with respect to both human settlements and protected land and sea areas;

- ✦ Strengthening of the decision-making capacity of local environmental and development authorities;

- ✦ Increased decision-making powers for local fishing cooperatives;

- ✦ Effective participation of local fishing cooperatives in the use and management of fisheries resources;

- ✦ A substantial increase in funds resulting from decentralization of taxation;

- ✦ A significant reduction in the rate of population growth, because of restrictions on immigration; and

- ✦ Control over external public and private interests seeking to exploit tourism and fishing resources.

Lessons learned

In developing countries, where the practice of democracy is usually more theoretical than real, conflicts are often resolved in favour of small elites. This rarely leads to improvements in the lives of the less-privileged segments of society. Furthermore, environmental strategies appropriate to developing nations may differ from exclusive models of park management originating with conservationists in the international science and education communities. The possibility of conflict occurring increases when local groups are excluded from participating in the planning process of conservation initiatives. In order to minimize conflicts over resource use between opposing interests in or around a protected area, it is important that distributional issues, such as power, costs, and benefits, be addressed. The planning process itself should be participatory in nature and empower and support the marginalized stakeholders while, if necessary, excluding those who might use their power to derail the proceedings.

In the Galapagos, some of the factors that contributed to the escalation of conflict were the very different degrees of power held by the various stakeholders, the fact that the cost of applying sustainable models of management were higher for the weaker players (limits on certain fisheries with no alternatives or compensation), and the failure of government to propose plans attractive enough to the weaker players to enlist their cooperation in applying models of sustainable resource management.

Although the local fishing sector was a heterogeneous group, its members shared a disadvantage in terms of balance of power, which likely fostered a common identity. The formation of the fishers cooperative was instrumental in the evolution of the group's interest in issue oriented negotiation; an empowering process of self leadership resulted in the transformation of the group from weaker player to social actor. In this way, the local fishing sector increased its bargaining power substantially and achieved the same rank as the other key stakeholders. This enabled them to accept reasonable restrictions in exchange for controlled access to certain fishing grounds.

This case study also reflects the more intricate issues intertwining governance and distributional equity through the park–province duality and related tension between national governance and aspirations for local control. Partial resolution of this tension included empowering park authorities to collect tourist fees to finance the collectively accepted management plan. Whereas some groups need to be empowered to participate effectively, others have to be deliberately left out. It may sometimes be necessary to exclude some important interest groups that, because of their economic power and political influence, might frustrate strategic alliances at some point in the negotiations. This exclusion helps level the playing field on which stakeholders must interact. Nonetheless, it is possible that, if an excluded group is powerful enough, it will exert enough pressure to recover the rights it has temporarily lost. In the case of Galapagos, although it is difficult to predict whether a conflict management process that excluded one of the important interest groups will succeed over the medium term, it seems that a national consensus has been reached in favour of conservation. In this context, it is unlikely that the commercial fisheries' lobbyists will gain the necessary support to introduce modifications to the law, although they can still influence several pending aspects for full enforcement, such as the new management plan and zonation of the marine reserve, and specific regulations concerning fisheries.

In addition to issues of distribution of power, the participatory process itself must be carefully considered. A common failing is the belief that a participatory approach to resource management can be reduced to holding one or two meetings — as if to meet some formal requirement. A participatory negotiating process aimed at community management of resources implies a systematic process whereby the various interest groups must be prepared to make concessions, but one in which they can also expect to receive concrete benefits or to be compensated for their losses in some cases. These processes may be time-consuming and complex and will require

- ✦ Application of clearly defined procedures: who is to participate, with what status, and how will decisions be made;

- ✦ Delimitation of the scope of discussion: clarifying the issues, objectives, goals, and outcomes;

- ✦ Use of appropriate materials and instruments, with a view to making as effective as possible the participation of the various interest groups, especially the weaker ones; and

- ✦ Selecting skilled facilitators who are, above all, neutral, so that they can assess the various points of view impartially.

The importance of a carefully thought out participatory process is made clear when viewing the potential negative consequences of a poorly established one. Violent confrontation could occur if the process underestimates the capacity of stakeholders who have a key role to play but are in a relatively weak position in terms of voicing their demands. Stakeholders of this kind may react with unexpected force if one or several of the following elements is present:

- ✦ If they perceive a threat to their interests because decisions are repeatedly made without their participation or consent and are seen to be unfair;

- ✦ If there is a lack of reasonable alternative proposals; or

- ✦ If they perceive that other stakeholders have won unfair advantages or are not subject to the same restrictions.

Yet, even confrontations can be converted into opportunities if, as in the case of the small-scale fishing community of the Galapagos, there is appropriate mediation and proper recognition of people's traditional user rights and their aspirations to benefit from the use of resources. In this case, in addition to an imbalance of power, conflict escalated because of the lack of an appropriate mediator. The National Fisheries Institute was unacceptable in this role because, at one point, it had been funded by the commercial fishery and was not seen as trustworthy by the local community. The Ministry of the Environment was considered a more acceptable mediator by all stakeholders.

When the marine reserve was created, conflict occurred because no effort was made to involve key users of the resource in the process through information-sharing, persuasion, or negotiation. The reserve was created without consultation or attempt at compensation. Lip service is regularly paid to such concepts as "sustainable resource management," "local participation," "compensatory measures," etc. However, in many cases the legal framework, financial resources, or imagination are lacking to formulate new and effective strategies and persuade the local populace to form lasting alliances for conservation and sustainable use of natural resources (on the basis of equal participation and responsibility). If community people are to be induced to make changes in their personal habits or activities to cooperate in the sustainable management of resources, it is essential that

- ✦ Decisions are made with the participation and consent of all the players involved;

- ✦ Alternative measures and reasonable compensation are considered for those affected by the changes (exchanging the free-access regime for one of community management of natural resources is a powerful incentive for involving the local populace); and

- ✦ The "sacrifices" accompanying change are shared fairly among all stakeholders, and this is done in a transparent manner.

In conclusion, the Galapagos is an exceptionally valuable area in terms of conservation, both domestically and worldwide. The degree of decentralization achieved through the new legal regime is unprecedented in the country and is even more remarkable when one considers that the island population is so small that is has very little political clout. This case is an example of how conflict over natural resource management between conservation and livelihood interests was harnessed to facilitate resolution resulting in greater equity and sustainability. To do so, a change in the distribution of power, costs, and benefits needed to be brought about, as well as a truly participatory process. Finally, very diverse stakeholders were involved in the conflict resolution: local, national, and international; powerful and weak; government and private; prodevelopment and proconservation.

In the short term, it is likely that the powerful groups that were excluded will use their influence to lobby Congress to modify the law and retain access to the fishery resources of the reserve. Over the medium term, the fishing cooperatives will propose changes to increase their individual production capacity. Perhaps, the best way to avoid future conflict is to strengthen the institutional capacity of the cooperatives to comply with the rules and provisions of the management plan. A new era of local participation has started that may make compliance and enforcement of regulations easier to achieve. However, it is too soon to predict whether commitment among and within groups will be strong enough to find common ground now that the "common adversary" is out of the way and new sets of sensitive issues are under discussion.

Acknowledgments

I thank the many people who contributed information for this report. I appreciate and respect the organizations, institutions, and individuals who over the last several years have devoted their time, resources, and energy to seeking authentic, participatory, and successful solutions to the important problems addressed here. The results could well be taken as a precedent, not only in Ecuador, but also in many other parts of the world. I salute the people of the Galapagos, especially the fishing community, and all the young professionals who are working so effectively for the conservation of these islands.

References

Coello, S. 1996. Situación y opciones de manejo de las pesquerías de Galápagos. *In* Estudio de factiblidad para el Banco Inter-Americano de Desarrollo y la Comisión Permanente para las Islas Galapagos [interim report]. Inter-American Development Bank, Washington, DC, USA. 447 pp.

Congreso Nacional, Plenario de las Comisiones Legislativas. 1998. Ley de régimen especial para la conservación y desarrollo sustentable de la Provincia de Galápagos. Congreso Nacional, Quito, Ecuador. 42 pp.

de Miras, C. 1995. Las Islas Galápagos un reto económico tres contradicciones básicas. Paper presented at the Symposium on Perspectivas Científicas y de Manejo para las Islas Galápagos, 8–9 Nov 1995, Quito, Ecuador. Charles Darwin Foundation for the Galapagos Islands; Institut Français de Recherche Scientifique pour le Développement en Coopération, Paris, France. 16 pp.

El Comercio. 1998. Fundación Natura rechaza veto a la ley especial para Galápagos. El Comercio, Quito, Ecuador, 26 Feb.

Epler, B. 1996. El turismo en Galápagos. *In* Gesellschaft für Organisation, Planung und Ausbildung. Estudio de factiblidad para el Banco Interamericano de Desarrollo y la Comisión Permanente para las Islas Galapagos [interim report]. Inter-American Development Bank, Washington, DC, USA. 447 pp.

GOPA (Gesellschaft für Organisation, Planung und Ausbildung). 1996. Estudio de factiblidad para el Banco Interamericano de Desarrollo y la Comisión Permanente para las Islas Galapagos [preliminary report]. GOPA; Inter-American Development Bank, Washington, DC, USA. 40 pp.

Heylings, P.; Cruz, F. 1998. Common property, conflict and participatory management in the Galapagos Islands. Charles Darwin Research Station, Puerto Ayora-Galapagos. Paper presented at the 8th

Annual Conference on Common Property of the International Association for the Study of Common Property, Jun 1998, Burnaby, BC, Canada. 20 pp.

IEFANVS–SPNG (Instituto Ecuatoriano Forestal de Areas Naturales y Vida Silvestre; Servicio Parque Nacional Galápagos) 1995. Plan de manejo del Parque Nacional Galápagos. United Nations Educational, Scientific and Cultural Organization; United Nations Develpment Programme; Comisión Permanente para las Islas Galápagos; Charles Darwin Foundation for the Galapagos Islands, Puerto Ayora, Galápagos, Ecuador. 166 pp.

Macdonald, T., Jr. 1997. Conflict in the Galapagos Islands: analysis and recommendations for management. Report for the Charles Darwin Foundation. Harvard University, Center for International Affairs, Program on Nonviolent Sanctions and Cultural Survival, Cambridge, MA, USA. 15 pp.

Ospina, P. 1997. La pesca industrial en Galápagos. Fundación Natura, Quito, Ecuador. 12 pp.

PDR–CPIG (Presidencia de la República; Comisión Permanente para las Islas Galápagos). 1992. Plan de manejo de la Reserva de Recursos Marinos de Galápagos. PDR, Quito, Ecuador. 143 pp. Aprobado mediante Decreto Ejecutivo no. 3573, R.O. no. 994, 6 Aug.

Rodríguez, J. 1993. Las Islas Galápagos. Estructura geográfica y propuesta de gestión territorial. Abya Yala Press, Quito, Ecuador. 276 pp.

SPNG–CHDRS (Servicio Parque Nacional Galápagos [Galapagos National Park Service]; Charles Darwin Research Station). 1997. Primera instancia de un proceso participativo local para la revisión del plan de manejo de la Reserva Marina de Galápagos: justificación y puntos de consenso de los usuarios e instituciones representadas en Galápagos [document-based points agreed to during the Workshop–Dialogue, 5–7 Jun 1997, Puerto Ayora, Galapagos, and the work of the Grupo Núcleo formed by representatives of the local fisheries, tourism and conservation organisations]. 17 pp.

Concept

Peace

Chapter 9

PEACE AND CONFLICT IMPACT ASSESSMENT

Kenneth D. Bush and Robert J. Opp

*In this chapter, we explore how community-based natural resource management inter-
ventions affect the "peace and conflict environment" in which they function.
Development interventions may generate or exacerbate conflict or they may build the conditions for more harmonious communities on a sustainable basis. The conventions of
political and economic life — "the rules of the game" — are generally weighted against
community responses in natural resource management as in other areas, there is a case
for instituting peace and conflict assessment. Such research will guide interventions in
ways which minimize conflict and build harmony, ultimately helping to generate new
development opportunities and ways of working.*

Researchers and development workers are well aware of the limitations imposed on their
work by the ebb and flow of violent and nonviolent conflict in various locations. However,
we are only slowly turning our attention toward systematic consideration and measurement of the impact of our development work on the dynamics of peace and conflict. It
became clear that development does not necessarily equal peace — it may also generate
or exacerbate conflict (for example, by challenging traditional values or authority structures, disrupting gender or other socially determined roles, raising the stakes of economic
competition, creating "winners" and "losers," and so on). Conversely, development projects may have peacebuilding impacts that are unintended and, thus, undocumented and
unable to inform future development work.

Interventions designed to affect access to, and control over, natural resources are
located in areas in which the propensity for conflict (both violent and nonviolent) is perhaps higher than in other areas of development activity. This is particularly the case when
issues are cast in zero-sum terms and when the stakes include economic livelihoods, a

sense of community, issues of political autonomy and control, as well as fundamental issues of justice, injustice, sustainable development, and exploitation.

The community-specific focus of this book requires us to bear in mind the general tendency for the "rules of the economic and political game" *not to be weighted toward communities*, whether in the area of natural resource management or in other areas of activity. Given the politicized, high-stakes, conflict-prone setting of community-based natural resource management (CBNRM), it is appropriate to develop and institutionalize a systematic process for assessing its impact on the "peace and conflict environments" (and vice versa). The costs of not doing so are exceptionally high in economic terms, but, more important, in human terms.

Peace and conflict impact assessment

Peace and conflict impact assessment (PCIA) is a means of anticipating and evaluating the impacts of proposed and completed development interventions on the structures and processes that strengthen the prospects for peaceful coexistence and decrease the likelihood of the outbreak, recurrence, or continuation of violent conflict; and the structures and processes that increase the likelihood that conflict will be dealt with through violent means (Bush 1998). In essence, PCIA is a means of systematically considering the positive and negative impacts of development projects on peace and conflict dynamics in conflict-prone regions. This applied research is supported by the International Development Research Centre and seeks ultimately to make peace and conflict issues an integral component of our development thinking and programing.

The integration of peace and conflict concerns into our development thinking calls for a number of tools to be used in the full range of development activities in conflict-prone regions from traditional development projects in agriculture, communications, and health to more overtly political projects in good governance, democratic development, and human rights. The kit would include tools for preproject proposal assessment, in-project monitoring and decision-making, and postproject evaluation and training.

Such tools would be used by a range of development actors — although different actors might rely on them in different ways. International donors might use them to guide project selection, funding decisions, and monitoring. Implementing or operational agencies might well use them to design projects and guide operational decisions. Communities in violence-prone regions may use them to assess the utility, relevance, and efficacy of development initiatives sponsored from outside. Although there have been a number of notable assessments of international initiatives in postconflict reconstruction and humanitarian intervention (Millwood 1996; CMI–NCG 1997; OED 1998), no equivalent to gender analysis or environmental impact assessment has developed to allow us to anticipate, monitor, and assess the impacts of our work in peacebuilding and postconflict reconstruction.

The examination of CBNRM through the lens of PCIA is an opportunity to develop a better understanding of both. The cases described in this volume are not, for the most part, set in "postconflict settings." Nonetheless, the combination of the social, political, and economic environments within each case and the sensitivities inherent in natural resource management justify the definition of these cases as "conflict prone." The term "conflict" does not necessarily entail violence.

Ideally, PCIA would be most useful if it helped us to understand not only the dynamics of conflicts but also, specifically, the escalation toward violence, so that preventive and tension-reducing actions might be taken. Such actions need not be grandiose high-profile initiatives. They could be local-level changes in our interventions designed to build trust and understanding or identify common interests between groups in a volatile setting. In other words, the changes may well focus on the way we do our work, rather than the type of work we do. Thus, whether our particular concern is CBNRM, health initiatives, or credit schemes, the question remains the same: What is the impact of this intervention on the dynamics and structures of peace and conflict in a particular area?

The nature of conflict

PCIA first requires a consideration of the nature of conflict itself. Conflict is not necessarily a negative or destructive phenomenon. In essence, development — including CBNRM in the current context — is *inevitably* conflictual, destabilizing, and subversive because it challenges established economic, social, or political power structures, which inhibit individuals and groups from pursuing their full potential. However, there is a need to maintain a clear conceptual distinction between violent and nonviolent conflict. Although PCIA focuses more on violent conflict, it has a special interest in those liminal moments at which nonviolent conflict "turns" ("re-turns") violent and is militarized. In this context, the presence or absence of conflict-mediating mechanisms and institutions are central factors influencing whether a conflict passes the threshold into violence — this might include representative political systems, a transparent and fair judicial system, an equitable social system, and so on.

One such example is the case of Cahuita National Park in Costa Rica, in which a local Committee of Struggle organized a peaceful takeover after the government orchestrated a sharp increase in park entrance fees without consulting local communities who depend on tourist revenue for their livelihoods (Weitzner and Fonseca Borrás, this volume). Why did the conflict not turn violent? One clue can be found in the statement of a community leader: "We knew we were right, because we knew that the law backed us." Simply put, the community did not lose faith in the legitimacy and ability of the judicial system to guarantee local peoples' rights in the face of national government action. Equally important, the legal structures proved able to deliver a ruling that was seen to be just. This sustains a mutually reinforcing dynamic, whereby the "given" legitimacy of legal structures underwrites the legitimacy of the court's ruling, in turn reinforcing general acceptance of the ruling, which feeds back into the perceived legitimacy of the system.

Some have argued that violent conflict is the ultimate expression of the breakdown of a society's systems of governance and that reconstruction, therefore, rests primarily on the renegotiation and refashioning of new systems of governance at the community, subnational, and national levels (Tschirgi 1994). Thus, the movement from conflict "management" toward conflict "resolution" or "transformation" requires strategies and interventions that promote institutional arrangements that can facilitate and sustain the transition from violent conflict toward sustainable development. An appealing feature of this kind of approach is the way its analysis of the problem is tied directly to an understanding of the nature of solutions.

A further example is the case of land conflict in Copan, Honduras, where the unresolved murder of a Chorti peasant leader illustrates the inability of the judicial system to mediate the conflict, as well as the problems inherent in a situation where large disparities of power and wealth exist (Chenier et al., this volume). It is interesting to note that, in this case, the Chorti did not resort to violence, even though this is the kind of environment within which such a move by the less powerful actors in the struggle for equitable land redistribution would indicate dissatisfaction with existing legal and political mechanisms and the perceived need for extreme tactics. This suggests that the absence of legitimate sociopolitical structures may be a necessary, but not necessarily sufficient, condition for a turn to violence.

In this example, we also see that the perceived failure of the Honduran judicial system is combined with the "structural violence" inherent in disparities of power and wealth. Thus, the manifestation of overt violence in the cause of land reform is better seen as an escalation and transformation of violence (from structural to physical), rather than simply the reactive frustration of peasants. Although it is still too early to assess the efficacy of its interventions, the innovative approach of the Honduran Network for Collaborative Natural Resource Management deserves close monitoring because it explicitly builds on the understanding that natural resource access and power disparities are intimately related and thus must be addressed in an integrated fashion.

To the extent that the judicial system is seen to support an unjust status quo, it encourages extrajudicial means to achieve justice and affect change. Such extrajudicial means need not entail violence: consider, for example, the *satyagraha* of Mahatma Gandhi, and the everyday forms of resistance by peasants toward exploitative authorities, such as tardiness, inefficiency, subtle subversion, and disrespect. However, in time, it is almost inevitable that an authority system (political, economic, judicial, social) that subsidizes or employs violence as a means of control will evoke a violent response by some individuals or subgroups from within the "victim community." But in examining the motives behind such violent acts, we should bear in mind that violence is but one response among many. In our efforts to explain them, we must do more than explain why there was dissent, *we must explain why such dissent was expressed violently.* Answering this question will require us to consider the full range of contributing factors including structural conditions, proximate or triggering events, as well as the random element of chance.

Despite an emphasis on the institutional dimensions of violence and peacebuilding, it is important to appreciate the variations of and the connections–disconnections between different manifestations and types of violence. In South Africa, for example, there is a disturbing tendency to disconnect the "political," structural violence of the apartheid past from the "criminal" violence of the postapartheid present. The danger of this disconnection (conceptually and pragmatically) is twofold: it inhibits us from examining the relations between political and criminal violence, the legacy of apartheid, and the full nature of contemporary violence in South Africa; and it tends to limit the scope of our responses to the legal–policing realm, rather than the socioeconomic–political realm. If the source of the contemporary violence is political, social, or economic, then a rigid legal–policing response will be as problematic in the postapartheid transition as it was during apartheid.

The common argument in South Africa is that the removal of the violence-dampening institutions of apartheid led to the current explosion in violent crime. However, this argument uses the term "violence" in a very narrow and conservative way. It makes sense to recognize the structural violence inflicted upon South Africans in the form of poverty, infant mortality, stifled advancement, and so on. If we accept that the term "violence" may have a variety of meanings and manifestations, then we can begin to see that the postapartheid era reveals, not so much a rise in violence as a change in the *type* of violence characterizing social, political, and economic relations. Contemporary manifestations of violence in South Africa *or any country* are not *sui generis*. They follow the trajectory of a country's historical, societal, and political developments. An understanding of the present requires a consideration of its linkages to the recent and distant past. The implication for the development of a PCIA is that it underscores the need to peel away the multiple layers of violence to build a sense of its dynamics, history, and trajectory.

The CBNRM cases mentioned above highlight the fact that the application of PCIA in conflict-prone settings can raise difficult moral questions concerning the place of violence in efforts to effect change, because violence may be used to either maintain *or overthrow* an unjust system. Thus, the avoidance of violent conflict does not necessarily serve the cause of social justice. Indeed, it *may be* that overt physical violence is necessary to overthrow a system that is unjust and founded on different forms of structural violence. As a minimum, it is reasonable to expect that challenges to an unjust status quo — for example, an unfair land tenure system — will almost inevitably increase conflict between those benefiting from the existing system and those exploited by it. The central issue is not simply whether a conflict may be "managed" nonviolently, it is also whether the outcome will be just, equitable, and sustainable. And while such consequentialist logic (that is, the ends justify the means) might justify or legitimize the use of violence, experience shows that violence is a particularly blunt instrument that is prone to generating consequences that are unanticipated, unintended, and uncontrollable (Sahnoun 1994; Bush 1997).

The case of the Galapagos Islands (Oviedo, this volume) — in which a segment of the local population threatened to take tourists hostage and burn parts of the island in its battle against the national park — suggests that even the threat of violence may generate a counterproductive backlash from former supporting constituencies. Nonetheless, although support for the groups calling for the use of violence evaporated, this episode was a critical juncture because it created conditions propitious for negotiation, which included the participation of the local fishing community. In other words, the impact of the threat of violence was, in fact, ambivalent.

Finally, and somewhat paradoxically, we should bear in mind that violent conflict may *generate* new development opportunities and ways of working. The experiences of Zimbabwe, Nicaragua, Eritrea, Somaliland, and South Africa suggest that violent conflict may serve as the anvil on which new and progressive social and economic structures, political solutions, and development opportunities may be formed. This particular point was underscored in a case study of the War-Torn Societies Project of the United Nations Research Institute for Social Development, in which the Eritrean partners stated emphatically that their society was war born, not war torn (Tschirgi, personal communication, 1998[1]).

Critical questions regarding the context of conflict:

✦ What are the legacies of the conflict(s) in the immediate area of the proposed intervention (for example, in the areas of the local economy; food security; the physical and psychological health of the community; personal security; availability of leadership; physical infrastructure; intergroup relations; women, children and vulnerable populations; and so on)?

✦ What are the political–social dimensions of the conflict (for example, religion, cultural factors, group identities, political structures and institutions)?

---

[1] N. Tschirgi, personal communication, 1998; see http://www.unrisd.org/wsp.

The interplay of resources in conflict-prone settings

Conflicts over natural resources do not occur solely at the material level; they inevitably have symbolic elements as well. Understanding the relationship between identity and geography is crucial for tracing the ways in which CBNRM interventions in conflict-prone environments may exacerbate conflict or contribute to peaceful development.

If we are to develop a clear sense of the dynamics of peace and conflict in a particular case, we need to employ a broad understanding of the term "resources" to allow us to trace the ways in which they interact (see Uphoff 1990). Here, it is essential to consider the ways in which struggles over natural resources can be harnessed to other battles by political entrepreneurs. It is quite possible that the boundaries of group identity may be manipulated and politicized as part of the struggle for natural, economic, or political resources. Thus, for example, the mobilization of group identity and the mobilization and extraction of natural resources may be mutually reinforcing in certain cases.

Identity resources

The mobilization of identity is a process whereby particular axes of identity within heterogeneous groups become more politically salient, thereby affecting both intragroup and intergroup boundaries. This process highlights, or even inserts, markers of difference between and within groups while obscuring possible markers of similarity. It appears that the mobilization of one group may stimulate countermobilization by other groups. Although this process is largely catalyzed and articulated by mobilizers, it is channelled through existing state and social structures, processes, networks, and institutions. The mobilization of identity merits attention because it sheds lights on the drawing of the dividing cum battle lines; it is a critical component in the construction and maintenance of a subgroup's claim to legitimacy that, consequently, affects both the efficacy of group boundary maintenance and the mobilization of resources.

This dynamic is illustrated in the case study of the Nuba Mountains, Sudan (Suliman, this volume). Although the roots of the conflict in this region lay in the increasing scarcity of resources, as a result of drought and incursion of mechanized farming operations, group identity was increasingly mobilized and politicized the longer the conflict persisted. The polarization of the Baggara and the Nuba made differences *within* groups less salient than the differences *between* groups. Internal divisions were overcome through a process that consolidated a sense of identity based, not necessarily on ancestry or religion (for at times, these two elements are shared between the groups), but on resource use — one group defining itself as nomadic traders in need of grazing land; the other, as agriculturalists. In this case, we see that the battle lines were drawn up on the basis of politicized identities tied implicitly to resource use.

Any attempt to manage or resolve the conflict taking place in the Nuba Mountains, then, must take into account the politicized and layered symbolic elements used to define the struggle itself. It will not be enough to work out material agreements on resource use. Peace structures will also need to build on the presence of the new-found "Nubaness" in the region, as the management or resolution of a multifaceted conflict must, by definition, also be multifaceted. Thus, Suliman succeeds in demonstrating that despite the many efforts to describe and "explain" Sudan as a case of "ethnic conflict," such analyses are incomplete and often misleading. Although group identities are an essential feature of the dynamics of conflict, Suliman points out that to understand their mobilization and politicization, we must appreciate the catalyzing impact of resource scarcity on the volatility of intergroup relations. Identity on its own does not create conflict, no more than does resource scarcity. However, when combined, the result is more unstable and volatile that each ingredient on its own.

A complementary example is provided by case of the Nam Ngum Watershed (Hirsch et al., this volume), which details the intersection of several dimensions of resource conflict, including competition between neighbouring villages from different ethnic groups, which is wrapped up in distinct traditional production systems, population movement, and the residual effects of wartime devastation.

Critical questions about identity resources:

+ Will the intervention affect access to, or distribution of, a natural resource in ways that may be seen as favouring one group over another (regardless of the basis of social differentiation, whether ethnic, linguistic, clan, kin group, economic, and so on)?

+ Does the natural resource involved in a particular intervention cut across territory that is associated with different identity groups?

+ Has the area affected by the intervention experienced intergroup tensions in the past? What is the likely impact of the intervention, and how can it be minimized or managed?

+ How likely is it that "ethnic mobilizers" will attempt to score political points at the expense of the CBNRM intervention?

+ Can CBNRM be structured in a way that builds cross-group interest *and participation* in the success of an intervention?

Symbolic contests over resources

If we can cast identity as a resource, then we are better able to appreciate the symbolic elements of contestations over natural resources. Moore (1993) has highlighted the importance of symbolic contestations over resources in the context of Eastern Zimbabwe. Using a "Gramscian perspective" on resource conflicts, he shows how local communities, threatened by the expansion of a national park, draw on social memories such as the association of imposed government policies with the former colonial administration as "symbolic capital" to argue for changes in the park boundaries. In this framework, culture and politics must be seen as interdependent:

> Values and beliefs mobilize action, shape social identities, and condition understandings of collective interests ... . Ideologies contribute to the formation of productive relations and do not derive, mechanically, from them. Struggles over symbolic processes are conflicts over material relations of production, the distribution of resources, and ultimately power.
>
> (Moore 1996)

Although Moore's work is based on a detailed ethnography of one locale, it is still useful in pointing out the necessity of employing a culturally–historically informed analysis of processes of conflict and dialogue. In cases such as the Cahuita National Park in Costa Rica, for example, the importance of understanding competing views of "conservation" between the state and local communities can be seen. Moreover, in cases such as the

Nam Ngum Watershed, the complex interweaving of ethnicity and historical events inevitably affects the ways in which "traditional" villages and resettled communities interact and compete with one another for scarce resources. Without understanding the social fabric of the context (and consequently the symbolic elements of the struggle), much of the nature of the resource conflict will be lost to an outside observer.

Critical questions about symbolic elements:

+ What is the cultural significance of the area affected by the intervention? In other words, what does it *mean* to the communities involved?

+ To the extent that an area is valued culturally by different groups in different ways, what will be the impact on the intervention, and how will it balance, broker, or accommodate these different values?

+ Might the symbolic value of an area affect community participation? Might it increase the volatility of community responses?

+ Does the symbolic significance of an area affect *whether* or *how* an intervention can be undertaken?

The neutrality of outside interventions

Although CBNRM efforts often take place within extremely charged and sensitive environments, they are typically viewed as neutral initiatives undertaken by nonpartisan actors seeking to create — or provide a neutral space for — public discussion among principal stakeholders. In many cases, CBNRM interventions are contrasted with more "traditional" mediation or advocacy approaches, whereby organizations align themselves with one or more stakeholders. Inevitably however, despite their professed neutrality, such interventions will have a different impact on different actors (implicitly, as well as explicitly) when the aim of an external actors is to "balance the playing field."

Power relations can never be assumed to be equal in such situations; actors cannot be expected to possess the levels of confidence, authority, and power resources that would allow them to participate equally in a dialogue:

> In nation-states and local communities composed of rural and urban women and men from vastly different class backgrounds, the peasant and the bureaucrat command neither equal cultural capital nor economic resources ... their relative participation or exclusion from "policymaking" is fundamentally shaped by power, history, and social relations.
>
> (Moore 1994)

The observation made by Gayle Smith (1993) concerning neutrality and evenhandedness in humanitarian interventions is equally applicable to CBNRM:

> The principles of humanitarianism require unobstructed loyalty to civilian populations and political impartiality ... . While aid providers should not take partisan political stands (except, perhaps in extreme cases such as Nazi Germany, and Khmer Rouge Cambodia), providing aid in a conflict [note: conflict-prone setting, in the current context], is in its impact and implications, an extremely political act. If the political environment ... is disregarded, there is a high risk that relief work by outsiders will intensify conflict or fall victim to manipulation by one or more parties to the conflict.

When it comes to assessing the impact of a CBNRM intervention on the peace and conflict environment, the variability of its effect on different actors, as well as the charged social conditions in which the process occurs, should give us pause in considering whether the role of the facilitator is really neutral. Although an external actor may avoid assuming advocacy roles, which involve direct challenges and opposition to other stakeholders on behalf of one, it is unlikely that an external intervener can be apolitical. In fact, everything about the CBNRM process is politicized, as it entails direct and strategic struggles over the material and symbolic elements of natural resources and will, thus, be seen to challenge the existing balance of power. Thus, from a PCIA perspective, no CBNRM intervention could be labeled neutral. The common perception of neutrality that pervades most developmental interventions in conflict-prone regions inhibits our ability to appreciate the political implications *and impact* of our work.

Within this very politicized environment, it is possible that claims to neutrality might be made instrumentally; that is, interventions may be portrayed as neutral to gain entry and to increase the chances of achieving their desired outcome.

Critical questions regarding neutrality of the intervention:

◆ What are the likely direct and indirect impacts of the intervention on the balance (or imbalance) of political, economic, and social power in affected areas? Does it maintain or challenge the status quo?

◆ What is the relationship between those involved in the CBNRM initiative and the local government? What is the initiative's latitude of action, that is, how independent is it from interference by vested interests, both governmental and societal?

Natural resource conflicts and "upscale and downscale linkages"

Our examination of CBNRM conflicts often focuses narrowly on the immediate, local level. However, conflicts over natural resources are not necessarily bound geographically, but may have linkages to larger systems and processes — political, economic, social, ecological, and so on.

A case in point is the conflict in the Nuba Mountains, Sudan (Suliman, this volume). Although local populations of Baggara and Nuba struggled over local areas, the conflict was strongly linked to the much larger situation of generalized conflict in the Sudan. The Nuba found themselves as "natural" allies of the Sudanese People's Liberation Army rebel groups in the south of Sudan, as the Baggara were supported and armed by the Jellaba government in Khartoum. Thus, local groups found themselves manipulated by macro-level actors with very different political and ideological objectives. Without understanding the dynamic of these linkages and their implications for local arenas, it is impossible to analyze adequately arrangements for management of natural resources in the area.

Under a political–economic lens, the Nam Ngum case suggests the catalytic importance of government reforms within the Lao PDR transitional economy from the mid-1980s onward — reforms that sought to move away from collective production within socialist central planning toward a market economy. As Hirsch et al. (this volume) write,

> The market reforms are particularly significant in encouraging intensified resource use instead of subsistence-based production. The reforms also involve an outward orientation of macroeconomic policy, based on attracting foreign investment to develop the country's natural resources for export; within this, hydropower has received particular attention. The Nam Ngum case thus provides something of a microcosm and a baseline for anticipation of the local implications of such policies.

Conflicts over natural resources may also be exacerbated by international pressures. In many parts of the developing world, structural adjustment policies and continuing debt burdens force national governments to make difficult trade-offs resulting in policies that increase local conflicts, as in the cases of Cahuita Park, Costa Rica, Nusa Tenggara, Indonesia, and the Galapagos Islands, Ecuador. At the same time, the international arena may also become the direct focus of struggle for local people, such as in the case of the Chorti of Honduras, who were able to take advantage of their government's international commitment to a global agreement enshrining the rights of indigenous peoples. In this case, international agreements became the fulcrum used by local communities to leverage issues onto the national agenda and to spur their government into action.

In terms of assessing the impact of CBNRM interventions, we must compare local contexts with wider processes to understand motivations and the direction of unfolding events. Not only may national and international structures and process affect the peace and conflict impact of CBNRM efforts at the local level, but such efforts may also have a "bottom-up" impact on regional and national levels as well. The case study of the Coastal Development Plan (CDP) in northern Philippines (Talaue-McManus et al., this volume) suggests that the resolution of tensions over coastal development in Bolinao had a positive effect on the process of municipal governance when the Municipal Council endorsed "the whole consultative and participatory process used in the CDP" and announced that it "should be iterated and incorporated in the formulation and passage of municipal legislation."

Critical questions about linkages:

✦ What are the most likely international sources of influence (positive and negative) on the intervention, for example, fluctuations in commodity prices, structural adjustment policies, flows in the tourist trade, regional destabilization (political, military, economic), parallel initiatives, and so on?

✦ What might be the direct and indirect ripple effects of the intervention beyond its immediate area of impact, for example, demonstration effects, creation of legal or political precedents for others to build on, the introduction of new mechanisms for CBNRM, and so on?

Deconstructing "community"

A closer look at the notion of "community" reveals a particularly interesting set of issues for the current study because it highlights the spatial dimension of collective identity. What is community? Put simply, it is a shared belief in a common identity that is rooted in *an attachment to place*. It is a phenomenon that is catalyzed at the intersection of psychology and geography. A group's sense of attachment to place and to each other may be maintained — even sharpened — when a community is separated from its geographic referent. This is evident, for example, in the attachment of some refugee or diaspora "communities" to a homeland that no longer exists. This phenomenon represents the elements of the "symbolic construction" of community, where "the consciousness of community is ... encapsulated in perception of its boundaries, boundaries which are themselves largely constituted by people in interaction" (Cohen 1985, p. 13).

In the context of CBNRM, attachment to place may also be sharpened by the threat of displacement, as a direct result of the struggle over access to, or control over, natural resources. Here, "dis-placement" refers both to physical eviction and to the sociological and psychological disequilibria that result from the loss of the familiar. When threatened with displacement, it is natural for members of a community to work to consolidate their symbols and boundaries of self-definition. As we have seen in a number of the case studies, at times this has involved the development of the organizational skills needed to protect individual and community rights and interests.

By definition, CBNRM is anchored in a very particular, very physical, package of territory. Although the case studies illustrate the clashes of interest between local communities and outside actors (forestry departments, private business, and so on), it would be incomplete to analyze such conflict as simply the competition for control over natural resources. Further, although we may *describe* the various interests of different groups, it is problematic to *define* groups in terms of their interests as this inhibits us from asking (let alone addressing) such critical questions as Why are these interests being articulated and pursued at a particular point in time? Within heterogeneous communities or other social units (including organizations or subcommunity groups), exactly whose interests are being served?

Central to the competition between groups is the struggle to define the "essential" meaning of contested space. The battle to define the space is intimately tied to self-definition of the community that inhabits that space. In one case, in a Canadian indigenous community's struggle to prevent an outside corporation from implementing a "super quarry" project on sacred territory "being opposed to the quarry became an expression of ethnic identity ... . The issue presented an opportunity to publicly define Mi'kmaq culture in opposition to mainstream values" (Hornborg 1994).

Among the studies presented here, this concept is illustrated by the case study of the Nusa Tenggara uplands of Indonesia which are defined as sacred by major clan groups (Fisher et al., this volume). In stark contrast, outside interests seek to define that same space narrowly in terms of its tourism potential. Each definition determines the range of activities that may be legitimately undertaken there. The sacredness of the mountains is essential to the clans' sense of identity. A perceived challenge to that sacredness is not simply an issue of land use. It may be perceived as a threat to a common identity that is rooted in *an attachment to place*. To the extent that such competition is framed in terms of community identity, then the intransigence and intractability of conflict increases.

When, therefore, does an external threat serve to consolidate a community (its ability to function as a social entity) or consolidate its sense of community (its ability to define itself as a social entity)? Conversely, when, why, and how do external threats weaken these abilities? What types of threats are presented? Do different types of threats evoke different types of responses? These are some of the questions that must be answered to understand the peace and conflict environments in which CBNRM interventions take place.

The case of the Wanaggameti Conservation Area (WCA) in Indonesia (Fisher et al., this volume) again offers insights into some of these issues. The kinds of tensions generated by the contestation over the definition of community within the context of natural resource management as local government moved to relocate communities from the periphery of the forest reserve can serve to consolidate the sense of community and have the potential to be used by community leaders to mobilize opposition to government authorities. It might be argued that, to the extent that such efforts at displacement fail, their mobilizational utility for community organizers *increases*, as it sharpens the sense of threat by providing an illustration of what *could happen* in the absence of organized resistance and community response. Indeed, in the WCA case, "Fear of escalating conflict and concern over the lack of a comprehensive management plan for the WCA led to the organization of a series of participatory surveys and collaborative planning measures" (Fisher et al., this volume, p. 67).

Finally, it should be noted that communities are not always as united as they may appear, either in their resistance to external threat or in their representations stemming from local people or outsiders. Communities, often assumed by national governments or development agencies to be homogenous in their composition and interests, contain a multiplicity of social actors engaged in contests of meaning and representation. Although a community leader may present a picture of unity, the social reality is more likely one of heterogeneity, social differentiation, and possibly conflict (Murphy 1990; Scott 1990). Members may be differentiated by class, race, ethnicity, gender, age, and a number of other lines of division, experiencing life from a variety of perspectives, and holding a number of different skills and knowledge.

In the case of Cahuita National Park, Costa Rica (Weitzner and Fonseca Borrás, this volume), these differentiations were evident in the stated dissatisfaction of community members with the legitimacy of representation found on the local management commit- tee, set up to make decisions on natural resource use. Relations within the management committee are also revealing: the two government representatives seem to wield dispro- portionate amounts of power compared with the three community members, setting the agendas, chairing the meetings, and even taking the minutes. Their vastly different per- spectives are illustrated by one community representative's statement that government representatives "feel they have supremacy over us community people … . For the time being we're at an impasse … because the MINAE [Ministry of Environment and Energy] representatives think that their ideas should prevail" (cited in Weitzner and Fonseca Borrás, this volume, p. 141).

The multiplicity of perspectives held by community members (and those external to communities) provides us with an important clue to understanding the origin and nature of social conflict. As Long and Villareal (1994) point out,

> If … we recognize that we are dealing with "multiple realities," potentially conflicting social and normative interests, and diverse and fragmented bodies of knowledge, then we must look closely at the issue of whose interpretations or models … prevail over those of other actors and under what conditions. Knowledge processes are embedded in social processes that imply aspects of power, authority and legitimation; and they are just as likely to reflect and contribute to the conflict between social groups as they are to lead to the establishment of common perceptions and interests.

Recognizing the role of multiple realities in establishing authority and shaping power relations extends beyond the boundaries of local communities to comprehending how CBNRM processes, involving both local and external actors, can be shaped by contesta- tions of knowledge. External organizations, national government agencies, and powerful local actors may create and enforce particular representations of community that suit pol- icy purposes or even for personal gain (Murray Li 1996).

Understanding how representations of community (or community-based manage- ment processes) are established and for what purpose is crucial for PCIA, as it points to unequal power relations and marginalized perspectives.

Critical questions about "community":

+ Given the heterogeneity of groups, exactly whose interests are being served by an intervention? Are internal divisions being created (exacerbated) by the intervention?

+ To what extent is an intervention likely to divide groups (for example, cause friction over the management of resources or the distribution of benefits) or unite groups (for example, by stimulating mutual interests or by creating a common enemy)?

+ How might the intervention contribute to the creation of an overarching sense of community within which its constituent "subcommunities" feel secure?

Toward a CBNRM-specific PCIA tool

This chapter has sought to examine some of the major themes to consider in examining the impact of CBNRM on the dynamics of peace and conflict. A more systematic means of assessing this impact is necessary to understand better how CBNRM processes resolve, exacerbate, or manage conflict. Accomplishing this goal will require a more careful analysis of such issues as the nature of conflict itself, the interplay of material and symbolic resources, the neutrality of external interveners, the upscale and downscale linkages of resource conflicts, and the contestations over the notion of "community."

The following set of questions might guide our analysis and interpretation of the peace and conflict impact of CBNRM interventions. They are meant to stimulate discussion on where and how we might or should look for peace and conflict impact. The "sample questions" are divided into two general categories: those related to the peace and conflict context or environment in which interventions may take place; and those related to the intervention itself and its impact on its surroundings.

Many of these questions may already be part of the standard repertoire of those involved in CBNRM. We hope that by articulating and categorizing them, we may move ahead in a more self-conscious, systematic, and self-critical manner. They are not definitive or exhaustive, but suggestive. And most importantly, they represent a starting point, not an end point. With such a wealth of experience behind us, it behooves us to ask not only what lessons have we learned, but what lessons should we learn. The following questions are proposed as part of this process.

Assessing context

The questions concerning context are intended to guide the systematic consideration of contextual factors that may have an impact on a CBNRM conflict management intervention. These are some of the questions that may be asked before, during, or following a CBNRM initiative.

Situating conflict

+ What will be the geographic extent of intervention?

+ Will it be located in politically or legally ambiguous or contested territory?

✦ What is the state of relations between community groups in the proposed intervention site and the other principal actors, including decision-makers, regionally and nationally?

✦ What are the legacies of the conflicts in the immediate area of the proposed intervention (for example, in the areas of the local economy; food security; the physical and psychological health of the community; personal insecurity or security; availability of leadership; physical infrastructure; intergroup relations; women, children and vulnerable populations; and so on)?

Timing

✦ Will the intervention coincide with other interventions in the region or country that might help or hinder its progress?

✦ Is it possible to identify or anticipate "external" political, economic, or security developments that might affect the intervention positively or negatively?

✦ What is the history or legacy of past interventions or events in the region?

Political dimensions of conflict

✦ What is the level of political support for the intervention locally, regionally, and nationally?

✦ What is the nature of formal political structures conditioning relations between the state and civil society (authoritarian, "transitional," partially democratic, democratic, decentralized, participatory, corrupt, predatory), and what are their possible impacts?

✦ Will the intervention involve politically sensitive or volatile issues (directly or indirectly)? What are the crucial issues which must be considered?

Social dimensions of conflict

✦ What are the dominant features of the social landscape in the locale of the intervention (ethnic, cultural, religious, class groups)?

✦ What are the sources of differentiation and division among actors involved in the resource conflict (economic, religious, ethnic, etc.)? How do these contribute to differential power relations?

✦ What factors might account for the violence or nonviolence of the resource conflict?

✦ Has identity been mobilized to contribute to the conflict? How?

Other potential factors affecting the impact of the conflict on the intervention

✦ What is the nature of the institutional context; leadership; colonial legacy; national and international political economic factors, such as economic infrastructure, structural-adjustment programs, and fluctuations in commodity prices; and the impacts of the conflict on type and availability of resources (especially natural and human resources)?

Assessing interventions

Similar to assessing a peace and conflict context, assessing an intervention involves asking questions before, during, and after the process. The purpose of each question is to stimulate thinking surrounding the design and the procedure of CBNRM interventions with specific reference to their impact on the peace and conflict environment. The questions presented here have been divided into four potential areas of impact, which should be regarded by the reader as simply notional, rather than rigid.

Institutional capacities to manage or resolve conflict, promote tolerance, and build peace

+ Did or will the intervention affect organizational capacity of individuals, or collectivities (institutions, social groups, private sector) — positively or negatively — to identify and respond to peace and conflict challenges and opportunities (for example, will it help to identify mutually acceptable alternatives)? If so, which groups? To what degree? How and why?

+ Did or will the intervention increase or decrease the capacity to imagine, articulate, and put into operation realities that nurture rather than inhibit peace? ("Organization capacity" might include the ability to *conceptualize and identify* peacebuilding challenges and opportunities; in the case of organizations, to *restructure itself* to respond; and to *alter standard operational procedures* to respond more effectively and efficiently in ways that have a tangible positive impact, for example, in ways that enhance fairness, equity, "evenhandedness," accountability, and transparency.)

+ What were or might be the obstacles to a sustainable and generally acceptable CBNRM regime?

+ How might the beneficial effects be amplified or made more sustainable, both during and following the intervention?

Human security

+ Did or will the intervention affect individuals' sense of security?

+ Did or will the intervention affect the military, paramilitary, or criminal environment directly or indirectly, positively or negatively? If so, how?

+ Was there or will there be tangible improvements in the political, economic, physical, food, security? If so, what are they and to whom do they apply? To what degree? How and why?

+ Did or will the intervention deepen our understanding or increase capacity to address the nonmilitary irritants to violent conflict, such as environmental degradation, resource scarcity, political manipulation, disinformation, mobilization, and politicization of identity, etc.?

+ To what extent did or will the intervention contribute to the "demilitarization of minds" (for example, through the dismantling of the cultural and sociopsychological predisposition of individuals and groups to use militarized violence as a first, rather than last, resort)? More generally, what was or might be the impact of the intervention on the role military weapons in social, political, and economic life; the delegitimization of a gun culture; and the evolution of nonviolent modalities of conflict management?

Political structures and processes

✦ Did or will the intervention help or hinder the consolidation of constructive political relationships within and between state and civil society? (For example, how did or will the intervention affect the understanding, composition, and distribution of political resources within and between state and civil society?)

✦ Did or will the intervention have a positive or negative impact on formal or informal political structures and processes — either within the formal arena of institutionalized state politics (for example, constitutional or party politics) or within the informal arena of civil society (for example, traditional authority structures)? If so, how?

✦ Did or will the intervention contribute to the development of the capacity of individuals and collectivities to participate constructively in democratic political processes?

✦ Did or will it contribute to increasing the transparency, accountability, representativeness, and appropriateness of political structures?

✦ Did or will the intervention influence policy processes or products? If so, in what ways?

✦ Did or will the intervention help defuse intergroup tensions? If so, how? Has it considered how to control tensions when they rise?

✦ What was or will be the impact of the intervention on human rights conditions within a country or region (for example, awareness, legislation, levels of abuse or respect)?

Social reconstruction and empowerment

✦ Did or will the intervention contribute to the development or consolidation of equity and justice or the means of providing basic needs?

✦ Were the benefits of the intervention shared equitably (or will they be)?

✦ Did or will the intervention include members from the various communities affected by the conflict? How?

✦ Did or will the intervention seek explicitly to benefit or build bridges between the different communities? Did or will it help foster an inclusive — rather than exclusive — sense of community? Did or will it facilitate the ability of individuals and groups to work together for mutual benefit?

✦ Did or will the intervention facilitate positive communication or interaction between and within groups? Is this sustainable? How might the quality of dialogue between groups be characterized?

✦ Did or will it provide or generate the skills, tools, and capacity for individuals and communities to *define* issues and problems to be addressed, *formulate* solutions to those problems, or *resolve* those self-defined problems?

✦ Did or will the design of the intervention take into consideration the history and legacy of conflict? For example, did or will it consider the specific impact on children, women, and other vulnerable groups, such as displaced populations and the politically, socially, and economically marginalized?

✦ Did or will the intervention increase contact, confidence, or trust between the communities? Did it dispel distrust? Did or will it create common interests or encourage individuals and groups to recognize their common interests and modify their behaviour to attain them?

✦ To what extent did or will the intervention incorporate or favour the views and interests of affected indigenous populations?

✦ Who defines the "space" for participation in the intervention? Who is representing the community or external interests? How were representatives chosen?

References

Bush, K.D. 1997. When two anarchies meet: international intervention in Somalia. Journal of Conflict Studies, 17(1), 55–78.

———— 1998. A measure of peace: peace and conflict impact assessment (PCIA) of development projects in conflict zones. Peacebuilding and Reconstruction Program, International Development Research Centre, Ottawa, ON, Canada. Working paper 1.

CMI–NCG (Christian Michelsen Institute; Nordic Consulting Group). 1997. Evaluation of Norwegian assistance to peace, reconciliation and rehabilitation in Mozambique. Royal Ministry of Foreign Affairs, Oslo, Norway. Evaluation report 4.97.

Cohen, A.P. 1985. The symbolic construction of community. Tavistock Publications, London, UK.

Hornborg, A. 1994. Environmentalism, ethnicity, and sacred places: reflections on modernity, discourse, and power. Canadian Review of Sociology and Anthropology, 31(3), 260.

Long, N.; Villareal, M. 1994. The interweaving of knowledge and power in development interfaces. *In* Scoones, I.; Thompson, J., ed., Beyond farmer first: rural people's knowledge, agricultural research and extension practice. Intermediate Technology Publications, London, UK. pp. 41–51.

Millwood, D., ed. 1996. The international response to conflict and genocide: lessons from the Rwanda experience: joint evaluation of emergency assistance to Rwanda (5 volumes). Steering Committee of the Joint Evaluation of Emergency Assistance to Rwanda, Copenhagen, Denmark.

Moore, D.S. 1993. Contesting terrain in Zimbabwe's eastern highlands: political ecology, ethnography, and peasant resource struggles. Economic Geography, 69(4), 390.

———— 1994. Optics of engagement: power, positionality, and African studies. Against Power, 64 (transition issue), 126.

———— 1996. Marxism, culture, and political ecology: environmental struggles in Zimbabwe's eastern highlands. *In* Peet, R.; Watts, M., ed., Liberation ecologies: environment, development, social movements. Routledge, London, UK. pp. 125–147.

Murphy, W.P. 1990. Creating the appearance of consensus in Mende political discourse. American Anthropologist, 92(1), 24–41.

Murray Li, T. 1996. Images of community: discourse and strategy in property relations. Development and Change, 27, 501–527.

OED (Operations Evaluation Department). 1998. The Bank's experience with post-conflict reconstruction. World Bank, Washington, DC, USA. Draft, 23 Feb.

Sahnoun, M. 1994. Somalia: missed opportunities. United States Institute of Peace, Washington, DC, USA.

Scott, J. 1990. Domination and the arts of resistance: hidden transcripts. Yale University Press, New Haven, CT, USA.

Smith, G.E. 1993. Relief operations and military strategy. In Weiss, T.G.; Minear, L., ed., Humanitarianism across borders: sustaining civilians in times of war. Lynne Reinner Publishers, London, UK. pp. 97–116.

Tschirgi, N. 1994. Linking development and security research. IDRC Reports, 22(3), 12–13.

Uphoff, N. 1990. Distinguishing power, authority and legitimacy: taking Max Weber at his word by using resource-exchange analysis. Polity, 22(2), 295–322.

Part 3
Land Use

Chapter 10

THE NUBA MOUNTAINS OF SUDAN:
RESOURCE ACCESS, VIOLENT CONFLICT, AND IDENTITY

Mohamed Suliman

*Since 1987, a violent conflict between the Nuba people of southern Kordofan and gov-
ernment forces supported by indigenous Arab Baggara has been raging in the Nuba
Mountains. The armed conflict has brought great misery to the inhabitants of the mountains, especially the Nuba and has had a severe impact on relations between the Nuba
and Baggara, who have shared the mountains in uneasy peace and guarded cooperation
for the last 200 years. The government persuaded the Baggara to join its crusade against
the Nuba by giving them arms and promising them Nuba lands after a quick victory. The
Baggara, intoxicated by military power and greed, rejected all calls for peace with the
Nuba. The war continued unabated for years. The Baggara lost some of their traditional
lands, many people, and animals. Their trade with the Nuba collapsed. Losses forced the
Baggara in several areas to negotiate peace with the Nuba. This chapter attempts to
explain the complex web of cooperation and conflict that binds the Nuba and the
Baggara. It also documents three peace agreements reached between the two warring
groups.*

The conventional assumption that violent conflicts in Africa emanate from ethnic, religious, or cultural differences is limited and misleading. In the Sudan, scarcity — resulting
from denying or limiting access to natural resources and from growing environmental
degradation — stands out as probably the most important factor behind conflict among the
peoples of the country. However, ethnic, religious, and cultural dichotomies are strong in
people's minds, and the longer a conflict persists, the more these factors come into play.
In a prolonged conflict, when the initial causes have faded away, abstract, ideological

ethnicity can become a material and social force, and change from consequence to apparent cause of such conflicts.

Ecological degradation can act as a cause or catalyst of violent conflict (Beachler 1993; Homer-Dixon 1994). However, the focus on degradation of the natural resource base tends to limit conflict resolution to tackling its specific causes — land-use, human and animal population growth, and climatic variations. Proposed resolution mechanisms are thus more technical than economic, political, or cultural: better water management, soil conservation, reforestation, family planning, etc. The crucial issues of the economy, the state, politics, and identity are inadvertently pushed aside. Persistent inequity in resource allocation, which is inherently political and economic, and the role of the beneficiaries and perpetrators of the status quo are thus taken out of the limelight. However, in all the group conflicts we scrutinized in the Sudan, access to natural and social resources expressed in terms of justice, fairness, equitable sharing, and equal development, was the primary concern of the people in arms.

Fragile ecology, fragile social peace

In the Sudan, as in most other parts of the continent, human and animal life depends on the delicate balance of soil, climate, water, and flora. Since the mid-1970s this equilibrium has been upset, particularly in the vast arid and semi-arid areas of the northern half of the country. Not only the persistent drought, but also the unsustainable methods of land use, such as large-scale mechanized rain-fed farming and overgrazing in marginal lands, are destroying the Sudano-Sahelian ecozone, where 70% of the population lives. Millions of people have been forced to abandon their homelands and have become displaced; so many in fact that the Sudan has the highest proportion of internally displaced people in the world — one in every six.

The slow processes of natural wear and tear on the environment have been accelerated enormously by the unprecedented exploitation of natural resources. This is being carried out by members of the northern Sudanese traditional merchant class (the Jellaba), prompted by their integration into the world market in the restricted role of extractors of primary resources. In addition, loan conditions imposed by the World Bank and the International Monetary Fund have considerably boosted the restructuring of Sudan's resource use away from local needs and the local market toward the demands of the international market (Suliman 1993).

This situation has been compounded by a steady decline in international terms of trade, brought about by the collapse of primary commodity prices, which had an effect on the local market, where terms of trade have also worsened. To maintain their living standards, peasants and pastoralists have had to produce more from a shrinking resource base. If they fail to do this, they have no option but to join the millions of dispossessed and assetless poor.

In the past, those in distress simply moved to a richer ecozone nearby. However, this option is increasingly hampered by an expanding population, large-scale mechanized farming, political and ethnic tensions, and the general worsening of the environmental situation. As central-government control of law and order in the countryside is weakened, physical security is becoming increasingly important in the decisions of people to abandon their homelands and move to urban centres where food is in greater abundance and physical security is relatively better maintained.

The movement of people and herds from one affected ecozone to another that is already occupied by a different ethnic group is a recipe for tension and hostility. Conditional agreements used to be reached when the need for sharing land was occasional, but now that this need is for prolonged periods (or even for permanent sharing), the strain is much greater. These difficulties are particularly prevalent in the south and in the drought-stricken areas of Darfur and Kordofan. They are one of the causes of the armed conflict raging in the Nuba Mountains of southern Kordofan (Suliman and Osman 1994).

The people of the Nuba Mountains

The Nuba Mountains lie in southern Kordofan, covering an area of 50 000 km^2 almost exactly in the geographic centre of the Sudan (Figure 1). The Nuba hills rise sharply to some 500 to 1 000 m above the plains. The area is classed as a subhumid region. The rainy season extends from mid-May to mid-October, and annual rainfall ranges from 400 to 800 mm, allowing grazing and seasonal rain-fed agriculture.

The term "Nuba" is often used to refer to the inhabitants of the Nuba Mountains; they number 1.5 million. The various Nuba people make up some 90% of the population of the area. The other 10% are Baggara (cattle herders) — mainly Hawazma and Misiriya Arabs. The Baggara moved into the mountains from the west and north in about 1800. There is also a smaller minority of Arab traders, the so-called Jellaba.

The Nuba

The term "Nuba" refers to "a bewildering complexity" of ethnic groups (Nadel 1947). Stevenson (1984) identified more than 50 languages and dialect clusters, falling into 10 groups.[1] Many authors have argued that the term "Nuba" was originally an alien label used to group together all peoples living in the hills area who were seen as "black Africans," as opposed to the Baggara Arabs (Nadel 1947; Baumann 1987). When the Nuba use the term to describe themselves, it has is not always consistently applied. Nadel (1947) commented that

> The people of a certain tribe will describe all similar groups of which they know or with which they come in contact as being their "race" but would be uncertain into which category to place other groups outside their kin ... . In the opinion of a Korongo man all the surrounding tribes were Nuba, but not the people of Dilling, whom he believed to be Arab.

Despite the problem involved in using the term, one can reasonably assume that the ethnic type presented by the Nuba today was widespread in the Sudan but was forced to retreat by Arabs coming into the mountains, where they found adequate water and easy defence. As MacMichel (1912) wrote,

> In the earliest days and for thousands of subsequent years the ancestors of the Nuba probably held the greater part of this country (i.e., what is now known as Kordofan) except the northern-most deserts. Beaten back by other races that ruled the Nile banks in successive generations, by tribes from the interior, and finally by the nomad Arabs, the Nuba have now retired to the mountains of southern Kordofan.

---

[1] This section on the history of the Nuba people draws extensively on Stevenson's (1984) book.

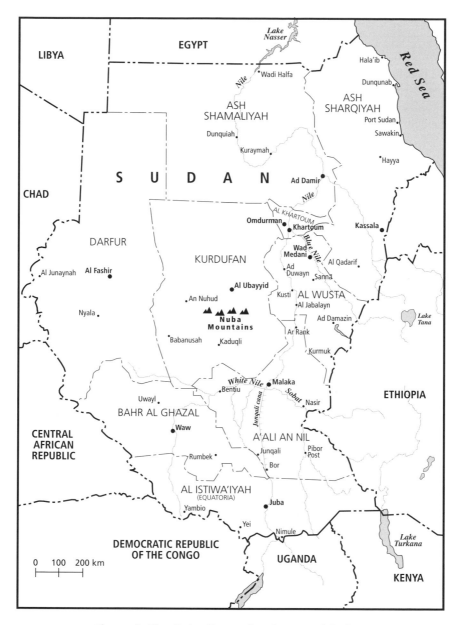

Figure 1. The Nuba Mountains in central Sudan.

In spite of the previous difficulty in using the term Nuba for all non-Arab inhabitants of the mountains, successive calamities have imposed a common destiny on these peoples and have been conducive to the development of a loose unity and a growing feeling of a common "Nubaness" among them. Their common historical experiences — the slave raids, the Turkish and British invasions, and Jellaba domination — as well as the existence of something akin to a common Nuba culture, permit commentators now to speak of one Nuba people.

This classification is also justified by the identification of the Nuba by others and the consequent implications of this identification on individual Nuba in relation to non-Nuba and among themselves. Thus, in a sense, a common ethnicity has been forced on these diverse peoples by the actions and definitions of other more powerful groups. The Nuba identity is, therefore, subjectively defined in contrast to the Baggara Arabs of Kordofan and Darfur regions (what the Nuba are not) and objectively determined by shared space, comparable cultural values, and similar economic activities (what the Nuba are).

Because they have no written language, the distant history of the Nuba peoples has largely been forgotten. As Nadel (1947) noted,

> The traditions and memories of the peoples themselves yield sparse information. It often seems as if historical traditions had been cut short by the overpowering experience of the Mahdist regime (1881–1898).

Of all Nuba peoples, those of Tegali have the best historical records because of the strong links they had with the Funj Kingdom of Sennar. The more recent history of the Nuba goes back to the early 16th century, at the point when large groups of Juhaina pastoral tribes began to move southwestward into the plains of northern Kordofan, ultimately confining the Nuba to the region now known as the Nuba Mountains. This great movement coincided with the establishment of the Kingdom of Sennar by Umara Dungas around 1504.

In spite of the lack of certainty about the Nuba's distant past, most authors seem content to assume that the Nuba have lived in the area they now occupy for a very long time. Some of Nadel's (1947) informants seem to attest to this. When asked about previous places of settlement, the people replied, "We have always lived here." It is also possible to assume that during most of their recent history, the Nuba have been farmers living mainly on the plains.

The Baggara enter the mountains

In about 1800, the Baggara tribes, which had previously roamed the plains of Kordofan and Darfur, began to move into the valleys of the Nuba Mountains in search of water and pasture for their growing herds. The Baggara are said to have divided the plains among themselves and driven the Nuba uphill. A large part of the Nuba area fell to the Hawazma (a Baggara tribe). The advent of the Baggara in the mountains coincided with the beginning of slave raiding. The fact that Nuba people were sturdy soldiers worked in a curious way to their disadvantage, because it encouraged continuous attacks from slave raiders who were looking for potential soldiers.

Driven into the hills, the Nuba turned to terrace farming of the relatively barren hill soil. Gradually barter-trade relations began to unite the two communities in a strong reciprocal, albeit asymmetric, relationship. Sargar (1922) mentions relations of cooperation, which stretch across the Nuba–Baggara divide: "Each sub-tribe of Baggara protected, as far as possible, the hills of its own zone, in return for supplies of grain and slaves."

These local Baggara–Nuba relations frequently created inter-Baggara rivalries, when a Baggara subtribe defended "their" Nuba from the machinations of another Baggara group. In some areas, Baggara–Nuba relations were even closer than the protection agreements indicated: some Baggara assuming titles and positions in Nuba tribes. Intermarriages were also recorded (Suleiman 1993). However, the extent and limits of these cross-cutting ties varied greatly from one area to another.

These sporadic good relations should not obscure the fact that the most prominent feature of Baggara–Nuba relations was the slave raids by the Baggara on the harassed Nuba communities. These raids were especially widespread during the Turkish rule (the Turkiyya), which began with the conquest of the Sudan by Egypt in 1821. The Turkish governors of Kordofan led many expeditions into the Nuba Mountains in search of gold and slaves but never made serious attempts to govern the area directly. As Stevenson (1984) noted, "With this strange mixture of trade and enslavement, the Nuba people continued through, and endured the Turkiyya."

The Mahdiyya and its consequences

The rise of the Mahdist movement in the 1880s brought fresh trouble to the peoples of the mountains. Some supported the Mahdi (a person believed to be the one who would lead Muslims to salvation); others resisted him. This difference in attitude toward the Mahdi was to be characteristic of Nuba relations with central governments in the future, dividing them into rebellious and government-friendly Nuba. After the death of the Mahdi, his successor, Khalifa Abullahi, sent a force under Hamdan abu Anja and al-Nur Muhammed Anqara to subdue the Nuba. More than 10 000 Nuba perished and even more were enslaved.

Brutal harassment of the Nuba people continued after the defeat of the Mahdist state by the allied forces of Egypt and Britain at the battle of Omdourman in 1898. In spite of their devastating experience during the Mahdiyya, the Nuba did not welcome the new colonial administration. As Stevenson (1984) remarked, "Hills which had managed to beat off the Mahdists at different times thought themselves impregnable to attack, notably Dair, Nyimang, Katla, Fanda and parts of Koalib." It took almost 30 years to subdue the various Nuba peoples and bring them in line with the rest of the country. With state authority at last established in all the Nuba Mountains, intercommunal raiding was minimized and community leaders were empowered by state appointment. "Friendly" Nuba were recruited to pacify Nuba rebels.

During this period of peace, many Nuba began to come down from the protection of the hills to farm and even live in the plains. This natural adaptation to peaceful times was supported by the desire of the central government to bring the Nuba down to the accessible plains for the purpose of effective administration and control by the state, which grew weary of the stubborn resistance of the Nuba to the new regime in Khartoum.

The new regime brought about far-reaching changes in the Nuba Mountains over a relatively short period, which transformed, in many respects irreversibly, the way the Nuba lived. One such change was the introduction of modern agricultural practices, with cotton as a cash crop. The success of large-scale mechanized production of cotton brought the mountains to the attention of international companies and, subsequently, to the attention of the Sudanese Jellaba. Another major change was the introduction of modern school education, although the Nuba had to wait until 1940 before the government introduced large-scale modern schooling into their area. The emergence of an educated Nuba elite was to have far greater implications for the subsequent history of the Nuba people than any single event or process. Education would later emerge as one of the strongest unifying factors, a pillar on which to build the edifice of a unified Nuba people.

The postindependence period

Independence, established in 1956, accelerated the opening up of the mountains to all the winds of change and catalyzed movement of the Nuba people toward the urban centres of the Sudan and foreign countries. The Nuba Mountains were also now open to economic and social intrusion by national and international agents of trade and politics and to cultural exchange. Going out to meet the world meant coming home to understand one's own identity. Many Nuba discovered their Nubaness in the towns of the Sudan, where their cultural diversity was reduced to a single Nuba identity.

Economy of the region

The Nuba practice a range of productive activities, including animal husbandry, hunting, and foraging; however, agriculture is the mainstay of their economy. It is fairly widespread throughout Nuba communities and is certainly one of the elements that distinguish the Nuba from some of their neighbours.

The basic farming unit is generally the nuclear family. Its members farm land that is, according to tradition, individually or family owned. Farmland is divided into three basic types based on its location: house, hillside, and far farms. These usually determine the choice of the crops grown and the family members responsible for their care. House farms are generally within a village, are used to grow a variety of early maturing crops (maize, bulrush, and millet), and are the responsibility of the women. Hillside farms (terraced plots on the hillside) are planted with later maturing grains. Far farms are situated on the clay plains that have been used by the Nuba since "pacification" of the area under Anglo-Egyptian rule and are worked traditionally by men. Land holdings are thus fragmented. This means that a large amount of time is spent traveling between home and the various plots, and the use of modern agricultural machinery is impractical for any one farm. The advantage is that the spread of plots tends to spread the risk of all crops failing in any one year.

The Nuba practice a form of shifting agriculture. Land is planted with a selection of crops and farmed until a new plot is needed. As a result, the regular demand for new land is an integral part of the farming system. This demand and the need to allow used land to regenerate is upheld in the traditional Nuba land laws. In any given area, the Nuba recognize three types of land: individually owned land, vacant land that is recognized as being communally owned by a village or hill community, and vacant land that does not belong to anyone. Any, usually male, member of a village community has the right of access to communal lands. All he or she has to do is to clear and cultivate the land to make it his or her own.

The patterns in Nuba agricultural production reveal several risk-spreading factors. For example, a range of crops grown on a range of plots relieves the land from the pressures of monoculture. Harvesting times are staggered to allow for lean times. Families try to produce a range of crops to cover most of their subsistence needs. Leaving large tracts of land unused gives herders room for grazing without interfering with crop production. However, now that the practice of large-scale mechanized farming is spreading, this integrated system is being eroded. The ability of Nuba farmers to respond to erratic rainfall and climate change has been severely limited by the expansion of mechanized farming. As is the case in many areas in the Sudan where mechanized farming has displaced traditional farming, the mere subsistence of millions of people is severely affected.

Sources of the current conflict

Current Nuba society is an excellent example of what Chevalier and Buckles (this volume) call a heterocultural society. The Nuba have never been a monocultural group. They are generally aware of the common destiny and other values that unite them, but they are also conscious of differences among them. After 200 years of sharing the mountains with the Nuba, the Baggara exhibit similar heterocultural features. This intragroup diversity has arisen out of Baggara–Nuba interdependence and the relative isolation of the two groups in their fairly secluded hill clusters. Nuba and Baggara cultures have permeated each other. However politically improper it may sound today, every Baggara embodies dynamic elements of Nuba culture and vice versa. Nuba–Baggara relations, be they cooperative or conflictual, have been instrumental in shaping their heterocultural societies; because these relations are in constant flux, Nubaness and "Baggaraness" are dynamic identities, impossible to solidify in monocultural or multicultural casts. War in such a society is particularly tragic, because it cuts deep wounds where the two groups have intermingled, amalgamated, and enriched each other.

In the past, problems arising from land and water disputes were resolved at an annual conference of Nuba Mekks and Arab Sheikhs. These meetings usually took place on neutral ground, both sides abided by the agreements reached, and the Nuba Mountains enjoyed decades of peace and relative prosperity. Recently, however, forces have conspired to bring the two groups into direct violent conflict. The major causes of the armed conflict are

✦ Allocation of the best lands to absentee Jellaba landlords; and

✦ The drought, which has brought large numbers of Baggara and their animals to the mountains.

Land ownership

The single most important issue behind the outbreak of the conflict in the Nuba Mountains is the encroachment of mechanized agriculture in an area of Nuba smallholder farming. This devastated the economic and social life of the Nuba and ultimately destroyed friendly relations with the Baggara.

In 1968, the Mechanized Farming Corporation, which was established with credit from the World Bank, supervised the introduction of large-scale mechanized farming at Habila, between Dilling and Delami. Of 200 mechanized farms supported by the State Agricultural Bank in the Habila area, 4 were local cooperatives, 1 was leased to a group of Habila merchants, 4 were leased to individual local merchants, and the rest (191) were leased to absentee Jellaba landlords, mainly merchants, government officials, and retired generals from the north (Suleiman 1993). A community leader from Korongo Abdalla told *African Rights* (1995) that

> Land is a big problem. At Abu Shanab, the local people prepared the land, but the government brought its tractors and began to prepare cultivation. We asked them to go to another side. They refused.

Two witnesses from Delami described the spread of mechanized farming: "The merchants came with tractors and ploughed right on top of people's cultivation. They could do this, because anyone who objected will be arrested" (African Rights 1995). A leading Nuba civil servant (who must remain anonymous) provided me with the following testimony:

> The mechanized farming problem has two ways of taking our land: the government planned mechanized farming schemes which are given from Khartoum, from the Ministry of Agriculture and regardless of the reality of the area, land is just allotted to certain people, who are mainly retired army generals or civil servants, or wealthy merchants from northern Sudan, or to local Jellaba who have been living in the area for a long time and here accumulated wealth. They have links with Khartoum and the central Sudanese government, because they originally come from the north. These people acquire land and then go and tell their relatives that they too can acquire land through the ministry. They join forces together and acquire more land.
>
> Because the Nuba are not wealthy only a small number of them are involved in this distribution of land. The government just demarcates land regardless of the realities of the area. They do not care if there are villages in this land or not. In the area of Habila, mechanized farms have circled many villages. There is no more land for the Nuba, no land for farming and no land for the animals to graze … . The Nuba are squeezed and have to choose between two options: either leave the area to work for the government as soldiers, or become workers in a mechanized farming scheme. This phenomenon is becoming massive.
>
> Besides the planned mechanized farms, there is the unplanned land acquisition. Here you have somebody who is powerful and wealthy, who just comes in and cleans up a piece of land, which is actually owned by the community. But because he is powerful he just cleans it and brings in his tractors and his workers and begins to farm. And then, if any resistance happens, he will go to the authorities to protest and ask them to protect him. Because he can bribe the authorities, he can pay and do whatever he likes. Otherwise, he has a politician friend, or an army officer, who is powerful and can send an order down here, so his friend can get the land. There are also other ways of getting land, for example burning down a village and forcing its inhabitants to move on.
>
> You can find no intention of keeping some of the land for the Nuba. The land is either taken by the Arab nomads for grazing, or taken by the wealthy landlords who come from the North. What remains for the Nuba is to fight back against these things. The Nuba have to find a way to protect themselves. They have already started to build their own political organizations or activate old ones.

The drought

Since 1967 rainfall in western Sudan has been less than half the annual average. As a result, Arab nomads, not local to the area, are seeking long-term or permanent shelter in the wet hills. Coupled with large increases in human and livestock populations, the persistent drought is a major cause of tensions.

The Jellaba mechanized farmers and the Baggara pastoralists have forged a temporary alliance to dislodge the indigenous people and take over their land. It remains to be seen whether this "marriage of convenience" can endure the conflicting interests of its partners, all seeking to eat the same cake. There are already signs that the powerful Jellaba will use the Baggara to secure their objectives, then deny them access to the best lands.

Escalation to violence

The scissors effect created by the drought and the incursion of mechanized farming alerted the Nuba people to the possibility of being squeezed out of their best farming lands. Thus, when civil war broke out in the south in 1983, the Nuba were generally sympathetic with the proclaimed aims of the Sudanese People's Liberation Movement (SPLM) and the

Sudanese People's Liberation Army (SPLA), and individual Nuba even moved into liberated areas and joined the movement.

The SPLA made its first incursion into the Nuba Mountains in July 1985. In response, the government began to arm the Baggara as a militia. *African Rights* (1995) reported that

> [It is] one of the deepest tragedies that the Baggara Arabs, who have implemented so much of the government's policies against the Nuba, are themselves an impoverished and marginalised group in the Sudan.

Almost at the same time (June–July 1985), the Khartoum government decided to arm the Baggara, namely the Misiriya Zurug and Humur. This mission was entrusted to the then minister of defence, Fadllala Burma Nasir, who was a Misiriya Zurug. He created the Misiriya militia, known as the Murahaliin, which spread terror throughout the mountains.

Although the Murahaliin militia had been created as a progovernment force against the SPLA, the Baggara groups had their own agenda. They immediately began raiding Nuba communities, increasing Nuba distrust of the Baggara, the central government, and the Arab north as a whole. The mistrust was reflected in substantial support for the Sudan National Party, a Nuba party headed by the Reverend Philip Ghaboush. As the government became aware of this change in the Nuba political situation it began to replace Nuba administrative and security officials with non-Nuba people, mostly Arabs.

In 1985, a Nuba militia group attacked the Baggara in the El Gerdud region. Rumour had it that the Nuba leader, Yusuf Kuwa, led the attack. The rumour was false, but Baggara girls lamented the breakdown of traditional friendship between the Nuba and the Baggara, singing "Yusuf Kuwa has forsaken our brotherhood and entered el Gerdud by force." A marked escalation of the war occurred in 1989, when an SPLA unit (the New Kush Battalion, headed by Commander Yusuf Kuwa Mekke) entered the region to establish a base in the eastern part of the Nuba Mountains and take the guerrilla war into Kordofan. The SPLA quickly occupied the area around Talodi and began recruiting Nuba youths.

The response of the Khartoum government

The response of the ruling Umma government to the turbulence in the mountains was highly irresponsible. Without authorization from the Constituent Assembly, it reorganized the Misiriya militia as a paramilitary force, the Popular Defence Force (PDF) and coordinated its actions with the army. By 1988, systematic killing of Nuba civilians by the army, the military intelligence, and the PDF had begun. This pattern of violence — elimination by attrition — became well established in the following years, which saw the SPLA advance close to Kadugli, the administrative centre of the Nuba Mountains.

The new regime of the National Islamic Front (NIF) offered no respite to the Nuba. In October 1989, it passed the *Popular Defence Act*, which had not been formally promulgated by the previous government. In effect the new Islamic regime had legitimized the Murahaliin militia. *Africa Watch* (1992) documented an upsurge in violence against Nuba civilians by the army and the military intelligence, the main targets of which seemed to be young educated Nuba men. Some Nuba believe that the army had drawn up lists of all educated people, whom it planned to kill.

In 1992, massive human rights violations against the Nuba were recorded. The Kordofan state government declared *Jihad* or holy war to implement a "final solution" to the "Nuba problem." A *fatwa* (an authoritative ruling on a religious matter) was issued in 1993 by a group of Muslim leaders supporting the *Jihad*. In its report, "Eradicating the Nuba," *Africa Watch* described a litany of killings, destruction of villages, and forced removals of Nuba people (Africa Watch 1992). In addition to the burning of villages and the disappearance of civilians, a large-scale plan of forcible relocation began to be implemented. Tens of thousands of Nuba are now scattered in small camps all over northern Kordofan. Many other thousands were taken hundreds of miles from home and abandoned. The scale of the killings and relocations reached the level of genocide.

In October 1993, First Lieutenant Khalid Abdel Karim Salih, who was in charge of security in Kordofan and was a personal bodyguard to the Governor of Kordofan (who is also his brother) from May 1992 to February 1993, made a statement in a press conference in Bern, Switzerland. He announced that, during a 7-month period, the army and the PDF had killed 60 000–70 000 Nuba. He stressed that these ethnic-cleansing operations made no distinction between Muslims and Christians. Churches and mosques, missionary centres and Quranic schools were all shelled indiscriminately.

Resolving the conflict

Since its inception in 1956 Sudan has been a Jellaba state; thus, government troops have always been fighting Jellaba wars by proxy. Earlier attempts at conflict resolution in the south and west focused almost entirely on sharing political power, often maintaining the economic status quo — a state of affairs most welcome to its beneficiaries, the Jellaba elite.

Given the complex relations between the Nuba, the Jellaba, and the Baggara, two independent approaches to conflict management and resolution can be proposed. First, the only way to resolve the relationship between the Nuba and the Jellaba is to stop the incursion of large-scale mechanized farming into the Nuba Mountains and return all stolen lands to their original owners, the Nuba. Second, in terms of the relationship between the Nuba and Baggara, there is a need for some sort of a temporary and equitable sharing of the available resources, mainly land and water. This should not be difficult, as the two groups have had working agreements in the past that have secured an uneasy peace in the mountains for almost 200 years. Cooperation is in the long-term interests of both groups.

Peace agreements between the Nuba and the Arabs

Since 1993 several peace agreements have been reached between the Nuba and the Baggara: the Buram agreement (1993), the Regifi agreement (1995), and the Kain agreement (1996). A precarious peace is still holding. During negotiations, several reasons were cited for the necessity of establishing peace — notable among these are the following:

- ✦ The Baggara lamented that they have lost many men and animals and some were forced to abandon their homes;

- ✦ The Baggara admitted that the government deceived them (it told them that the war against the rebels would only take a month or two, whereas it is now more than 10 years old);

- ✦ The Baggara said that they need trade with the Nuba (they want to trade their consumer goods for cereals grown by Nuba peasants);

- ✦ The Baggara told the Nuba that their politicians (for example, El-Mahdi, the leader of the Umma party) have already left the Sudan and are working with the SPLM against the NIF regime;

- ✦ The Nuba emphasized the fact that they are fighting against the government, never against the Baggara; and

- ✦ The Nuba said that they also need to trade with the Baggara (they especially need to exchange cereals and animals for clothes, salt, and other industrial goods that the Baggara bring from Khartoum).

Both sides emphasized that

- ✦ They had been living together in peace for 200 years;

- ✦ They intermingled through marriage and sharing of cultural and religious values;

- ✦ Most of the Nuba and the Baggara fighters have been poor;

- ✦ Outsiders, mainly rich Jellaba, seem to be the only beneficiaries of the war;

- ✦ Both sides have lost many people and animals for no good reason; and

- ✦ The outsiders come and go, but the people indigenous to the mountains will stay and have to find ways to live together in peace.

Nuba leaders are well aware of the need to win over the Baggara in the war against the government. In March 1989, Commander Yusuf Kuwa entered the mountains with six well-armed battalions. In an interview, he indicated that he was aware that the Baggara were assembled at Lake Abiad, and that his troops intentionally avoided them. However, the Baggara followed their trail and attacked the Nuba at Hafir Nigeria, unaware of how strong the Nuba fighting force was. The Baggara suffered huge losses and many were taken prisoner. A few days later, all prisoners were freed and given letters from Yusuf Kuwa to their sheihks asking them to either join the struggle or refrain from siding with the government. He recalled the case of a Baggara trader called Abdulla who carried his message to Baggara sheihks that the SPLA is not at war with them.

Several Baggara groups responded positively (including Sheikh Sanad). They kept open the dialogue with the Nuba leadership through letters and emissaries. The farsighted decisions of the Nuba leadership not to retaliate, to refrain from attacks of revenge, and to seek talks with the Baggara have at last yielded good results. Even so, it took 6 years, from 1987 to 1993, for the first peace agreement between the Baggara and the Nuba to materialize.

The Buram agreement

The first peace negotiations between the Baggara and the Nuba took place in February 1993 in Buram in the southern Nuba Mountains. The initiative came from the Misiriya in response to written appeals from Yusuf Kuwa. This agreement spelled out conditions and commitments for peace that have been echoed in all future agreements:

- ✦ Both sides will immediately stop all military actions against each other;

- ✦ Both sides have the right to move freely in the other's territory;

- In case of dispute or violation of the peace, a joint committee will intervene to settle the matter;

- All animals stolen will be returned, and the thieves will be punished;

- Killings will be investigated, and those responsible will be punished;

- Trade will be safeguarded;

- Information, especially of military relevance, will be exchanged; and

- Travelers to either side will have safe passage and, when necessary, will be assisted to reach their destination.

This peace agreement opened up a trade route into Buram and adjacent areas. The Misiriya traders brought in essential goods, such as salt, matches, clothes, and medicine, and the Buram trade flourished until the end of 1993 when government troops overran Nuba positions in the area and stopped it. Although sporadic trade still goes on and an uneasy peace still holds in the area, the government has succeeded in weakening the accord that began so well. Disheartened, a group of Nuba rebels joined the government and were used by its security forces to attack the Baggara and rekindle the feuds between them and the SPLA. However, it is also important to note that a number of Baggara fought with the Nuba troops against the government in Buram and continue to honour their agreement with the Nuba rebels.

The Regifi agreement

The Buram agreement gained a new lease on life in the 11-point Regifi accord signed on 15 November 1995, which reiterated pervious commitments to peaceful cooperation and mutual assistance. The Baggara delegation was keen to distance itself from the Khartoum government. Again, they told of their great losses in men, animals, and trade. Both sides agreed that peace is crucial for their existence in the precarious situation in the mountains.

The government did all it could to sabotage the agreement. It targeted the leaders of the Baggara who signed it: Abdalla, the Misiriya leader at the negotiations, was shot dead; others were assassinated or imprisoned. A few were bribed and skilfully used by the government to undermine the spirit of trust and cooperation between the Baggara and the Nuba, which had begun to spread in the region.

The Kain agreement

In June 1996, the Nuba took the initiative toward peaceful cooperation with the Rawawga Baggara. A delegation of five sought the Rawawga on neutral ground in Zangura, west of Tima, Lagowa region, and invited them to move their market close to a liberated area. The Baggara traders accepted the invitation and met with a Nuba delegation headed by Ismail El-Nur Galab. The accord reached was almost identical to the previous ones. However, a special trade committee was established this time to oversee the fairness and safety of mutual trade. It is remarkable to note that

- The Rawawga were so confident in the stability of the agreement that they began to bring in ammunition and army uniforms to sell to the Nuba;

✦ The Baggara traders began to come unarmed to the markets and were gradually accompanied by women and children; and

✦ The first test of the agreement came shortly after signing it, when an Arab attacked a Nuba, took his weapon, and left him for dead: the Baggara brought the weapon back, paid for treatment for the victim, and promised to deliver the attacker to the Nuba authority.

Once again, the government began to sabotage the agreement through murder, imprisonment, and bribery. Government spies began to appear in the marketplaces. The Nuba leadership became alarmed at the implications for military security and ordered the closure of the markets. A Nuba official told me that the markets would only be reopened when they could be supervised properly. Peace is still holding.

Lessons learned and final outcomes

Issues troubling the Nuba–Baggara peace accords

A number of obstacles have affected all the peace agreements signed so far. The most serious problems are the following:

✦ The government sabotaged the agreements, targeting the leaders on both sides for murder, imprisonment, and bribery. Especially vulnerable are the leaders of the Baggara. In one known case, government officials offered a would-be assassin 4 million Sudanese pounds and a licence for a mill in return for killing a leading Nuba signatory to the agreement (in 1999, 2 576 Sudanese pounds [SDP] = 1 United States dollar]).

✦ The government's propaganda and indoctrination machinery have influenced people on both sides to rally behind its Islamization and Arabization programs against peace and reconciliation in the region.

✦ Not all Baggara and Nuba recognized the peace accords. Many Nuba have been fighting with the government in the PDF. In fact, one of the biggest offensives against the Nuba rebels (the 1997 dry-season offensive) was commanded by a Nuba officer, Brigadier Mohamed Ismail Kakum, nicknamed Amsah (the Eraser) for his brutality.

✦ Difficulty in communication among the troops scattered all over the southern and western mountains resulted in clashes between armed groups unaware of the peace agreements.

✦ Security and financial interests occasionally dominated the actions of some Baggara traders. On one hand, they traded with the Nuba and even sold them ammunition; on the other, they supplied the government with information about rebel troops.

✦ Landlocked and cut of from the main SPLA forces in southern Sudan, the Nuba rebellion has been fairly isolated, nationally and internationally. This made both the Nuba and Baggara vulnerable to government pressures and atrocities.

✦ Old animosities die slowly. The Nuba have not forgotten the role of the Baggara in the slave trade, nor how arrogantly and abusively they behaved toward them, when the El-Mahdi's government armed the Baggara in 1900 and left the Nuba open to their blackmail.

Nubaness: from perception to cause of conflict

Before the onset of violent conflict in the Nuba Mountains, the diverse Nuba people were fully aware only of their clan affiliations. They neither perceived themselves as a Nuba nation nor actively sought to be one. Their relations with their Arab neighbours, the Hawazma and Misiriya, were tolerable. They exchanged goods and services, and inter-marriage was an acceptable practice especially among Arabs and Muslim Nuba. At the beginning of the conflict, many Nuba even sided with the government, because they per-ceived the conflict to be a political discord, rather than an ethnic or economic strife.

Along with other factors, the war has been crucial in bringing out and solidifying the awareness of the Nuba as members of a united and quasi-homogeneous ethnic group. As a result, the conflict is increasingly being perceived by many Nuba as an ethnic conflict. There is even a small core of angry Nuba, who believe that all Arabs should be thrown out of the Nuba territory in a final, radical solution! For this group, ethnicity has already crossed the threshold from perception to cause of violent conflict. And the longer the war continues, the greater the probability that more Nuba people will join the ranks of those who fight for the ethnic cause. One hopeful sign that the current differences might not build an insurmountable ethnic divide between the Baggara and the Nuba is the unani-mous agreement among all the Nuba leaders I interviewed that peace and long-term coop-eration between the two groups are fundamental for them all.

Most violent conflicts are over material resources — actual or perceived. However, with the passage of time, ethnic, cultural, and religious affiliations seem to undergo trans-formation from abstract ideological categories into concrete social forces. In a wider sense, they themselves become contestable material social resources and, hence, possible objects of group strife and violent conflict. Although usually by-products of fresh conflicts, ethnic, cultural, and spiritual dichotomies can invert, with the progress of a conflict, to become intrinsic causes and, in the process, increase its complexity thereby reduce the possibility of managing, resolving, and ultimately transforming it. The Nuba armed conflict is a living proof of this transformation.

References

Africa Rights. 1995. Facing the genocide: the Nuba of the Sudan. African Rights, Jul, 42–43.
Africa Watch. 1992. Sudan: Eradicating the Nuba. Africa Watch, 4(10) (Sep).

Baumann, G. 1987. National integration and local integrity: the Miri of the Nuba Mountains. Clarendon Press, Oxford, UK.
Beachler, G. 1993. Conflict and Co-operation in the light of human–ecological transformation, Swiss Peace Foundation, Bern, Switzerland. ENCOP Occasional Paper No. 6.

Homer-Dixon, T.F. 1994. Across the threshold: empirical evidence on environmental scarcities as causes of violent conflict. International Security, 19(1).

MacMichel, M.A. 1912. The tribes of northern and central Kordofan. Cambridge University Press, Cambridge, UK.

Nadel, S.F. 1947. The Nuba. Oxford University Press, Oxford, UK.

Sargar, J.W. 1922. Notes on the history, religion and customs of the Nuba. Sudan Notes and Records, 5.

Stevenson, R.C. 1984. The Nuba of southern Kordofan: ethnographic survey. Khartoum University Press, Khartoum, Sudan.

Suleiman, R. 1993. The crisis in the Nuba Mountains. Presented at a workshop on the Sudanese Civil War, Mar 1993, St Anthony's College, Oxford University.

Suliman, M. 1993. Civil war in the Sudan: from ethnic to ecological conflict. The Ecologist, 23(3).

Suliman, M.; Osman, O.A. 1994. War in Darfur: the desert versus the oasis syndrome. Institute for African Alternatives, London, UK.

Chapter 11

Copán, Honduras:
Collaboration for Identity, Equity, and Sustainability

Jacqueline Chenier, Stephen Sherwood, and Tahnee Robertson

Social oppression dating back to the Spanish conquest has created a legacy of poverty for the Chorti people of Copán, in western Honduras. Continued domination and exploitation has led to grave injustices and increasing conflict and violence. Population pressures and degradation of the natural resource base have added to the prospect of a grim future for all but a few of Copán's people. In 1997, following the assassination of indigenous leader Cándido Amador, the Chortis marched on Tegucigalpa where they conducted a hunger strike to publicize their cause. In response to national and international pressure, the Honduran president intervened and decreed the use of public resources for the allocation of several thousand hectares of land to the Chortis. However, this was only a first step toward effective social change and progress in Copán. Community-based natural resource management (CBNRM) efforts initially focused on strengthening the position of the Chortis. After less than 1 year, as a result of participatory processes, disputes have been diffused, and the Chortis are better organized and equipped to advocate their interests in local and national forums. Although many challenges lie ahead, valuable experience and useful lessons have been learned with respect to establishing CBNRM.

In Central America, growing populations and gross exploitation by private interests are placing increasing pressure on the limited and ever-decreasing natural resource base. Furthermore, government restructuring has led to delegated management of natural resources, giving local interest groups and nongovernmental organizations (NGOs) expanded roles. The transition has led to a sharp decline in administrative mechanisms and effective communication among rural stakeholders — agriculturists, cattle ranchers, sawmill owners, environmentalists, government officials, and local communities. Disparities in access to natural resources, lack of consensus, and misinformation are particularly common in rural settings.

This paper draws on the experience of the Network for Collaborative Natural Resources Management (COLABORA) with the Chorti people of Copán in western Honduras. Established in 1994, COLABORA is an informal group of organizations concerned with strengthening community-based natural resource management (CBNRM) processes in Honduras and a member of the regional Meso-American Network for Socio-environmental Conflict Management. Founding members of COLABORA include the NGOs Caritas, Global Village, the Guayape Valley Project, and World Neighbours, as well as Cornell University and the Pan American School of Agriculture (Zamorano). Subsequently, the Honduran forestry agency and various municipal governments have become increasingly involved. Our experience suggests that the establishment of CBNRM can help to resolve disputes and promote more responsible and democratic change by facilitating communication and learning among diverse parties and by placing decision-making power in the hands of stakeholders.

The setting and the conflict situation

The region

Honduras occupies an area of about 112 000 km² in the heart of mountainous Central America. Agricultural commodities contribute about 22% of the country's gross domestic product, with chief earnings coming from the export of bananas, coffee, cattle, sugarcane, and tobacco. The per capita gross national product is about 879 United States dollars (USD), but income disparity is great: 20% of the population accounts for 64% of the national income. The illiteracy rate is about 43%. Half of the country's nearly 6 million people are subsistence maize and bean farmers, and 80% of these farmers are considered poor to extremely poor (World Bank 1994).

The vast majority of Hondurans are of mixed European and Native American descent (referred to locally as *mestizos*) (Newsome 1992). Honduras' indigenous and ethnic groups have declined to less than 10% of the total population, and today this social group represents the country's most disadvantaged people (Rivas 1993). Nowhere in the country are poverty and social disparity more egregious than in Copán, especially among the people who are most directly descended from the Mayans — the Chorti.

The city of Copán in mountainous western Honduras has a population of about 6 000 people. However, its Mayan archeological ruins draw over 150 000 tourists annually from around the world (Director, personal communication, 1998[1]). Most of the city's population is *mestizo*; the Chorti inhabit the villages on the surrounding hillsides (Figure 1).

The Chortis are commonly of mixed Mayan–Spanish ancestry, and only a few dozen retain their indigenous language (Herranz 1996). Nevertheless, their cultural identity is largely intact and, in 1994, the Honduran government officially acknowledged the Chortis as one of its remaining seven indigenous and ethnic groups.

---

[1] Director, Honduran Anthropological Institute, personal communication, 1998.

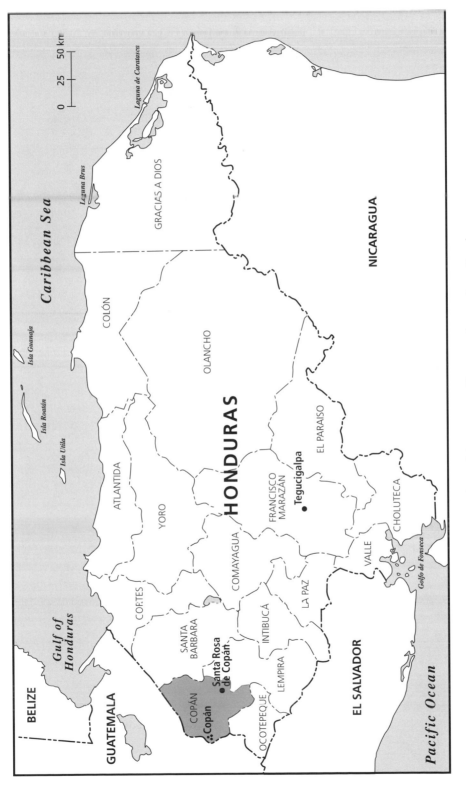

Figure 1. Copán and its surrounding area in western Honduras.

About 8 000 Chortis have been relegated to the hillsides as subsistence farmers and day labourers for local plantation owners (the *terratenientes*, who are usually of direct Spanish descent) and live in conditions of extreme poverty (Martínez 1997). Illiteracy rates reach 90% and more, the infant mortality rate is about 60%, and more than half of the children are malnourished. The average life expectancy is 49 years for men and 55 years for women. Against continuing social and economic pressure, the Chortis are struggling to preserve their customs and to reconstruct their identity, language, and livelihood.

A history of disparity

In the early 1500s, the Spanish claimed ownership of all natural resources and people in Honduras. The governing rights were distributed to conquistadors (Newsome 1992). As the Roman Catholic Church increased its role in the latter part of the century, it briefly distributed governing rights to native *caciques* who had converted to Catholicism, but later gave primary control to *criollos* (descendants of the Spanish, born in America). As a result, six *criollo* families emerged as large landowners in the Copán Valley (Martínez 1997).

During the 18th and 19th centuries, immigration of *criollos* and *mestizos* increased the population of the Copán Valley, further consolidating the privatization of resources and displacing the Chortis from their native land (Martínez 1997). Although the Roman Catholic Church made provisions for indigenous access to territory, many Chortis were forcibly removed from their land. In the early 1800s, the determination of political boundaries between Guatemala and Honduras divided the Chorti nation. In the 20th century, social domination became increasingly institutionalized.

Current social conflict

In the 1950s, powerful landowners purchased thousands of hectares throughout the Copán Valley, extending into Guatemala (Martínez 1997). Many Chorti communities were located in this territory, and their inhabitants were forced to work as farm labourers to survive. As part of the Honduran land reform policies of the 1970s, the Instituto Nacional Agrario (INA, national agricultural institute) provided new land to 3 of the 17 Chorti communities in Copán. Although the redistribution was very limited and the land awarded was largely infertile, the action provided much needed relief to swelling communities.

During the 1980s, rural communities formed farmers' unions to demand the right of access to land and credit (Martínez 1997). In 1991, more than a dozen union members in Copán were assassinated. Anthropological research and the International Labour Organization's (ILO's) Agreement 169 for Indigenous and Tribal Villages of Independent Countries, which aimed to protect and benefit indigenous communities, improve their access to land, health, and housing, and ensure their basic needs, heightened Chortis sense of cultural identity. In November 1994, with the help of the National Confederation of Autochthonous Villages of Honduras and the National Pedagogical University, local leaders created the National Chorti Indian Council of Honduras (CONICHH) to advocate concerns, in particular the recovery of lost indigenous territory.

On 12 April 1997, Chorti leader Cándido Amador was assassinated. Although authorities have still not fully determined the circumstances of the assassination, the events further consolidated Chorti nationalism and incited protests. In May 1997, nearly 1 000 Chortis marched on the Honduran capital, Tegucigalpa, and conducted a hunger strike that captured the attention of the nation as well as that of the international community. They demanded further investigation into the death of Cándido Amador and the restoration of tribal land.

The Farmers' and Ranchers' Organization of Copán Ruins (AGRACOR), representing the interests of plantation owners, lobbied the Honduran government to prevent redistribution of land. Among other issues, they challenged the ethnicity of the Chortis. However, despite AGRACOR's strong ties to members of the Honduran Congress, the media and public pressure demanded presidential intervention to end the hunger strike. The government decided to support the Chortis' cause and awarded them 2 000 ha of productive land and 200 000 Honduran lempira worth of credit for housing (Table 1) (in 1999, 14.24 Honduran lempira [HNL] = 1 United States dollar [USD]).

In December 1997, the INA transferred 350 ha of the total land awarded to the Chortis, to be administered by CONICHH. However, this move aggravated existing relations among stakeholders for a number of reasons. The government purchased largely nonarable and unproductive land from *terratenientes* at exorbitant rates (often three times the market value). INA awarded public land, causing problems with the local municipal government, as a result of unclear legal responsibilities. Furthermore, only 5 of 17 Chorti communities received land, and they questioned the actual number of hectares distributed. Finally, the government made no provision for financial or technical support to enable the Chortis to become productive farmers. The Chortis, who had worked primarily as labourers for the last few generations, had lost much of their farming knowledge.

Table 1. Chorti perspective on important events in their history.

Time	Event
Before 1502	Mayan descendants freely farmed the Copán Valley.
1502	Spanish conquered indigenous population, with limited resistance.
1560s	Spanish crown distributed land and the people to Spanish conquerors.
1600s	Chortis subsisted on small plots farmed both individually and communally.
1800s	Criollos established tobacco and coffee plantations.
1950	Juan Ramón Cuevas purchased land inhabited by Chorti communities to cultivate sugarcane and raise cattle. When he died, his sons inherited the land and Chorti communities and began to exploit labour.
1970s	Land reform occurred in Honduras. A few Chortis organized in farmers' groups (about 10%) were allocated land by the government.
1987	Increased community organization occurred, followed by heightened repression.
1991	Several Chorti leaders were killed for claiming rights; ILO's Agreement 169 was established for Indigenous and Tribal Villages of Independent Countries.
1994	CONICHH was created.
1995	CONPAH was created.
April 1997	Two Chortis, including leader Cándido Amador, were assassinated. Pilgrimage was made to Tegucigalpa, and protests for rights occurred.
May 1997	Agreements were reached with the central government for the distribution of 2 000 ha to Chorti communities. Chortis contacted COLABORA (via Caritas) for support.
December 1997	Five Chorti communities received 350 ha of nonarable and unproductive land from INA. Decisions began to be made on how to use and distribute the land.

Note: COLABORA, Network for Collaborative Natural Resources Management; CONICHH, National Chorti Indian Council of Honduras; CONPAH, National Confederation of Autochthonous Villages of Honduras; ILO, International Labour Organization; INA, Instituto Nacional Agrario (national agricultural institute).

The critical issues

The ongoing conflict in Copán emerged from a multiplex of issues. Discrepancies over ownership and distribution of land divided Chorti communities. The Chortis were also concerned about government noncompliance with the July 1997 agreements and had grown mistrustful. Tobacco farmers discouraged community organization by threatening CONICHH members and excluding them from employment opportunities or access to land. Furthermore, historical social tensions, especially between *criollo* descendants and indigenous peoples as well as between the urban wealthy and rural poor, aggravated the situation. The principal stakeholder groups and their concerns are listed in Table 2.

Mediating change through CBNRM

Following the violence and protests of 1997, CONICHH sought organizational and technical support from development agencies. Its leaders approached the Catholic NGO Caritas, which was conducting projects in western Honduras and was an active member of COLABORA. Caritas and COLABORA joined forces to help CONICHH ameliorate the situation in Copán.

Intervention

In late 1997, COLABORA representatives began to visit Copán regularly to acquire a cursory understanding of the situation and establish a CBNRM process. The most pressing initial need was to prevent further violence and to establish an environment more conducive to dialogue. As the weaker party in the community, CONICHH and its constituents also needed to strengthen their collective ability to negotiate with stronger parties, in particular the large landholders and other private business interests.

Table 2. Principal stakeholder groups in Copán.

Stakeholder group	Description	Primary concerns
Chortis	Largely tobacco-farm labourers, who can be categorized into two groups: those who belong to CONICHH and those who do not	Access to land and economic opportunities, self-governance
Plantation owners	Primarily six families owning land in and around the city of Copán	Control over land and labour
Government (local and national)	Local municipality (mayor's office) that oversees administration of public laws and national-level government institutions (president's office and INA) responsible for the enforcement of public policy	Peace and economic development in Copán
NGOs	Development organizations: Caritas, Mennonite Social Action Committee, Christian Organization for Integrated Development of Honduras, government extension project (Plandero), and others that organize community members and provide technical assistance	Access to resources and economic opportunities for project beneficiaries
Tourism industry	Local businesses that serve tourists, provide thousands of jobs, and bring millions of dollars into the economy annually	Peace and avoidance of confrontations that could disrupt tourism

Note: CONICHH, National Chorti Indian Council of Honduras; INA, Instituto Nacional Agrario (national agricultural institute).

COLABORA responded with workshops and exchanges involving Chorti representatives and organizations dealing with similar situations in other parts of the country
(Guayape Valley, Olancho; Las Marias, Olancho; Yeguare Valley; Comayagua). Through
visits, participatory research, and workshops to exchange and develop conflict management methods and strategies, COLABORA was able to help diffuse threats of violence and
achieve commitment to a long-term CBNRM process (Rios et al. 1998). Table 3 summarizes the activities carried out during this stage.

Following initial CBNRM activities, CONICHH became concerned with ameliorat-
ing social conflicts over natural resources, in particular those between landowners (those
who sold land to the government and those who did not), Chortis communities
(CONICHH members and nonmembers), the municipality, the INA, and the president's
office. As a follow-up step and a means to strengthen their ability to participate in broader
decision-making processes, the Chortis identified the equitable distribution and productive
use of awarded land as a priority (Figure 2).

CONICHH felt that addressing community conflicts over land distribution and management would help resolve the immediate differences between the Chortis, and it would
strengthen overall consensus and organization. In view of food scarcity and the approaching May planting season, they requested that COLABORA begin by working with the five
communities that had already received government land grants. Between January and
April 1998, COLABORA sent a team of three action researchers to help these communities conduct stakeholder analysis and resource assessments, produce collaborative plans,
and implement short-term land management projects.

Results

Early goals of the CBNRM process were to facilitate information exchange and to enhance
community understanding of the origins of the current situation. Through participatory
rural appraisals in the five communities that received land under the May 1997 presidential decree, COLABORA and CONICHH tested assumptions and confronted prejudices.
For example, one major source of community concern was over the actual quantity of land
distributed by the government; so COLABORA also contracted an external technical team
to measure land allocations. Early CBNRM processes helped to clarify misunderstandings
and reorient future action (Table 4).

Table 3. Participatory research activities conducted in Copán by COLABORA.

Activity[a]	Purpose
Community maps	To determine ownership boundaries, land in dispute, roads, water sources, basic services, population, geographic extension, land-use classification criteria, perceptions among adults, youth, and children, and sexes
Agricultural cost–benefit analysis	To determine agricultural feasibility, potential for substituting production and labour, capability and knowledge of agriculture production, and financial requirements
Assessment of community expectations and hopes for the future	To interpret community dreams and goals, define preferences and activities, and develop local planning capabilities
Chorti stakeholder analyses of land-tenure conflict and other community concerns	To perceive community interpretation of land-tenure conflict, generate potential solutions, and understand preoccupation with land

[a] Activities were gender- and age-sensitive to facilitate more sophisticated analyses and planning.

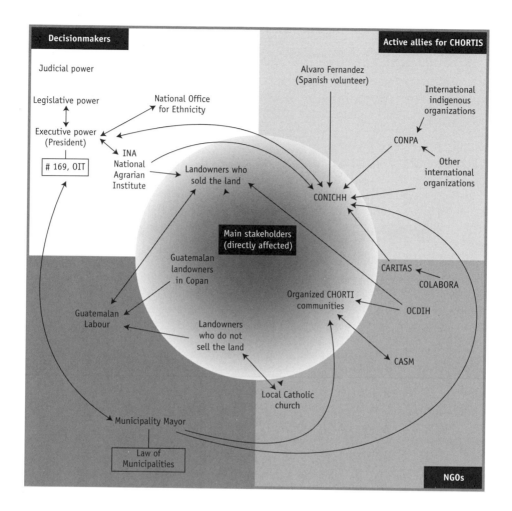

Figure 2. CONICHH analysis of relationships among the principal stakeholders with regard to land tenure (⟷ , power support).

Table 4. Learning as a result of early CBNRM processes.

Mistaken assumptions of CONICHH and the community	New understanding as a result of rural appraisals and technical studies
The government allocated less than the 350 ha promised for the first distribution.	Land allocated by the government was more than expected — a total of 416 ha.
Allocated land was suitable for farming, exceeded community needs, and could provide for the 12 communities that had not yet received land.	Allocated land was not suitable for farming (water for irrigation was scarce, land was rocky and compacted because of overgrazing, slopes commonly exceeded 35%).
Communities could easily reach consensus on how to cultivate the land, what crops would be grown, and how management would be carried out.	Sharp differences over land management divided communities and required special attention.

Note: CONICHH, National Chortis Indian Council of Honduras.

Chorti suspicion and distrust of the national government abated, and CONICHH began to focus on helping communities achieve consensus over use and management of awarded lands. Because of the low fertility of soils and limited production potential, CONICHH and the five communities rejected the option of moving families from communities that did not receive land or of allowing outside families access to it. Instead, they pledged to help those villages win their own land. Furthermore, they decided that

✦ Land would be distributed based on total area allocated per community, soil fertility, and family size.

✦ Agricultural land would be distributed to families, but for the approaching emergency season it would be cultivated collectively. Community members would collaborate in planting crops and support additional activities. Coffee plantations that existed on 30% of the awarded land would be expanded and harvested for overall community benefit.

✦ Forested areas would be zoned according to three use categories: watershed, forest reserve, and timber and firewood extraction.

CONICHH asked the government and local NGOs for agricultural assistance and financial support to enable more productive and sustainable land management. Concerned over the large number of development organizations that claimed to represent Chorti interests, CONICHH established collaboration rules. It proclaimed that NGOs and the government organizations wanting to help the Chorti cause and work with communities must obey the following five articles:

✦ Seek approval from CONICHH before contacting communities;

✦ Design interventions with community participation;

✦ Present an activity plan to CONICHH and receive its approval;

✦ Periodically inform CONICHH of project evaluations and progress; and

✦ Coordinate efforts with other development organizations to prevent redundancies and methodological conflicts.

CONICHH and Caritas organized workshops for community representatives on how to improve communications between community members and how to enhance organizational capacity. Participants reviewed proposals and chose community projects and implementing organizations by consensus. Subsequently, CONICHH established contracts, agreements with collaborators, and dates for evaluation meetings.

CONICHH reviewed early CBNRM efforts and concluded that effective outcomes were

✦ Access to new information on community demographics and resources;

✦ More accurate assessment of awarded land and boundaries;

✦ Clearer understanding by CONICHH of multiple community perspectives;

✦ New opportunities for community participation in decision-making processes;

- ✦ Alternatives for increasing land productivity and assuring its equitable distribution;

- ✦ Alternatives for addressing the needs of landless families;

- ✦ Greater consensus on immediate land use and management;

- ✦ Enhanced consolidation of organizations and greater ability to articulate and represent concerns; and

- ✦ New channels of communication and more positive attitudes among stakeholders toward plans for addressing broader community concerns.

Future challenges and lessons learned

Challenges ahead

Although CONICHH and participating communities feel that the contributions of COLABORA and, especially, Caritas have been positive, clearly the Chortis have only begun to address their needs. Eleven communities still do not have land, and those active in organizing are still denied employment opportunities. The Chortis are aspiring to change a long history of social domination and violence and face severe institutional obstacles, including highly biased social, economic, and political structures. Clearly, the most important and difficult tasks lie ahead.

Table 5 summarizes CONICHH's immediate plans for the future. First and foremost, the Chortis need to engage the array of actors more fully. In particular, establishing new relations with the *terratenientes* and encouraging their involvement in CBNRM processes pose new challenges.

Lessons

At the most basic level, COLABORA views CBNRM as a useful tool for not only improving natural resource management, but also evolving systemic, highly complex social arrangements. There is no blueprint for achieving effective CBNRM. By its nature, natural resource management involves multistakeholder situations characterized by diverse perspectives, interests, and needs. CBNRM is necessarily a creative process built on iterative and adaptive learning and action involving a wide variety and ever-changing assembly of individuals and organizations over time. CONICHH and the Chortis have only begun efforts in this area. Nevertheless, through the research in Copán, we gained valuable insight into the mechanics of CBNRM and, from that experience, draw some lessons for our future work that may be useful to others.

At the heart of CBNRM lies participation — not just the presence of multiple actors, but also shared control over decision-making and policy formulation. For those who have worked in community development, in such areas as agriculture, health, literacy, and organization, CBNRM may be just a natural progression in that preparation. We drew heavily on the experience of established adult-education, planning, and conflict resolution methods. Consistent with popular grass-roots development approaches, we used technical themes to take on more social concerns, and we engaged relatively overwhelming structural issues by starting small, that is, addressing more manageable problems before tackling

Table 5. CONICHH's immediate follow-up plans for CBNRM in Copán.

Needs	Obstacles	Opportunities	Strategies	Activities and external participants
Information and documentation Communication system Further understanding of stakeholders Continued record of facts, outcomes, agreements	Illiteracy and limited formal education	Media have effectively represented the situation and disseminated information to a broader public	Assure that researchers are objective and perceived that way Maintain confidentiality	Review status of land tenure (Caritas, INA, COLABORA) Conduct a new stakeholder analysis (COLABORA) Produce radio programs and information bulletins on the Chortis reality (NGOs, Radio Católica, Radio Sta. Rosa)
Capacity-building and learning Participatory appraisals and analyses Democratic decision-making Broad understanding of CBNRM processes	Illiteracy and limited formal education Limited understanding of history Lack of consensus on causes of problems	Numerous interested development organizations (NGOs)	Promote understanding of identity through training Develop understanding of participation and ability to use participatory methodologies	Closely involve Chortis in research activities (Caritas, COLABORA) Meeting to plan training and integrate resources (Ministry of Education, NGOs) Produce educational radio programs (Comunica, Radio Católica, Radio Santa Rosa)
Relationships and organization (CONICHH) Balanced power between CONICHH and communities Democratic leadership and community participation Interaction between CONICCH and farmer organizations Community consensus and planning over the use of awarded land	Division between communities Little tradition of participatory decision-making Large land owners active resistance to Chortis organization Tradition of authoritarian leadership and paternalism History of dependency	Numerous interested development organizations (NGOs)	Link research with organization Build leadership from the local context Start with small projects and use success to inspire Establish mechanisms of technical support Strengthen relationships with other stakeholders	Workshop on organizational development for CONICHH (Caritas, NGOs) Enable CONICHH to develop its own proposals and projects (Caritas, COLABORA, NGOs) Conduct visits and exchanges with other stakeholders

Note: COLABORA, Network for Collaborative Natural Resources Management; CONICHH, National Chorti Indian Council of Honduras; INA, Instituto Nacional Agrario (national agricultural institute); NGO, nongovernmental organization.

increasingly complex concerns. (For explanations of the general development methods used, as well as other pertinent conceptual matters, please see Korton [1980], Fisher and Ury [1981], Chambers [1983], Bunch [1985], Chambers et al. [1990], Freire [1990], Lee [1993], and Uphoff [1996].)

Because COLABORA's participation in Copán began relatively recently, the following lessons emerged from the initial stages of CBNRM, in particular problem identification, analysis, and planning.

Encourage local participation and leadership

✦ Participation was not automatic, but rather achieved. Early on, leaders and communities alike had limited interest in CBNRM. However, small successes, such as the measurement of awarded land and accurate documentation of community interests, enhanced local participation. When people felt heard, their confidence in CONICHH grew, and they became increasingly supportive of the organization.

✦ Representation in organizations was not always a fact. Healthy scepticism enabled us to see that, although well-intentioned, CONICHH did not necessarily represent the interests of communities. By building capacity, CONICHH was able to engender greater community participation and better represent constituent perspectives in projects and political circles, thereby strengthening the legitimacy of CBNRM outcomes.

✦ Low-profile leadership was best. Conventional authoritarian leadership can interfere with CBNRM processes. Differences were not effectively resolved if actors did not become fully engaged in learning and action processes and if they did not take responsibility for decisions. Transforming conventional demagogic leadership styles into new, low-profile ones through participation and collaboration permitted more democratic and effective decision-making and overall better leadership.

Address power imbalances and link stakeholders

✦ Peaceful protests helped to level the playing field. Chorti marches and hunger strikes won significant public attention, both nationally and internationally. Mass media played a decisive role in raising awareness of injustices and pressuring the government to take on issues previously all too easy to ignore. As a result of ensuing government action, the Chortis' position was strengthened and legitimized.

✦ Strengthening weaker stakeholders provided for new, more peaceful alternatives. Armed with better information, new analytical skills, and stronger organization, the Chortis no longer needed to resort to drastic measures, such as hunger strikes. In addition, stronger parties realized that power abuses would no longer be tolerated. Under such conditions, stakeholders became increasingly prepared to negotiate with others and collaborate.

✦ Common ground could be found (or established). Recognizing interests and needs and promoting mutual understanding increased people's interest in negotiation. Regardless of initial differences, stakeholders have been able to identify or build common ground for dialogue. At the end of the day, poor or rich, we are all humans and share basic needs and concerns that unequivocally link us together.

✦ Historical and social analysis improved decisions. Intragroup stakeholder analyses, in particular gender- and age-sensitive studies, provided important insight into diverse local perspectives. When solutions included this complexity, constituents were more willing to accept outcomes and cooperate with change and needed action.

Understand legal rights and the limitations of government

✦ Laws and knowledge of them were powerful tools. ILO's Agreement 169 clearly had an impact on the Chortís' cause. CBNRM participants should be familiar with the policies that are created to serve them, such as those governing access to natural resources and human rights, so that they can appropriately advocate their own interests.

✦ Government action was limited. Despite good intentions, governments of developing countries rarely have the wherewithal to administer their own policies. Pressuring the government can be productive in terms of obtaining contracts, such as the decree awarding land to the Chortis, but agencies were often limited in their ability to execute policy. NGOs that had access to independent funds for community projects played important roles as both advocates and administrators of policy goals.

Mediate creatively, dynamically, and locally

✦ Local people and organizations were the best mediators. Whereas conflict resolution methods tend to rely on external arbitrators, we found that local human and organizational assets, such as Caritas, were often effective in fulfilling such roles. They often understood histories and were less likely than outsiders to overlook relevant issues. Furthermore, by developing the mediation capacities of local actors, we left behind valuable resources for the future.

✦ Interveners wore many hats. As stated previously, CBNRM is a highly dynamic process that demands tremendous resourcefulness. Caritas and COLABORA provided diverse types of support to the efforts in Copán, including technical assistance, capacity-building, advocacy, convening, linking, and awareness-raising. Interveners needed to "wear many hats" during CBNRM activities. As problems were resolved and new situations arose, organizers needed to withdraw from or join the mediation process, depending on their relative neutrality, authority, and legitimacy.

✦ Teamwork heightened flexibility. Rather than having individuals organize CBNRM events, COLABORA used a team approach for planning, facilitating, and documenting activities. Group thinking and coordination sometimes introduced confounding factors and was, therefore, arduous, but the resulting diversity led to improved planning that better reflected the broad concerns of CBNRM participants.

Conclusion

Power imbalances have marginalized the Chortis in Copán and left them vulnerable to exploitation. Historically, this situation has led to nonsustainable exploitation of resources and concentration of wealth, which have disrupted human relationships and contributed to disparagement, protest, and violence.

Through CBNRM, COLABORA helped CONICHH improve relations among Chorti communities and strengthen the participation of its constituent members. As a result, the Chortis began to address priority concerns through models of leadership that increasingly centred on participation and democracy and that contributed to outcomes more consistent with overarching aspirations. After less than 1 year of COLABORA support, CONICHH and Chorti communities became more unified and increasingly able to promote their own interests.

Despite much progress, the bulk of work in Copán lies ahead. The Chortis continue to be unjustly dominated and exploited, and severe economic, political, and social obstacles block further progress. Now that the Chortis are better prepared to enter negotiations with the more powerful sectors in Copán, other stakeholders may not accept the authority and neutrality of COLABORA as a mediating force. Consequently, the network cannot afford to rest on its laurels. COLABORA must continue to search for creative ways to resolve conflicts and enable diverse parties to reach consensus on how best to manage their resources and achieve progress for Copán and its people.

COLABORA has learned that early stages of CBNRM — especially participatory rural analyses and appropriate conflict management training — can help communities, government agencies, NGOs, and other actors to address very difficult and complex issues. This experience demonstrates that innovative multistakeholder approaches to collaborative learning and action hold great promise for social change contributing to more sustainable and socially equitable futures.

Acknowledgments

Caritas and COLABORA are grateful to the numerous contributors to the efforts in Copán. Gilberto Rios, Sergio Larrea, and Myriam Paredes made up the documentation team and facilitated field visits and participatory research with CONICHH leaders Antonio Ramírez, Jesus and Victoriano Pérez, and Dionisio and José Rufino. Octavio Sánchez, Coordinator for COLABORA, and Reina López and Lesbi Valladares from Caritas, provided valuable coordination and logistical support to the documentation team. Daniel Buckles and Gerret Rusnak from the International Development Research Centre (IDRC) provided valuable comments on earlier versions of this paper. IDRC provided financial support for this project. We thank Caritas, the Cornell International Institute for Food, Agriculture and Development, the Cornell Center for the Environmental, as well as the other members of COLABORA, for their continued support for CBNRM processes in Honduras. The authors take full responsibility for any errors or misrepresentations that appear in this paper.

References

Bunch, R. 1985. Two ears of corn: a guide to people-centered agricultural improvement. World Neighbors, Oklahoma City, OK, USA. 268 pp.

Chambers, R. 1983. Rural development: putting the last first. John Wiley & Sons, New York, NY, USA. 246 pp.

Chambers, R.; Pacey, A.; Thrupp, L.A. 1990. Farmer first: farmer innovation and agricultural research. Intermediate Technology Publications, London, UK. 219 pp.

Freire, P. 1990. Pedagogy of the oppressed. Continuum Publishing, New York, NY, USA. 186 pp.

Fisher, R.; Ury, W. 1981. Getting to yes. Houghton Mifflin, MA, USA.

Herranz, A. 1996. Estado, sociedad y lenguaje. Editorial Guaymuras, 1 Ed. Tegucigalpa, Honduras. 532 pp.

Korten, D.C. 1980. Community organisation and rural development: a learning process approach. Public Administration Review, 40(5), 480–511.

Lee, K. 1993. Compass and gyroscope: integrating science and politics for the environment. Island Press, Washington, DC, USA. 243 pp.

Martínez, A. 1997. La fuerza de la sangre Chortí. Centro Editorial, Tegucigalpa, Honduras. 92 pp.

Newsome, L. 1992. El costo de la conquista. Westview Press, Boulder, CO, USA. 529 pp.

Rivas, R. 1993. Pueblos indígenas y garífunas de Honduras: una caracterización. Editorial Guaymuras, Tegucigalpa, Honduras. 492 pp.

Ríos, G.; Larrea, S.; Paredes, M. 1998. Situación de las comunidades chortis afiliadas al CONICHH: Informe sobre jornada de diagnóstico y documentación participativa con ocho comunidades chorti del 14 de febrero al 6 de marzo de 1998. Red COLABORA, Tegucigalpa, Honduras. 78 pp.

Uphoff, N. 1996. Learning from Gal Oya: possibilities for participatory development and post-Newtonian social science. Intermediate Technology Publications, London, UK. 300 pp.

World Bank. 1994. Social indicators of development. Johns Hopkins University Press, Baltimore, MD, USA.

Chapter 12

THE LAGUNA MERIN BASIN OF URUGUAY: FROM PROTECTING NATURAL HERITAGE TO MANAGING SUSTAINABLE DEVELOPMENT

Carlos Pérez Arrarte and Guillermo Scarlato

This chapter describes a case study in the management of natural resources in a Uruguayan watershed over a period of 10 years (1987–96). It focuses on the tensions between development and environmental interests and ways to resolve them and on new approaches to sustainable development. The study takes place in a region where "modern" commercial farmers and livestock producers operate according to business practices, private ownership of productive resources, and fully developed markets for factors, services, and products. The analysis is organized around two distinct periods and experiences: protecting the natural heritage and managing sustainable development. Each coincided to some extent with an action-research project conducted by the Centro Interdisciplinario de Estudios Sobre el Desarrollo (interdisciplinary centre for development studies).

Development and the environment in the Lake Merin basin

The Lake Merin watershed is on the Atlantic coast of South American in the temperate zone; it occupies some 6 million ha between 31° and 34° S and between 51° and 55° W (Figure 1). The western half covers 18% of Uruguay; the other half lies in Brazil. This area is representative of a broad pampa region of 270 000 km² that includes the southern part

Figure 1. Map of the Lake Merin watershed.

of the state of Rio Grande do Sul in Brazil, the northern part of Uruguay, a large part of Argentina's Mesopotamia (the northern portions of Entre Rios, Corrientes, and part of Misiones), and part of the Chaco in southern Paraguay (Figure 2). The natural landscape consists of gently rolling country and broad plains typified by grassland, wetland, and natural forest ecosystems along the banks of the many waterways that drain the region. The climate is subtropical, with an annual rainfall of 1 200–1 500 mm.

Until recently, these grasslands and pampas, with their rich biodiversity, had been only slightly disturbed by livestock grazing on large ranches. However, in the last 20 years, the spread of irrigated and mechanized rice growing has introduced a new dimension of transformation and its associated conflicts over natural resources.

In Uruguay, a 1-million-ha portion of the Lake Merin basin forms a vast plain, with deep soils, numerous waterways, and a wealth of flora and fauna. Toward the southern boundary of the basin, natural drainage is more limited, and the plain becomes a large wetland, known as the Bañados del Este or the Bañados de Rocha, which originally covered 350 000 ha. The wetland extends to the Atlantic coast, where it is associated with a system of lagoons connected to the ocean. This zone contains the most valuable ecosystems in terms of biodiversity, water-regulation capacity, beauty of landscape, and the tourist

Figure 2. The extent of the livestock–rice growing region.

industry. It was because of this region and its importance as a waterfowl habitat that Uruguay signed the Ramsar Convention on Internationally Significant Wetlands in 1984. The United Nations Educational, Scientific and Cultural Organization has declared the area a World Biosphere Reserve.

Unlike many of the other biodiversity reserves of the world, the basin is privately owned, essentially by ranchers who make their living from it; it contains no significant expanses of public property. From the earliest days of settlement, the area has been used for extensive livestock grazing. Large ranches take advantage of the expanse of natural grasslands and marshes to pasture animals. These operations require little in the way of human resources or infrastructure. The gaucho on horseback is the classic figure in this landscape.

In addition to livestock production, the area has been developed for other uses. Food and commercial crops are planted by resource-poor inhabitants. Tourism has become an important activity on the Atlantic coast. This is putting pressure on coastal resources, but at the same time it gives a large portion of the country's urban population an opportunity to see the wetlands region and understand its problems.

Irrigated rice cultivation began in the region about 30 years ago. Since then the area under cultivation has expanded to 100 000 ha and now accounts for about 70% of Uruguay's rice crop. Rice growing is now the mainstay of the regional economy: the sector is a heavy user of farm inputs and services and generates gross revenues per hectare 30 times those produced by raising livestock. Yields, which range from 5 000 to 7 500 kg/ha, compare favourably with those of more developed parts of the world. In addition to satisfying local needs, rice is among Uruguay's top three exports in financial terms.

Since its beginnings this activity has been a major factor in the transformation of the environment, altering the physical and biological setting, as well as the social one. The abundance of virgin land, the production techniques used, and state policies have encouraged a model of development with enormous ecological costs. Rice growers move to new land after every few cycles of rice production, putting pressure on previously untouched soils and quickly transforming large areas of the natural ecosystem. This contrasts with models of intensive crop–livestock rotations. The model of itinerant development not only destroys natural ecosystems but also fails to allow for the development of the long-term infrastructure needed to link the isolated farms and local communities.

In recent years, the possibility of further expansion within the Lake Merin basin is being exhausted. New technologies and investments in regional infrastructure and more intensive crop–livestock rotations are assuming growing importance. Work is under way to drain wetlands, protect flood-prone zones, introduce rural electrification, etc. However, the old itinerant model is continuing outside the basin, where a "land rush" is on to open new lands in areas with natural ecosystems.

The rice industry in Uruguay employs about 700 growers. Farm production units are relatively large: the average farm under rice cultivation is 200 ha and requires heavy investment in machinery, infrastructure, and labour. A high proportion of the key resources for rice growing — land and water — do not belong to the growers. Tenant farming arrangements predominate; the livestock ranchers retain ownership of the land; and they and other agents, including large industrial companies, own the water resources and irrigation systems. Only 11% of farmers own their own land and the water they use for their crops; 8% lease water; 35% lease their land; and 46% lease both basic resources (Tommasino et al. 1996). The growers are associated with about a dozen industrial and commercial concerns. One of these firms alone controls more than 50% of the business; three of the larger firms are vertically integrated agroindustrial concerns. The high degree of vertical integration of these industrial firms is characteristic of the sector: the mills process and market the grain, but they also supply the farm units with the necessary inputs, and may also lease land and water to them and provide access to capital goods, financing, etc.

The Uruguayan government has played a role in the creation and development of the rice economy through a number of specific policies. The country's development bank, the Banco de la República [bank of the republic], extends lines of credit for cultivation and for industrial and marketing activity, and has frequently made debt refinancing arrangements in times of crisis. With the establishment of the Eastern Experimental Station in 1970, the public sector — working closely with private interests — assumed an important role in generating and disseminating rice-growing technology. At the same time, the state carried out a series of infrastructure works that were of great assistance to the industry — roads, irrigation systems, wetland drainage, rural electrification — and channeled loans from multilateral agencies (the Inter-American Development Bank, the World Bank) that were vital to the expansion of cultivation over the low-lying areas of the basin. Since the

1980s rice growers have enjoyed rebates on indirect taxes and, in some years, this has represented a significant boost to their incomes.

In 1995, the total population of the Lake Merin basin was 185 000. The rural population is highly dispersed, only 1.09 people/km². Most rural dwellers depend on livestock activities. Some 80% of the population lives in urban centres, of which 3 have more than 25 000 inhabitants, 13 have 1 000–10 000, and 17 have fewer than 1 000 people. The rice industry is an important business for these smaller towns and cities, whose populations provide various business services and urban amenities — housing, electricity, water, sanitation, communications, etc. — and are engaged in jobs created by local governments. Along the Atlantic coast, tourism is increasingly the mainstay of income generation.

Conflict over protection of the natural heritage

The conflict analyzed in this chapter was triggered by a lawsuit launched in 1987 by a group of nongovernmental organizations (NGOs) to block a state-sponsored project to channel a river to protect adjacent rice plantations from periodic flooding. The project threatened an important area in terms of biodiversity and tourism. Tensions also rose over access to water, the most significant factor affecting further rice expansion. Water for irrigation comes from natural sources, such as Lake Merin, and from publicly or privately constructed reservoirs. Various interests — ranchers, who usually own the natural water sources, rice growers, and rice processors — have been scrambling to control these sources, which are the determining factor in the amount of surface area that can be cultivated. Finally, the distribution of the costs and benefits of land rental, water rights, and the services that support production (transportation, drying, processing, and marketing) has also caused tension. For example, at harvest time the farm-gate price for rice is set through a process of negotiation among the groups involved in the various stages of rice marketing. These groups have different capacities to negotiate shares in the profits. The industrial process is concentrated with a few companies whose costs of production are not public knowledge and who can dictate their terms. Transportation companies are small, numerous, and unorganized, leaving them with little negotiating power. Producers receive a residual price for their product, after the costs and profits of the other agents have been determined. These differences in negotiating power are a key source of tension.

Sectors not involved in rice growing constituted a heterogeneous interest group motivated by their common opposition to rice. Small-scale livestock producers and local residents who use resources of the natural ecosystem have been affected by the expansion of rice production. Businesses engaged in tourism have suffered from the decline in the quality of the recreational areas near the ocean, which have been polluted by runoff from large-scale drainage operations.

By March 1985, at the end of the dictatorship period, there were already a number of studies and demonstrations by social agencies (NGOs, universities) highlighting the importance of the eastern wetlands, the degradation they were being subjected to, and the need to protect them. The country's return to democracy created a particularly propitious climate for social protest, and one of its major manifestations was the environmental movement and its demands for conservation measures. The epicentre of this movement was in Rocha, a southern area typified by its vast, rich wetlands. This region also includes an extensive shoreline along the Atlantic Ocean, a tourist area, and other valuable habitats, which added to the complexity of the issue and opened up other collateral problems that aroused the urban public.

The major interest groups or stakeholders involved were the producers, the conservationists, and the local government:

✦ The "production" bloc was committed to business at all costs and exerted continuous pressure for new infrastructure to carry on the traditional exploitation of the wetlands. It consisted of the rice sector (growers, processors, technicians, etc.), certain sectors among the large-scale livestock community who benefited from the increased value of their land generated by the new works, together with various central-government agencies, such as the Ministry of Livestock, Agriculture and Fisheries and the Ministry of Transport and Public Works (which regulates everything to do with water). The recently created Ministry of Housing, Lands and Environmental Management played a marginal or passive role in this confrontation.

✦ The bloc pressing for a "conservationist" approach to natural resources portrayed the rice business in a negative light. It was made up of a heterogeneous assortment of groups: small-scale livestock raisers, local people affected by drainage activities, environmental organizations, the six NGOs active nationally — which had formed a network called Agrupaciones Uruguayas por un Ambiente Sano (AGUAS [the Spanish word for water], Uruguayan group for a healthy environment) — and a number of other organizations that, to varying degrees, involved themselves in the conflict: the Uruguayan network of environmental NGOs, university groups, etc.

✦ The local government in the region — the Intendencia Municipal de Rocha (municipal government of Rocha) — played a strategic role advocating sound land management. It threw its support behind the environmentalists, publicly denouncing the central government for its "centralist" actions and for listening too closely to the complaints of the business lobby that was in league with the rice sector and demanding public policies and action seen as destructive of the country's basic resources.

The NGOs mobilized in a number of ways, holding information sessions and workshops, bringing pressure on the media and government agencies, and publicizing their interpretation of events at national and international forums. The greatest impact internally was the stir that was caused by the screening of two videos dealing with the region — *Bañados de Rocha: the secret of the waters* and *India Muerta* — which were prepared by Imagenes, a member of the AGUAS network. These videos were shown during an initial campaign in 40 urban centres in this part of the country, in public halls, followed by a public discussion period. Subsequently, the videos were circulated through normal channels. During this time, the production proponents failed to take account of the claims of the conservationist front, and they made no effort to build a better public image. This attitude began to change toward the end of the period.

Analysis of the situation by the Centro Interdisciplinario de Estudios Sobre el Desarrollo (CIEDUR, interdisciplinary centre for development studies) (Damiani 1993; Scarlato 1993a, 1994; Pérez Arrarte 1994, 1995; Tommasino et al. 1996) indicates that these protests had various impacts:

✦ No additional public works were carried out in the region during this period; however, the private sector continued to work on infrastructure projects without permission from the authorities.

✦ The public image of the rice sector suffered because of its affect on the environment, and this should be seen as a turning point. Until the second half of the 1900s, the rice sector enjoyed almost unrestricted local power, which allowed it to do things that had a terrible effect on the environment without having to seek permission or be accountable afterward. This situation changed dramatically. As a director of the rice growers' association remarked, "Now when we go to a meeting, the first thing we have to do is explain that we rice growers are not out to destroy the environment."

✦ Regional and national awareness was slowly created with respect to the value of wetland ecosystems and biodiversity in general, and people began to appreciate the real tensions between development and environment. Within the region, an environmental movement was taking root with the appearance of a number of NGOs and a network of activities.

✦ Thanks to efforts of the United Nations and the Universidad de la República, the Program for Conservation of Biodiversity in the Bañados del Este (PROBIDES) was developed and approved, with funding from the Global Environmental Facility for a period of 5 years (1993–98). PROBIDES was an ambitious undertaking carried out under the auspices of the Faculty of Sciences of the Universidad de la República [university of the republic], the Ministry of Housing, Lands and Environmental Management, and the municipal government of Rocha. The general goal of the project was to conserve the biodiversity of the Bañados del Este by promoting sustainable regional development. Specifically, the project was to increase the knowledge of the natural resources of the region, strengthen human resources for research and advocacy, increase the flow of information on the environment, and facilitate the participation of local public- and private-sector actors.

✦ A tremendous flow of field data and research information — on the natural resources, the productive systems, and the society and economy of the region — was generated, assembled, and analyzed (see Rilla and Rudolf 1992; Chabalgoity and Piperno 1993; Damiani 1993; Irigoyen 1993; Rubio et al. 1993; Scarlato 1993b; Carballo and Di Landro 1994; Pérez Arrarte 1994).

Toward participatory management for sustainable development

By the early 1990s, conditions were right for bringing about a substantial change in the behaviour of the various parties involved and in their relative strengths and bargaining power. Implementation of the PROBIDES project in the Rocha region represented a milestone and, in effect, launched a new stage in the management of the conflict. The presence of the Universidad de la República as project leader, the involvement of the Rocha municipal government as a second partner, the enlisting of the new ministry responsible for the environment, and the active participation of the national United Nations Development Programme office all lent a high degree of legitimacy to the private organizations that had mobilized earlier to defend the interests of conservation. As the local environmental movement matured, the NGOs and other agencies based in Montevideo tended to withdraw from active involvement in the Rocha area.

Perceptions of the tensions between "los Bañados del Este" and the economy of rice and livestock that dominated the region can be summarized as follows:

◆ There was a recognized need to adopt a watershed-wide focus to address problems of sustainable development and to bypass the debate over purely local issues (in the *bañados* area, which covered only a third of the wetlands and a tenth of the watershed basin).

◆ The problem of resource use for rice growing included a number of key political, sectoral, technological, and institutional issues. The productive system had severe inefficiencies as a result of the lack of local linkages not adequately addressed by market forces. There was no systematic rotation of crops and pastures, which would have increased land-use intensity and made crop growing and livestock production more complementary. The infrastructure — irrigation, roads, energy, and storage — that had developed to support itinerary rice production remained underused after the growing period. Suboptimal use of these fixed investments was reflected in poor living conditions for workers and poor long-term warehousing facilities for equipment and commodities.

◆ Difficulties arising from the lack of land-use guidelines and the absence of local land-use authorities with effective power over a defined area were obvious in the lack of control over local production interests, the exclusion of low-income or minority social groups, and disregard for the broader interests of the citizenry.

◆ The equity perspective, which was eclipsed by the dominant paradigm of productivity, needed to be highlighted and promoted. In the absence of specific alternative mechanisms, definition of land use and production goals, resolution of environmental problems, and development of local urban centres were determined by the rice growers and the big ranchers, who had the greatest lobbying power.

◆ A great deal of information was available, but was generally not considered in the decisions of the various players.

Based on this summary of the situation, an action-research project was identified, and support for it was obtained from the Program for the Management of Natural Resources and Irrigation Development (PRENAER), which was being implemented in Uruguay with resources from the World Bank. The project related to the issue of the rice–livestock production system in the Lake Merin basin and stressed interaction with decision-makers in four areas: mid-sized growers, the technology-policy sector at the microregional level, and development of protected areas. The conceptual and methodological framework was inspired by Dourojeanni (1991), Nelson et al. (1992), and Poggiese (1994).

A priority of the project was to establish roundtables or workshops for interaction and negotiation among the stakeholders involved in each area; technical experts acted as facilitators and suppliers of the information needed to see the negotiations through to a conclusion. The final outcome was to be a document containing the points on which consensus had been achieved. This would be circulated to the various interest groups, the institutions involved, the policymakers, and the community at large.

For each area of the project, a lead institution was identified and others were invited to serve as participants. In some cases, invitations were sent out more widely for specific events. Leadership in the mid-sized growers' component was assumed by the Rice Growers' Association; its manager, directors, and advisors took part in the group's meetings. Also attending were experts from two bodies under the Ministry of Livestock, Agriculture and Fisheries (MGAP): the Office of Agricultural Programming and Policies and the Directorate of Economic Research. The Directorate of Natural Resources, which was also invited, declined to take part. Other participants included experts from the Agricultural Planning Office (a parastatal program for livestock development), representatives of various firms in the rice industry, independent experts, and officials of the Banco de la República, the state bank, which is the primary source of financing for rice growing.

In the technology-policy area, activities were concentrated at the National Agricultural Research Institute's (INIA) experimental station in the Lake Merin basin, which carried out research on rice growing. The project was managed by the Rice Working Group, with involvement of the research team for each activity, plus a group of leading producers and technical advisors.

For the local development area of the project, community people were encouraged to form a group that became known as the Committee for the Electrification of the Séptima Baja (the "seventh lowland"), which was the first need identified by the group. This was an area with a long history of rice production that had seen frequent conflicts over scarce water resources controlled by a few relatively powerful family businesses. In both the technology-policy and local-development areas, the local government — the Intendencia Municipal de Treinta y Tres — played a key role, first by lending legitimacy to the project and later by helping out with its execution.

A fourth decision-making group had been planned to identify and develop a protected natural area in the department of Treinta y Tres. However, this project area had to be canceled after the initial work of making contacts and identifying the site had been completed. The Directorate of Natural Resources of the MGAP forced the financing agency to block progress in this component, claiming that such activity was an encroachment on its legal jurisdiction.

Outcomes of an inconclusive experiment

The project was to be carried out over 3 years, but difficulties with the MGAP forced it to close after only 15 months. Nevertheless, the results of three of the project areas can be summarized as follows:

- ✦ In the mid-sized growers' component, there was extensive debate with the other major players about the factors that affect the sustainability of this mode of production, which is so important in the rice–livestock sector in Uruguay. The group met regularly and had in-depth discussions following a previously agreed on agenda and often making use of specially prepared working documents. Guidelines were developed for improving policies related to credit for growers, including specific measures to support small-scale producers (such as setting up a guarantee fund). A training project for farmers was sketched out and is currently being negotiated with the association. Problems impeding rotation of crops between rice and pasture were analyzed (given that new pastures could stimulate the local livestock economy), and the results became the basis for an extension program carried out under the agricultural plan in the rice-growing area. The relationship between rice growers and the processing industry was examined, as was the role of the land and water owners, the various types of contracts in use, and how they affect the environmental and social sustainability of rice growing.

✦ Under the technology-policy area, an initial meeting was held to present the objectives of the undertaking. Subsequently, participants met at the INIA–Treinta y Tres Experimental Station to prepare its "Medium-Term Indicative Plan," which established the focus of work in this area over the next 5 years. In addition, for the 15 months of the project, they took part in all technical discussions in the region, expanding their contacts and introducing the sustainability perspective. The INIA technical staff were given all relevant information available on the objective of the work. Surprisingly, the group encountered great difficulty in establishing a fruitful dialogue among those engaged in formal technological research and technicians working for companies involved in rice growing.

✦ The Committee for the Electrification of the Séptima Baja was launched in a satisfactory manner. Once the first meetings had been held to sound out local leaders, broader gatherings were held in which a neighbourhood committee was set up, with electrification of the region as its primary objective. The committee worked reasonably well, carrying out a major survey and making the necessary contacts with local and national authorities. It established links with the state electricity enterprise, Administración de Usinas y Transmisiones Eléctricas (UTE, administration of electrical utilities and transmissions) and began work in accordance with the agency's guidelines for providing service; electricity is used in homes and for economic ends, primarily as power for pumping water for rice irrigation. A survey of the neighbourhood was carried out (150 homes and farms spread over 70 000 ha) to determine energy demands. Work began on the outline of a project, and meetings were held with the local authorities and the electric company to promote it. Currently UTE is completing plans for the distribution of electricity, and expects to begin work on building the transmission lines.

The results of the action project should be evaluated in light of several problems:

✦ The execution time was short. Given the nature of such activities, it would have been better to carry them out over at least 3 years, as was originally planned.

✦ The proposed project was novel for Uruguay. It was proposed by a private organization (CIEDUR) in a country with a strong tradition of state leadership, and it was an action project with no promise of investment funding or financing for the activities of the presumed beneficiaries.

✦ A section of MGAP, the Directorate of Natural Resources, which supervised the execution of the PRENAER project that financed this activity, decided halfway through the first year of the project that it conflicted with the ministry's prerogatives and should not proceed. It tried to cancel the project and later prevented work from being completed as originally negotiated.

In general, the process of change was typified by a shift in the centre of gravity of the conflict away from defending the natural heritage toward seeking a form of development that would be consistent with preserving that heritage. The first stage, consisting of protests, helped slow down the increasing rate of environmental degradation of a sensitive subregion (the *bañados*); the second marked the beginning, partial and slow, of a search for sustainable development involving the various stakeholders.

The most notable outcome of the process was the change in behaviour of some of the key actors. The demands of NGOs and other institutions moved from shrill statements and agitation to more carefully informed proposals and a search for common ground in terms of development that would consider environmental values. On the other side, organizations representing business interests, and in some cases the businesses themselves, began to include environmental issues in their pronouncements — often as a superficial gesture, no doubt, but in some cases reflecting a genuine change in their perception of the problem and in their basis for decision-making. Surprisingly, the rice sector, which at first seemed to be the most hostile, showed itself open and ready to talk, to find solutions that would suit everyone and to consider the central issues of sustainability. On the other hand, the livestock interests represented a large, mixed, poorly organized group, with divergent interests depending on their scale and location, which made it difficult to engage them in dialogue and negotiations.

The stakeholders that appeared most impervious to change and most opposed to finding common ground were, to a large extent, the organs of the central government (ministries, the development bank). Less marked, but still significant, resistance could also be detected in INIA, a nonstate public entity. Finally, within the public sector, the local governments were the most amenable to change, in some cases in sharp conflict with the central-government agencies.

Bañados de Rocha, the most fragile and conflictual subregion, has continued to move along its own particular path. On one hand, the PROBIDES project, which is peculiar in that it is governed by a board made up of a relatively independent body (the Universidad de la República), a central-government agency (Ministerio de Vivienda, Ordenamiento Territorial y Medio Ambiente [Ministry of Housing, Land Use Planning and Environment]), and a local government (the Intendencia Municipal de Rocha), is now in its fourth year of operation and is succeeding in channeling vast sums of money into the area, in public recognition of the environmental value of the region's natural resources and the tensions that a traditional approach to development had provoked. It may be viewed as the major institutional success to date. Final evaluation of the project, to be carried out in the fifth year, will allow us to determine whether it has achieved its objectives and justified the high expectations it aroused among so many players when it was approved.

Lessons learned: the winding road to community participation

An overview of the processes and events that occurred during a decade of efforts to promote sustainable development in the Lake Merin watershed makes it clear that community participation is a broad and complex process of actions and reactions (Viola 1992). In fact, it often necessitates a realignment of power, whether from the national or the local level. Yet, as those who now hold such power will not give it up graciously, each new arena for participation must be conquered.

In the cycle of conflict, the process of recognizing the less powerful interest groups, or those with more diffuse interests, is costly and laborious. The more powerful elements will attempt to conceal their privileged position from local and national eyes and will do their lobbying discreetly and in a way that closely targets the sources of power. It will take public events and demonstrations to make different positions clear and to open a phase of negotiation and searching for possible points of agreement. Negotiations come about as the more powerful stakeholders realize that they have something to lose. Things may have to go through periods of instability, which will place some pressure on the various players to continue the dialogue.

In the case of the Lake Merin watershed, the importance of this two-stage process — awareness raising then negotiations — becomes clear. Lawsuits, information sessions, workshops and demonstrations by social agencies, such as NGOs and universities, served to make the issues known to a wide range of people. This both raised awareness about the value of the wetlands and tarnished the public image of the rice sector, forcing it to begin to consider its effect on the environment and establishing the need for negotiations. The negotiation process itself, although incomplete, allowed the various stakeholders to move away from extreme positions and begin searching for a common ground.

The declining influence of specific national policies in current models of development — inspired by the focus on macroeconomic equilibrium, international trade and liberalization of investment, and market mechanisms — is reflected in the behaviour of central-government ministries involved in economic production. They face increasing operational problems, but they continue to be strongholds of bureaucratic resistance, and they refuse to experiment with the new forms of management that sustainable development demands. Yet, the accepted tools of development — public policies on regional or sectoral development, financing, and technological development — represent the original source of major territorial and environmental impacts, and of their associated conflicts, externalities not included in conventional assessments (Scarlato 1996).

We need to define a "new" institutional arrangement in which participation by civil society is more suitable and effective. The fields of action for the new kind of participation explored in this case study involve multiple levels and dimensions. These include the sectoral dimension, which allows direct interaction with decision-makers who apply private resources to production and investment, and the regional–local dimension, through the growing weight of local governments and other local and regional stakeholders in the social processes that affect their sphere of influence. The processes of decentralization and strengthening of local governments and communities occurring in countries throughout Latin America will encourage a form of management that is closer to the people and to the natural resources in question (Bervejillo 1994).

The experts who are closely tied to technology, production, and business — engineering agronomists, civil engineers, economists, etc. — have been trained in the paradigm of "productivity" (in the sense used by Trigo [1994]). This makes them a barrier to the participation of civil society, because their one-sided perception of the development process and their close links with business and political interests make it difficult for them to support actions that question the "powers that be." The agencies that now make up the national agricultural-research system are "demand driven" by highly focused sectoral interests; they emphasize short-term productivity in all their projects and maintain a low profile when it comes to research relating to natural resource conservation and sustainability.

There is a need for a comprehensive research approach that includes identifying the key points of dispute and posing alternatives. Such an approach should be seen as independent and trustworthy by the various interests involved, including the poorest and most marginalized sectors of society. Institutes that are most firmly rooted in civil society (NGOs and the like) and are engaged in independent action research can objectively promote and facilitate negotiations between various interests and, at the same time, defend the diffuse rights of the citizenry when necessary.

Acknowledgments

We are grateful to the International Development Research Centre and the Program for Natural Resource Management and Irrigation Development, Uruguay, for their support for our basic research.

References

Bervejillo, F. 1994. Nuevos procesos y estrategias de desarrollo: territorios en la globalización. Prisma, 4.

Carballo, G.; di Landro, E. 1994. Estudio del uso de la tierra en relación a su aptitu, en la Cuenca de la Laguna Merín. (Procesamiento digital de imágenes satelitales). Centro Interdisciplinario de Estudios Sobre el Desarrollo, Montevideo, Uruguay. Investigaciones 119. 26 pp.

Chabalgoity, M.; Piperno, P. 1993. Atlas socioeconómico de la Cuenca de la Laguna Merin-Uruguay. Vol. I. Centro Interdisciplinario de Estudios Sobre el Desarrollo, Montevideo, Uruguay. Investigaciones 109. 158 pp.

Damiani, O. 1993. Marco jurídico-institucional de la gestión ambiental del Departamento de Rocha. Centro Interdisciplinario de Estudios Sobre el Desarrollo, Montevideo, Uruguay. Investigaciones 107. 51 pp.

Dourojeanni, A. 1991. Procedimientos de gestión para el desarrollo sustentable (aplicados a municipios, microregiones y cuencas). Comisión Económica para América Latina, Santiago de Chile, Chile.

Irigoyen, R.M. 1993. La integración arroz-ganadería en la Cuenca de la Laguna Merin. Centro Interdisciplinario de Estudios Sobre el Desarrollo, Montevideo, Uruguay. Investigaciones 113. 47 pp.

Nelson, M.; Couto, W.; Seré, C.; Chaparro, F.; Li Pun, H. 1992. Action research in resource management: the use of knowledge in decision-making systems. Regional Office for Latin America, International Development Research Centre, Montevideo, Uruguay. Internal document.

Pérez Arrarte, C. 1994. Bases para el ordenamiento territorial de la Cuenca de la Laguna Merín: relaciones entre el uso y la aptitud de los suelos para el cultivo de arroz. Centro Interdisciplinario de Estudios Sobre el Desarrollo, Montevideo, Uruguay. Seminarios y talleres 82. 10 pp.
————— 1995. Arroz: cultivo vs. sistema. Arroz, Montevideo, 3, 12–15.
————— 1996. Grupo de trabajo Medianeros y Sistemas Arroceros. Arroz, Montevideo, 5, 28–30.

Poggiese, H. 1994. Metodología FLACSO de planificación-gestión (planificación participativa y gestión asociada). Facultad Latinoamericana para las Ciencias Sociales, Buenos Aires, Argentina. Serie de documentos e informes de investigación 163.

Rilla, F.D.; Rudolf, J.C. 1992. Fauna del Area de Ramsar Uruguay. Centro Interdisciplinario de Estudios Sobre el Desarrollo, Montevideo, Uruguay. Documento de trabajo 75. 13 pp.

Rubio, L.; Scarlato, G.; Stenger, H. 1993. Programa de evaluación de modelos arroz-ganaderos. Centro Interdisciplinario de Estudios Sobre el Desarrollo, Montevideo, Uruguay. Documento de trabajo 85. 14 pp.

Scarlato, G. 1993a. La actividad arrocera en la Cuenca de la aguna Merin: perspectiva histórica. Centro Interdisciplinario de Estudios Sobre el Desarrollo, Montevideo, Uruguay. Investigaciones 108. 168 pp.

———— 1993b. Desarrollo y ambiente en la Cuenca de la Laguna Merin: un panorama sobre los conflictos y las respuestas. Centro Interdisciplinario de Estudios Sobre el Desarrollo, Montevideo, Uruguay. Documento de trabajo 84. 33 pp.

———— 1994. La actividad arrocera uruguaya, marco general y perspectiva regional. Montevideo, Centro Interdisciplinario de Estudios Sobre el Desarrollo, Montevideo, Uruguay. 109 pp.

———— 1996. Agricultural dynamics in subtropical zones of South America: productive systems, land use and public policies. Centro Interdisciplinario de Estudios Sobre el Desarrollo, Montevideo, Uruguay.

Tommasino, H.; Scarlato, G.; Salgado, L. 1996. Análisis regional de las formas de acceso a la tierra y el agua. Arroz, Montevideo, 6, 28–31.

Trigo, E. 1994. Investigación agropecuaria, innovación institucional y desarrollo sostenible: el papel de las instituciones nacionales de investigación agrícola. PROCISUR(IICA), Montevideo, Uruguay. Dialogo XLII.

Viola, E. 1992. De la denuncia y concientización a la institucionalización y el desarrollo sustentable. Nueva Sociedad, 122.

Chapter 13

MATAGALPA, NICARAGUA:
NEW PATHS FOR PARTICIPATORY MANAGEMENT IN THE CALICO RIVER WATERSHED

Ronnie Vernooy and Jacqueline A. Ashby

This chapter describes current progress on the International Centre for Tropical Agriculture's Hillsides project in Nicaragua. This action-oriented research project aims to provide decision-makers at various levels with the strategic information and instruments they need to improve the management of the natural resource base in the fragile and degraded hillside environment of Central America. The main activities are described briefly, with emphasis on the organizational principles and actions that are guiding the project. We conclude with a summary of the impact and lessons learned so far.

The research site and context

The International Centre for Tropical Agriculture (ICTA's) Hillsides project is an action-oriented research project aimed at providing farmers, farmers' associations, nongovernmental organizations (NGOs), and policymakers with strategic information and methods for improving the management of the natural resource base in the fragile and degraded hillside environment of Central America. Research is being carried out in four watersheds: three in Honduras and one in Nicaragua. The project is funded by the Swiss Development Corporation, International Development Research Centre (IDRC), and the Inter-American Development Bank. The fieldwork in Nicaragua is being carried out by an interdisciplinary team of researchers that includes the coordinator, research associate, Jorge Alonso Beltrán,

and research assistants, Nohemi Espinoza, Dominga Tijerino, and María Eugenia Baltodano. ICTA staff based in Cali, Colombia, and Tegucigalpa, Honduras, provide additional
support in such areas as geographic information systems and soils research.

In Nicaragua, the area of research is the Calico River watershed, located in the
southern part of Matagalpa, about 125 km northeast of the capital, Managua (Figure 1).
The Calico River is a tributary of the Great Matagalpa River, and its watershed covers an
area of about 170 km². In 1997, the total population was about 23 800 people, living in
17 rural communities (about 13 000 people) and the town of San Dionisio, the municipal
capital (Baltodano et al. 1997).

The climate of the watershed, which forms part of the central-hillsides range of the
country, is semi-arid (800–1 600 mm annual rainfall; temperature range, 22.5° to 25.0°C).
The land ranges from 350 to 1 250 m above sea level. Agricultural activities are based
mainly on small-scale farmers' production systems: a combination of corn and bean crops
(one cycle of corn, two cycles of beans), dual-purpose livestock (milk sold to the factory,

Figure 1. Map of Nicaragua showing general location of San Dionisio.

cheese produced for the local market), and coffee in the higher altitudes (for export). Land tenure varies; there are still a significant number of landless households, a large number of smallholders (less than 2 ha), but also a few large landowners.

The major problems people face are poverty, characterized by lack of health and education facilities and poor housing conditions; a strong dependence on corn and beans, with no, or very few, production alternatives; soil degradation; a scarcity of water; and deforestation. According to a 1996 study, 76% of the population in the San Dionisio municipality is considered poor, and the municipality is among the poorest in the country (Arcia et al. 1996). Data that we gathered in 1997 confirm that this very high percentage of people does live in poverty. Local people explain that one of the main factors contributing to these conditions is the land-tenure situation, which forces many to rent land and others to work as day labourers to earn some additional income (Baltodano et al. 1998).

The problems for people in the watershed were further aggravated by the devastating impact of hurricane Mitch at the end of October 1998. The Calico River watershed was badly hit by the hurricane, which destroyed 150 houses, secondary roads, and the bridge over the Great Matagalpa River (disconnecting the area from the south and east of the Department of Matagalpa) and damaged rural schools, health-care centres, and crops in the fields. A preliminary evaluation estimated that about 80% of the bean crops and 40% of the corn yield were lost. Coffee, sorghum, fruit, and vegetable crops were also affected. Hundreds of trees were uprooted and washed away. People from San Dionisio described the newly formed shores of the Calico River as *playa*, or beach; the force of the water had dramatically enlarged the river bed.

Problems, conflicts, and opportunities for alternative management arrangements

In September 1997, a participatory workshop on watershed management brought together a mixed group of 30 local men and women (farmers, NGO staff, and local-government officials), who identified the key problems affecting land management and the livelihoods of people in the Calico area at various levels — community, microwatershed, and watershed. These problems included land degradation leading to lower yields, deforestation causing soil erosion and loss of wildlife, water scarcity, and water pollution (Vernooy 1997). Survey data collected in 1997 as part of our watershed-wide study on poverty confirmed these findings.

At the beginning of the Hillsides project, the situation in terms of organization could best be described as the uncoordinated presence and intervention of a number of NGOs — Programa Campesino a Campesino (Farmer to Farmer Program) – Unión Nacional de Agricultores y Ganaderos (national union of farmers and ranchers), Cooperative for American Relief Everywhere (CARE), PRODESSA–UCOSD, ODESAR, Indigenous Association of Matagalpa. Each of these NGOs operates in one or more of the 17 communities in the watershed, providing technical support in terms of soil conservation techniques, reforestation, diversification, postharvest treatment, credit, marketing support, and training. Several organizations sometimes independently serve the same rural households. There is also a Municipal Development Council, made up of municipal-level representatives of the ministries of health, education, water, and social action, members of the municipal council, and the coordinator of the Campesino a Campesino program. This council focuses mainly on infrastructure — the construction and repair of roads, schools, and health-care centres. At the community level, there are several Drinking Water Committees in charge of maintaining the water system, as well as Parent Committees that oversee the programs implemented in rural kindergartens and primary schools, and a variety of active church groups that deal with health issues and cultural events. The ministries of agriculture and livestock, natural resources and the environment, and agrarian reform had virtually no presence in this organizational context.

The main problem leading to conflict in this watershed regards access to, and use of, drinking water. Tensions have arisen between the owners of land in the upper reaches of the river and downstream communities that depend on these sources for their supply of drinking water. Downstream users complain about the negligence of the landowners in terms of water-source maintenance and deforestation of the surrounding areas. They are also regularly faced with threats by the landowners to cut off the water supply. A second area of tension is between neighbouring communities where one of the communities depends on another for drinking water; an example of this type of tension is found in the communities of Susuli, which has a water source, and El Jicaro 2, which does not have its own source and depends on Susuli for water. Some farmers use river water illegally for irrigation, a practice prohibited by municipal law. Municipal authorities are powerless to stop this. Downstream users complain because water flow is reduced, limiting the amount available for domestic use and consumption.

Access to, and use of, land is another source of conflict. Uncertainty about the legality of the agrarian land-reform process and its results continues to cause trouble, especially for farmers organized in cooperatives. Several cooperatives in the watershed have received expropriation notices from former landowners who have returned to Nicaragua after the 1996 election of neoliberal President Arnoldo Alemán Lacayo.

We examined this situation in terms of opportunities for action:

- ✦ Looking at natural resource management problems at the watershed and microwatershed levels;

- ✦ Improving rural people's participation in decision-making at the municipality level;

- ✦ Stimulating coordination among NGOs, the Municipal Development Council, and ministries (to increase the impact of efforts and avoid duplication); and

- ✦ Facilitating *concertación* (cooperation, harmonization), where relevant, focusing on the resolution of conflicts over natural resources and, perhaps, the development of an integrated natural resources management plan.

In meetings and conversations with NGO staff and members of the Municipal Development Council, we learned that they were aware of the lack of coordination, the duplication of efforts by NGOs, and the existing opportunities for more concerted action, but that no one was interested in taking the initiative to do anything about the situation. However, a few months after our arrival in the area, we proposed reviving one of the ideas developed by the Campesino a Campesino program and the municipality — reforestation of a tract of the Calico River. Coordination was rapidly achieved; a project proposal and planning process were outlined, with input from most local actors; and work was spearheaded by the mayor of San Dionisio.

Activities under way in the Calico River watershed

Enhancing local organizational capacity

In terms of strengthening organizational processes in the area, the ICTA Hillsides team came to an agreement with the Campesino a Campesino program in San Dionisio to form a number of Comtés de Investigación Agricola Local (CIALs, local agricultural-research committees). The idea behind these committees is to provide local communities with a way to carry out participatory research, focusing on and solving a locally felt natural resource management problem (identified through participatory problem analysis), thus enhancing local organizational capacity (Ashby et al. 1997). CIALs are also seen as key building blocks for an organizational structure at the watershed level to deal with cross-boundary natural resource management problems and opportunities.

Eight CIALs have been formed so far, and they are functioning fairly well. A considerable number of people have been involved in the various stages of the research process (represented by an *escalera*, or ladder). Experiments (identification of promising, unknown varieties of corn and beans) have been carried out, the results have been seen as successful by the CIALs and community members, and a commitment has been made to continue experimenting in 1999 on a larger scale. A number of new farmer–leaders are emerging, and CIALs have been involved in watershed-level initiatives. CIALs are linked to each other to exchange ideas and results within the watershed and with research and technology organizations, such as the Nicaraguan Institute for Agricultural Technology.

Reforestation of the watershed

The revival of a local initiative and the formation of an interinstitutional committee on reforestation of the Calico River area constitute a second activity facilitated by the ICTA team. Members for this committee were selected from the Municipal Development Council. In addition, a CIAL member and a farmer with land along the Calico River were included on the suggestion of the ICTA team. Based on a diagnostic study of the natural resources along the banks of the river, which was coordinated by ICTA, the committee prepared a project proposal. Funding for the project was obtained, and a tree nursery was established. Planting of trees along the river, with the involvement of committee members, local farmers, and students from secondary schools in San Dionisio, was completed in September 1998. This experience demonstrated to local people, community organizations, and NGOs that the focus on the watershed level was relevant to the discussion of problems and to testing potential solutions. The Municipal Development Committee in San Dionisio has indicated an interest in using the watershed approach in future activities it spearheads.

Funds for local management

A third initiative concerned the establishment of a small-grants fund for small natural resource management projects in the rural communities, to be managed by an association of rural community organizations representing a variety of interests or user groups, with the support of one ICTA team member (who would serve simply as an adviser, without a formal function). As one of its first tasks, this Association of Community Organizations will support local-level group or community initiatives to improve water, soil, and tree management. The association is also expected to create the environment for a more demand-driven process of technology development and development assistance as well as for building managerial capacity. During the first half of 1998, the association, with the support of the ICTA team and through a participatory planning process, defined its goals, objectives, activities, rules, and regulations. Its members have also expressed interest in establishing chapters at the community level.

One of the participants in the Association of Community Organizations is the Association of Drinking Water Committees, which is an umbrella organization for the local Comités de Agua Potable (CAPs, drinking water committees) that exist in most of the 17 communities. With support from the Campesino a Campesino program, the municipality, and the government department dealing with drinking water, the CAPs are responsible for the repair and maintenance of the local drinking water system. They collect small user fees for this service. The organizations that support the CAPs all agree that strengthening the committees would help solve some of the current conflicts about access to, and use of, drinking water and prevent future conflicts.

Participatory research and environmental analysis

During 1998, the Hillsides project carried out a series of participatory microwatershed analyses, involving small groups of local key informants in each of the 15 microwatersheds (farmers, local *tecnicos* [technicians], *promotores* [promoters], and assistant mayors). Factors being examined include land use (agroecological zones), the state of forests, water resources, crops, wildlife, domesticated animals, pastures, and local soil indicators. In addition, participants are identifying the limitations, as well as opportunities, for agricultural production and natural resource management in the area (Espinoza and Vernooy 1998). Based on their findings, a set of natural resource indicators has been developed for monitoring and comparisons between diverse microwatersheds.

The aim is to present the results of these analyses to key local decision-makers, such as the Mayor of San Dionisio, state agencies, and NGOs operating in the watershed, as well as to the recently created Association of Community Organizations, which we consider will be a key stakeholder. The results will allow decision-makers to identify priority zones for action where natural resources are already in bad shape or are at high risk or, alternatively, offer opportunities for alternatives. The analyses will also be helpful as a pre-Mitch overview of the state of the natural resource base and will allow for comparison with the post-Mitch situation.

To get a better idea of the extent of destruction and damage caused by the hurricane, the Association of Community Organizations, with funding from IDRC, will coordinate a study to evaluate the impact of hurricane Mitch on the natural resource base across the watershed. The study aims to provide detailed data as input for the development of a broad reconstruction and rehabilitation program, in collaboration with local NGOs, the municipalities, and government ministries at the regional and national levels.

Establishing a planning process

Building on the microwatershed analyses and considering the new, posthurricane situation, the Hillsides team aims to facilitate a multistakeholder, participatory planning process to look at organizational or institutional aspects, decentralization, and policy-making at the watershed level, within the context of reconstruction, rehabilitation, and disaster prevention and mitigation. The intent is to examine the organizational activities and structures that currently exist (community, NGO, and government based), where they operate, and what they do. The next step will be to determine how these processes and structures can be organized at the watershed level to facilitate more participatory, effective, and efficient natural resource planning and management, to rebuild what was lost as a result of hurricane Mitch, and renew agricultural production. Although it is still too early to measure the impact of these new forms of experimenting, planning, and organizing, so far people have accepted the ideas with enthusiasm and invested considerable effort. The participatory research process is providing local people with the opportunity to analyze and reflect on their own situation and to discover gaps and linkages among various levels of local ecology and socioeconomic organizations in the watershed. New paths are being explored for dealing with issues affecting people's livelihoods, and a collective sense of the social structure of the watershed is emerging.

Lessons learned

Action research in the Calico River watershed in Matagalpa, Nicaragua, points to lessons regarding effective methods and organizational principles.

Methods

Watershed resources are needed by a variety of direct and indirect users with different and sometimes opposing or conflicting interests. This is especially the case in agroecologically diverse hillside environments such as the Calico watershed. Identification of these stakeholders is therefore critical to organizing for sustainable management at the watershed level. Because the stakes can change over time, a continuous analysis of the configuration of stakeholders and interests is also needed (Ravnborg and Ashby 1996).

An interdisciplinary perspective is also critical. Soils and microwatershed analyses important to management decisions need to be placed in the context of user groups, multiple interests, and other socioeconomic features. Interdisciplinarity also increases the understanding of the interconnectedness of various levels of analysis, from the plot, farm, and community to the microwatershed and the watershed. A combination of "diagnostic" research (for example, dividing the watershed into agroecological zones, identification of critical areas for intervention) and participatory action research (for example, the CIALs, the formation of multistakeholder committees, the formation of associations of local groups, the development of indicators to be used by local people, the participatory evaluation study of the impact of the hurricane) helps to provide multidisciplinary information on the state of the resource base at various levels. It also enhances the involvement of the users of the resources in problem and opportunity analysis and facilitates the rapid transition from research to action. Farmer–experimenters, local leaders, and extension workers have an important role to play, together with the technical people and researchers from NGOs and government ministries.

Local-level monitoring of resource use is required to ensure compliance and regulation. In order to achieve better resource management practices through cooperative action, rules, and sanctions, it is important that local people and those cooperating with them have a good understanding of ecological processes, such as soil dynamics, nutrient flows, and water cycles. Resource assessment and resource-use monitoring are, therefore, key activities in any effort to improve management practices and regulatory arrangements. Monitoring will help to raise awareness among local decision-makers about the inter-dependence of resources and, if carried out collectively, can easily impart skills and credi-bility and create a sense of ownership and confidence.

There is a need to develop methodological tools that local people can use to analyze the local situation; discuss constraints, problems, and opportunities; take action; and mon-itor results. The microwatershed seems to be a useful level for intervention and action to develop and test these types of tools.

Organization

The nature and scale of watersheds require some form of collective action for their sus-tainable management (Malanson 1993). Thus, strengthening and involving local organi-zations is needed to change the ways they interact with each other and with broader society (Campbell 1994; Anderson White and Ford Runge 1995). The goal is greater and more equitable control over resources, amplifying the range of options of less privileged people (women, ethnic minorities, the landless), enhancing their involvement in policy-making at the regional or national level (providing space for more people to make their voices heard), and improving the quality of their involvement. The strengthening or estab-lishment of interest groups, however, is not an easy process. Collective action does not emerge automatically, even when, from the outsider's point of view, potential gains seem obvious (Cernea 1989). Building trust is key, but this takes time. Recognizing the strengths and weaknesses (comparative advantages) of different players is also a key principle — it helps to build the required trust.

Our experience suggests that to get things going it is useful to deal with different organizational levels simultaneously in an iterative process that seeks to identify interde-pendencies between the community, microwatershed, and watershed levels. This should build on existing initiatives, such as the projects carried out by NGOs (for example, CARE and the Campesino a Campesino program in San Dionisio) and local community organi-zations (the CAPs). Organizing should focus on defining rules and norms for equitable resource use. This will require informed communities (user groups, stakeholders) with the capacity to engage in dialogue and undertake particular tasks. This, in turn, requires an appropriate level of community or grass-roots organization, based on managerial capacity (Bromley and Cernea 1989) and leadership at the local level, involving both formal and informal rural organizations (see, for example, Claridge and O'Callaghan 1997) .

The CIALs and the Association of Community Organizations have also proven to be good starting points. They provide a means for local people to organize around a specific issue (for example, challenges of natural resource management and agriculture) and solve locally felt problems. There is a need for more support for these kinds of local initiatives and to involve these local forms of organization in municipal and watershed affairs, such as land-use planning, reforestation, water distribution, and conflict management.

The experience of the project suggests that it is useful to start by planning activities to bring people together to learn by doing (presenting ideas, working together, collectively planning, participatory monitoring) (Uphoff 1992). This creates a forum for discussion of problems and solutions and allows people to assume responsibility for new initiatives, such as the reforestation project. There is room for more and more meaningful interaction between community groups, NGOs, the Municipal Development Committee, government ministries, ICTA, and other organizations in Matagalpa. However, the starting point is the strengthening of local groups and the building of bridges among them.

The integration and coordination of planning efforts, from the farm to the micro watershed and watershed levels, is also critical to developing more sustainable management practices. This requires bringing together the direct users of the resources who are living or working in the watershed. However, outside or external users of the resources may also have interests different from those of the people living in the area. Steps are needed to involve them in planning efforts as well and bridge the gaps or negotiate internal versus external interests in the watershed.

Horizontal and vertical links among stakeholders can be strengthened by addressing key institutional and organizational gaps. In Calico, this involves creating and linking horizontally local groups of farmer–experimenter (the CIALs) and facilitating, through ICTA, vertical links with the national research and technology-transfer centres. ICTA has also facilitated, through workshops and meetings, horizontal links between organizations operating at the community level and between these organizations and NGOs, ministries, and the municipality. Creating these links helps local actors identify sources of technical assistance and exert pressure on governments for the services they deserve. It also helps to integrate governments into the local planning process and influence broader policy agendas.

The experience of the Hillsides project suggests that researchers should operate as facilitators for local analysis and action, building bridges between local knowledge, initiatives, and forms of organization, on the one hand, and external sources of information and resources, on the other. Local people are interested in new knowledge, but they frequently lack the channels to access it. This new role for researchers requires the art of skilful listening, asking the right questions, fostering group synergy, and assisting in problem diagnosis and mission definition.

References

Anderson White, T.; Ford Runge, C. 1995. The emergence and evolution of collective action: lessons from watershed management in Haiti. World Development, 23(10), 1683–1698.

Arcía, G.; Mendoza, H.; Iachan, R. 1996. Mapa de pobreza municipal de Nicaragua. Report to the Fondo de Inversión Social de Emergencia, Managua, Nicaragua. 49 pp.

Ashby, J.A.; García, T.; del Pilar Guerrero, M.; Patiño, C.A.; Quiroz, C.A.; Roa, J.I. 1997. Supporting local farmer research committees. *In* van Veldhuizen, L.; Waters-Bayers, A.; Ramirez, R.; Johnson, D.A.; Thompson, J. Farmers's research in practice. Intermediate Technology Publications, London, UK. pp. 245–263.

Baltodano, M.E.; Tijerino, D.; Vernooy, R. 1997. Proceso de identificación y características de la sub-cuenca del estudio, río Calico-San Dionisio, Matagalpa. *In* Proyecto ICTA Laderas América Central. Reportes de progreso 1997. Centro Internacional de Agricultura Tropical, Managua, Nicaragua. pp. 69–86.

———— 1998. Análisis de bienestar en la sub-cuenca del río Calico, San Dionisio, Matagalpa. Centro Internacional de Agricultura Tropical, Managua, Nicaragua. 17 pp.

Bromley, D.W.; Cernea, M.M. 1989. The management of common property resources. World Bank, Washington, DC, USA. World Bank Discussion Paper 57. 66 pp.

Campbell, A. 1994. Community first: landcare in Australia. International Institute for Environment and Development, London, UK. Gatekeeper Series 42. 21 pp.

Cernea, M.M. 1989. User groups as producers in participatory afforestation strategies. The World Bank, Washington, DC, USA. World Bank Discussion Papers 70. 70 pp.

Claridge, G.; O'Callaghan, B., ed. 1997. Community involvement in wetland management: lessons from the field. Incorporating the Proceedings of Workshop 3: Wetlands, Local People and Development. International Conference on Wetlands, 9–13 Oct 1997, Kuala Lumpur, Malaysia. Wetlands International, Kuala Lumpur, Malaysia. 278 pp.

Espinoza, N.; Vernooy, R. 1998. Las 15 micro-cuencas del río Calico, San Dionisio, Matagalpa: mapeo y análisis participativos de los recursos naturales. Centro Internacional de Agricultura Tropical, Managua, Nicaragua. 100 pp.

Malanson, G.P. 1993. Riparian landscapes. Cambridge University Press, Cambridge, UK. 296 pp.

Ravnborg, H.; Ashby, J.A. 1996. Organizing for local-level management: lessons from the Río Cabuyal watershed, Colombia. *In* ICTA Hillsides Agro-ecosystem Program Annual Report 1995–1996. Centro Internacional de Agricultura Tropical, Cali, Colombia. pp. 131–151.

Uphoff, N. 1992. Learning from Gal Oya. Cornell University Press, Ithaca, New York, USA. 448 pp.

Vernooy, R. 1997. Memoría del taller. Manejo sostenible de cuencas: una introducción. Centro Internacional de Agricultura Tropical, Managua, Nicaragua. 40 pp.

Concept

Policy

Chapter 14

POLICY IMPLICATIONS OF NATURAL RESOURCE CONFLICT MANAGEMENT

Stephen R. Tyler

Conflicts over natural resources have always played a role in human society, but recent conditions have led to an increase in their intensity, public profile, and complexity. Policies have paid relatively little attention to the broader perspective of conflict management. It is increasingly important to sort out new mechanisms and institutions to manage these conflicts and resolve them productively in the interests of both long-term sustainability and short-term economic feasibility. This chapter reviews the experiences documented in the case studies and draws lessons from them relevant to public policy in support of conflict management.

The changing policy climate for natural resource conflicts

The policy environment for natural resources management has changed dramatically in recent decades. Population growth, agricultural settlement, and growing trade, investment, and economic activity have increased pressure on all resources. Natural resources once used only locally have been appropriated for the manufacture of industrial products (fibres, oils, timber, minerals) or international foodstuffs (coffee, beef, fruits). Both large-scale resource development for export and local overpopulation cause resettlement of rural resource users to ever more vulnerable and unproductive sites, in search of land suitable for the agriculture on which they base their livelihood.

There are no more "resource frontiers." Virtually every change of land use, new development, or expansion of any resource use now involves conflict (Ayling and Kelly 1997). Natural resource use also continues to be an aggravating factor in armed conflicts around the globe (see Suliman, this volume), and even in cases where the true sources of the conflict may extend beyond disputed resources, resource conflicts are often the most visible and symbolic causes of the dispute (Tungittiplakorn 1995).

Historically, conflicts at the local level were often dealt with through customary or traditional dispute resolution mechanisms. Traditional societies did not necessarily share the instrumentalist perspective of the modern global economy. Conflicts not only took place in an economic context in which risk minimization was generally preferred to profit maximization but were also based on culturally specific notions of value and spirituality that defined the sacred, the secular, and the field of play between these. However, with the breakdown of traditional practices and the penetration of global economic forces to the local level, such conflicts now often come under the jurisdiction of the state. The extending reach of the industrial–consumer society has also transformed the definition of natural resource conflicts (see Chevalier and Buckles, this volume).

In peripheral regions, the state has often acted to assert its authority for reasons of national security, national identity, and nation-building against the interests of local resource users (de Koninck 1994; Michaud 1994). But the state is increasingly constrained in its ability to act unilaterally, even in matters over which it may have constitutional jurisdiction, such as natural resources. Global information flows can quickly place local conflicts on the regional or world stage. Even in isolated and obscure conflict situations, access to telephone, the Internet, and other electronic communication tools makes it increasingly difficult even for the most authoritarian regimes to stop the release of contradictory information or prevent public scrutiny of conflict interventions. This is becoming a thorny problem for policymakers around the world. (Examples of these trends in Southeast Asia are documented by Poffenberger [1990], Laohasiriwong and Kongdee [1995], and Posgate [1998].)

One response has been to increase the effort devoted to resource planning; another has been to revise central policies dealing with natural resource management. The emphasis tends to be on technocratic solutions that establish rules for allocation of resources between conflicting uses. Although these efforts at conflict avoidance are sometimes useful, they are often unsuccessful (and may even be counterproductive). Yet, fundamentally, the key players involved in resource conflicts usually want to resolve them, because the uncertainties surrounding unresolved conflicts increase everyone's commercial and livelihood risks. Appropriate government policies can support the application of innovative conflict management mechanisms.

Public policy as a cause of natural resource conflict

An important initial step in identifying potential policy contributions to the management of local resource conflicts is to recognize the ways public policy can exacerbate such conflicts. There is ample evidence from case studies of how specific policies, government programs, and their implementation have generated or aggravated conflicts, even when the intention was to reduce the conflict. Such contradictions suggest that the nature and dynamics of local resource conflicts are poorly understood and that conventional interventions can be counterproductive.

There are, of course, cases where the direct political interests of central or national elites conflict with those of the local, marginalized poor (Chenier et al., this volume; Fisher et al., this volume). In these cases, the policy tools of the state may be applied in a deliberately one-sided fashion. However, two important lessons can be drawn from these political conflicts:

✦ Even when direct interests clash in the arena of local natural resource use, neither party has a completely free hand. For a variety of reasons, and despite the imbalance of political power, a satisfactory solution for either group may require that both parties reconcile their fundamental interests before either can make use of the contested resources. For example, landowners in Copán, Honduras, came to recognize that in spite of their politically powerful position, their own interests would be better served by selling some of their land than by forcing the government to continue the confrontation (Chenier et al., this volume). In a politically lopsided situation, the tools of the state are not helpful; because of the political conflicts, the government is widely perceived as lacking legitimacy, and any government interventions are likely to exacerbate the problems.

✦ Although fair policy frameworks for natural resource management may be in place, such policies may be ignored or perverted in their implementation under the pressure of influential elites. This situation may persist because of traditional cultural deference, opaque government procedures, or lack of information. Once again, such situations are becoming less tenable, which begins to shift the balance of political power. Policy responses will need to adjust to reflect these changes.

There are a variety of other ways in which the direct actions (or inactions) of policy-driven government agencies can contribute to local resource conflicts.

Uncoordinated planning and investment

Sectoral agencies typically prepare land and resource plans, zoning strategies, and maps that reflect their own objectives; however, these plans may be contradictory at the local level. This is a particular problem in protected areas, where conservation-oriented managers can gain strong international and national political support for excluding other resource users. This is not just a matter of physical exclusion from the protected area, but also, typically, a case of conceptual and ideological exclusion: other interests have often been assumed to be secondary to the ("urgent, imperative, previously overlooked") conservation objectives, and hence it is thought that these other, nonconservationist interests can be ignored by the planners and managers of the protected area.

Each of the case studies dealing with protected areas in this volume provides an illustration of how government officials concentrated on their conservation mandate for the protected areas, paying little attention to the legitimacy of other claimants (Fisher et al.; Oviedo; Weitzner and Fonseca Borrás, this volume). In Bolinao, even the proposal for a protected marine area exacerbated latent conflicts in the community (Talaue-McManus et al., this volume). Similar arguments apply where government agencies are charged with resource planning and investment in their own sectors (for example, forestry, agriculture, mining, industrial development). Within the local community, various resource users are represented within different sectors and receive contradictory signals from different government agencies in dealing with the same resource base. In Uruguay, government incentives for industrial agricultural expansion were in conflict with conservation and other resource interests (Pérez Arrarte and Scarlato, this volume). Government officials are typically unaware themselves of the conflicts and confusion caused by the contradictory regulations, procedures, and plans of their various agencies (Fisher et al., this volume).

Inadequate information or consultation

Inadequate or obsolete data and a limited understanding of local resource uses are common problems in many developing countries. Sometimes these problems are not recognized (that is, central-government officials think they understand the situation better than they actually do), but often decisions are made in full knowledge that the available data are inadequate. Surprisingly, even in cases where data gaps are recognized, local consultation is seldom attempted as a way to improve understanding before devising or implementing a policy. As a result, plans and programs may actually worsen the problems they are intended to address. For example, in Laos, government policy supporting community resource management was implemented in such a rigid way that village demarcation or boundary changes created new conflicts (Hirsch et al., this volume).

Discriminatory or unclear tenure policies

Many countries have tenure systems for land and resources that either reflect historical inequities in wealth and political power or have been recently modified to encourage large-scale industrial agriculture and capital investment. The interests of small-scale and marginalized farmers have been widely ignored. As a result, these people become involved in disputes over resources that they have traditionally used or managed, but to which they have no legal claim. Such situations have frequently arisen as a direct result of government policies intended to promote industrial agriculture or forest plantations (Posgate 1998; Pérez Arrarte and Scarlato, this volume).

Population displacement and migration

A frequent result of major development projects supported explicitly by government policy is the displacement of resident populations. In many countries, there are also policies supporting (or even forcing) migration and resettlement away from more populous regions to the agricultural frontiers. In addition, a variety of regional development policies are intended to attract voluntary migration to target regions of large countries. There are crucial differences between voluntary and involuntary resettlement, but both can lead to deprivation and conflict, even when they are planned and supported financially by government or other project sponsors (Cernea 1988).

The resource conflicts that concern us here typically arise at the resettlement site, when migrants establish farms or begin to use resources that had previously been available to local groups. In many cases, the migrants have a different cultural background from that of the local residents. They share no common tradition or recognition of resource values and taboos. They do not share a common social framework to identify resource rights and processes. They are not party to established mechanisms for arbitration, benefit-sharing, and managing common property. They are also highly stressed — typically with little knowledge of the local resource base and limited reserves of food or cash. They are forced to be opportunistic in their use of resources, a situation that can degenerate into open access.

This situation calls for the external imposition of rules and order, together with initial dialogue and monitoring. Yet, governments typically underestimate the impact and disruption caused by resettlement and fail to recognize the conflicts that arise. For example, in the Vangvieng District of Laos, where repatriated refugees were settled without adequate attention to existing resource users, the ensuing conflict made it impossible to introduce pilot projects to improve management (Hirsch et al., this volume).

A piecemeal approach to reform

In response to local natural resource management concerns or conflicts, many governments have introduced tenure reforms, decentralization of administrative authority, or organizational changes in resource management. However, the scope of the reforms is often limited to the sector of the responsible agency (for example, social forestry, irrigation), with the result that closely related local institutions remain unchanged. Thus, for example, reform of the local-government administrative system in the Philippines has given greater authority to local-government units to manage natural resources. However, technical support, planning and coordination, credit, and extension and marketing systems are not equipped to provide the tools to allow them to take advantage of this increased authority. The result can be greater frustration and even increased conflict, as internal factions or adjacent municipalities follow their own interests or struggle to deal with multiple contradictory projects of different agencies (Talaue-McManus et al.; Fisher et al., this volume).

Vague policy direction

Policies drafted by central-government officials may be poorly communicated to the local-government agencies responsible for their implementation. Thus, a regulation that may be clear to the officials who developed it and the political authorities who approved it may be interpreted entirely differently by local implementing officials. The sense and intent of the national-level legislation may not be an overriding concern for local officials dealing with the practicalities and constraints of their own situation. Neighbouring districts may implement the same laws or regulations in contradictory ways, leading to new conflicts among resource users who were accommodated under previous arrangements (Hirsch et al., this volume).

Inadequate support for reforms

Some elements of reformed or enlightened resource management frameworks can be found in most of the cases described in this volume. However, such reforms are almost always inadequately supported. Decentralization of authority is not accompanied by adequate funding, training, or capacity-building among the officials charged with implementing the policies. As a result, enlightened policies may either fail to be implemented or be implemented very differently at the local level than intended by the policymakers.

An essential element in effective policy responses to natural resource conflicts is the ability to recognize and anticipate these kinds of counterproductive government activities. Avoiding or correcting such problems will result in a solid policy base on which to build conflict management processes in natural resource administration. Some of the problems are deeply entrenched in the political system, but simply recognizing them can be a major step on the road to conflict management.

Innovative policy responses

The parties involved in resource conflicts often press governments to intervene directly to resolve them. One rationale for this can be found in economic theory. In complex natural resource disputes, it is usually neither feasible nor economically attractive for the parties directly involved to organize conflict resolution efforts. Transaction costs are high and many of the benefits do not accrue to the participants themselves, so government involvement is justified on a "public-good" basis. Governments also typically have constitutional and legal authority in the specific field of natural resource management and may, therefore, be legally obliged to intervene in cases of conflict. In many cases, the state is also one of the claimants to contested resources.

However, precisely because the state is not a disinterested party, its role in resolving natural resource conflicts can be limited. The parties in conflict may not perceive the state to be a legitimate arbitrator. But the state may be a crucial stakeholder because of its statutory responsibilities for natural resource management. Regardless of its role in the conflict, the support of the state may be essential to successful outcomes because of its powers of enforcement and support for collateral implementation efforts (for example, investment, training, technical advice). This dilemma has several important policy implications. First, the role of the state and its agents in natural resource management is likely to have to change to respond to the need for better conflict management. Second, innovative mechanisms to resolve natural resource conflicts are likely to lead to policy support for new institutions and processes outside the formal realm of state authority and the emergence of new actors and skills to manage conflict situations. Third, the importance of procedural transparency and access to information in resolving conflicts begins to define how these roles, players, and processes are likely to have to interact and how policies can foster or impede such interaction.

Sweeping guidelines that policymakers can apply across the board when confronted with volatile local natural resource conflicts are unlikely to emerge. A principal lesson from the experiences described in this book and elsewhere is that conflict resolution and local management of natural resources rely on locally specific solutions. There are few general rules for the kinds of interventions that might be appropriate, although useful diagnostic tools are available for evaluating the nature of the conflict and the potential for facilitating various kinds of solutions (for example, Bush and Opp, this volume; Ramírez, this volume). Policy responses should recognize and empower local stakeholders to become more effective in assessing their own needs, negotiating with other resource users, understanding and interpreting technical assessments of resource quality, and implementing consensus solutions. In short, much progress can be made in conflict management through policy responses that improve *governance* at the local level.

The role of research as a catalytic tool

The cases demonstrate repeatedly how information plays a catalytic role in conflict management. The process of exposing, validating, and sharing information about the resource base and its use is, in all cases, a crucial first step in the process. Typically, the various parties in conflict do not share a common set of data (for example, Oviedo, this volume; Pérez Arrarte and Scarlato, this volume). Although information alone is insufficient to lead to a resolution of resource conflicts, it is a prerequisite in building consensus-based plans. Information collection improves the understanding of all parties and engages the attention of those at the periphery of the issues. It also requires the engagement of all parties in providing, often contradictory, information.

Because the offended parties in a conflict are unlikely to share information openly, they have to be treated with respect and dignity to gain their participation. Meeting this requirement is an excellent way to start any consensus-based conflict management process. Participatory research methods that give a large degree of control and initiative to the groups and individuals who provide information in the first place can be useful tools in helping information collection agents (for example, government officials) change their own attitudes about the various parties to the conflict. Research can also provide a method for politically weaker stakeholders to elucidate their needs and validate assumptions about the conflict situation, as well as potential solutions, thereby providing a more robust basis for an eventual resolution (Chenier et al., this volume).

Any resolution of a conflict situation must rely on a detailed understanding of the idiosyncracies of each unique local context. Such understanding is always time-consuming to obtain, never transparent, usually much more complex than anticipated, and best learned from the mouths and experience of the local people themselves. Therefore, the process by which information is collected, validated, analyzed, and shared is a fundamental element of any natural resource conflict management exercise.

But the importance of information in the conflict management process does not end with its collection. Many of the cases emphasize the importance of the timely *sharing* of information and the use of it to build links between interest groups or between local and central authorities to better define interests and engage various stakeholders in the process (Fisher et al., this volume). Transparency of information and analysis is essential to building and maintaining the trust needed to identify mutual interests and develop consensus-based decision-making.

New approaches to administration

In many cases, the state's conventional role of administering and arbitrating natural resource use has come under such pressure through conflict situations that the nature of the administrative mechanism has had to be changed. This kind of change may be implemented on an experimental or pilot basis in a few test cases, but it will eventually involve statutory changes in the authority of the responsible agencies. Two kinds of administrative change can be described: devolution of authority from central to local governments and comanagement.

These innovations are broadly consistent with a number of other trends affecting public administration, which vary from country to country but include the following:

- ✦ Structural-adjustment programs that require cuts to central-government spending in the name of fiscal restraint;

- ✦ Efforts to make government more responsive to specific local or regional conditions, in the interests of greater effectiveness and accountability;

- ✦ A stronger role for civil society and various public organizations in influencing the public-policy agenda;

- ✦ More vocal policy commentary by an increasingly educated public, with better access to information; and

✦ Fewer alternatives for local livelihoods among people affected by central policy decisions.

Although the specific approaches, policy rationale, and context vary from one country to the next, it is striking that these kinds of changes are under way in many jurisdictions with widely varying political systems (Tyler 1995).

The case studies in this volume include good examples of this kind of change. In Costa Rica, the government had to abandon its independent administrative authority over the Cahuita protected area in the face of persistent and effective local action. The initiative to demand more say in the uses of the protected area and in its day-to-day management clearly originated from the community and was resisted by state authorities. The novel comanagement mechanism that was developed to resolve this conflict has provided important lessons to both the professional reserve managers acting as agents of the state and the community itself as it grapples with its new responsibilities (Weitzner and Fonseca Borrás, this volume). This administrative model has already become an alternative to the traditional protected-area management approach in Costa Rica. It may be further refined and formalized as experience is gained, and it may be replicated in other situations, where appropriate.

In the Philippines, in contrast, formal administrative devolution of natural resource management and jurisdiction preceded the development of the local institutions needed to exercise such management authority. In the case of coastal marine resources, where resource mobility, jurisdictional boundaries, overlapping tenure, and navigational uses compounded the management issues, the problems were especially acute. The development of a novel local environmental-planning body, featuring multiple stakeholders and a consensus-based decision process, offered local governments a new mechanism for exercising their resource management authority (Talaue-McManus et al., this volume).

The adoption of local comanagement by the powerful state forestry departments in India illustrates both the potential and the hazards of this kind of administrative reform (Kant and Cooke, this volume). The reforms have formalized a role for the community in forest management but have done so in a centralized and bureaucratic fashion. Unlike the other cases, where the initiative and structure of innovations came largely from the communities themselves, the new administrative structure for joint forest management (JFM) was standardized by the state and applied in a "cookie-cutter" fashion to thousands of diverse and heterogeneous village situations. In some cases, it has worked reasonably well; in others, it has failed utterly. Ironically, for an initiative that was intended to address problems of conflict between village forest users and the state (in its role as manager of the forest lands), JFM has typically *not* developed tools or processes for conflict management. The result is that persistent local conflicts over forest use, management processes, accountability, and equity threaten the feasibility of this approach.

Recognition of the legitimacy of multiple stakeholders

Typically, under state management systems, resource rights are recognized for only a single user or a small number of users. These entities are issued licences, titles, or other legal documents to certify their claim on the resources. In exchange, the state taxes the commercial gains from exploitation of these resources. These arrangements are most often formulated so that large-scale industrial resource users can have access to the volume of raw material they need to be competitive in international markets. However, in reality the resources are often shared by multiple users, who may have large- or small-scale, extractive or nonextractive claims on them.

The inevitable conflicts cannot be resolved if the state recognizes only one set of legitimate users. Indeed, that practice may exacerbate a latent conflict situation (Suliman, this volume). A crucial policy step is to recognize that there are multiple stakeholders, with varying degrees of legitimacy, in any situation of contested resource use. Resolution of conflict situations will require their engagement and commitment to solutions.

In the Galapagos Islands, for example, management of the protected marine areas could not be effective without the development of a consensus-based plan that involved the commercial fishing and tourist industries (Oviedo, this volume). Although the powerful protected-area managers, who had strong international support, assumed a consensus on resource management objectives, there was actually a wide range of heterogeneous views and conflicts even between diverse groups in the fishing community. Until all of the relevant stakeholders were recognized and sat down together to reach consensus on management, attempts to enforce the authority of the state and its official management plans only increased the tension and conflict.

The creation of a forum in which stakeholders could legitimately represent their interests and contribute equally to the resolution of the conflict situation was also an essential element of success in the case in Bolinao, Philippines (Talaue-McManus et al., this volume). There, stakeholders representing diverse interests within the community first had to organize to be able to select representatives to participate in the multistakeholder group. The planning process undertaken by this group was also consensus based and required the group to deal with intense conflicts that, in the past, had been dominated by the powerful elites of the community. A mark of the success of the process was that the local government recognized the group's value and sought to regularize the multistakeholder body, even after the original conflict had been resolved.

New roles for government officials

The kinds of change discussed above often involve major shifts in the role of government officials. The conventional duties of natural resource management officials include collecting and analyzing data on resource use, administering official resource tenures, planning and establishing targets, providing direction to local officials and resource users, etc. However, administrative innovations to support conflict management will require these officials to learn a whole new set of skills. Policies to support these new roles will be essential if innovative conflict resolution mechanisms are to contribute to community-based natural resource management. The new roles are facilitative, rather than directive. Although sanctions may still be needed, government officials will have to become accustomed to sharing power. In developing resource management plans, they must master participatory and consultative methods. Rather than being experts who make administrative decisions, officials will need to be more like advisors who can help communities in conflict to distil facts, identify common interests, and reach a consensus. This change is not a minor retooling; it involves a fundamental paradigm shift.

In India, the implementation of joint forest management has been greatly hampered by the lack of recognition that a fundamental change is required from the professional forest managers (Kant and Cooke, this volume). It is only to be expected that local forest officers, whose status and power come from their administrative control of resource management and use, will be reluctant to share the authority to make these decisions, regardless of the formal directions they receive from their superiors. Attempts to identify local innovations to improve resource management in Laos quickly focused on the crucial role of district officials in facilitating, leading, and supporting community resource management planning (Hirsch et al., this volume). The key to introducing a successful local management process and to recognizing its potential to contribute to conflict management was the training and skills development provided to the district agriculture and forestry officers, in combination with their enthusiasm and commitment. In a variety of cases, formal government agencies responsible for resource planning and administration were forced to adopt new consultative roles, new decision-making processes, and changes in their conventional planning and coordination mechanisms. When such reforms proved particularly difficult for the government or when formal government agencies faltered in their new roles, the conflict management process also faltered (for example, Pérez Arrarte and Scarlato, this volume).

New roles for independent mediators

There are many limits to the kinds of roles that even the most reform-minded government can play in conflict management. The state's responsibilities for natural resource management mean that it is almost never a disinterested party in resource conflicts and may often be an important cause; the skills needed to support conflict management processes are not those for which government officials have been trained; and the requirements for sharing power and ensuring equal standing of stakeholders with formal and informal claims do not always sit easily with officials who have spent most of their careers enforcing only one set of resource claims. Thus, policies that support conflict management must recognize the crucial importance of a new set of actors in resource management: external mediator–facilitators independent of government.

This role is perhaps not so new after all. Most traditional societies recognize and value the role of mediator, distinct from the authority of elders or leaders, as a matter of practical social necessity (Chevalier and Buckles, this volume). The context of mediation is crucial. In many Asian cultures, it is extremely difficult for governments to be involved in mediation processes, particularly senior officials, as a result of the social imperatives of status, deference, and authority. Therefore, with no direct stake in mediation processes or outcomes, senior officials can be dismissive of results obtained through efforts at a lower level. One solution in the Asian context is to build linkages between organizations with similar experiences and to build them from the grass-roots level back up to government agencies and policymakers, as ways of converging on consensus when mediation is culturally difficult (Fisher et al., this volume).

Government policies can create opportunities for mediation during disputes. However, they must include mechanisms for judging the prospects of success at the outset and adopting contingencies to ensure the mediators' security if situations deteriorate. For example, where one or more parties is intransigent or believes its objectives can be achieved unilaterally, mediation is unlikely to succeed. Situations can change quickly, and many conflict situations are extremely volatile.

The role, tasks, required skills, and modus operandi of a successful mediator will depend on the specific context of any dispute. Although a North American perspective would tend to emphasize neutrality and impartiality (based on our legal dispute resolution system), strongly traditional societies might adopt a quite different approach, in which neutrality and impartiality may be inappropriate (Chevalier and Buckles, this volume).

The crucial characteristic of an effective mediator–facilitator in natural resource conflicts is credibility with the main parties in the dispute, whether that credibility comes from technical expertise, professional experience, social status, kinship, or wisdom ("authority" is usually a poor criterion for selecting mediators). A successful mediator–facilitator is likely to be highly skilled in this practice and to have no direct economic stake in the outcome of the conflict. The mediator–facilitator typically understands the nature of "community development" and its associated tasks of negotiation, leadership development, and education. These tasks and skills help in the process of identifying stakeholders and facilitating productive interaction. In some cases, formal institutions with mandates for mediation in disputes may already exist and may be adapted to play a crucial role in the resolution of resource conflicts. For example, in the case of the Cahuita protected area, the government ombudsperson provided a legitimate channel for public complaint and took the initial steps toward a consensus solution (Weitzner and Fonseca Borrás, this volume).

In both Indonesia and Honduras, the mediator role was played by a technically competent nongovernmental organization (NGO). The engagement of the mediators arose in different ways in each case. The Nusa Tenggara Uplands Coalition was initiated and led by an NGO that saw the need to shift its position from one of advocacy to one of facilitation, trying to improve and develop its mediation skills as it went along (Fisher et al., this volume). In Honduras, the NGO was asked to become involved initially because of its strong technical skills, its clear independence of the interests in the dispute, and its international credibility and connections (Chenier et al., this volume). But reliance on NGOs is not always appropriate: the important factor is the competence and credibility of the mediator. In the Galapagos, professional mediators were hired to facilitate the multistakeholder discussions on management of the marine reserve (Oviedo, this volume). In all cases, the successful outcomes were attributed in part to the crucial contributions of the mediators–facilitators.

The importance of a trained, skilled mediator in facilitating the conflict management process may appear to be self-evident. However, among technocrats who have not been exposed to the practice of conflict management, the need for such skills is far from obvious, and the need for these skills and tools becomes self-evident to policymakers only after they have seen them in action. For example, the first formal dispute resolution training program in Thailand was established recently at Khon Kaen University, with minimal support from external donors. Various administrative elements of the Thai government had been embroiled in increasingly bitter disputes with the public over the past decade, yet there had been few attempts to develop tools and methods to deal with these conflicts more effectively. In the short time since its inception, the new program has trained thousands of Thai officials, at the expense of the Thai government, and its methods have been praised and widely adopted (Armstrong 1998).

A policy framework for management of natural resource conflicts

The experiences described above suggest an outline of the kind of public policy framework in which natural resource conflict management can best be applied. The core of this framework is the recognition of the need to engage the key parties, rather than abstracting data, analyzing, and generating expert-driven technical solutions: "The innovative and practical ideas required to solve difficult issues are more likely to be revealed if those who are affected by the resolutions are given some responsibility for designing them" (Grzybowski 1998, p. 92). Conflict management requires acceptance, especially by government agencies but also by other parties, of the need for mutual responsibility and joint problem-solving.

Administrative coordination

The first element of a policy framework is better local coordination of natural resource administration. Planning by sectoral agencies should be closely linked and coordinated at the local level, where conflicts typically arise. Such coordination is likely to involve an enhanced role for the local-government administrators, external groups, or both. In some cases, where local administrators lack the required skills or other resources, coordination might be handled by technically competent and committed NGOs or by a special agency (or commission) at a senior level of government assigned specifically to carry out this function. The coordinating function may be ongoing or aimed at addressing a specific conflict situation. This function may be ameliorated by the development of specialized tools for coordinating spatial and resource data (databases, geographic information systems, expert systems).

Information-sharing and communications

The importance of shared information was stressed in many cases. Sharing of information can result from better administrative coordination by sectoral agencies, when these groups actually have data to share. Or it may result from specific research, undertaken by credible independent parties. Information-sharing can increase transparency, build trust, resolve issues of fact, and distinguish these from issues of interest. The process of undertaking research and sharing information can also serve as a valuable means to identify and engage various stakeholders.

Stakeholder identification and analysis

Stakeholder recognition may arise from information exchange or through research. The recognition of a range of stakeholders with legitimate interests may in itself be an act of redistributing political power, if the state has previously assumed sole responsibility for management decisions. The application of specialized analytical tools to diagnose the range of interests and the capacity of various stakeholders strengthens the ability of mediators to guide the process (Ramírez, this volume).

Engagement of a legitimate intermediary

A legitimate intermediary may be an outside mediator, a credible independent public agency (for example, ombudsperson), or a culturally appropriate "insider." Conflict management is a process rather than a specific package of standard solutions. The process needs expert guidance from individuals and institutions able to gain the trust of all parties. In many cases, it is impossible for the government to play this role, and public policy must make provisions for the recruitment of external professionals. It is also often impractical for the courts to play this role, even where a well-developed and independent judiciary exists. The issues are typically not amenable to legal definition and adjudication, and attempts to define them in terms of narrow "rights" through formal legislation are both clumsy and inflexible.

A process of interaction

Information-sharing and stakeholder identification represent the beginnings of an interaction process. Depending on the depth and severity of the conflict, it may not be possible to begin interaction on any of the specifics. Building trust and shared understanding can start with peripheral, less controversial issues. Interaction may take a variety of forms, depending on the context and the actors involved, from multistakeholder consultations (roundtables) to formal negotiations or mediation.

These interactions are best built on traditional practices of dispute resolution mechanisms, when vestigial traditional institutions exist and can be modified to include the parties and context of the contemporary problem (Lindsay 1998). As participants on all sides of the issue learn more at each successive stage of interaction, issues can become more clearly focused and the likelihood of successful resolution of the conflict will increase. When methods are used to increase transparency at each step by sharing information, reviewing conclusions, and discussing evidence openly, all participants can increase their commitment (CORE 1994).

A legal framework and procedural equity

For the process to move from ad hoc crisis management to systematic practice, some sort of legislative umbrella is required. The intent would be to confer some legitimacy and structure on the process without overly constraining it. Participation must be voluntary, but at the same time, mechanisms should also be found to ensure the commitment of all parties (especially the government) to a mutually agreed course of action.

Although many traditional cultures have agreed to social procedures for addressing resource disputes, there can be difficulties in building on these as legal instruments ("traditional law"). Traditional law is not law in the statutory sense, but rather a range of dynamic social conventions. It may not measure up to increasingly rigorous standards of transparency and fairness and may suffer from lack of recognition in cases of cross-cultural disputes. Thus, although traditional dispute resolution processes provide strong clues for the design of interactions to construct mutual solutions, they may not be helpful as a basis for robust and generalizable enabling statutes.

Issues addressed by such an umbrella statute may include criteria for fairness and procedural equity to ensure that reasonably affected parties can participate fully, the nature of procedural oversight and appeals, and access to information and tools to make sense of it. This may also require provision of certain minimal resources to enable all parties to participate (funds for travel, translation, printing, communications, independent analysis).

Strong local government

Local governments are typically not well qualified or equipped to deal with conflict interventions. Strengthening of skills, oversight procedures, increased transparency, and provision of expertise will all be needed to improve the ability of local government to cope with these issues. Appropriate resolution of conflicts through properly mediated interventions can strengthen the legitimacy of local governments by clarifying roles and mandates and by providing for local enforcement of consensus-based solutions to the benefit of affected parties (for example, Truong 1998; Oviedo, this volume).

External support

There are many areas in which external support for a local conflict management process is vital: information collection, validation, and sharing; skills development; mediation; legitimizing outcomes. Such support is particularly important once a conflict management process has generated a positive outcome. Implementation of consensus-based conflict solutions will usually require services, investment, monitoring, and feedback. In many cases, local resources for these activities are insufficient, and external support, whether from the state or from other donors, will be essential, particularly in the early phases. Resolutions of serious conflicts are always initially fragile, and policies should recognize the need for flexible but urgent support under these conditions.

Research

In most of these dimensions of policy response, there is an important role for locally dri-ven, applied interdisciplinary research to determine the basis of a shared data set, adapt tools for administrative coordination, identify and analyze stakeholders, experiment with various procedural innovations, and develop new institutional forms and enabling statu-tory tools at the local and senior-government levels. These areas of research require a wide range of expertise in fields ranging from natural sciences through information technolo-gies, behaviourial sciences, economics, and law. The research methods and the results gen-erated will not fit within a single discipline but will require a synthesis of the methods and procedures of several disciplines. These processes are premised on principles of mutual learning and change and adaptability through interaction, which are very similar to those employed in the practice of participatory action research (PAR). Recent experience using interdisciplinary PAR in the rebuilding of societies that have suffered violent conflict has demonstrated the effectiveness of rigorous and neutral research in contexts analogous to, if even more severe than, those of local natural resource conflicts (Stiefel 1998).

Time

The management of natural resource conflicts, through application of some of these tools and the interaction of the parties directly involved will require time. Information-sharing, representation, negotiation, argument, acceptance — each step requires time, and there is no shortcut to a solution. Under pressure from political or economic interests, this factor is often neglected.

Challenges in creating a supportive policy environment

Successful conflict management requires cooperation among the various stakeholders and identification of mutually dependent actions and interests. Parties design their own solu-tion cooperatively. This approach to problem-solving is *not* consistent with the reduction-ist view of the modern technocracy. We have elaborate systems of specialized study, training, analysis, and institutional organization for choosing the "best solution" on technical, economic, political, religious, or even multivariate grounds. We do not have well evolved systems to foster and support stakeholders in decisions to design solutions collaboratively. In the absence of such systems, even the stakeholders themselves often back away from the responsibility and expect somebody else (often the state) to solve the problem.

Any of the policy innovations described above would support the application of conflict management tools and methods, such as the ones described in the case studies. Taken as a package and implemented together, these measures would amount to a powerful commitment, not only to consensus-based conflict management, but also to a new community- and user-centred paradigm of natural resource management. However, change agents, whether inside or outside government agencies, should be aware that introducing a new paradigm is a lengthy and painful process. Changes are never easy. The case studies suggest that it may often be the central government that is most resistant to these kinds of innovation (Pérez Arrarte and Scarlato, this volume). Most of the required changes involve government agencies delegating, devolving, or relinquishing some of their authority over natural resource management and use. It is rare for any public agency to voluntarily reduce its power; those who try to implement such innovations must recognize the difficulties they face.

Part of the problem is that the changes suggested above are inconsistent with the conventional self-image of a modern professional, expertise-based organization. Professionals in the public service are employed on the basis of their specialized expertise. They expect to analyze technical information and make professional judgments about "optimal" solutions to complex problems. They do not expect to turn over problem-solving to groups of local people or "outsiders." However, the government officials most directly responsible for local resource management must adopt a facilitative role, requiring new knowledge and skills, to support participatory and consensus-based conflict management processes. The magnitude of the change required should not be underestimated. Changes in organizational structure, job titles, and job descriptions are easily accomplished on paper, but changes in attitude and assumptions can only be achieved over the long term.

Reorganization and human-resource changes will have to recognize the internal incentive systems of the public agencies involved (promotions, transfers, awards) and restructure these in support of the new policies. The perceived loss of certain direct authorities and independent decision-making powers will be highly threatening to individuals and the organization as a whole. In any bureaucracy, conceding line authority (that is, the ability to spend money on local projects and make decisions about what happens on the ground) is dangerous. It reduces not only the agency's direct influence with clients but also its relative power within the government. Career prospects and promotion paths will be threatened. One way to tackle these problems is to identify them explicitly and ensure that a reformed resource management agency, along with the professionals within it, receive the greatest possible credit for their successes and for the difficulty of their task, in the face of diminished fiscal impact and political authority.

The perception that the package of policy measures discussed above might "weaken" traditional resource management agencies can also be addressed by reinforcing the importance of state agencies' continuing to play a legitimate role in protecting public interests. In a number of respects, the adoption of policies more supportive of conflict management approaches will actually increase the importance of certain administrative roles, particularly in relation to coordination of various resource agencies, validation and provision of information, and monitoring of consensus-based management outcomes. All of these activities can build on the traditional roles of these agencies.

The devolution of conflict management and resource-planning authority will also require that the government adopt monitoring (not control) procedures to ensure that public interests are represented and protected from narrow parochial interests. For example, many natural resource problems cross local political boundaries, and consensus decisions within one jurisdiction may be detrimental to those "downstream." Policy innovations to provide more opportunities for conflict management will still have to take place within a framework that ensures comprehensive resource management, administrative fairness, and effectiveness (CORE 1994). This will continue to pose both technical and professional challenges.

Thus, many of the obstacles to introducing these policy innovations can be seen as challenges of presentation and perception. There will be a continuing need for strong central professional expertise and leadership, in spite of the loss of some direct authority and control at that level. But there will also be a need for new skills and behaviours to ensure the introduction and successful application of conflict management to address natural resource conflicts.

Unresolved issues

A number of difficulties remain in our policy framework. A central issue is resolving the dynamic between local actors, including local governments, and the state. Mutually devised, multistakeholder consensus-based conflict resolution puts both responsibility and initiative in local hands. Yet, there must remain a strong and legitimate role for the state. For example, several cases demonstrate that the community alone cannot implement or enforce solutions without the sanction of senior government (Hirsch et al.; Talaue-McManus et al., this volume).

The community also needs the authority of the state to strengthen its ability to deal with large and powerful external interests, such as multinational corporations. It would be helpful to describe and report on other mechanisms to provide community stakeholders with the tools and support needed to engage on a more equitable basis with the state and external interests (NGO networks and consortium-building have been suggested in some cases, for example, Fisher et al., this volume).

The policy interventions needed to support a mature conflict management system are costly and will require effort over a long period. They involve a lot of organizational learning and retooling, not only within the administrative system but also among the participants in each conflict. Participatory methods, research, information-sharing, and better communications will all require time, staff support, and expertise. The high costs of attempting these methods (combined with the even higher costs of failure) suggest the need for broader and more systematic sharing of experience. What are we learning about how to do this better? How can we improve practices, develop supportive information management tools, improve skills, strengthen local institutions, and select and train mediators? What are the key contextual parameters influencing the success of various mediated processes? How transferable are successful innovations within the same country, the same culture, or across cultures? A strategic research and networking effort would help governments identify best practices and resource materials.

Natural resource conflict is not going to go away. Permanent resolution of these conflicts is not likely. Management of the inevitable resource conflicts is important as a public good in the economic sense and, therefore, merits policy support. But there are no magic solutions, no quick technical fixes. The challenge for governments is to create opportunities for new institutions and processes supportive of mutual solutions and joint responsibility, redefine their own roles and foster new ones in these processes, and encourage the creativity and courage needed to learn from the experience of these new institutions and roles.

Acknowledgments

The author acknowledges the helpful comments of David Brooks, Daniel Buckles, and Ronnie Vernooy on an earlier draft of this paper.

References

Armstrong, G., ed. 1998. What works? A case study of successful Canadian governance programming in Thailand and Cambodia. Southeast Asia Fund for Institutional and Legal Development; Canadian International Development Agency, Ottawa, ON, Canada.

Ayling, R.; Kelly, K. 1997. Dealing with conflict: natural resources and dispute resolution. Commonwealth Forestry Review, 76(3), 182–185.

Cernea, M. 1988. Involuntary resettlement in development projects: policy guidelines for World Bank projects. World Bank, Washington, DC, USA. Technical Paper 80.

CORE (Commission on Resources and Environment). 1994. Provincial land use strategy. Vol. 4: Dispute resolution. CORE, Queen's Printer for British Columbia, Victoria, BC, Canada.

de Koninck, R. 1994. Forest policies in Southeast Asia: taming nature or taming people? In de Koninck, R., ed., Le défi forestier en Asie du Sud-Est. Groupe de recherche en amélioration des céréales, Université Laval, Québec, QC, Canada. pp. 33–48.

Grzybowski, A. 1998. Public policy conflict analysis framework. In Grzybowski, A.; Morris, C.; Johnson, H.; Owen, S., ed., Building democratic institutions and practices in Cambodia: proceedings from the Cambodia Commission on Human Rights Capacity Building Project. Institute for Dispute Resolution, University of Victoria, Victoria, BC, Canada. pp. 79-94.

Laohasiriwong, S.; Kongdee, W. 1995. Dispute resolution in Thailand: working together for peace and prosperity. Proceedings of a workshop in Khon Kaen, Thailand, June 1995. Institute for Dispute Resolution, Khon Kaen University, Khon Kaen, Thailand.

Lindsay, J. 1998. Law in community-based natural resource management. Paper presented at the International Workshop on Community-based Natural Resource Management, 10–14 May, Washington, DC, USA. Economic Development Institute of the World Bank, Washington, DC, USA; International Development Research Centre, Ottawa, ON, Canada; Ford Foundation, New York, NY, USA.

Michaud, J. 1994. Montagnes et forêts frontalières dans le nord thaïlandais: l'état face au montagnards. In de Koninck, R., ed., Le défi forestier en Asie du Sud-Est. Groupe de recherche en amélioration des céréales, Université Laval, Québec, PQ, Canada. pp. 89–114.

Poffenberger, M., ed. 1990. Keepers of the forest: land management alternatives in Southeast Asia. Ateneo de Manila University Press, Manila, Philippines.

Posgate, D. 1998. Rural development and conflict in northeastern Thailand: a background paper. *In* Armstrong, G., ed., What works? A case study of successful Canadian governance programming in Thailand and Cambodia. Southeast Asia Fund for Institutional and Legal Development, Canadian International Development Agency, Ottawa, ON, Canada.

Stiefel, M. 1998. Rebuilding after war: a summary report of the War-torn Societies Project. United Nations Research Institute for Social Development, Geneva, Switzerland.

Truong Van Tuyen. 1998. Toward an improved management of common property in Tam Giang Lagoon, Vietnam. Paper delivered to International Association for the Study of Common Property conference, 10–14 Jun, Vancouver, BC, Canada.

Tungittiplakorn, W. 1995. Highland-lowland conflict over natural resources: a case of Mae Soi, Chiang Mai, Thailand. Society and Natural Resources, 8(2), 279–288.

Tyler, S.R. 1995. The state, local government and resource management in Southeast Asia: recent trends in the Philippines, Vietnam and Thailand. Journal of Business Administration (special edition), 22–23, 51–68.

Appendix 1

CONTRIBUTING AUTHORS

Porfirio M. Aliño
Marine Science Institute
University of the Philippines
Diliman, Quezon City, Philippines

Carlos Pérez Arrarte
Researcher
Centro Interdisciplinario de Estudios Sobre
    el Desarrollo
Montevideo, Uruguay

Jacqueline A. Ashby
Director
Natural Resources Management
International Center for Tropical Agriculture
Cali, Colombia

Daniel Buckles
Senior Program Specialist
International Development Research Centre
Ottawa, ON, Canada

Kenneth D. Bush
Independent Researcher
Geneva, Switzerland
and
Research Fellow
Dalhousie University Centre for Foreign
    Policy Studies
Halifax, NS, Canada

Jacqueline Chenier
National Coordinator
Pastoral de la Tierra y del Medio
    Ambiente/CARITAS
Tegucigalpa, Honduras

Jacques M. Chevalier
Professor
Department of Sociology and Anthropology
Carleton University
Ottawa, ON, Canada

Roshan Cooke
Program Associate
United Nations Development Programme
Nairobi, Kenya

Larry Fisher
Director
Program on Environment and Community
Center for the Environment
Cornell University
Ithaca, NY, USA

Marvin Fonseca Borrás
School of Geography
University of Costa Rica
San José, Costa Rica

Philip Hirsch
Division of Geography
School of Geosciences
University of Sydney
Australia

Shashi Kant
Assistant Professor
Faculty of Forestry
University of Toronto
Toronto, ON, Canada

Ilya Moeliono
Coordinator
Studio Driya Media
Bandung, West Java, Indonesia

Robert J. Opp
Project/Research Officer
International Development Research Centre
Ottawa, ON, Canada

Paola Oviedo
Centro de Educación y Promoción Popular
Quito, Ecuador

Khamla Phanvilay
Department of Forestry
Faculty of Agriculture and Forestry
National University of Laos
Lao People's Democratic Republic

Ricardo Ramírez
International Support Group: Linking Local
    Experience in Agroecosystem Management
Guelph, ON, Canada

Gerett Rusnak
Research Officer
International Development Research Centre
Ottawa, ON, Canada

Tahnee Robertson
Associate Director
Program on Environmental and Community
Center for the Environment
Cornell University
Ithaca, NY, USA

Severino G. Salmo, III
Marine Science Institute
University of the Philippines
Diliman, Quezon City, Philippines

Guillermo Scarlato
Researcher
Centro Interdisciplinario de Estudios Sobre
    el Desarrollo
Montevideo, Uruguay

Stephen Sherwood
Associate Expert
International Potato Center
Quito, Ecuador

Mohamed Suliman
Director
Institute for African Alternatives
London, United Kingdom

Liana Talaue-McManus
Marine Science Institute
University of the Philippines
Diliman, Quezon City, Philippines

Kaneungnit Tubtim
Nam Ngum Watershed Resource
    Management Study
Lao People's Democratic Republic

Stephen R. Tyler
Senior Program Specialist
International Development Research Centre
Ottawa, ON, Canada

Ronnie Vernooy
Senior Program Specialist
International Development Research Centre
Ottawa, ON, Canada

Viviane Weitzner
Natural Resources Institute
University of Manitoba
Winnipeg, MB, Canada

Stefan Wodicka
Southeast Asia Area Representative
World Neighbors
Ubud, Bali, Indonesia

Alexis C. Yambao
Marine Science Institute
University of the Philippines
Diliman, Quezon City, Philippines

Appendix 2

ACRONYMS AND ABBREVIATIONS

ADR alternative dispute resolution
AGRACOR Farmers' and Ranchers' Organization of Copán Ruins
AGUAS Agrupaciones Uruguayas por un Ambiente Sano

BATNA best alternative to a negotiated agreement
BKSDA Center for Natural Resources Conservation
BPN Land Registration Board

CAPs Drinking Water Committees
CARE Cooperative for American Relief Everywhere
CBNRM community-based natural resource management
CBCRM Community-based Coastal Resources Management
CDP Coastal Development Plan
CIALs Comtés de Investigación Agricola Local (local agricultural-research
   committees)
CIEDUR Centro Interdisciplinario de Estudios Sobre el Desarrollo (interdisciplinary
   centre for development studies)
COLABORA Network for Collaborative Natural Resources Management
CONICHH National Chorti Indian Council of Honduras
CONPAH National Confederation of Autochthonous Villages of Honduras
CPAWM Centre for Protected Area and Watershed Management
CRC Costa Rican colon
CWG Conservation Working Group

DAD decide–announce–defend

EP	ethnoenvironmental politics
FPC	Forest Protection Committee
HNL	Honduran lempira
ICTA	International Centre for Tropical Agriculture
IDRC	International Development Research Centre
ILO	International Labour Organization
INA	Instituto Nacional Agrario (national agricultural institute)
INIA	National Agricultural Research Institute
INR	Indian rupees
JFM	joint forest management
KAISAKA	Municipcal-wide Federation of People's Organizations for Coastal Resource Management
KOPPESDA	Research Coordination Team for Natural Resources Management
LGCAMC	Lingayen Gulf Coastal Area Management Commission
LP3ES	Institute for Economic and Social Research, Education and Information
MCDB	Multi-sectoral Consultation on the Development of Bolinao
MGAP	Ministry of Livestock, Agriculture and Fisheries
MINAE	Ministry of Environment and Energy
NEDA	National Economic Development Authority
NGO	nongovernmental organization
NIF	National Islamic Front
NTCDC	Nusa Tenggara Community Development Consortium
NTFP	nontimber forest product
PAR	participatory action research
PCIA	peace and conflict impact assessment
PDF	Popular Defence Force
PDR	Peoples Democratic Republic
PHP	Philippine peso
PRA	participatory rural appraisal
PRENAER	Program for the Management of Natural Resources and Irrigation Development
PROBIDES	Program for Conservation of Biodiversity in the Bañados del Este
RAAKS	rapid appraisal of agricultural knowledge systems
SINAC	National System of Conservation Areas
SPLA	Sudanese People's Liberation Army
SPLM	Sudanese People's Liberation Movement

UNDP	United Nations Development Programme
UNESCO	United Nations Educational, Scientific and Cultural Organization
UNHCR	The United Nations High Commission for Refugees
UPMSI	University of the Philippines' Marine Science Institute
USD	United States dollar
VFPC	Village Forest Protection Committee
WCA	Wanggameti Conservation Area
WDP	Watershed Development Program
WWF	World Wide Fund for Nature

About the Publishers

The International Development Research Centre (IDRC) is committed to building a sustainable and equitable world. IDRC funds developing-world researchers, thus enabling the people of the South to find their own solutions to their own problems. IDRC also maintains information networks and forges linkages that allow Canadians and their developing-world partners to benefit equally from a global sharing of knowledge. Through its actions, IDRC is helping others to help themselves.

IDRC Books publishes research results and scholarly studies on global and regional issues related to sustainable and equitable development. As a specialist in development literature, IDRC Books contributes to the body of knowledge on these issues to further the cause of global understanding and equity. IDRC publications are sold through its head office in Ottawa, Canada, as well as by IDRC's agents and distributors around the world. The full catalogue is available at http://www.idrc.ca/books/index.html.

The World Bank Institute (WBI) provides training and other learning activities that support The World Bank's mission to reduce poverty and improve living standards in the developing world. WBI's programs help build the capacity of World Bank borrowers, staff, and other partners in the skills and knowledge that are critical to economic and social development.

WBI is located at World Bank headquarters in Washington, DC. Many of its activities are held in member countries in cooperation with regional and national development agencies and education and training institutions. The Institute's distance education unit conducts interactive courses via satellite links worldwide. While most of WBI's work is conducted in English, it also operates in Arabic, Chinese, French, Portuguese, Russian, and Spanish. Additional information about the World Bank Institute and its publications is available at http://www.worldbank.org/wbi/.

About the Editor

Daniel Buckles holds a PhD in Rural Sociology from Carleton University (Ottawa, Canada). While working as a Rockefeller Foundation Post-Doctoral Fellow and later as a Senior Scientist with the International Maize and Wheat Improvement Centre in Mexico, he undertook research on the social and economic aspects of ecological agriculture and on participatory approaches to technology development and farmer-to-farmer extension. Previous research examined the impact of modern society on the political and economic life of the indigenous peoples of southern Veracruz, Mexico. His project-development work with IDRC focuses on collaborative approaches to natural resource management and on the application of biodiversity research to the development of policies that address local concerns and aspirations. Among Dr Buckles publications are *A Land Without Gods: Process Theory, Maldevelopment and the Mexican Nahuas* (with J. Chevalier, Zed / Fernwood, 1995) and *Cover Crops in Hillside Agriculture: Farmer Innovation with Mucuna* (with B. Triomphe and G. Sain, IDRC / CIMMYT 1997).